Bigfoot to Mothman

Bigfoot to Mothman

A Global Encyclopedia of Legendary Beasts and Monsters

Margo DeMello

BLOOMSBURY ACADEMIC
NEW YORK • LONDON • OXFORD • NEW DELHI • SYDNEY

BLOOMSBURY ACADEMIC
Bloomsbury Publishing Inc, 1359 Broadway, New York, NY 10018, USA
Bloomsbury Publishing Plc, 50 Bedford Square, London, WC1B 3DP, UK
Bloomsbury Publishing Ireland, 29 Earlsfort Terrace, Dublin 2, D02 AY28, Ireland

BLOOMSBURY, BLOOMSBURY ACADEMIC and the Diana logo are trademarks
of Bloomsbury Publishing Plc

First published in the United States of America 2024
Paperback edition published 2026

Bloomsbury Publishing Inc does not have any control over, or responsibility for,
any third-party websites referred to or in this book. All internet addresses given
in this book were correct at the time of going to press. The author and publisher
regret any inconvenience caused if addresses have changed or sites have
ceased to exist, but can accept no responsibility for any such changes.

Library of Congress Cataloging-in-Publication Data
Names: DeMello, Margo, author.
Title: Bigfoot to Mothman: a global encyclopedia of legendary beasts and
monsters / Margo DeMello.
Description: New York: Bloomsbury Academic, 2024. | Includes bibliographical
references and index. |
Audience: Ages 15–21 | Audience: Grades 10–12
Identifiers: LCCN 2023031504 (print) | LCCN 2023031505 (ebook) |
ISBN 9781440877254 (hb) | ISBN 9798216170860 (ebook) | ISBN 9781440877261 (epdf)
Subjects: LCSH: Monsters–Encyclopedias, Juvenile. |
Cryptozoology–Encyclopedias, Juvenile. | BISAC: SOCIAL SCIENCE /
Folklore & Mythology | SOCIAL SCIENCE / Conspiracy Theories
Classification: LCC QL89 .D386 2024 (print) | LCC QL89 (ebook) |
DDC 001.944–dc23/eng/20231023
LC record available at https://lccn.loc.gov/2023031504
LC ebook record available at https://lccn.loc.gov/2023031505

ISBN: HB: 978-1-4408-7725-4
PB: 979-8-7651-1245-8
ePDF: 978-1-4408-7726-1
eBook: 979-8-216-17086-0

Typeset by Deanta Global Publishing Services, Chennai, India

For product safety related questions contact productsafety@bloomsbury.com.

To find out more about our authors and books visit www.bloomsbury.com
and sign up for our newsletters.

Contents

Preface

It has often been said that while paleontology studies creatures that existed in the past, and that have left documentable evidence, but that no human has ever seen, cryptozoology looks at creatures that are said to exist today, for which there is (as of yet) no actual evidence, but countless people have seen them. This encyclopedia attempts to take a closer look at these beings whose very existence is up for debate as well as at those people who have an interest in them.

This one-volume encyclopedia will explore the world's cryptids—those hidden or secret animals believed to exist at the margins of human society. It includes well-known creatures like Bigfoot, Yeti, the Loch Ness Monster, and the Jersey Devil, as well as hyperlocal and not well-known creatures like Bunyip or Mamlambo.

Alphabetically arranged entries will profile specific cryptids, examining the geography, history, folklore, sightings, and attempts to debunk the creature. The focus of the entries is to look at the cultural beliefs surrounding these cryptids, rather than focusing on scientific measures of proof. Entries include information on the cultural manifestations of these creatures—what do people around the world find scary or upsetting, and why? Because cryptids are firmly located in the realm of folklore and popular culture, whenever possible, entries include a snippet of folklore or folk song about the creature.

Ultimately, this book will provide those with an interest in cryptids and cryptozoology, as well as those with an interest in folklore, mythology, and even zoology, an overview of the field of cryptozoology, the major issues associated with the field, as well as an in-depth look at cryptids from around the world.

Alphabetical List of Entries

Cryptids

- Ahool
- Akkorokamui
- Almas
- Altamaha-ha
- Barmanou
- Batutut
- Bearilla
- Beast of Bladenboro
- Beast of Bray Road
- Beast of Exmoor
- Beast of Gévaudan
- Bessie
- Bigfoot
- Bunyip
- Cadborosaurus
- Champ
- Chessie
- Chupacabra
- Dingonek
- Dobhar-Chu
- Ebu Gogo
- El Hombre Caimán
- El Cuero
- Encantado
- Fouke Monster
- Grootslang
- Honey Island Swamp Monster
- Issie
- Jersey Devil
- Lizard Man
- Loch Ness Monster
- Loveland Frogman
- Mamlambo
- Mapinguary
- Merfolk
- Moehau
- Moha moha
- Mokele-mbembe
- Mongolian Death Worm
- Mothman
- Nahuelito
- Nandi Bear
- Orang Pendek
- Ozark Howler

Extinct, Invented, or Mythical Creatures Similar to Cryptids

Geographical List of Entries

North America

United States

- Altamaha-ha
- Bearilla
- Beast of Bladenboro
- Beast of Bray Road
- Bessie
- Bigfoot
- Chessie
- Chupacabra
- Fouke Monster
- Honey Island Swamp Monster
- Jersey Devil
- Lizard Man
- Loveland Frogman
- Mothman
- Ozark Howler
- Pope Lick Monster
- Skunk Ape
- Thunderbird
- Wendigo

Canada

- Bigfoot
- Cadborosaurus
- Champ
- Wendigo

Latin America

- Chupacabra
- El Cuero
- El Hombre Caimán
- Encantado
- Mapinguary
- Nahuelito

Europe

Russia

- Almas

Great Britain

- Beast of Exmoor
- Bownessie
- Dobhar-Chu
- Loch Ness Monster

France

- Beast of Gévaudan

Germany, Austria, Switzerland

- Tatzelwurm

Iceland

- Lagarfljót Worm

Africa

- Dingonek
- Grootslang
- Mamlambo
- Mokele-mbembe
- Nandi Bear

Asia

East Asia

- Akkorokamui
- Issie
- Mongolian Death Worm
- Yeren

Central Asia

- Barmanou

Southeast Asia

- Ahool
- Batatut
- Ebu Gogo
- Orang Pendek

South Asia

- Yeti

Australasia

- Bunyip
- Moehau
- Moha moha
- Thylacine
- Yowie

Global

- Merfolk

Thematic List of Entries

HABITAT

Air Creatures

- Ahool
- Jersey Devil
- Mothman
- Thunderbird

Water Creatures

Lake Monsters

- Akkorokamui
- Bessie
- Bunyip
- Cadborosaurus
- Champ
- Chessie
- Dobhar-Chu
- El Cuero
- Issie
- Lagarfljót Worm
- Loch Ness Monster
- Nahuelito

Sea Monsters

- Merfolk
- Moha moha

Swamp Monsters

- Bunyip
- El Hombre Caimán
- Honey Island Swamp Monster

River Monsters

- Altamaha-ha
- Bunyip
- Encantado
- Grootslang
- Lizard Man
- Loveland Frogman
- Mamlambo
- Mokele-mbembe

Land Creatures

- Almas
- Barmanou
- Batutut
- Bearilla
- Beast of Bladenboro
- Beast of Bray Road
- Beast of Exmoor
- Beast of Gévaudan
- Bigfoot
- Chupacabra
- Dingonek
- Ebu Gogo
- Fouke Monster
- Mapinguary
- Moehau
- Mongolian Death Worm
- Nandi Bear
- Orang Pendek
- Ozark Howler
- Pope Lick Monster
- Skunk Ape
- Tatzelwurm
- Thylacine
- Wendigo
- Yeren
- Yeti
- Yowie

Taxonomy

Human-Animal Hybrids or Shapeshifters

- Almas
- Barmanou
- Batutut
- Bearilla
- Beast of Bray Road
- Bigfoot
- El Hombre Caimán
- Encantado
- Fouke Monster
- Honey Island Monster
- Lizard Man
- Loveland Frogman
- Malambo
- Merfolk
- Moehau
- Mothman
- Skunk Ape
- Yeren
- Yeti

Beasts

- Ahool
- Bearilla
- Beast of Bladenboro
- Beast of Bray Road
- Beast of Exmoor
- Beast of Gévaudan
- Bessie
- Bigfoot/Sasquatch
- Chupacabra
- Dingonek
- El Cuero
- Emela-Ntouka
- Grootslang
- Issie
- Jersey Devil
- Moha moha
- Mokele-mbembe
- Mongolian Death Worm
- Nandi Bear
- Ozark Howler
- Tatzelwurm
- Thylacine

Animal Kin

Primates

- Ahool
- Almas
- Barmanou
- Batutut
- Beast of Bray Road
- Bigfoot
- Ebu Gogo
- Fouke Monster
- Honey Island Monster
- Moehau
- Orang Pendek
- Skunk Ape
- Yeren
- Yeti
- Yowie

Canines

- Beast of Bladenboro
- Beast of Bray Road
- Beast of Gévaudan
- Chupacabra
- Dobhar-Chu
- Nandi Bear

Bats

- Ahool

Felines

- Beast of Bladenboro
- Beast of Exmoor
- Ozark Howler
- Tatzelwurm

Bears

- Bearilla
- Ozark Howler

Fish

- Merfolk

Goats

- Pope Lick Monster

Horses

- Jersey Devil

Invertebrates

- Akkorokamui
- El Cuero
- Mongolian Death Worm
- Mothman
- Tatzelwurm

Dolphins, Otters, and Seals

- Dobhar-Chu
- Encantado

Serpents

- Altamaha-ha
- Bessie
- Cadborosaurus
- Champ
- Chessie
- Grootslang
- Issie
- Lagarfljót Worm
- Loch Ness Monster
- Malambo
- Moha moha
- Nahuelito

Birds

- Thunderbird

Amphibians and Reptiles

- El Hombre Caimán
- Lizard Man
- Loveland Frogman
- Moha moha
- Mokele-mbembe

Sloths

- Mapinguary

Pangolin

- Dingonek

Unknown

- Bunyip
- Wendigo

Mythic and Legendary Creatures

- Al-mi'raj
- Black dog
- Cerberus
- Chamrosh
- Emele-ntouka
- Gamayun
- Hodag
- Kelpie
- Kishi
- Kitsune
- Lavellan
- Milk Hare
- Nittaewo
- Popobowa
- Rolling Calf
- Sarimanok
- Selkie
- Steller's Sea Ape
- Swan Maiden
- Tanuki
- Tengu
- Tikbalang
- Zanzibar Leopard

Hoaxes and Inventions

- DeLoy's Ape
- Dinosaur Man
- Elwetritsch
- Feejee Mermaid
- Great Mammoth Hoax
- Jackalope
- Minnesota Iceman
- Monkey Man of Delhi
- Montauk Monster
- Rat king
- Sea Rabbit of Coney Island
- Skvader

Former Cryptids

- Bili Ape
- Moa
- Quagga
- Ulama

Alien Cryptids

- Flatwoods Monster
- Fresno Nightcrawler

Introduction

Cryptids are, according to the subculture that hunts and studies them, hidden or secret animals, or animals whose existence has not yet been substantiated by science. Cryptozoologists are people who believe in the existence of, and study, these creatures. According to most scientists, however, cryptids are not real but, instead, live in the realm of folklore.

This book looks at cryptids around the world and will attempt to make sense of the wide variety of creatures that are thought to live in the lakes, swamps, forests, and deserts of the planet, hidden from mainstream science but very much alive in popular culture. The book will not attempt to either prove or debunk the claims of cryptozoologists about the reality of cryptids as biological creatures. Instead, we will focus on alternative ways of seeing and understanding these beings that seem to stubbornly exist outside of the realm of the natural sciences.

A Variety of Approaches

Cryptids and, indeed, the field of cryptozoology, which is dedicated to the study of cryptids, straddle a number of different intellectual realms and thus must be looked at through a variety of lenses. This encyclopedia takes an approach that argues that the most fruitful lens through which to view cryptids is a cultural one. Their biological existence aside, there is no question that cryptids have long existed within the realms of the imagination—in the stories, myths, and legends that we tell each other, and ourselves, about the world in which we live. This type of approach does not preclude scientific inquiries into cryptids; it simply allows us to better understand the historical and cultural context in which they live. To the author of this text, the question of whether cryptids exist as physical beings subject to the laws of nature is no more important than the question of how cryptids came to be and why they are so important to us—especially in this precarious time in planetary history.

Besides a cultural lens, a natural science approach is the one that is used by most cryptozoologists who seek, after all, to prove the existence of cryptids as biological creatures. If the goal of cryptozoologists is to prove—or disprove—the empirical existence of hidden animals like Bigfoot or the Chupacabra, then this goal can only be met through a scientific lens: collecting evidence, assessing that evidence through scientific measures, and coming to a conclusion based on the strength of that evidence. Cryptozoologists, who rarely have any training in the natural sciences, borrow liberally from biology, locomotion studies, ecology, paleoanthropology, and other scientific fields but do so without a background in those disciplines. In addition, cryptozoologists also use the many folktales, myths, and legends about these creatures as another way to provide proof of their existence, often without a broader understanding of the linguistic, cultural, and historical contexts in which they developed.

As noted earlier, this book will primarily use a cultural approach to understanding cryptids. An approach like this means that the empirical existence of cryptids is not the goal. Instead, we will focus on cryptids as social constructions: beings that—whether or not they actually exist–were created and given shape by humans. Looking at Bigfoot, for example, this way means locating the creature culturally and historically; this helps us to understand how a creature like this functions in different cultural settings and how beliefs about (and sightings of) this creature are linked to the very specific cultural, social, and historical context in which it is found.

We might also try to understand these creatures through a psychological perspective. How are cryptid sightings, for example, linked with mass hysteria? Or moral panics? Beliefs about cryptids spread through culture virally but are not accepted by everyone. How does the psychological makeup of the believer play a role in whether or not one accepts the existence of cryptids?

Finally, anthrozoology provides another lens through which we might understand creatures that—whether or not they run out to be real—exist in the human's mind. Anthrozoology (also known as human-animal studies or animal studies) is a relatively new, multidisciplinary and interdisciplinary field that looks at the relationships between humans and other animals—both real and imaginary. It takes as one of its basic principles the idea that animals—that DO clearly exist in reality—are still social constructions—their existence is shaped largely by humans' understandings of them, which of course are shaped by the cultural, social, and historical context in which they exist. Thus any biological understanding of animals is always linked to a cultural one. Anthrozoology also allows us to investigate how beliefs in cryptids are linked to our understanding of ourselves vis-à-vis the natural world. This, to this author, makes anthrozoology an obvious choice to study cryptids.

Cryptozoology and Mainstream Science

This encyclopedia was written during 2021–22—in other words, during a time when the world was grappling with a global pandemic that has changed us in ways that we will probably not understand until many years into the future. But I think it's safe to say that many of the social movements that developed or reemerged during the pandemic—such as the Black Lives Matter movement, the fight for LGBTQ+ rights, the fight for reproductive rights, the "great resignation," and the rise of conspiracy theories and movements like QAnon—are linked to the traumas and uncertainties associated with the pandemic and the various social inequalities that it exposed.

How is this related to cryptids? Cryptids are not accepted by Western science. This means that cryptozoology, by inference, is a pseudoscience, and those who practice it are naive at best and nuts at worst. While cryptozoologists draw on findings from various scientific disciplines, they are not scientists and are not bound by the scientific method. It does not help that many cryptozoologists and cryptid enthusiasts share beliefs in other fringe beliefs like the existence of aliens.

In addition, the fact that cryptozoologists lack scientific training, and thus are shunned by the scientific community, shapes cryptozoologists and their beliefs. Any social group that feels

Figure 1 *Ahools exist because we need them—today more than ever. Copyright © 2023 Heidi Scheidl. All rights reserved.*

that their voices are not being heard, and that is continually invalidated by those with more power, will fight back and often double down on their beliefs. This is certainly the case with cryptozoologists who tend to view scientists with suspicion. In addition, there is ample evidence to show that people who are attracted to beliefs that fall outside of the mainstream—like Flat Earthers or QAnon supporters, or even Americans who believe that Donald Trump won the 2020 presidential election—do so in part because they have a suspicion of authority that stems from being excluded from spaces where their voices might matter.

Cryptozoologists also, largely, stem from rural areas. Almost by definition, cryptids live on the margins of human society. With very very few exceptions, cryptids—like most wildlife—live outside of cities, which means that virtually all cryptid sightings occur "in nature," that is, in forests, deserts, and swamps, as well as in various waterways, which means they will be most common among people who live in rural areas and/or who hunt and fish or regularly engage in other outdoor activities. This poses a credibility problem; besides the obvious fact that cryptozoologists are uncredentialed, and excluded from scientific spaces, the fact that most sightings are made by people who, again, may lack scientific education continues to shape the field and the ways in which cryptozoologists—many of whom see themselves as citizen scientists—engage with science.

In addition, in recent years young earth creationists have been joining cryptology in an attempt to find evidence to support the idea that the earth is just a few thousand years old. If, for example, the Loch Ness Monster turns out to be real, then creationists argue that finding a so-called living dinosaur living alongside of humans will disprove evolution once and for all.

In the United States, where this book was written, we are more polarized in terms of our political beliefs than ever before, thanks in part to all of the issues and conspiracies that emerged during the pandemic. American cryptozoologists in particular may move further away from the mainstream as beliefs, no matter how outrageous, become markers of identity and as distrust of authority—including scientists and government officials—continues to grow.

We should also remember that Western, scientific systems of knowledge are not the only ways that knowledge is produced; indigenous science, for example, refers to traditional ways of knowledge production that are only now becoming recognized and valued outside of those cultures and which might offer us a new way to understand creatures that exist outside of Western science. The history of science tells us that science does not exist outside of history or culture; it is shaped by both. Nor is science always neutral; a rigorous focus on the scientific method does not mean that science is objective. It is shaped by all of the same social, cultural, and historical factors that shape all of us and should be treated as such. Yet Western science continues to maintain that it is objective, and that through the use of the scientific method, "objective truth" can be achieved, even as the notion of objectivity continues to be challenged by nonscientists. Cryptozoologists, operating outside of that world, will never see their work accepted or their beliefs validated, and because they are shunned by scientists, their hypotheses very rarely are subject to review or evaluation outside of what is functionally a closed community.

History of Cryptozoology

Cryptozoology began as a specialized field in the late 1950s with the publication of Bernard Heuvelmans's *On the Track of Unknown Animals* (1955) and Ivan Sanderson's *Abominable Snowmen: Legend Come to Life* (1961). But people have had an interest in "monsters" for thousands of years, as is indicated by the inclusion of such beings in religious texts and bestiaries of cultures throughout the Old World, where animals both real and unreal are used to teach moral lessons. But early scientist-philosophers like Pliny the Elder studied and wrote about animals outside of the lens of religion, giving us one of the first natural histories, called, fittingly, encyclopedic *Naturalis Historia* (Natural History), written in 77 CE. But natural history, which covered all aspects of the natural world, began to give way to biology, physiology, zoology, geology, and other more specialized sciences by the seventeenth and eighteenth centuries. It was in the eighteenth century that Carl Linnaeus published his *Systema Naturae*, which provided a taxonomic system for understanding plant and animal life on this planet along with a new system of scientific nomenclature that we still (largely) use today.

But even as the biological sciences, with their new scientific rigor, emerged, monsters remained a part of science. The first five editions of *Systema Naturae* included a number of species that were believed to exist but which we now consider to be mythical creatures, including the hydra, unicorn (what Linnaeus called a Monoceros), siren, and the phoenix. By the nineteenth century, most of today's natural sciences had emerged, and monsters were no longer included in scientific treatises. In addition, scientists themselves changed, from wealthy amateur naturalists, whose wealth and leisure time afforded them the ability to explore, think, and write, to professional scientists with university training and degrees. From this point forward, an interest in monsters was relegated primarily to the field of folklore as well as, briefly, a scientific field called teratology: the study of human monsters, or what we in contemporary society would know as people with disabilities.

With the publication of Charles Darwin's origin of species in 1859 and the dissemination of the theory of evolution by natural selection, combined with the first fossil discoveries of dinosaurs, proto-humans, and other extinct species, an interest in wondrous beings reemerged. For the first time, it became clear that there were once animals on this earth that no longer exist. Some of those animals, such as Plesiosaurs, the first fossil of which was found in 1823, would be valuable in providing not only the physical characteristics of cryptids like the Loch Ness Monster but also one of the most significant theories to explain their presence: the evolutionary relic. It is not a coincidence that the first sightings of the modern Loch Ness Monster began in this same period, after the first plesiosaurs were discovered. Bernard Heuvelmans located the origin of the field with the 1892 publication of Anthonie Oudemans's article, *The Great Sea-Serpent*.

Heuvelmans, who coined the term cryptozoology in 1955, was a trained zoologist with an interest in finding hidden animals. His book, *On the Track of Unknown Animals* (1955), was the first major cryptozoological study and essentially kick-started the field. Another zoologist, Ivan Sanderson, was also an extremely important early researcher. (It wasn't until 1983 that J. E. Wall coined the term cryptid, in an attempt to move away from sensational terms like monster.)

I think it's notable that the field itself took off in the 1950s, when the Cold War was still new and terrifying, nuclear war was an ever-present worry, and science itself offered both promise and danger. It's not a coincidence that so many horror and science-fiction films from the period focused on the dangers of this new scientific age.

Cryptids as Animals

Most cryptids are classified by cryptozoologists as beasts, that is, they are animals but have not yet been discovered or accepted by science, like the chupacabra of Latin America or the many alien big cats like the Beast of Exmoor. Some are hybrid creatures, carrying characteristics of two or more creatures. Of the beasts, many are canine or feline, pointing to the importance of those animals in human society. In addition, cryptids tend to be carnivores. This makes sense if one of the functions of cryptid stories is to provide a warning system for young children: a child is more likely to heed his or her parents' warning about a big, aggressive, flesh-eating creature than one who is an herbivore that favors flowers. But the emphasis on large carnivores may be just a reflection of the human bias toward predators and away from prey animals.

For those who believe that cryptids are animals, or that they might be real animals, zoology (as well as other related disciplines like ethology) might seem to be the most appropriate lens with which to study them. And in fact, those animals that were once thought to be mythical but that actually turned out to be real—the giant squid is the best example—they do in fact enter the realm of zoology, ethology, and all the other disciplines that take animals as their focus.

Other animals have come to the attention of Western scientists only in the recent past—think of the okapi, the gorilla, the platypus, or the Komodo dragon, all of which are examples given of mythic creatures that turned out to be real. But these animals never existed in the realm of the imagination. Rather, they were long known by locals and only came to the attention of Europeans much later. In fact, after European explorers began bringing back biological specimens from Australia starting in the seventeenth century, some European scientists concluded they could not be real. But European ignorance about animals that they had never seen does not mean they were cryptids.

Technically, any creature that is the subject of myth, folktale, or legend can be a cryptid—the most important part of most definitions is the fact that the cryptid is unknown to science.

Once an animal has been "discovered" scientifically, it is no longer a cryptid but moves into the "former cryptid" category and thus out of cryptozoology and into zoology.

Cryptids as Monsters

Many cryptids are described as part animal/part human and include ape-like creatures like Bigfoot as well as creatures that walk on two legs like the Loveland Frogman. These creatures may be interpreted as evolutionary holdovers from the past; water serpents like the Loch Ness Monster are thought to be modern plesiosaurs that somehow survived the extinction of the other dinosaurs, and ape- men like Bigfoot are thought to be modern descendants of extinct hominids like Gigantopithecus. These are examples of what Darren Naish calls the prehistoric survival paradigm. In addition, a small percentage of cryptids is wholly anomalous and may not resemble or share characteristics with other creatures. Australia's Bunyip and the Fresno nightcrawler are examples of cryptids with no known living or extinct relatives, which moves them further into the monstrous category.

While most cryptozoologists would like to help prove the existence of cryptids as biological beings, not everyone in the cryptozoology community shares this wish. There is a small element that sees at least some cryptids as magical beings. This is most common among those who had a firsthand encounter as well as within the Bigfoot community. In this subculture within a subculture, creatures like Bigfoot are not, and never have been, of this world. They are supernatural beings, which often is used to explain why they can stay undetected by humans or can appear and disappear magically.

Even when the supernatural nature of the beast is not highlighted, many cryptids are described with characteristics that defy a natural explanation: glowing red eyes, breath that smells like sulfur, multiple heads, or the ability to shapeshift. Some of these supernatural characteristics are then used to help explain how, for example, a 10-feet-tall ape-man living in Northern California can not only escape detection for hundreds of years but can also, as some believe, speak telepathically.

While those with an interest in cryptids as biological organisms tend to reject the more far-out supernatural theories and rightly recognize that they pose a threat to the acceptance of cryptozoology by mainstream science, there is still an element of the fantastical in witness reports from even the most practical of witnesses. In fact, Westerners' first-person reports often have an uncanny feel. People report that, for example, they thought the creature was staring at them, attempting to communicate with them, or that they had an otherwise strong, but unsettling feeling. These stories share some similarities with dolphin–human encounters, either in the wild or in a captive setting like a swim-with-dolphins facility. Dolphins are very real creatures with no (known) supernatural abilities, but dolphin encounter stories emphasize the uncanny, even spiritual nature of the contact. Part of the reason for this is a misunderstanding of dolphin facial features (the curved rostrum or jaw of a dolphin makes it seem as if dolphins are always smiling), and part of it comes from the representation of dolphins in popular media.

Bernard Heuvelmans, known to many as the father of cryptozoology, wrote that a cryptid must be "truly singular, unexpected, paradoxical, striking, or emotionally upsetting" because it's that very singularity that allows the creature to enter folklore where they get their name. In anthropology, we might refer to cryptids as monstrous, in the sense that they are anomalies, unusual beings that do not conform to our current understanding of the world around us. While the goal of many cryptozoologists is to prove the existence of these creatures, doing so would remove the very unexpected and striking elements that attracted Heuvelmann, and many people like him, to the subject.

Sightings and the Rules of Evidence

The existence—or lack thereof—of cryptids is the central concern of cryptozoology. Everything else—their nutrition, ecology, reproduction, and behavior—are all secondary to the central question of their existence. Cryptozoologists recognize multiple forms of evidence. Physical sightings whether done by members of the general public or cryptologists remain one of the most important forms of evidence supporting the existence of cryptids. Eyewitness accounts of cryptids—especially well-known cryptids like Bigfoot or the Loch Ness Monster—are reported in the mainstream media as news and are collected by cryptozoology groups and treated as data points.

Besides actual sightings, the other major form of evidence sought by cryptozoologists is the materials that they leave behind. This includes hair or fur, footprints, feces, and, for carnivorous creatures, the carcasses of dead and mutilated animals. All of these forms of evidence must then be analyzed and interpreted in order to make a sound argument in favor of a cryptid's existence, but here again, the fact that cryptozoology exists outside of the bounds of science only hurts it. In order to determine the provenance of, say, a fur sample or a bit of feces, typically those samples must be given to a scientist who has the skills and equipment necessary to analyze the sample. But it is the scientific establishment, as well as the government, that not only does not believe in the existence of cryptids but is (most likely) also engaged in covering up their existence. This explains why cryptozoologists may reject any scientific conclusion that points away from the veracity, or they may conduct the analysis themselves.

Interpreting animal remains accurately is required to understand who the predator is as well as to understand the behaviors of predators—whether they are operating alone or in a group, whether they are sick or healthy, and whether there have been any changes in the environment that might impact predator–prey behavior. This requires training in not just the anatomy of animals and the ways in which different predators hunt, kill, and otherwise engage with the carcasses of other animals but with a wider understanding of the micro- and macroecological factors that shape predator–prey behavior.

What's behind most of the sightings? It is difficult to generalize, but it's probably true that only a very small percentage of sightings are hoaxes. While there have been a number of well-known hoaxes involving the most famous cryptids like Bigfoot or the Loch Ness Monster, most witness reports are most likely given in good faith, even if they may be misinformed.

One thing that we know from criminology is the way that first-person witness accounts of crimes are notoriously unreliable. The shock that a witness to a crime—but especially a violent one—changes how we see and understand what we are seeing. In addition, many people are simply not very good at remembering details. But we also cannot dismiss the importance that cultural memory plays in what we see and how we interpret it. Every American knows who Bigfoot is, what he looks like, and some basic elements of his ecology and behavior. We have a vast cultural library to draw from when thinking about him, and, especially for those in the pacific northwest, entering a mountainous forest immediately conjures an image of Bigfoot. (It doesn't help that every town in or even near redwood forests where Bigfoot is thought to live is chock-full of Bigfoot paraphernalia.) Given the way that beliefs about some cryptids circulate through the culture, and especially through mass media, it would be more surprising if there were no sightings at all.

Sightings make up by far the greatest category of what cryptozoologists collect as evidence for the existence of cryptids. Witness reports, then, are an extremely important part of the field. But they also function as a passport of sorts. Having had a personal encounter with a secretive, perhaps even magical creature that is the subject of so much attention would be a momentous, perhaps even life-altering, experience. Encounter narratives, then, offer the witness a place in a new community, one that validates one's experiences and helps provide a framework through which to understand what was seen. The cryptozoological community is a place where witness accounts are not ridiculed but accepted, no matter how incredible. This is extremely important as a belief in cryptids, but especially a firsthand experience with one, is often ridiculed and shamed by those outside of the community.

Because so much of the evidence for the biological existence of cryptids is not subject to review, evaluation, or analysis outside of the community, it gains acceptance with the community if the community's experts accept it. That means as each new piece of unverified evidence arrives and is found to be credible if not empirically true, it becomes another card in an evidentiary house of cards that, at least from a scientific perspective, may collapse at any moment.

Cryptozoology is, among many other things, fundamentally about the production of knowledge—who has the right to produce knowledge, under what conditions, and with what methods and under which assumptions. What method of knowledge production is best suited to creatures whose existence is almost entirely found in the realm of human belief as well as popular and mass media. Is the scientific method even appropriate here?

In the absence of the scientific establishment taking any interest whatsoever in these creatures, it has essentially been up to the amateurs who are most invested in the subject to develop the theories, borrowing basic methods from scientific disciplines, if not a well-developed grasp about science itself.

Science relies on (some might argue that it fetishizes) the concepts of objectivity and neutrality, universal truth, and a rigorous methodology. In contrast, folk knowledge, where so much of what we know about these creatures comes from, is deeply intertwined with local conditions, traditions, languages, and worldviews and is less focused on objective truth than on lived experience. Folk knowledge is also intended for a specific, local audience who shares in that worldview. Cryptozoology often uses folk knowledge—transmitted by travelers, explorers, missionaries, and others without a background in the culture, to bolster their scientific evidence in a way that conventional science rejects and in a way that ignores the context and intent of this knowledge.

One of the challenges, if not dangers, of using folklore and myth from indigenous cultures in-service to cryptozoology, besides the obvious problem of losing all cultural nuance, is the fact that in many of these cultures there isn't a strict line between human and animal or between nature and culture. In fact, many cultures see animals as potential clan members, ancestors, separate nations, or intermediaries between the sacred and profane worlds. For instance, the Evens, a Siberian pastoralist and hunting society, consider animal spirits as the parents to humans so that when they hunt, the parents (the reindeer) allow themselves to be hunted and eaten by the children.

In a Eurocentric context, the border that separates nature and culture, human and animal, is absolute, making it difficult for many of us to comprehend the worldviews of those who see things differently. Borrowing folk beliefs from cultures with very different concepts of nature, culture, human, and animal will necessarily result in a distortion of those views. Just because the Salish, for example, believe in a wild man figure who guards nature does not necessarily mean that wild men exist as biological flesh-and-blood beings who can be discovered, analyzed, and tamed.

The Functions of Cryptids

Why does every culture have beliefs, stories, and myths about strange animals that seem out of this world? And does the presence of these stories point toward real animals?

Stories about cryptids, like much of folklore and mythology, serve a number of purposes. They are explanatory and can, like the "just so" folktales, explain how a place or thing came to be. They can also be used to explain the unexplained or as a way to provide meaning when a tragedy has occurred. In the mountains of Northern California, an area known as the emerald triangle because of the extensive marijuana farms (both legal and illegal) there, a number of young men have disappeared or turned up murdered. These disappearances and deaths have often been attributed to Bigfoot, as that area is known to be Bigfoot habitat, although police in the area believe the deaths are due to the dangers in the illegal drug market. And of course, cryptid tales are used as cautionary tales, offering parents a boogeyman to use to teach their children not to get into trouble. Beliefs in cryptids are found in every culture, testifying to the importance of these stories.

Psychologically, beliefs in cryptids function the way that beliefs in other unusual beliefs, conspiracies, and urban legends do: they offer a way for us to deal with our fears and anxieties. But they go further than that and provide validation for those fears. Stories and beliefs about cryptids offer a focal point for a whole variety of concerns and fears—not only surrounding nature and the unknown but also surrounding the government and the so-called scientific elite. (This is one reason why cryptozoology took shape during the Cold War when much of the world lived under the ever-present fear about nuclear war.) Beliefs in cryptids—like other anomalous beliefs—are thus self-reinforcing.

Beliefs about cryptids, like other beliefs, spread from place to place and take on local attributes in each new locale in which they find themselves. This might explain the wide variety of Bigfoot-like creatures found in North America. Either Bigfoot beliefs traveled via diffusion from the pacific northwest to other parts of the continent, taking on names like The Skunk Ape, Honey Island Swamp Monster, the Fouke Monster, and Momo, or else they were independently invented in each locale, which seems unlikely given the similarities in lore.

Cryptids are liminal creatures in that they exist at the borders of human society, but more importantly, they exist at the edge of the fantastical, a realm where secret creatures guard secret knowledge. They are neither real nor are they fake; instead, they are found at the intersection of reality and fantasy, nature and culture, and faith and science.

Finally, cryptids, and the explosion in cryptozoology that has occurred in recent years, testify to a longing to reconnect, not just with nature but also with the wild untamed nature that has been largely conquered, scientifically analyzed, and, in some cases, been wiped out—all by us. We are living in a time where human impacts on the planet are at an all-time high. One of the results of human activity is what many scientists are calling the sixth great extinction: we are literally watching as much of this planet's biodiversity is disappearing, and there is no scientific debate about the fact that it is human activities that have caused this.

The fact that the thylacine—an Australian marsupial that looks like a cross between a coyote and a tiger, which went extinct in the 1930s—is now considered by some to be a cryptid whose possible (re)existence is being documented by activists throughout Australia points toward hope (or perhaps guilt) as one of the motivations for cryptozoology. Finding a thylacine, alive, somewhere in Australia would go far toward alleviating some of the responsibility and guilt that Australians hold for the extinction of the thylacine. Finding that thylacines are alive after all would provide hope for cryptozoologists (and animal lovers) everywhere that perhaps there is still time to reverse the damage that we have done to our planet.

Cryptids, like all monsters, exist because we need them—today more than ever. They offer us a tool with which to think about and work through our deepest fears about ourselves and the world around us. With an acceleration of urbanization, and as the tentacles of late capitalism continue to tighten around us, has come massive environmental degradation and a creeping sense of alienation. Cryptids embody the untamed forces of nature. Not too long ago, those forces were threatening and dangerous. Today, nature has been wiped clean of its dangers and been rendered not just safe but also comprehensible. There's something inevitable about what we have done to the planet, especially in a culture like the United States with its focus on constant progress. The presence of monsters—unknown, unchecked, inscrutable—may be the only thing we have left that reminds us of what once was but that can never be again.

Further Reading:

Arment, C. (2004). *Cryptozoology: Science & Speculation*. Coachwhip Publications.

Bauer, H. (2014). Cryptozoology and the Troubles with "Skeptics" and Mainstream Pundits. *Journal of Scientific Exploration*, 27(4), 690–704.

Brotherton, R., & French, C. C. (2014). Belief in Conspiracy Theories and Susceptibility to the Conjunction Fallacy. *Applied Cognitive Psychology*, 28, 238–48. doi:10.1002/acp.2995

Bubandt, N. (2019). Of Wildmen and White Men: Cryptozoology and Inappropriate/d Monsters at the Cusp of the Anthropocene. *Journal of the Royal Anthropological Institute*, 25(2), 223–40.

Dagnall, N., Denovan, A., Drinkwater, K., Parker, A., & Clough, P. J. (2017). Urban Legends and Paranormal Beliefs: The Role of Reality Testing and Schizotypy. *Frontiers in Psychology*, 8, 94.

French, C. C., & Stone, A. (2013). *Anomalistic Psychology: Exploring Paranormal Belief and Experience*. Palgrave Macmillan.

Hurn, S. (Ed.). (2016). *Anthropology and Cryptozoology: Exploring Encounters with Mysterious Creatures*. Routledge.

Mullis, J. (2019). Cryptofiction! Science Fiction and the Rise of Cryptozoology. In *The Paranormal and Popular Culture*. Routledge, 240–52.

Regal, B. (2011). *Searching for Sasquatch: Crackpots, Eggheads, and Cryptozoology*. Springer.

Rossi, L. (2016). A Review of Cryptozoology: Towards a Scientific Approach to the Study of "Hidden Animals". In F. M. Angelici (Ed.), *Problematic Wildlife, A Cross Disciplinary Approach*. Springer International Publishing, 573–88.

The Encyclopedia

Cryptids

A

AHOOL

Name: Ahool
Alternative Names: n/a
Related Cryptids: Thunderbird
Location: Indonesia
Most Recent Documented Sighting: 2015 (in Portugal)

The ahool is a mysterious giant bat from Southeast Asia and, more specifically, Indonesia.

The ahool is huge, larger than any known flying mammal, with a wingspan ranging anywhere from 12 to as large as 28 feet. For comparison the flying fox, which is the largest species of insect-eating bat, and also the largest flying mammal, only has a wingspan of 5 feet. In appearance, they are sometimes described as having the appearance of a primate, specifically an ape, with gray fur, dark eyes, and usually described as having red wings with claws on the forearms. The face has been described as primate, hominoid or human-like, and descriptions emphasize the flattened snout associated with primates. Some descriptions suggest that it has feet that point backward. This is significant because in cultures with a belief in witches, one of the most common identifying features of a witch is having either organs or body parts that are backward, upside down, or inside out. This indicates that, at least in some areas, the ahool is thought to be associated with witchcraft. On the other hand, bats' feet point backwards, so the description may point more toward the anatomical understanding of bats.

Like other bats, it flies. While most bats are insect eaters, the ahool hunts and eats fish, small animals, as well as much larger animals, and they have been known to attack and kill humans. They are mostly associated with the island of Java, and the name itself is an onomatopoeia: the Javanese word ahool is the sound that the creature makes. Today, the ahool is known not only throughout the entire Indonesian archipelago but also throughout much of Southeast Asia as well including Vietnam and the Philippines.

Indonesia has come under the influence of a wide variety of cultures, including other indigenous cultures in Southeast Asia, as well as Islam, Hinduism and Buddhism (from India), and Confucianism (from China), and their myths reflect that diversity. Many of the ancient indigenous spirits of the forests and waterways have been associated with gods, spirits, and demons from the newer religions after they arrived.

What is the ahool exactly?

The ahool could, like all of the other flying cryptids, simply be the result of misidentification of other wildlife, such as a large raptor. An owl would be a good candidate because it is large and the sound that it makes could easily sound like "ahool." The largest owl in the world is the Blakiston's fish owl, with a wingspan of about 6 feet. Another possible candidate for the ahool could be the hammer headed bat, which is Africa's largest bat with a wingspan of 3 1/2 feet,

Figure 2 *Ahool. Copyright © 2023 Heidi Scheidl. All rights reserved.*

but aside from the fact that hammer headed bats look more like dogs than primates, this bat is native to Africa and has not been known in Asia. The best candidate is most likely the Bismarck fruit bat, which has a wingspan of between 5 and 6 feet and is native to New Guinea, which puts the bat directly in the region. Another possible explanation is the one given for the existence of the Thunderbird as well as other large mythic birds: they are simply surviving populations of previously thought to be extinct species, usually a pterosaur. In other words, the ahool is a relic or holdover species.

The ahool was largely unknown outside of Southeast Asia until the first Europeans arrived in the sixteenth century and definitely after the colonization of Indonesia by the Dutch in the early seventeenth century. But it took until the twentieth century for the first written account to leave Indonesia. Ernst Bartels, a Dutch naturalist, grew up in Java and in 1927 heard the cry that is associated with the ahool. This account of the creature, which Bartels said encountered twice (in 1925 he said it had flown directly over him while he was exploring the Selek Mountains), was given during an interview with cryptozoologist Ivan Sanderson.

Giant bats are relatively rare in cryptozoology. The ahool shares many similarities with the ropen, a mythical bat from the easternmost island in the archipelago, New Guinea, which is similarly huge, and glows while it flies, and was first reported by a Westerner in 1935. Another close relative is the Orang Bati. This is another giant flying creature with the face of a primate, but reports about the creature are much more sinister than regarding the ahool. Orang Bati are known to swoop down from the sky in order to kidnap small children, which it then takes back to its lair to be eaten later. The Orang Bati, which is primarily associated with the Indonesian island of Seram, is clearly linked to witchcraft beliefs, which are extremely popular in Indonesia, even while witchcraft itself is illegal. According to a 2012 poll, 69 percent of Indonesians believe in witchcraft, and one of the witch's most notable characteristics—and this is found in witch lore from around the world—is the idea that witches fly through the air at night and kidnap and eat children, especially babies. Think as well of the flying monkeys in *The Wizard of Oz*, which act as familiars to the Wicked Witch of the West (in the film but not the book). One unusual aspect of the connection between flying creatures and witches is that, at least in many parts of Indonesia, there is no known association between bats and witches, perhaps because Indonesian bats are fruit and insect eaters, while witches are known to be carnivorous.

Other cultures have flying bats as well, including the Bat Beast of Kent and Batsquatch of Washington, although these creatures seem to be very much the product of modern lore. More relevant to the flying bats of Indonesia are those of Africa: the olitiau, a flying bat from Cameroon, Kangomoto, a giant flying beast from subtropical central Africa, and the sasabonsam, from Ghana.

See also: Gamayun, Thunderbird

Further Reading:

Forth, G. (2021). Ambiguous Birds: Ideas About Bats on Flores Island and Elsewhere. *Journal of Ethnobiology*, 41(1), 105–20.
Sanderson, I. T. (1972). *Investigating the Unexplained: A Compendium of Disquieting Mysteries of the Natural World*. Prentice-Hall.

AKKOROKAMUI

Name: Akkorokamui.

Alternative Names: n/a

Related Cryptids: n/a

Location: Uchiura Bay, Japan

Most Recent Documented Sighting: n/a

Akkorokamui is a giant octopus or squid from Japan's Uchiura Bay, off of the island of Hokkaido.

Akkorakamui (or Atkor Kamuy, the Ainu name) is one of the oldest creatures on the island, dating back at least to the time of the Ainu, Japan's indigenous people.

It is described as enormous, as large as a hectare in size, and can swallow boats, thus posing a major risk to sailors and fishermen.

Akkorakumui is a yokai, one of many of Japan's indigenous spirits. These spirits inhabit the mountains, rivers, lakes, and oceans in and around Japan and provide safety and protection but can also tease, harass, and even harm people. As a tiny island nation surrounded by ocean, it's no wonder that Japan is host to a large number of ocean creatures. Besides Akkorakamui, Akura is a gigantic fish, Akaei, a stingray, Ika no Kōan, a cuttlefish, Suiko, a water tiger, Hōnengyo, a bipedal fish-reptile monster (and the inspiration for Godzilla), and the Ningyo, Japan's mermaid.

In addition, Akkorakumui is not Japan's only giant octopus, either. Other tentacled beasts include Ikuchi, a giant sea serpent that is usually depicted with giant tentacled arms. Like Akkorakumui, Ikuchi can swallow a ship whole by enveloping it within its tentacles. One of the more interesting variants is Tako nyōbō, which is a shapeshifter. They take as their main shape the octopus but can transform into human women and marry human men. This puts them into the category of animal brides—magical female animal beings who, while in their human guise, take on a life with a human with whom they have fallen in love. Once married, unless their secret is detected, they can make very good wives. Unlike selkies, swan maidens, and other animal brides, the skin of the Tako nyōbō is not used to control her. However, if the husband figures out who she really is, she will return to the sea, never to return.

See also: Kitsune, Selkie, Swan Maiden

Further Reading:

Jankiewicz-Brzostowska, M. (2020). Depictions of Animals in the Satirical War Prints of Kobayashi Kiyochika. *Art of the Orient*, 9(1), 134–54.

Mouritsen, O. G., & Styrbæk, K. (2021). Strange Beings from the Depths of the Sea. In O. G. Mouritsen, K. Styrbæk, J. D. Mouritsen, & M. Johansen (Eds.), *Octopuses, Squid & Cuttlefish: Seafood for Today and for the Future*. Springer International Publishing, 5–16.

Srinivasan, A. (2017). The Sucker, the Sucker! *London Review of Books*, 39(17), 23–5.

ALMAS

Name: Almas

Alternative Names: Alma, Almesty

Related Cryptids: Bigfoot, Yeti, Yowy, Yeren

Location: Central Asia, but especially Mongolia

Most Recent Documented Sighting: 1992

The Almas, or alma, is a hominoid creature found throughout much of Central Asia, including Mongolia, Russia, and Siberia. If most regions of the world have a hominoid, or "ape-man" creature, the Almas fills that niche in this part of the world.

Almas are tall (ranging between 5 and 6½ feet), strong, hairy (usually with hair of a reddish hue, but it has also been described as yellow, brown, and black) but not covered with fur, and human-like (in fact, they are seen as more human than animal), and they hunt and eat small animals and forage for wild plant foods. They are more stocky than humans, weighing approximately 500 pounds, and they can be male or female, with the females distinguished by the large pendulous breasts. They have a foul odor, something that is common with wild men in other locations.

They live in the most isolated mountain ranges, occasionally bothering or even kidnapping humans. The almas is said to use simple stone tools, which is different from other ape-men, such as Bigfoot, which are usually seen as having no tool use as well as no language. They live in the mountains of Mongolia, and especially in the west of the country, in caves and holes or other depressions in the earth, and are known to fear fire and water.

The almas is the Central Asian example of what are called wild men, ape-men, ape-human hybrids, or sometimes just Bigfoot. That is to say that these are all names given to creatures that are part of the myths, legends, and folktales of people around the world but that have not been accepted as real, living beings by any of the scientific disciplines.

In Central Asia, wild men can be found in Mongolia, Kyrgyzstan, and Kazakhstan, and these wild men are described in much the same way that wild men of China are. And these beliefs are similar to those found in Iran and India. In fact, we can see a gradual continuum between these beliefs from as far east as Japan to as far west as the British Isles, which tells us that wild men, and the beliefs about them, spread through the Old World in the same way that other material and nonmaterial phenomena have traveled: east to west and west to east, from Asia to Europe and back again.

Why do people believe in wild men, and why is it such a prevalent belief around the world? Does the presence of, and commonalities between, all of these belief systems mean that the creatures or real, or does it speak to something else that these creatures may represent? From Enkidu in the Mesopotamian legend of Gilgamesh to England's Green Man, there are countless versions of a primitive, hairy, man-like creature living in the forests, generally at the edge of human society. They have been included in the natural history of many early naturalists, such as Pliny the Elder who describes a race of creatures called silvestres that live in India and whose description sounds an awful lot like gibbons, India's lesser ape. But putting aside the misrepresentation of primate species—famously, Hanno the Navigator, a fifth-century Carthaginian explorer, thought that the gorillas that he saw were a tribe of hairy women who he called the gorilla tribe—there must be other reasons for this pervasive belief in a world inhabited by humans as well as by near-humans who lurk around the borders of our world.

Humans everywhere are interested in the natural world and our place in it. In many non-Western societies, nature and animals are not necessarily categories that are easily opposed to culture or humans. In fact, many cultures see (or saw) animals as potential clan members, ancestors, separate nations, or intermediaries between the sacred and profane worlds. Many of these cultures share a belief in animism, a worldview that finds that humans, animals, plants, and inanimate objects all might be endowed with spirit and, thus, are sentient. In addition, we know that humans look for images of ourselves around us. We see Jesus in a grilled cheese sandwich or Aunt Mary in a raincloud, and we anthropomorphize or zoopomorphize everything from trains to cars. We are highly attuned to looking for, and seeing, faces in both animate and inanimate objects, so it should not surprise us that an idea that there are beings who are not only like us but also are wilder, less civilized makes a lot of sense.

Philosophers have been debating what makes humans humans and what makes animals animals. Because the human-animal border did not develop as a hard and fixed idea until after the domestication of animals, prior to this time, the idea of a part human–part animal creature would have been very normal. As societies develop, and especially with the development of agriculture and the domestication of animals, the idea that humans now occupy one world—civilization—and animals occupy another—nature—becomes fixed. Wild men occupy the space in between—they are not civilized but they are not entirely natural either. In addition, wild men provide the exception that proves the rule: humans are very different from animals, although there are monstrous freaks that blur that border. It is exactly the presence of these creatures that reinforces the separation between nature and civilization, human and animal.

While cryptozoologists translate almas to mean ape-man, the Mongolian word almas actually means demon or witch, and almas, or derivations of the word, is used throughout Central Asia, including Turkey and Iran. Like so many other people, Mongols saw supernatural spirits as always engaging in the natural world; some were good, some neutral, and many were dangerous. Many had very specific tasks; one might make childbirth difficult for women. By the time that Westerners began reporting on stories about the almas, the creature had morphed into one that was primarily folkloric, rather than real. And today, in the modern world, almas have changed again, reflecting the changing human environment. Almas today can be male, female, or even juvenile, and while almas have always been implicated in kidnappings and other minor to major harassments, a newer notion is the idea that after kidnapping a victim, they will have sex with them. Typically, when this type of a belief is found associated with a mythical being, there is a concern about sexual promiscuity, sex before marriage, and, importantly, premarital births. Having a belief that accounts for the occasional presence of a baby being born to a young unmarried girl or woman can provide cover for those women. It is said that these almas babies are larger, stronger, and hairier than human babies.

Many almas stories are relayed in the same way that urban legends are: they are told in the third person, and the storyteller asserts that while they did not encounter the creature, their friend/aunt/cousin/cousin's friend did. It is the using of the name of a witness that confers legitimacy. Greater legitimacy, however, can be had if the witness had firsthand experience with the creature. This gives the witness status in the community and makes them somewhat worthy of fear.

While there are stories of wild men who were shot and killed, there has never been a verified body, body part, or even a bit of fur associated with the almas. The scientific interest in almas emerged in the 1950s and early 1960s but then dropped off until after the fall of the Iron Curtain at the end of the 1980s and beginning of the 1990s. Today, the belief in almas has gotten a boost thanks to the interest of cryptozoologists, many of whom have traveled to the region to try to find the creature. With Western cryptozoological interest comes the conflating of almas characteristics with wild men from other regions and the distancing of almas stories from the cultural, historical, and social context in which they originally circulated. In recent years, Almas have also been blamed for one of Russia's most mysterious events—the Dyatlov Pass Incident, when a group of nine Soviet college students met a violent end while on a hike through the Ural Mountains in 1959.

With this comes a shift in what the creature is thought to be. Like so many other wild men and ape-men that have come to the attention of cryptozoology, almas are now theorized as evolutionary relics, modern survivors of either ancestors, like Homo Erectus, or the cousins of our ancestors, such as Neanderthals or Denisovans. Perhaps even more importantly, many cryptozoologists who see almas as real, rather than folkloric, beings understand the almas to represent the population from which Bigfoot and all of the other north (and south) American hominids evolved. The hypothesis is that just as humans crossed the Siberian land bridge to North America perhaps 20,000 years ago, Almas, or almas-like creatures, came over with them, dispersing and populating the continent.

The first detailed reports of the almas to reach the Western world emerged at the end of the Victorian era, an era where much of what would come to be known as cryptozoology was starting to develop. Almas were slotted into a body of popular science that was developing at the time and which would eventually link almas to Bigfoot, yeti, and yeren, even though there are significant differences between these creatures. Yeti and Bigfoot, for example, are more animal-like than human-like, and are both larger than the almas. The Chinese yeren, another seemingly close relative, is also more ape-like than human. Even the orang pendek, Sumatra's wild man, is closer to an animal than a human being.

Functionally, almas stories probably serve many of the same purposes that other wild men, as well as a wide variety of monsters, play. They are probably used to help socialize children and to teach them a healthy fear of the forests. They probably help to explain when, for example, livestock are killed by an unknown creature. Finally, they may also help to make sense of what we now call feral children. In 1850, Zana, either a feral child or an almas, was caught in the Caucasus Mountains and was raised as a human. She was also impregnated by several men, giving birth to multiple children who were described as both very dark and very strong (but not hairy).

Abhishek Chakravorty argues that the Yahoos, ape-like creatures in Jonathan Swift's *Gulliver's Travels*, published in 1726, were based on the almas and argues that stories of wild men from Central Asia had been seeping into Europe since the Middle Ages. Swift's description of the Yahoos certainly sounds like the descriptions we have of the Almas:

> Their Heads and Breasts were covered with a thick Hair, some frizzled and others lank; they had Beards like Goats, and a Long Ridge of Hair down their Backs, and the fore parts of their skins, which were of a brown Buff coluor... The Hair of both sexes was of several colours, brown, red, black and yellow. (Swift, 209)

Swift also describes their behavior, with an emphasis on their sexual practices:

> For they are cunning, malicious, treacherous and revengeful. They are strong and hardly, but of a cowardly spirit, and by consequence insolent, abject, and cruel. It is observed that, the Red-haired of both sexes are more libidinous and mischievous than the rest, whom yet they much exceed in strength and Activity. (Swift, 248)

This tracks with Mongolian accounts of Almas that would rape and impregnate human females.

Debbie Argue, on the other hand, suggested in an essay in the cryptozoological journal, *The Relic Hominoid Inquiry*, that it was Bigfoot that influenced Swift who may have heard stories from travelers to the North American colonies about indigenous beliefs.

While there's no way to know definitively whether or not Swift's Yahoos were based on Mongolian Almas, American Bigfoot, or any other creature, it seems likely that Swift was influenced by wild man stories.

See also: Bigfoot, Orang Pendek, Yeren, Yowie

Further Reading:

Argue, D. (2018). Does the Yahoo in Gulliver's Travels Represent an Eighteenth Century Description of the Sasquatch? *The Relict Hominoid Inquiry*, 7, 97–106.

Bayanov, D. (2012). Historical Evidence for the Existence of Relict Hominoids. *The Relict* Hominoid Inquiry, 1, 23–50.

Chakravorty, A. (2021). Wild men of Central Asia: A Cryptozoological Analysis of Jonathan Swift's Yahoo. *Research Journal Of English (RJOE)*, 6(3), 1–5.

Heaney, M. (1983). The Mongolian Almas: A Historical re-evaluation of the Sighting by Baradiin. *Cryptozoology*, 2, 40–52.

Rinčen, P. R. (1964). Almas Still Exists in Mongolia. *Genus*, 20(1), 186–92.

Stáhlberg, S., & Svanberg, I. (2017). Wildmen in Central Asia. *Anthropos*, 112(1), 51–62.

Swift, J. (1726). *Reprinted as Gulliver's Travels into Several Remote Nations of the World*. Lee & Shepard, 1876.

Wenzel, N. (2009). The Legend of the Almas: A Comparative and Critical Analysis. Independent Study Project (ISP) Collection. 801. https://digitalcollections.sit.edu/isp_collection/801.

ALTAMAHA-HA

Name: Altamaha-ha
Alternative Names: Alti
Related Cryptids: Bessie, Loch Ness Monster
Location: Georgia
Most Recent Documented Sighting: 2018

The altamaha-ha is a river monster that lives in the Altamaha River, in southeastern Georgia. It has been described as a giant sea serpent, Nessie-like in appearance, with a bony ridge on the top of the body, and measuring from 15 to 70 feet in length. It has no back legs and a set of front flippers, which it uses to navigate the waters in and around the river basin. It is gray or dark green.

The Altamaha River, and watershed that runs for 470 miles from its origin at the confluence of the Oconee and Ocmulgee Rivers to the Georgia coast where it empties into the Atlantic Ocean, is host to a wide diversity of animals, including sturgeon, snakes, the gopher tortoise, and the West Indian manatee.

It is also host to a sea serpent named after the river, which often appears around Butler and Darien islands, just off of the coast. Interestingly, Darien was founded in the eighteenth century by a group of Scots from Inverness, which famously borders Loch Ness.

The first European account of the Altamaha-ha comes from sixteenth-century French artist Jacques le Moyne de Morgues who accompanied René Laudonnière on an expedition to the New World; Laudonnière was attempting to colonize northern Florida (the Spanish were already in control of the southern half of the peninsula) on behalf of France. As with similar expeditions led by the English and the Spanish, the king ordered that an artist/cartographer accompany the trip in order to map and illustrate the new possessions for the crown. The expedition left France in 1564 where the group established Fort Caroline in what is now Jacksonville, Florida. The colonists were never able to develop a self-sufficient lifestyle and many eventually abandoned the colony. It finally met its end in 1565 after the Spanish killed the majority of the remaining settlers; le Moyne and a few others managed to escape the massacre and return to France, bringing with him his detailed illustrations.

During the year that the French were in Florida, they were in contact with the local native people, the Timucua, who provided food and other support to the struggling colonists, and le Moyne was tasked with documenting the landscape, plants, animals, and native peoples of the new land. His illustrations, later compiled into a 42-illustration volume published by de Bry, were the first images of any inhabitants of North America to reach Europe.

One of the most notable of his illustrations is an image depicting a group of Timucua Indians fighting what we know today to be an alligator—although in le Moyne's illustration, it is larger than any known alligator. The animal is easily the size of twenty men and has elements of sea serpent morphology, including a very large head and a surprisingly long neck. Le Moyne's illustrations probably reflect stories that the settlers learned from nearby Indians, who told of a being called an altamaha-ha, which was a scaly river monster.

It would take another 300 years before the story of the altamaha-ha was reported in an English-language newspaper; it was in 1830 that the *Savannah Georgian* paper published an interview with a Captain Delano, who saw a large sea serpent-like creature. It was spotted at the mouth of the river near St. Simons Island along the Florida coast. The newspaper printed the following:

> He repeated the . . . particulars precisely, describing the animal he saw as being about 70 feet long, and its circumference about that of a sugar hogshead, moving with its head (shaped like an Alligator's) about 8 feet out of the water. (*Savannah Georgian*, April 22, 1830)

Sightings over the next century occurred rarely, but the consensus of those reports was that the monster looked like an alligator or a giant snake but was enormous. The legend did not really gain traction until 1981 when two eel fishermen, Larry Gwinnett and Steve Wilson, saw the creature; the story was picked up by the tabloid *Weekly World News* and, from there, went international. Gwinnett was quoted as saying:

We were at an elbow in the river near Smith Lake pulling up our traps. There's a real deep hole there and we didn't have enough rope to drop a trap. All of a sudden a large wave—like one made by a large boat—almost tipped our boat. I looked around and saw these two humps about 5 feet apart like what would be on a serpent. They were as thick around as a man's body. It Had to be 16 to 20 feet long. I was scared. (*Weekly World News*, 1981)

It was not until 2018 that hard evidence of the existence of the altamaha-ha appeared, in the form of a corpse found on the beach in Wolf Island off of the coast of Georgia. It had the long neck of a classic sea serpent à la the Loch Ness Monster and unfortunately turned out to be a hoax, created by New York City performance artist Zardulu. She reported that the carcass was that of a shark supplemented by paper mache.

So far, there has been no evidence to support the existence of Altie, and sightings continue to be rare.

See also: Bessie, Champ, Chessie, Loch Ness Monster

Further Reading:

Interview with Captain Delano (1830). *Savannah Georgian*, April 22.
Miles, J. (2000). *Weird Georgia: Close Encounters, Strange Creatures, and Unexplained Phenomena.* Cumberland House Publishing.
Monster Serpent Lurks in Muddy American River (1981). *Weekly World News*. March 23.

B

BARMANOU

Name: Barmanou

Alternative Names: Jangali mosh

Related Cryptids: Yeti, Almas, Ebu Gogo, Orang Pendek

Location: Pakistan and Afghanistan

Most Recent Documented Sighting: 2019

The Barmanou is an ape-man from northern Pakistan and one of many such creatures in Central Asia.

Pakistani folklore has been influenced by the traditions and beliefs of a wide variety of cultures. The country has been under the influence of, over the years, Aryans, Persians, Greeks, Arabs, Turks, Afghans, Mongols, and the British, all of which have left their mark on the country. In addition, the country is home to multiple ethnic groups, all of which have their own folk traditions. In the south of Pakistan, much of the folklore surrounds historical events, while the folklore of the north tends to be focused more on supernatural events and entities.

In the north of the country is the region of Chitral, in the Hindu Kush mountains. This region is fairly isolated and much of their traditional cultural practices preserved, even after the British arrived in the country. The people who live here are called the Kho or the Chitrali, and their folklore and language are referred to either as Chitrali or Khowar. While today, it is technically a Muslim area, traditional beliefs are still strong.

Khowar folklore, which was heavily influenced by cultural traditions in ancient India, China, and Persia, includes a wide variety of spirits, monsters, and ghosts. Many are evil, some are good, and many are neutral and can help or hurt a person.

One of those beings is known as a barmanu or barmanou. It is a bipedal creature, covered in hair (except for the face, hands, feet, and, oddly, knees), often seen wearing animal hides, and emits a foul odor. Descriptions of the barmanu are very similar to those of the other wild men in Central Asia like the almas. Barmanou is a Sanskrit word that means "man of the forest." It is just one of many giants in Khower folklore, such as the deo, a fire giant that lives in caves, the nang, which is a giant underwater beast, and the barzangi, which is essentially a demon that lives in the most remote mountains and eats humans.

The barmanu is a dangerous being, because it attacks and kills livestock and abducts women for sex. It is thought to specifically pick out beautiful women to kidnap.

There are very few reports of firsthand encounters with a barmanou, although many people have allegedly heard its loud, agonizing, and terrifying cry, rather than seen it. Instead, it seems to operate more like an urban legend, in that stories about these encounters are typically told in the third person, about someone that the speaker knows, as the following account shared on Reddit does:

> Word on the street nawaz sharif was on his daala heading to his holiday house and Barmanou threw his car off the mountain. Many daalas owned by corrupt people including Zardari and Shabaz sharif have gone missing and Barmanou is assumed responsible. (akerbrygg 2020)

Another redditor shared this account:

> Personally I've never seen such a creature but I have heard stories and accounts. My father is an avid outdoorsman. Back in his day he used to spend up to 40 days in the mountains fishing, hunting and exploring places. From my childhood I have heard one particular story from him of a creature in Kashmir. He described it as small and with an elongated whitish face with a humanoid like body. From what he told me he and his friend heard some voices from the roof of a nomad's stone winter house. They took a local with them to inquire but only saw a glimpse of the creature I described above. (Agentweatherby 2020)

Those cryptozoologists with an interest in the barmanou, including the person who did the most research, zoologist Jordi Magraner, suggest that like so many other ape-men or wild men, the barmanou is a relic hominid, or members of a species that went extinct long ago but that survives in very small numbers today. Magraner, who was murdered while in his home in Pakistan, was one of the few cryptozoologists to dedicate themselves to one creature and one culture. He learned the Khower language, to make it easier to collect stories and interview witnesses, and was able to collect twenty-seven first-person accounts by witnesses who directly encountered the creature.

Besides these first-person accounts, the only other information that could be considered evidence of the barmanou is footprints. Witnesses reported seeing footprints that were too large and misshapen to be human.

One of the accounts that Magraner collected provides information about not only the beast's appearance but also its aggression:

> It was on an evening of July 1987, around 9:00 pm. The shepherd was returning to the village with his goats, lantern in hand. He suddenly found himself face-to-face with an adolescent hairy man who tried to touch Mohamed with his arms outstretched (a defensive rather than aggressive gesture). In defense, the shepherd hit the young hairy with his stick. The two opponents were on a slope with scattered trees and bushes at about 2,300 m. There was a large bush between them, around which they circled. According to the Pathan, the action lasted for about two hours, he hitting the young hairy, the latter trying to grab him. The young hairy man uttered guttural sounds, a kind of deep exhalation—"ahan!" The shepherd was

not afraid of being bitten but rather scratched—the young hairy was reaching with its long fingernails. Its smell was strong and unpleasant, like that of a rotting corpse. It was 1.1–1.2 m (43–47 in) tall and entirely covered with greyish-brown hair. Its head-hair was short; its face, the palm of its hands, and the sole of its feet were hairless. Its skin was dark, "like that of a Gujar." It did not wear any clothes. It had no forehead and a small flattened nose; its mouth had no lips and its teeth were similar to a Man's, without fangs. The arms seemed long, because of the long narrow hands and fingers. The feet were human-like but wider, especially in the front. Its chest was very developed. After two hours, the young hairy fled uphill to the nearby forest. (Magraner 2018)

Many of Magraner's stories included the element of the barmanu trying to kidnap a woman; other stories emphasized that it was the presence of a woman that attracted it. While the barmanou is primarily seen as male, there are a few accounts of encounters with female barmanou.

Some of the barmanou stories point toward some functions. For example, when a child goes missing or is found hurt or dead, it is clear to most that a barmanou was involved. It is understood that female barmanou may sometimes kidnap human children if they cannot have, or have lost, their own. In addition, the barmanou's habit of kidnapping, raping, and sometimes impregnating girls and women may have operated as a form of cover for women who might be having sexual relations outside of marriage.

See also: Almas, Ebu Gogo, Orang Pendek, Yeti

Further Reading:

Agentweatherby (2020). Does Anyone Have any Stories of the Barmanou. *Reddit, R/Pakistan*, May 12, https://www.reddit.com/r/pakistan/comments/hplbrd/does_anyone_have_any_stories_of_the_barmanou/.
akerbrygg (2020). Does Anyone Have any Stories of the Barmanou. *Reddit, R/Pakistan*, May 12, https://www.reddit.com/r/pakistan/comments/hplbrd/does_anyone_have_any_stories_of_the_barmanou/.
Bhutto, A. (2018). Invisible Monster: A Compromised Zoologist in Pakistan. *TLS. Times Literary Supplement*, 6024, 29–30.
Magraner, J. (2018). Relic Hominids of Central Asia: Extracts from the Report – Notes on Relic Hominids of Central Asia. *The Relict Hominoid Inquiry*, 7, 16–68.

BATATUT

Name: Batatut
Alternative Names: Rock Ape, Nguoi Rung, Little Bigfoot, Vietnamese Rock Ape
Related Cryptids: Orang Pendek, Yeren, Yeti, Ebu Gogo
Location: Vietnam
Most Recent Documented Sighting: 1975

The batatut, also known as a rock ape, is a cryptohominid or "ape-man" from Vietnam.

Like so many cryptids, the batatut is a combination of local folklore about a wild man, mixed with elements of wild men from neighboring cultures, and then appended onto a global theory developed by mid-twentieth-century cryptozoologists.

There may at one time have been a belief in two species of rock ape, one larger (6–7 feet) and one smaller. Like ape-men everywhere, they are bipedal and covered with reddish, brown, or black fur, although without fur on the face (like some monkey species). According to witnesses, they are not afraid of people, communicate using a series of sounds, are active both day and night, and appear to be solitary. They are thought to be omnivorous, supplementing fruit and leaves with the occasional scavenged or hunted small animal. The smaller variant has lighter hair, a smaller body, and is only active during the day. Neither type uses tools or possesses language.

Cryptozoologist Jeff Meldrum, one of just a handful of cryptozoologists with a scientific background (he's a biological anthropologist), takes the position, put forth decades earlier by Sanderson and Heuvelmann, that there are populations of relic hominoids and hominids all around the world. These relics are living members of species that went extinct hundreds of thousands or even millions of years ago but that managed to survive into the present, largely without being discovered. According to this approach, the existence of wild man stories across the world offers indisputable proof that these creatures were once, and are most likely now, real.

The batatut has been a figure of Vietnamese folklore for hundreds of years and is, in particular, linked with the indigenous people who occupy the mountain jungles of the central highlands. The dominant ethnic group, the kinh, once avoided the highlands because evil spirits were thought to live there. When Vietnam fell to French rule in the late nineteenth century, the French realized that the highlands were ideal for the establishment of plantations to grow cash crops for export. The French also encouraged the settlement of the highlands by the kinh, further disturbing and partially displacing the indigenous people.

The highlands are also home to a variety of animals, including the Asian elephant, the Indochine tiger, and a number of bovine species including the gaur, the water buffalo, and the banteng. In addition, there are twenty-four primate species in Vietnam, one of which is the gibbon, while the rest are monkeys, almost half of which are threatened with extinction. One of the regions most threatened monkey is the Grey-Shanked Douc Langur, which is only found in this region of Vietnam and is critically endangered.

Everywhere in the world that nonhuman primates and humans coexist includes those primates in their folklore and myths. Monkeys and apes are both symbolically important—they seem not only very much like us but unlike us as well, and their interest in us, their curiosity, and intelligence make them especially relatable. This can trigger a sense of the uncanny, a feeling also associated with cryptid sightings. This makes them good candidates to represent the hopes and fears of humans.

Indigenous Monkey lore in Vietnam was probably supplemented by beliefs and stories from elsewhere, such as China and India, both countries that had a significant impact on Vietnam.

Figure 3 *A young batatut collects rocks to throw at soldiers. Copyright © 2023 Heidi Scheidl. All rights reserved.*

It only came to the attention of people outside of Vietnam after stories about American soldiers getting attacked by these creatures made it back to America. Soldiers told of frightening and unexplainable encounters while in the jungles with a large, hairy creature that threw rocks at them, and even grenades, and otherwise scared and harassed them.

Soldiers at war—but especially in a place like Vietnam where the terrain was unfamiliar, conditions were harsh, and the tactics of the North Vietnamese and Vietcong vicious—face threats that most people can never imagine and experience PTSD (which was not yet named in at that time) in very high numbers. They also seesaw between long dull stretches of no action and very violent and frightening situations. It should not surprise us that these men might attribute scary noises and movements in the jungle to a mythical creature. In fact, it's not at all unheard of and has occurred in other wars.

Soldiers, often aided by government-sponsored propaganda, often demonize the enemy, turning them from people into monsters. Military and political leaders will tell stories about atrocities committed by the enemy in order to gain support for the war as well as to bolster soldiers' confidence. This also contributes to greater displays of violence by soldiers themselves. One can only wonder whether the practice of turning one's enemy into subhuman monsters also makes it more likely that supernatural monsters become part of the wartime experience.

During the First World War, in 1915, a German submarine attacked and sank the British ship *Iberian* near Ireland. The submarine's captain, Baron von Forstner, later wrote about seeing a twenty-meter-long sea monster that was thrown out of the water from the force of the torpedoes. Cryptozoologist Bernard Heuvelmann later concluded that what von Forstner had seen was a sea crocodile that had survived the extinction of others of its kind. Soldiers fighting in the trenches also reported accounts of monsters terrorizing them.

But it was the Vietnam War that has been associated with the most monster sightings. If war is hell, then American soldiers fighting in Vietnam experienced a double hell: the viciousness and uncertainties of war, combined with a tropical jungle environment filled with unknown—to the soldiers—animals. Countless stories emerged from Americans serving overseas, supplemented by those told by the South Vietnamese. Most reports describe an ape-man with orange-brown fur, a muscular body, and a bipedal stance. Oddly, they were also often seen in groups, which is extremely rare in any cryptid sighting but especially in ape-men. There were so many sightings of these apes (which got their nickname from throwing rocks at soldiers), especially on and around Sơn Trà Mountain near the Bay of Da Nang that soldiers called the mountain Monkey Mountain.

A sergeant in the army named Kregg Jorgensen wrote later:

Suddenly, according to the men, a few small trees located fifteen yards uphill began clearly shaking. The soldiers had trained for this, and as they got ready for combat to fight the expected VC soldiers jumping out the bushes, they never imagined what they saw next.

A long, cucumber-shaped head showed up. The face, the soldiers said, was covered in red hair with a pair of dark eyes and a huge mouth. The creature then stepped out of the vegetation into a clearing, allowing the group to observe the rest of its muscular body, which was also featured by the same type of red hair. It wasn't taller than five feet and walked upright. It stopped, looked at them as though scrutinizing each of the soldiers. (2001)

There were so many stories told about the creature that in 1982, a government-sponsored research team was tasked with finding and studying it. This team produced a number of articles from their time in the Himalayas, concluding that wild men did in fact exist. This resulted in the Vietnamese government creating Chu Mom Ray National Park by carving out land on Mom Ray Mountain for these beings.

Evidence for the biological existence of the batatut includes photos or casts made of footprints, witness accounts, hair and feces samples, and folklore. Jeff Meldrum, the American anthropologist and cryptozoologist, claims that the footprints are real, and that they show a big toe as well as an arch, both associated with humans, although considerably larger than human. Most scientists outside the community do not accept the footprint evidence, nor the idea that there is an ape-man, much less a relic human, living in Vietnam. In 2014, Brian Sykes et al. compared a couple dozen Bigfoot as well as hair samples to known animal species and concluded that they all represent living beings.

See also: Almas, Bigfoot, Yeren

Further Reading:

Bacon, A.-M., & Long, V. (2001). The First Discovery of a Complete Skeleton of a Fossil Orang-utan in a Cave of the Hoa Binh Province, Vietnam. *Journal of Human Evolution*, 41, 227–41.

Coleman, L., & Huyghe, P. (1999). *The Field Guide to Bigfoot, Yeti, and Other Mystery Primates Worldwide*. Avon Books.

Forth, G. (2008). *Images of the Wildman in Southeast Asia: An Anthropological Perspective*. Routledge.

Jorgenson, K. P. (2001). *Very Crazy, GI: Strange but True Stories of the Vietnam War*. Random House Digital, Inc.

Loxton, D., & Prothero, D. R. (2013). *Abominable Science: Origins of the Yeti, Nessie, and Other Famous Cryptids*. Columbia University Press.

Messner, R. (2001). *My Quest for the Yeti: Confronting the Himalayas' Deepest Mystery*. Macmillan.

Murray, C. E. (2019). Locating the Wild Man: Rain Forest Enchantments and Settler Colonial Fantasies Amid the Ruins of the Anthropocene. *Journal of Historical Sociology*, 32(1), 60–73.

Sterling, E., Hurley, M., & Le, M. (2006). *Vietnam: A Natural History*. Yale University Press.

Sykes, B. (2016). *Bigfoot, Yeti, and the Last Neanderthal: A Geneticist's Search for Modern Apemen*. Red Wheel Weiser.

Sykes, B. C., Mullis, R. A., Hagenmuller, C., Melton, T. W., & Sartori, M. (2014). Genetic Analysis of Hair Samples Attributed to Yeti, Bigfoot and Other Anomalous Primates. *Proceedings of the Royal Society B: Biological Sciences*, 281(1789), 20140161.

Taylor, D. C. (2018). *Yeti: The Ecology of a Mystery*. Oxford University Press.

Ward, M. (1997). Everest 1951: The Footprints Attributed to the Yeti-myth and Reality. *Wilderness and Environmental Medicine*, 8, 29–32.

BEARILLA

Name: Bearilla

Alternative Names: Gateway Werewolf

Related Cryptids: Nandi Bear, Ozark Howler; Skinwalker, Spottsville Monster, Werewolf

Location: The forests and caves of Kentucky; additional sightings in Michigan, Pennsylvania, Wisconsin

Most Recent Documented Sighting: 2011

Bearilla is a wolf-bear hybrid creature that is most associated with Kentucky, although it has been seen in other states and even Canada.

It is a large creature, about 7 feet in height, with the body of a bear and the head of a wolf, complete with long snout and large, protruding canines. It walks upright on two legs, has silvery or gray fur, and very large, very sharp claws.

There have been dozens of reported sightings of the creature dating back to the first in 1944, when a young boy was reportedly attacked by one (he survived) while fishing in Johnson County. Johnson County is located in the Gateway region of the state, between the flatlands and the mountains of the eastern part of the state, and this is one of the regions with the most sightings. (This is why one of the nicknames for Bearilla is the Gateway Werewolf.) Since then, there have been many more of sightings of the creature.

Bearilla was not seen again until 1972, when a hunter was attacked on the banks of Hinkston Creek, near Berry, Kentucky. It was this hunter whose description led to the name Bearilla: it was described as looking like a bear combined with a gorilla. After this, Bearilla was spotted by numerous observers in the cemetery in Ashland, and some people claim that someone was killed in 1981 by the beast, but there are no documented records to prove this. There have been a handful of reported sightings since then, in 1989, 1999, 2001, and 2005. Another sighting in March 2008 of a tall, wolf-like creature resulted in a new name: the Erlanger Werewolf, because it was seen in the region of Erlanger, a suburb of Cincinnati.

Because there have been so few (relatively speaking) sightings of Bearilla, it is thought that the creature is able to keep itself well hidden from people. Kentucky has a vast network of caves, making it a good place for such a creature to live. In addition, the vast Appalachian Mountain range provides Bearilla with lots of game species; it is thought that it hunts deer and elk and occasionally preys on livestock when other animals are not available. Great parts of the state are heavily forested, giving Bearilla a huge amount of space on which to hunt and also hide from the public.

Most Bearilla reports do not actually involve a sighting; instead, Bearilla is thought to be the cause of many cases of unexplained livestock deaths. As is the case for the Chupacabra, Bearilla is implicated whenever a farmer or rancher finds animals that are mutilated but don't appear to be eaten, because most people assume that "regular" carnivores like wolves and dogs do not kill without eating their prey. The reality is that wolves do sometimes engage in surplus killing, where they kill more than they can eat, and packs of feral (and even domestic) dogs regularly attack livestock for fun, mutilating their bodies and leaving the remains. (When dogs attack livestock, they often attack their faces, one area where they can gain purchase, tearing off skin, ears, and more.)

Cryptozoologist Ron Coffey has been tracking Bearilla for decades, and while he hasn't found any physical remains, he has created a plaster cast footprint that is purportedly from the beast itself.

Kentucky is host to a number of cryptids. Locals have been reporting seeing large black cats (or Alien Big Cats) for years, Bigfoot-like creatures have been spotted in the Ohio River Valley (such as the Spottsville Monster, which terrorized one family in 1975), and in Christian County, Kentucky, a number of creatures (which were thought to have been aliens but may have been great horned owls) nicknamed the Hopkinsville Goblin once terrorized locals in 1955. Kentucky even has its own lake serpent, the Herrington Lake Monster. But Bigfoot (or its many variants) has been spotted throughout the state, although mostly in Central and Western Kentucky, the area with the most extensive cave networks. It's most likely, then, that Bigfoot and Bearilla may live close by each other in similar ecological conditions.

The most well known of the Kentucky cryptids is the Pope Lick Monster, a goat-human hybrid that lives beneath a bridge in Louisville. More closely related to Bearilla is the Werewolf of Mayking, a humanoid-canine hybrid that killed a number of pets and livestock over a two-week period in 1995. Unusually for a creature like this, those who saw the Werewolf of Mayking reported that it was wearing pants and boots.

Bears are an extremely important animal with respect to its role in the mythology and folklore of cultures in much of the world. (Bears are found in North and South America, Asia, and Europe; the single African bear species, the Atlas Bear, went extinct in the late nineteenth century.) This may be because they are sometimes worshipped as a god in hunter-gatherer societies and present a real threat to farmers and their livestock in farming societies. In addition, because bears walk upright, they are often seen as being closely related to humans and in many cultures are thought to be ancestral to humans, which explains their totemic importance to many Native American tribes. (The Koreans, as well, traditionally believed that they were descended from a bear.)

Many cultures had bear gods or goddesses, and bears were often seen as being a mediator to the supernatural world. The Celts worshipped a bear goddess named Artio. Bear goddesses often were portrayed as very protective of their young, just as bears are. In particular, shamanistic cultures that live in the far north, such as the Sami and the Ainu, were often closely associated with bears. These cultures had bear cults in which a baby bear would be raised for a year, almost as a human child (they would be breastfed by a human woman), and then sacrificed in an elaborate ceremony, which was thought to bring good fortune to the community. In Pacific Northwest Native American cultures, bears are often portrayed as magical animals and, because they hibernate, are often thought to influence dreams.

Because the bear looks so human-like, it is also not surprising that we find a number of tales in which bears transform into humans, humans transform into bears, or humans marry bears. For instance, in the Haida tale, "The Bear and His Indian Wife," a maiden gets taken by a bear chief, who marries her and has two children with her, before she is finally taken from the bear and reunited with her people.

The idea that bears and people can transform into each other is found most readily in the various folktales classified by folklorists under the name "Bearskin." In these tales, found throughout Europe and Asia, a man or a woman is given a bear skin to wear, which provides them with luck and riches; alternatively, a bear is able to remove its bear skin in order to appear human (and often in order to seduce a bride).

A related cryptid to Bearilla is the Nandi Bear, a bear-man hybrid first spotted by a European explorer named Geoffrey Williams in Kenya in 1905 (although well known to the local Nandi people after whom the creature was named, although another tribe, the Lumbwa, call it "brain eater") and which disappeared in 1919.

One theory to account for the presence of Bearilla goes back to the early exploration of the state by French Canadian explorers in the seventeenth century. These early explorers were accompanied by allies from the Huron and Algonquin tribes who probably brought with them their beliefs in the Wendigo, a shapeshifting creature that kills and eats humans. Native beliefs in the Wendigo may then have combined with the beliefs of the French explorers and settlers, who believed in werewolves, and, later, with the folk beliefs of the Scottish and English settlers who began arriving in the eighteenth century. Ultimately, Bearilla is part werewolf, part Bigfoot, part bear, and part human with respect to its appearance, behavior, and its origins in the folk beliefs of both Europeans and Native Americans.

Ron Coffey, a cryptozoologist who founded the Gateway Paranormal Society and who has been hunting Bearilla for decades, suggests one explanation for the presence of Bearilla. He points toward an extinct animal called Amphicyonid, or bear-dog, as the possible origin for Bearilla. Bear-dogs were carnivorous animals that lived from about 45 million years ago until they disappeared from the fossil record about 8 million years ago. They once lived in the southern part of the United States, so it is plausible that, assuming these creatures continued to exist beyond the Miocene, they could have evolved into Bearilla. Unfortunately for cryptozoologists and other believers, no one has ever found any proof of the creature's existence, apart from Coffey's plaster foot cast.

The latest sighting of Bearilla was in 2011 when a man visiting Pennyrile Forest State Reserve Park saw a large, upright creature with the coat of a wolf.

Bearilla is featured in a number of popular country songs. The best known of these, "Bearilla Woman" (2010), by zydeco musician Leroy Thomas, opens like this:

I once met a girl
Her mom was a bear
Her old daddy must have been a gorilla

See also: Chupacabra, Ozark Howler, Wendigo

Further Reading:

Coffey, L., Coffey, M., Ed, R., & Coffey, R. (2018). *Kentucky Cryptids: "Monsters" of the Bluegrass State.* Independently published.

Erdoes, R., & Ortiz, A. (1984). *American Indian Myths and Legends*. Pantheon Books.

Nunnelly, B. (2007). *Mysterious Kentucky*. Whitechapel Productions.

Ogude, J., & Nyairo, J. (2007). *Urban Legends, Colonial Myths: Popular Culture and Literature in East Africa*. Africa World Press.

BEAST OF BLADENBORO

Name: Beast of Bladenboro

Alternative Names: Vampire Beast of Bladenboro, Vampire Beast

Related Cryptids: Chupacabra

Location: Bladenboro, North Carolina

Most Recent Documented Sighting: 1954

The Beast of Bladenboro is a still unknown creature responsible for killing a number of dogs and terrorizing a town for one week in 1953. For a frightening few days, townspeople were finding their livestock and their pets mauled, until one day when the monster attacked a person. The Beast of Bladenboro is an example of a one-time occurrence that has been turned into a cryptid via media exposure. It's also an example of a cryptid for which there is no hint of an underlying legend.

The story begins on December 29, 1953, when the first dog was killed by a large, black beast a few miles outside of town. Two nights later, on New Year's Eve, two more dogs, both from the same household in Bladenboro, were killed. The next day, another two dogs were killed, and the day after, January 2, 1954, yet another dog lost its life. Two more dogs were killed the next day, and by then, people were scared. All of the dogs appeared to have been mauled, and one of the dogs from the January 3 attack underwent a necropsy to determine the cause of death. The next few days brought more deaths, but this time the killer had expanded its choice of victims, killing a rabbit and a goat, along with another dog.

Only a handful of the attacks were witnessed, but of those that were, the witnesses reported that it was a black or very dark creature, either a canine, a feline, or perhaps a bear. On January 5, 1954, the *Robesonian* newspaper announced that a hunting party (which included four fraternity members from the University of North Carolina) was being formed to look for the beast:

> Armed posses roam the town after the discovery of three mutilated dog bodies recently. Police chief Roy Fores said the body of the latest victim was opened yesterday and it contained only a few drops of blood. he said the three dogs all had their bottom lips broken open and their jaw bones smashed back. he said the ear of one dog was chewed off and the tongues of the others chewed out. (Robesonian 1954)

Gruesome details like this, breathlessly reported by local media, and as the crisis went on, national media, only served to scare the people of Bladenboro further. One newspaper article included a photo of Chief Fores holding the head of one of the dogs.

Ultimately, the hunting party was not successful, although they did find paw prints that appeared to be from a large animal. That same day, another dog was attacked, and finally, that night, the first human, although she was not harmed. The headline in the January 5, 1954, *Raleigh News and Observer* shrieked "'Vampire' charges woman":

> A large marauding cat that has killed and sucked the blood of at least seven dogs charged a woman here tonight but turned and fled back into a swamp when she screamed and her husband rushed onto the scene.

> Mrs Kinlaw who lives in the mill village near Bladenboro Mills on highway 211 1 mile west of here said she heard the dogs whimpering one night and went out to investigate. Near the dogs she said was what looked like a big mountain lion. (*The News and Observer*, 1954)

The *Charlotte Observer*'s January 5 headline read "Vampire on loose Bladenboro beast attacks woman" and opened with: "The bleeder beast struck again tonight singling out its first human being to attack." That article also called the beast a "blood Hungry marauder" and an eerie killer. These articles, and the idea that the beast was now after people, terrified the local community. Over the next two days, hundreds if not thousands of people showed up to try to find the beast.

On January 13, a farmer named Luther Davis shot and killed a bobcat that had gotten caught in a trap. The next day, the front page of the *Raleigh News and Observer* announced, "Fallen Beast of Bladenboro? Citizens Cheer Killing of Bobcat." Bladenboro mayor W. G. Fussell told the paper, "I just hope this is it. It has certainly caused a lot of excitement around here." Davis brought the bobcat into town, so townspeople could look at it, and while many were relieved and grateful that the beast had been killed, not everyone was convinced. The bobcat seemed too small to inflict the damage that it had, and its stub tail (bobcats have a bobbed tail) conflicted with reports that had seen an animal with a long tail. Another local resident, Bruce Soles, hit a big cat with his car that same day, which he claimed was the beast. Ultimately, there was never any satisfying answer as to who or what the beast was—was it a bear, a wolf, a bobcat, a panther, a feral dog, or something else entirely—although the killings did end, for a time. In December of 1954, a full year after the killings began, five pigs and three chickens were killed on a farm outside of town, and, once again, it was reported that the animals had been drained of their blood. Luckily, that was the last of the killings.

After the whole crisis was over, the community has come to embrace its hometown creature and now throws an annual Beast Fest, held every October, to commemorate that strange and scary week.

See also: Beast of Bray Road, Beast of Gévaudan, Chupacabra

Further Reading:

Armed Hunting Party to Seek Bladenboro's "Vampire Beast". (1954). *The Robesonian*, January 5, 1.
Citizens Cheer Bobcat Killing (1954). *The Robesonian*, January 13, 1, 7.

Dresser, N. (2022). American Vampires. In D. Puglia (Ed.), *North American Monsters: A Contemporary Legend Casebook*. University Press of Colorado, 118–30.

Gallehugh, J. F. (1976). The Vampire Beast of Bladenboro. *North Carolina Folklore Journal*, 24, 53–8.

Hairr, J. (2013). *Monsters of North Carolina: Mysterious Creatures in the Tar Heel State*. Stackpole Books.

"Vampire" Charges Woman (1954). *The News and Observer*, January 6, 1, 6.

BEAST OF BRAY ROAD

Name: Beast of Bray Road

Alternative Names: Dog Man, Wisconsin Wolfman, Manwolf, Bear-Wolf, Indigenous Dogman

Related Cryptids: Beast of Bladenboro, Chupacabra

Location: Bray Road, outside of Elkhorn, Wisconsin

Most Recent Documented Sighting: July 2020

The Beast of Bray Road is a large canid of some kind that has haunted a rural road outside of Elkhorn, Wisconsin, for decades, starting in the 1980s. That makes it a relatively recent cryptid as well as one that is extremely connected to the location where it has been seen.

The story began in 1990 when local reporter Linda Godfrey heard about some odd reports about a creature.

Some people, however, point to a much earlier event as the beginning of the beast. One night in 1936, school night watchman Mark Shackleman was at work at the St. Coletta School for Exceptional Children (where Rosemary Kennedy, the sister of President John F. Kennedy, lived) in Jefferson, Wisconsin. That night, when patrolling the school grounds, he saw an animal that looked like a canine of some kind, except that when it stood up, it was in the shape of a tall, upright (but shaggy) man.

Jefferson County, where the school is located, is home to a number of effigy mounds, which are mounds created by Native Americans from the Hopewell culture. They were created around 300 CE and may have served a number of religious purposes, including human burials. According to Shackleman, the animal was digging into one of the burial mounds that were once located near the school. He also smelled rotting meat emanating from it before it disappeared into the woods. The next night, Shackleman saw the creature again, once again digging into the mound. When it growled at him, it sounded like a person but also an animal. He never saw it again, and there were no more reports of a strange beast. Not until the 1980s, when a series of sightings began on and around Bray Road, a rural road outside of Elkhorn and about a half an hour from the school where Shackleman first saw the creature.

Unlike a lot of cryptids, one woman is largely responsible for promoting the story of the beast. Linda Godfrey was a reporter working for the *Walruth County Week*, and after the first sightings came to her attention in 1990, she decided to investigate for herself. She reached out to those who had said that they had seen the creature and began interviewing witnesses to find out exactly what they saw.

One witness, Lorianne Endrizzi, recounted her experience, which occurred in the fall of 1989:

I was driving home one night on Bray Road, and I saw this thing on the side of the road. As I came up to it in my car, its back was to me so I saw it had ears and the whole bit. It was kneeling! Elbows were up and its claws were facing out, So I knew it had claws. I remember the long claws. And it was eating roadkill or something. As I drove by and saw all of this it looked right at me and didn't run, didn't get spooked or anything. And it had like glowing eyes, which probably were a reflection of my headlights. It was right on Bray Road, right before the Bray farm, on the curve. And I saw it. He was brownish-gray . . . and he had big teeth and fangs. And he looked at me. He turned his head to look at me.

It was about the size of an average man, 5-foot-7 maybe, about 150 pounds. It was holding the thing it was eating palms up, with the real long claws and the pointed ears. (Godfrey 1991)

Godfrey spoke to a half dozen people who had encountered the beast, and while she started out as a skeptic, not really believing the stories, she ultimately became convinced, and her story was published on December 29, 1991, in the *Week*. She also included another account, this time from a high school student named Doris Gipson who thought she hit an animal on Bray Road on her way home in October of 1991. She told Linda that she got out of the car to see what she had hit and said:

I walked to the end of the car, and here comes this thing—it was running right up to me! You could see the chest of this thing because it was big and it was hairy. It was fast, that's for sure because I see this thing, I get in the car and by the time I got inside the car, the thing had grabbed hold of the car. I just put my foot on the gas pedal and I started going. Maybe after I got going I looked back but at the time I was more interested in leaving. The way it was running you could suggest that it was on two legs because you could see the chest so well and it was pulsating as it was coming toward me . . . I've never seen a human run as fast as that and my uncle was a track star . . . it was bigger than any dog I've seen around here. (Ibid.)

Unlike a lot of cryptids, and especially canids, this beast is unusual in that it has never attacked a person or even harmed an animal. Instead, it is thought to eat roadkill, which might explain the rural roadside location where it is seen.

Godfrey's story ended up making international news and kicked off a new era of sightings. She drew the illustrations for her first article herself, and it is those illustrations that have now become the face of the beast.

It also changed Godfrey's life, because she has dedicated the last thirty years pursuing not just the Beast of Bray Road but other American monsters as well, eventually publishing four books.

There are still occasional sightings of the beast, but after the burst of encounters (some of which were probably prompted by Godfrey's articles) in the 1990s, they slowed down to a trickle.

What was (or is) the beast? It could have been a large dog, a wolf, a coyote, or, even, perhaps, a bear.

But the legend has stayed alive, thanks to Godfrey herself as well as the television shows, podcasts, movies, and books dedicated to the beast. The Beast of Bray Road even has its own song. Called the Beast of Bray Road, by the heavy metal band Cage, it begins like this: "Slashing, tearing, scanning and scaring . . . THE BEAST!" It is a terrific opening for a heavy metal song about a monster, except for the fact that the Beast of Bladenboro has never been known to kill, or even harm, a person or animal.

See also: Beast of Bladenboro, Chupacabra

Further Reading:

Godfrey, L. S. (1991). Tracking Down the Beast of Bray Road. *The Week*, December 29.
Godfrey, L. S. (2003). *The Beast of Bray Road: Tailing Wisconsin's Werewolf.* Big Earth Publishing.
Godfrey, L. S. (2006). *Hunting the American Werewolf: Beast Men in Wisconsin and Beyond.* Big Earth Publishing.

BEAST OF EXMOOR

Name: Beast of Exmoor

Alternative Names: n/a

Related Cryptids: Beast of Bladenboro, Ozark Howler

Location: Southwest England

Most Recent Documented Sighting: January 2022

The Beast of Exmoor is a cat that roams the moorland region in Southwest England known as Exmoor—particularly the area around west Somerset and north Devon. The Beast is an example of an ABC or Alien Big Cat.

Exmoor was once one of sixty-seven Royal Forests—land owned by the monarch—throughout England. These forests, since the Norman invasion in 1066, limited all hunting to the monarch and imposed strict penalties (including execution) on those who hunted within them. (The term "forest" doesn't refer to a place with trees, as in the American English usage, but instead just refers to land on which animals (especially deer) belong to the king.) Prior to the Norman conquest, humans had used this area for thousands of years—going back at least to the Mesolithic, with standing stones and other stone structures still standing today.

Animals have also lived in Exmoor for thousands of years. Wildlife includes red deer (which were, again, considered the property of the king until the end of Exmoor's Royal Forest status in 1815) as well as numerous birds. Notably, there is one species of feline native to England: the European wildcat (*Felis silvestris*), a small brown-gray cat, weighing from 5 to 15 pounds, which once roamed much of the island (including Exmoor). However, the cat disappeared from England sometime in the early nineteenth century and now can only be found (in Great Britain) in Scotland. Domesticated animals have also been part of the forest for at least 3,000 years, with sheep and ponies long roaming Exmoor.

It shouldn't surprise us that this region is host not only to a mysterious cat but also a wide variety of other supernatural creatures such as pixies, giants, milk hares, demonic hounds, and the Devil in a variety of guises. Many of these creatures are associated with the standing stones, stone circles, and cairns, which were erected anywhere from 3,000 to 5,000 years ago.

The Beast of Exmoor is, according to almost every recorded account, a large cat, ranging in size from 4 to 8 feet in length. The color of the cat varies widely, however, with many reporting a black cat, while others have seen cats with other types of coloring: tan, agouti, gray, or even striped or spotted. But by far the most common color for the beast is black. In the wild, black cats are either jaguars or leopards (and can occasionally be found in other species like bobcats) with a genetic mutation that results in an all-black coat.

The first reported sightings of the Beast of Exmoor occurred in the 1970s, but it wasn't until a major case in the 1980s that such sightings exploded. In 1983, a farmer from South Molton found over a hundred of his sheep mutilated. These attacks were attributed to the Beast of Exmoor and gained considerable media coverage, no doubt leading to more sightings.

Witnesses have produced a number of photographs of the beast over the years, most of which are vaguely blurry images of an indeterminate cat of some kind. Because the pictures are taken at a distance, it's often difficult to determine the size of the animal, leading to a number of sightings of beasts that may or may not be simply domesticated cats. The culprit behind some of the livestock deaths, however, is most likely a domestic dog (or pack of dogs), as England has only a handful of native predators (like foxes, owls, and eagles), most of which do not kill large animals like sheep.

On the other hand, there have been a number of cases of big cats being kept as exotic pets or big cats held in zoos, which escaped from their homes and may be responsible for some livestock attacks. Some may even have been intentionally released after the passage of the Dangerous Wild Animals Act in 1976, which mandated that people who want to keep a dangerous wild animal must obtain a permit to do so. One of the open questions is whether any of those cats have reproduced, either with other wild cats or with domesticated cats, creating a small population of wild cats or wild cat hybrids. Experts, however, have rejected the likelihood of there existing a breeding population of wild cats in England.

The Beast of Exmoor is not the only ABC in Great Britain. Other cats include the Surrey Puma, seen by hundreds of people in the 1950s and 1960s (and photographed in 1966); the Beast of Bodmin, spotted in Cornwall from the 1970s through the 1990s; the Nottingham Lion, seen by a handful of people in 1976; the Fen Tiger, filmed in Cambridgeshire in 1994; the Norfolk Panther, seen most recently in 2013; and the Cotswolds big cat, a black cat that was first spotted in 2012 and has been seen as recently as 2020.

Other unnamed big cats were seen, and sometimes even filmed, in Herefordshire (2009), Gloucestershire (2010 and 2017), Moray (2011), North Lanarkshire (2011), Somerset (2013, 2017), and West Midlands (2017). Typically, however, as soon as a person reports that they have seen a big cat, the British tabloids quickly coin a name for it: The Shooters Hill Cheetah, the Sheppey Panther, the Galloway Puma, the Beast of Buchan, and the Beast of Dartmoor are all examples of this phenomenon.

As with other creatures such as the chupacabra, big cat reports can stem from a sighting, but also can develop out of physical evidence (such as a paw print), or dead or injured pets or livestock. Sometimes, too, the animals have attacked people. A Monmouthshire boy was attacked by a large black cat in 2000; similar attacks occurred in 2005 in London and 2019 in Cornwall. Others were dead ends; a "lion" that was seen by a number of people in Essex in 2012 was most likely a Maine Coon cat.

As discussed before, one possible explanation for many of these sightings has to do with the presence of wild captive cats in Great Britain, which are either kept as pets or in institutions like zoos. Occasionally those cats have escaped and have roamed the countryside until they were either caught or killed.

One of the first such cases was in 1903 when a hunter shot and killed a Canadian lynx in Devon; while no one knows where the animal came from, it was clear from the animal's teeth that it had been living in captivity for some time.

Sightings and encounters with wild felines picked up in the 1970s as the popularity of wild cats as pets exploded in many places—including Great Britain. These include a clouded leopard captured in Kent in 1975, pumas that were caught in 1980 and again in 1993 in Scotland, a jungle cat that was killed in Shropshire in 1989 (and which may have produced offspring, which two girls claimed to have seen in 2013), a Eurasian lynx killed in Norwich in 1991, an ocelot or serval that was killed in 1994 on the Isle of Wight, a caracal that was killed in 1996 in Ireland, and another Eurasian lynx who was captured in 2001. One exciting case occurred in 2009 when an animal thought to be the Beast of Exmoor washed up on the shores of Croyde Bay; the animal turned out to be a grey seal, however. The latest episode was in 2017 when a black panther was reportedly hit by a car near Harworth (which ended up being a black dog).

(The English counties with the most sightings, as reported by the group Big Cats in Britain, include Devon (with the most sightings), Gloucester, Sussex, Cornwall, Kent, Somerset, Yorkshire, and Leicester.) Some people claim that the stories of the Beast first emerged after animal trainer and circus performer Mary Chipperfield released three pumas to the wild after her zoo, Plymouth Zoo, was closed down in 1978. (Interestingly, it was perfectly legal to release wild animals—even non-native animals—to the wild until 1981 when it was finally criminalized in England.)

Even after the passage of the Dangerous Wild Animals Act in 1976, it has been estimated that, as of 2018, 5,000 wild animals live in private homes throughout the country, including big cats. Given this situation, we should expect that sightings of ABCs will continue, and indeed they do. The latest sighting, at the time of this writing, occurred in Devon in May 2020 when a witness saw (and photographed) a mysterious large, black cat near Tedburn St. Mary. This encounter occurred just a couple of days after a farmer found a lamb with its head torn off and just days after another person photographed what looked like large paw prints in Newton Abbot—an area where other deceased animals have been found.

Big cat sightings are not limited to the modern era. ABCs have been seen throughout Great Britain for centuries. One early reported sighting was in the mid-eighteenth century when writer William Cobbett encountered a large cat in Surrey and another in New Brunswick.

But long before that, mysterious cats were an extremely common feature of the folklore of the British Isles. The thirteenth-century Welsh poem, *Pa Gwr*, tells of a monstrous cat called a *cath palug*, which was born to a pig. The cat killed 180 warriors during a mammoth battle to find and kill the creature. It was even said to have fought with King Arthur.

Why are the sightings of ABCs most often of black cats—especially when black cats are so rare in the wild? One reason may have to do with an ancient, pre-Christian folk belief, found in many parts of Europe but especially prominent in Great Britain, in a ghostly or demonic black animal—usually a Black Dog. While there are a variety of interpretations for the presence of this creature, one of the most common is that when a person encounters it (typically at night and often at a crossroads) death will follow. Another common belief is that the Black Dog is simply the devil in disguise. Like the ABCs, the Black Dog is larger than a regular domestic dog and also tends to have glowing eyes. While ABCs are not typically associated with death or the devil, the fact that most descriptions of the Beast of Exmoor include a black coat color may point to a connection between these two creatures.

Unlike dogs, though, cats seem both of this world and very much of some other, supernatural, world. Under Christianity, the reputation of cats in Europe suffered mightily. Cats were denounced both because of their high status in pre-Christian cultures and their nocturnal abilities that associated them with evil. Seeing cats on or near a grave, for example, was interpreted to mean that the deceased lost his soul to the devil. Cats could also bring good luck, although they often had to die to do so; in Medieval Europe, for example, cats were buried under the fields to ensure a good harvest and were buried in walls to protect houses from evil spirits.

Because cats are so mysterious and inscrutable, a number of British folktales deal with the mysterious behaviors of cats. In the English folktale, "The King of the Cats," a man either witnesses a funeral made up of cats or hears a cat telling of the death of someone. When the man returns home and tells of what he saw, his own cat shouts, "Then I am the king of the cats!" and disappears up the chimney, never to be seen again. This tale implies that cats live in, at least part time, a kingdom of their own. Many tales involve cats consorting with demons or other underworld figures (the three hairs on the tip of a cat's tail, for example, are called the devil's hairs). For instance, in "The Demon Cat," an Irish folktale, a cat used to come into a fisherman's home and eat all of his fish. The cat was large, black, and growled at the fisherman and his wife and no amount of yelling or beating would scare it away, until the fisherman's wife threw holy water at it, which burnt the cat until it disappeared, never to return again.

The Beast of Exmoor is one of Britain's—and the world's—most well known of the ABCs.

Thus far, there is no empirical proof for the existence of the Beast (or for any ABC, for that matter), although there has been ample proof (via both live captures and dead bodies, and even DNA evidence) that big cats have been roaming Britain for at least 100 years. But they may have been around much longer; the Tower of London famously held a menagerie of beasts from the thirteenth until the nineteenth century, some of which may have escaped. Wild cats had been part of the royal menagerie since the earliest days; Henry III had three big cats (probably lions, although they were called leopards), and over the centuries, tigers, leopards, and other big cats were added to the collection, along with a continuing presence of lions (one of the symbols of England). Even before that time, William the Conqueror kept wild animals at his estate in Woodstock.

There have been both government-sanctioned attempts to locate the creature and numerous personal attempts, by both cryptozoologists and normal citizens, to find and capture or kill the animal. The first such attempt was in 1988 when the British Ministry of Agriculture sent a squadron of Royal Marines to Exmoor to find it. While the animal was supposedly seen by some of the Marines, no hard evidence was located. Much more recently, two mutilated deer carcasses found in Gloucestershire were tested for DNA in 2012, with the evidence indicating that it was a fox that killed them.

The latest (at the time of this writing) sighting occurred in January of 2022 in Devon when Sam Aston spotted the beast while walking his dog.

"It was about 11.45am and I looked into a big open empty field to my left and 200 or 300 yards away a black animal was running. I couldn't make out what it was so I grabbed my phone and took a pic for identification purposes. I'm a bit of a wildlife photographer and I automatically went through a list—was it a dog, a deer, a cow?" Aston posted the photo he took to twitter along with the following:

> Genuinely think I may have seen a #BigCat on #Exmoor today. I'll put the cropped photo in the comments. It moved cat like, was running towards a wooded area, and I think it was a big cat, but may be wrong given the unlikelihood. The worst thing is, I'll never know. 🐾 (Aston 2021)

See also: Beast of Bladenboro, Black Dog

Further Reading:

Aston, S. [@SAstonWildlife]. (2021). *Genuinely Think I may Have Seen a #BigCat on #Exmoor Today. I'll Put the Cropped Photo in the Comments. It Moved Cat Like, was Running Towards a Wooded Area, and I Think it was a Big Cat, but May be Wrong Given the Unlikelihood. The Worst Thing is, I'll Never Know* 🐱 [Tweet]. Twitter, December 20, https://twitter.com/SAstonWildlife/status/1473005190395711492

Beer, T. (1984). *The Beast of Exmoor: Fact Or Legend?* Countryside Productions.

MacDermot, E. T. (1911). *The History of the Forest of Exmoor.* Barnicott & Pearce, Wessex Press.

Roberts, A. (1987). *Cat Flaps! A Survey of Mystery Cats in the North of England.* Brigantia Books.

Shuker, K. P. (1989). *Mystery Cats of the World: From Blue Tigers to Exmoor Beasts.* Robert Hale.

Watson, W. G. W. (1920). *Calendar of Customs, Superstitions, Weather-lore, Popular Sayings, and Important Events Connected with the County of Somerset.* Somerset County Herald.

BEAST OF GÉVAUDAN

Name: Beast of Gévaudan

Alternative Names: Wolf of Chazes

Related Cryptids: Beast of Bladenboro, Chupacabra

Location: South-Central France

Most Recent Documented Sighting: 1767

The Beast of Gévaudan was a wolf-like, or werewolf-like, creature that terrorized the people of Gévaudan, a small village in the south-central region of France, during the mid-eighteenth century.

Werewolves (*were* means man in Old English) are wolf-human hybrids that hunt and kill humans. They are found throughout Europe and date to the Middle Ages when the word werewolf appeared for the first time in print in the eleventh century. The idea of a person transforming into a wolf is much older than that, however, and can be found in the myths of Iron Age Indo-Europeans, which themselves probably date back to the Greek and Roman beliefs (described by Greek historian Herodotus as well as Roman naturalist Pliny the Elder) that humans could turn into wolves. The beliefs were most prominent in German-speaking regions of Europe as well as in the Slavic countries of Eastern Europe where wolves were once totemic animals. (The nomadic Turkic people of Central Asia believe that they descended from wolves; in particular, a she-wolf named Asena was said to have nursed a baby human, leading her to give birth to a race of half-wolf/half human-babies who became the Turkic people.)

The ability of the wolf to quietly stalk and viciously kill their prey (they are endurance predators rather than ambush predators) makes wolves both respected and feared predators. With the rise of Christianity, wolves started to be portrayed as amoral, greedy, and evil—even demonic. *The Malleus Malleficarium* (the Hammer of Witches), a guidebook for hunting witches, described wolves as either agents of the devil or agents of God to punish men. One of the reasons for this treatment has to do with the lifestyle of much of ancient Israel: the people were shepherds, raising flocks of sheep, cattle, and goats. This gave way to the Christian concept of Jesus as the Good Shepherd, who protects his flock of sheep (Christian followers) from wolves (the devil), and the continued demonization of the wolf. Ultimately, the wolf suffered greatly from this portrayal, as wolves have been subject to systematic slaughter in much of the Western world.

European and Asian folklore have a number of variants of what is known to folklorists as "The Werewolf's Tale." This story tells of a man, who has been cursed to spend half of his time in the body of a wolf, and his ultimate victory over his curse. The motif of a human transforming into a wolf is found in folktales in Western Europe (especially Germany and the Scandinavian countries), Eastern Europe, and China and often involves a curse that causes the person to transform into a beast. (The stories may have traveled from Scandinavia during the Viking Age into Russia, where the Vikings founded a state called Kievan Rus, and from there into the Balkans.) China, in fact, had a wide variety of such tales, focused on both wolf-humans and dog-humans. Werewolves are related to the Native American skinwalker, another creature that is half human, half beast, and the Wendigo, another Native American/First Nations creature that attacks and kills people. Similar to the skinwalker is the Mesoamerican *nagual* or *nahual*, which is a person who can shapeshift into an animal and can be good or evil.

In Europe, werewolf stories differ in the Eastern, Balkan countries from the tales told in the West. German and French werewolves were more like witches and in fact were subject to similar trials to the witch trials of Medieval Europe. Slavic werewolves, on the other hand, were described more like vampires or reanimated corpses: they are undead and drink the blood of the living.

The werewolf combines the vicious and destructive nature of the wolf with the transformative abilities of a witch, creating a terrifying creature that not only mutilates and kills their prey but can (in some beliefs) turn their victims into werewolves as well. They were not treated as mythical beings by either commoners or government and religious officials; instead they were included in legal codes, ecclesiastical writing, and other official documents.

One of the most frightening of all wolf-creature stories is the saga of the Beast of Gévaudan. Starting in the summer of 1764, both livestock and villagers began disappearing in the vicinity of the forest, sometimes turning up mutilated. The first survivor of the beast was a fourteen-year-old girl named Marie-Jeanne Valet who was attacked while crossing a river and only survived because she stabbed it with a wooden spear. (There is now a statue of Valet fighting the beast in the town of Auvers.)

The beast was described as huge, much larger than wolf, with red or gray fur, a stripe down its back, and blazing red eyes, and it could stand on four feet or just two. Some witnesses reported that it could repel bullets, disappear into thin air, or do other otherworldly things.

Before the crisis was over in 1767, over 200 people were attacked and over 100 killed, with an unknown number of animals losing their lives. The victims were maimed by their attackers, often having their faces or throats ripped open, and eyewitnesses and survivors of some of the attacks reported that the attackers were either dogs, wolves, or some sort of large, bipedal humanoid. Other witnesses reported seeing multiple animals: sometimes a pair and sometimes a mother and offspring.

After reports of the unexplained deaths reached King Louis XV, a number of hunters were dispatched to Gévaudan to track and kill the beast. A wanted poster printed in 1764 described the beast as follows, before offering a reward of 2,700 livres to the person who kills it:

> Picture of the monster desolating the Gévaudan, This Beast is the size of a young Bull, it likes to attack Women and Children, it drinks their Blood, cuts off their Heads, and carries them off. (Figure du monstre qui désole le Gevaudan, 1764)

Like many of the reports from this time, this poster emphasized the beast's interest in women and children as well as the vicious way that it attacks. Others emphasized the seemingly magical nature of the beast and the way that it appeared to be able to ward off bullets. Some of the drawings of the beast that were made at this time depict it as a large wolf, while others show a more ambiguous, human-like creature. In fact, one of the reasons why this is such a well-known case is because the eighteenth century was a time when the popular presses in Europe began to rapidly expand. European newspaper breathlessly covered the Beast of Gévaudan and most likely not only heavily embellished the stories of the attacks but also spread the story far and wide.

The first organized expedition to catch the monster was led by government official Étienne Lafont and infantry officer Captain Jean Baptiste Duhamel (who later described the monster as part lion). This effort involved a huge team of hunters, poisoned bait, hunting dogs, and even had soldiers dressed as women who were meant to entice the beast into attacking but ultimately the attempt was unsuccessful.

After the first hunters returned without having caught the beast, Francois Antoine, the King's Lieutenant of the Hunt, arrived in the region in June 1765. In June, Antoine shot and killed a gray wolf that was identified by some of the survivors as the culprit and later killed that wolf's family; the first wolf was stuffed and sent to Versailles to be presented to the king. English writer Horace Walpole was visiting France at the time and described the Beast in a letter:

> In the Queen's antechamber we foreigners and the foreign ministers were shown the famous Beast of the Gévaudan, just arrived, and covered with a cloth, which the two chasseurs (pageboys) lifted up. It is an absolute wolf, but uncommonly large, and the expression of agony and fierceness remains strongly imprinted in its dead jaws. (Quoted in Romero & Schwalb 2016: x)

Even though Antoine was both hailed for his bravery and paid generously, it was less than three months later that two young boys were attacked (and survived). This attack was followed by more attacks, and more deaths, until another wolf was killed by a local hunter named Jean Chastel on

June 19, 1767. Chastel used a silver bullet (which is known to be able to kill werewolves) to kill the creature. During the preparation of the body for stuffing, the last victim was allegedly found in its stomach.

Ultimately it is unknown how many animals were responsible for the attacks in Gévaudan, although it is now assumed that the killings were done by multiple wolves, perhaps working in a pack, although the killers could have been dogs as well. The killings could also have been committed by a lion or another big cat; these animals were kept in private menageries all over Europe and were known to escape from time to time. Whether it was one wolf, multiple wolves, or some other animal, well over 100 wolves were killed before the attacks ended.

Hundreds of years after the beast, or beasts, roamed the French countryside, mauling women and children, it remains a popular subject today. It even inspired a song about it, released by German power metal band Powerwolf in 2021, which begins by emphasizing one of the most frightening aspects of the beast: "Beast of Gévaudan, feared no sword and feared no gun."

See also: Beast of Bladenboro, Chupacabra, Kitsune

Further Reading:

Figure du monstre qui désole le Gevaudan (1764). *Gallica Digital Library* [Online]. https://gallica.bnf.fr/ark:/12148/btv1b84096673 (Accessed May 4, 2022).

Grant, J. (1867). The Wild Beast of Gevaudan. *The Argosy: A Magazine of Tales, Travels, Essays, and Poems*, 4(1), 54–62.

Lopez, Barry H. (1978). *Of Wolves and Men*. J. M. Dent and Sons Limited.

Marvin, Garry (2012). *Wolf*. Reaktion Books Ltd.

Romero, G. S., & Schwalb, S. R. (2016). *Beast: Werewolves, Serial Killers, and Man-Eaters: The Mystery of the Monsters of the Gévaudan*. Skyhorse.

Smith, J. M. (2011). *Monsters of the Gévaudan: The Making of a Beast*. Harvard University Press.

Thompson, R. H. (1991). *Wolf-hunting in France in the Reign of Louis XV: The Beast of the Gévaudan*. Edwin Mellen Press.

BESSIE

Name: Bessie

Alternative Names: South Bay Bessie, Lake Erie Chopper, Lake Erie Monster, Lemmy, Lem

Related Cryptids: Champ, Loch Ness Monster, Ogopogo

Location: Lake Erie, New York

Most Recent Documented Sighting: 1995

Bessie is a lake creature that lives in Lake Erie, one of the Great Lakes that borders Michigan, Ohio, Pennsylvania, New York, as well as Toronto, Canada. It is mostly visible on the south shore of the lake, alongside the cities of Cleveland, Akron, and Sandusky.

North America has sixty-two lakes with creatures in them, with forty-seven of those in the United States. Lake Erie, home of Bessie, is the fourth largest lake in the United States. In fact, the five largest lakes in the United States have their own lake monsters.

While some lake creatures have been a part of local legends or myths for hundreds of years or longer (especially in Japan and Africa), many, including Bessie, have appeared in much more recent times. Many lake creatures, in fact, jumped into public consciousness after the Loch Ness Monster became popularized in the 1930s, while some had their first rumored existence in the nineteenth century, the era when Plesiosaur fossils were being furiously dug up by amateur and professional archaeologists and naturalists. The late nineteenth century in particular was an extremely fertile time for anything Plesiosaur-related, and that includes lake monsters. (Sea serpents, on the other hand, predate Nessie by, in some cases, hundreds or thousands of years. It is the lake monsters, most of whom look like Nessie, that developed much later.)

The first sighting of the creature may, if the reports are true, have occurred in 1793, when a ship named *Felicity* encountered what the captain described as a 17-foot snake that rose out of the water.

It took another hundred years for the creature to make another appearance. It was in 1892 that a schooner heading from Buffalo, New York, to Toledo, Ohio, came across the creature for the first time. The story was covered in the May 21, 1892, edition of the *Cleveland Plain Dealer*, which described the creature this way:

> [The monster] was described to be about twenty-five feet long and about one and one-half feet in diameter through the largest part. Its head was large and flat. Above five feet from its head there appeared to be several large fins or slippers. Its color was black, mottled with brown spots. (1892)

A few years later, the daily paper from Sandusky, Ohio, the *Daily Register*, referred to that sighting as well as others:

> For a number of years, vague stories about huge serpents have come with each recurring season from Dominion [Canadian] shores, and now, at last, the existence of these fierce monsters is verified and the fact so well established that it can no longer be questioned. (*Daily Register* 1898)

This article went on to say that a local hunter had found four eggs on the shore of the lake and, after he brought them home, they hatched, revealing very long baby snakes. Ten years later, there was another report, this time of a "Wriggly Dragon, Grayish-Green and of Playful Disposition," which was spotted by workers at the Union Salt Company, located in Cleveland.

There were no more recorded sightings of a monster in the lake until July 1931, when two fishermen, Clifford Wilson and Francis Cogenstose, saw what they described as a sea serpent in Sandusky Bay. The men promptly subdued it by clubbing it and then putting into a crate; they told their story to a *New York Times* reporter who was in the area at the time, but once the Cleveland Museum of Natural History decided to investigate, they determined that it was a python. This was just two years before the first major sighting of the Loch Ness Monster.

Every few years, another report would appear, until the 1980s, when the monster was finally named South Bay Bessie (shortened to Bessie), thanks to a contest in the *Port Clinton Beacon*, after the Davis-Besse Nuclear Power Station that used to sit right on the lake.

Now that Bessie had a name, drawing tourists to the area specifically to see it, the sightings picked up. The September 28, 1990, edition of the *Daily Kent Star* featured an account by a man named Harold Bricker who told the paper that he saw a black, 35-feet-long creature with the head of a snake. After the publicity generated by Mr. Bricker's story, which was published in the *Los Angeles Times*, John Schaffner, the editor of *The Beacon*, in nearby Port Clinton, Ohio, set up a 1-800 number for people to call with sightings. This no doubt also increased the number of reports. In fact, it was also John Schaffner who came up with the idea of the contest to name the creature; without the name, and the 800 number, it is doubtful that Bessie would be as popular as it is today.

One of the oddest stories to emerge about Bessie was in 1992, when the tabloid *Weekly World News* had splashed across its cover the headline "Lake Erie Monster Sinks Sailboat," accompanied by an image of a giant beast taking down a sailboat. According to the article, three sailors died, with two surviving to tell their story.

That same year, beachgoers hanging out at Huntington Beach saw a huge monster rise out of the water. One of the onlookers, an eleven-year-old boy named Victor Rasgaitis, gave the following account:

My cousins were in from South Carolina—they wanted to see Lake Erie. And they were standing there on the walking path . . . and we saw these bubbles, like something rising, not even past the jetty. It came up a foot out of the water, just this crest. It looked like water—but sort of solid. . . . I was a little afraid to go in the water after that.

Bessie, like most lake monsters, is described as serpentine, snake-like, or like the classic lake monster, the Loch Ness Monster, like a modern plesiosaur: large body, two or four flippers, and a long, swan-like neck topped by a small head. She—like the grandmother of lake creatures, Nessie, Bessie is female—is anywhere from 15 to 40 feet long.

What is Bessie? Many people think it's a giant sturgeon; these ancient fish can, under the right conditions, grow quite large; in 2021, the largest known sturgeon was caught on the Fraser River in British Columbia and measured 11½ feet in length with a girth of 55 inches. It's easy to imagine seeing a 10- or 12-feet-long creature swimming just below the surface of the water and thinking it's a serpent.

Lake Erie is fed by the Cuyahoga River, and in the nineteenth and early twentieth centuries, it was massively polluted, thanks to all of the pollution dumped into the river from what was then a thriving Cleveland industrial sector. Some people think that the toxins in the river, combined with waste from the Davis-Bessie Nuclear Power Station, mutated some of the animals there, creating the monster in the process. This story is somewhat of a "nature bites back" story, because it positions Bessie as an avenger, punishing the city of Cleveland for polluting the river and lake.

Bessie is now a proud mascot for the entire south bay of Lake Erie, and its name and likeness can be seen throughout the region. One local businessman has offered a $100,000 plus reward for the live capture of Bessie, and an Ohio State University zoologist named Charles Herdendorf offered a possible scientific name for Bessie, *Obscura eriensis huronii*, and suggested that the lake was big enough to host perhaps 175 monsters like Bessie. Whether that is enough to provide enough genetic diversity to maintain a viable breeding population is another matter. It even was made into a gaffe: Baby Erie, or Erie Baby, as it was known, was billed as a dead infant monster. Larry Peterson, a local taxidermist, said that he found it on the shore of the lake with a fish hook in its mouth. He may indeed have found a dead fish, because that's what Baby Erie was, that he modified to look like a sea monster, complete with four flippers. It was purchased by the Creation Evidence Museum in Glen Rose, Texas, where it was treated as evidence that dinosaurs lived recently, the earth is only 6,000 years old, and evolution is a lie.

See also: Bownessie, Champ, Loch Ness Monster, Ogopogo

Further Reading:

Brown, R. (2009). *The Lake Erie Shore: Ontario's Forgotten South Coast*. Dundurn.
Cassady, C. (2009). *Paranormal Great Lakes: An Illustrated Encyclopedia*. Schiffer.
Lake Erie Sea Serpent: Said to Have Been Seen by Fishermen Near Oak Harbor (1892). *Cleveland Plain Dealer*, May 21.
McClelland, E. (2018). *Folktales and Legends of the Middle West*. Belt Publishing.
Radford, B., & Nickell, J. (2006). *Lake Monster Mysteries: Investigating the World's Most Elusive Creatures*. University Press of Kentucky.
Renner, J. (2012). *It Came from Ohio: True Tales of the Weird, Wild, and Unexplained*. Gray & Company.

BIGFOOT

Name: Bigfoot

Alternative Names: Sasquatch

Related Cryptids: Almas, Yeren, Yeti, Yowie

Location: The Pacific Northwest region of North America

Most Recent Documented Sighting: 2022 (Ohio)

Bigfoot is a large hairy ape-man or woman that lives in the redwood forests of North America. It is the world's most famous cryptid and the face of cryptozoology.

Bigfoot occupies two very different realms—folklore, both European and Native American, and popular science—that are combined by cryptozoologists to form Bigfoot lore. Cryptozoologists argue, on the other hand, that Bigfoot is a biological being whose study is properly the domain of natural science, including zoology, biology, ethology, paleontology, paleoanthropology, and more. For cryptozoologists, folklore about Bigfoot or Bigfoot-like creatures is used as a secondary source of evidence, to help prove that they exist in nature.

The descriptions of Bigfoot are highly standardized. It—Bigfoot is the rare cryptid that witnesses report can be male or female—is huge, ranging from 7 feet to as tall as 12 or 15 feet. They are muscular, and females have visible breasts. Their fur ranges from reddish brown to black, and they are bipedal, although they walk with a slightly hunched gait, perhaps because they do not appear to have a neck. Some witnesses have reported that their eyes glow red in the dark. They are said to have a strong odor, a feature that is common to a great deal of cryptids.

Not much is known about Bigfoot's behavior because, while there have been thousands of reported sightings, they are fleeting and reveal very little to tell us about behavior, social structure, reproduction, diet, or almost anything else. However, witnesses have often reported that the creature throws rocks when agitated, a behavior common to chimpanzees and gorillas. Most people feel that Bigfoot is not dangerous, although there are occasional stories of a Bigfoot attack on a person.

Bigfoot does not use tools and has no language. Instead, they communicate (perhaps only to humans) by smashing and breaking branches and other forest debris as well as through vocalizations. The descriptions of Bigfoot call very widely from howls to whoops to whistles and chattering, which most likely come from a variety of species.

They are thought to be solitary animals because they are only ever seen alone, although that describes virtually every cryptid in the world. The glowing eyes suggest an adaptation to night vision, but all monkeys and apes are diurnal, making it unlikely that Bigfoot would be nocturnal.

The first Europeans to settle North America in the seventeenth century brought their folk beliefs with them, which included a belief in a wild man who lives in the forest. These were mostly English men and women, but very shortly, Irish, German, and Dutch people began to arrive, followed by Swedes. All of these groups had legends or folktales about wild men who live in the forests, which themselves are most likely an amalgamation of Celtic beliefs in spirits combined with Roman creatures like the faun. Wild men were common beings in the ancient world, with the first written account of such a creature in the Mesopotamian Epic of Gilgamesh, dating back 4,000 years, and clearly represented wild untamed nature as compared to civilization.

With the permanent settling of North America by Europeans, these old-world beliefs were transplanted to the New World where they would eventually circulate alongside Native American beliefs.

Among Native Americans and First Nations people (the indigenous populations of Canada), there are a wide variety of wild man or hairy man beliefs—just as there are around the world. While such beliefs are not universal, they are extremely common. Besides offering a way to symbolically represent the wilderness at the edges of human culture, these beliefs had a number of other functions as well, some common (acting as a boogeyman to teach children to fear or respect nature or offering explanations for unexpected or unwanted events) and some specific to each tribe or language group.

It was in 1898 that the word Sasquatch entered the English language through anthropologist Charles Hill-Tout, who recorded a Nlaka'pamux story about a wild man; the term given to Hill-Tout was se'sxa, later anglicized to Sasquatch. Other tribes had similar creatures, but the specifics of their behaviors differed. Some were dangerous and could attack or even kill, some were nocturnal while others were diurnal, and some were cannibals. Most stories, however, treat these creatures as relatively harmless, although they might be blamed for stealing food.

By the twentieth century, much of the folklore that Europeans had brought with them had given way to a new form of folktale: the urban legend.

Urban legends, also known as contemporary legends, are fictional tales that are both orally transmitted and transmitted through modern media like the internet, fax, and email, and even television or print news, which are purported to be true. When they are told, the teller typically relates that the story happened to someone who is known to the teller—a cousin, a friend of a friend, a great aunt and so on. They are often localized, in that they carry elements of a local environment (city names, even street names), which make them more believable to the listeners. They often have a disgusting or macabre element to them—a person or an animal is often killed, sometimes in a gruesome fashion.

Sometimes urban legends have kernels of truth in them, in that they were inspired by real events, but the legends themselves are false. More than a story's truth or falsity, however, what folklorists find important is the ways in which these legends are shaped by, and in turn shape, our beliefs and feelings about a variety of subjects, such as technology, food, or the natural world. In addition, urban legends sound plausible—which accounts for their continued spread today.

Bigfoot, as we know it today, did not enter the picture until 1958, and it was through a hoax that it did.

Logger Jerry Crew was operating a bulldozer in the Six Rivers National Forest in Northern California when he reported that he discovered a massive footprint in the mud. Crew took a cast of the print and contacted a reporter named Andrew Genzoli of the *Humboldt Times*, the daily paper in nearby eureka. After the story, along with a picture of Crew's footprint, and Genzoli's name for the creature, Bigfoot, was published, it immediately began to spread. This was the first time that the name Bigfoot, and the story of a huge hairy creature that liked to tease loggers, made it into the press, and the story went international.

The modern legend of Bigfoot was born.

What would not be known for almost another fifty years is the fact that Ray Wallace, a logger who worked with Crew, created the prints that gave Bigfoot its name. By that time, Bigfoot had become truly legendary, the subject of hundreds of books, movies, an entire industry dedicated to Bigfoot-related memorabilia, and most critically, it was Bigfoot that helped launch the entire field of cryptozoology.

Once Bigfoot had a name, a physical description, a behavioral repertoire, and, thanks to the uncritical use of Native American lore, legitimacy, Bigfoot hunting and Bigfoot sightings began in earnest. One of the era's most influential cryptozoologists, Ivan Sanderson, encouraged the search for Bigfoot because he worried that the Russians were close to finding their own wild men.

But it was a decade later that the most important piece of Bigfoot evidence was released. Known as the Patterson-Gimlin film, it is a 59.5-second 16-millimeter black-and-white film that purports to show a female Bigfoot (now known affectionately as Patty) walking in the woods outside of Bluff Creek, California. The footage was taken by Bigfoot hunters Roger Patterson and Robert Gimlin and is viewed within the community as genuine. Today, the Patterson-Gimlin footage ranks alongside of the Zapruder tape of President Kennedy's assassination as one of the most important pieces of American popular culture.

Since the 1950s, there have been thousands of in-person Bigfoot sightings (primarily in Northern California, Oregon, Washington, and British Columbia), an unknown number of photos and videos, and footprint casts, hair, and feces samples. None of these items has been verified by scientists outside of the cryptozoological community, but, except for the obvious hoaxes, they are treated as evidence of Bigfoot's existence. Even though many Bigfoot researchers acknowledge the paucity of physical evidence, the lack of evidence is not seen as proof that it does not exist. In fact it is the Native American stories, as they have been retold by cryptozoologists, that provide the last mark of legitimacy. Bigfoot must be real, even if there's no physical evidence, because how else can one explain the indigenous stories?

Making sense of the myths and beliefs of people outside of one's culture is never easy. Anthropologists and folklorists specialize in this task, yet they also acknowledge that the process of translating the beliefs of one culture into the language of another can never be perfect. The values, experiences, and worldviews of the anthropologist will always be included at some level in the process, no matter how much the anthropologist attempts to maintain neutrality.

In the case of Bigfoot myths, most cryptozoological researchers lack the language skills as well as the cultural competence to collect these stories firsthand, from the cultures that possess them, much less interpret them in a way that honors the cultural context in which it was found.

Since Bigfoot entered popular culture in the 1950s, it has started to spread around the country. Today, regional Bigfoot variants exist throughout the country, such as the Florida Skunk Ape, the Fouke Monster in Arkansas, the Monster of Whitehall in upstate New York, Missouri's MomoMonster, Big Muddy Monster in Illinois, Honey Island Swamp Monster in Louisiana, and Mogollon Monster in Arizona, to name just a few.

For those who believe in the existence of Bigfoot, there are a few theories to account for its existence. By far the most popular is the idea that Bigfoot is an evolutionary relic—a member of a species of extinct fossil hominoid that somehow has survived hundreds of thousands or millions of years after the rest of the species disappeared. Because of Bigfoot's huge size, one fossil that is often chosen as Bigfoot's likely ancestor is Gigantopithecus, an extinct ape from the Miocene that lived in Southeast Asia and disappeared from the fossil record by 200 to 300 years ago. Cryptozoologist Grover Krantz suggested that an unknown number of these animals followed humans over the Bering Land Bridge into North America, where they dispersed and became Bigfoot.

Gigantopithecus was indeed enormous, but it was also an ape and not in the evolutionary line that would produce humans. As an ape, it would have been quadrupedal, while Bigfoot is fully bipedal. This would mean that bipedalism not only developed independently in Bigfoot, but that it did so in just a few hundred thousand years. Today, primatologists as well as paleoanthropologists consider Gigantopithecus to be an ancestor of the orangutan, not Bigfoot.

Another possibility would be the species of fossil hominin known as Australopithecus robustus, also known as Paranthropus robustus, which is also not considered to be ancestral to us, although it's much closely related to us. Unfortunately this species was only found in East Africa.

One of the problems with the evolutionary relic theory is that it tends to be based on a misunderstanding of evolution. Bigfoot hunters famously consider Bigfoot to be a "missing link" between humans and apes. Such a thing does not exist, because humans did not evolve from ape. Rather, we share a common ancestor who lived about 8 million years ago, and since that time, our line, as well as the rest of the large-bodied hominoids (which includes gorillas, chimpanzees, bonobos, and orangutans), has continued to evolve, as the fossil record in the Old World demonstrates. (No hominoid fossils have ever been found in the New World.)

Skeptics, on the other hand, argue that Bigfoot sightings, which make up the overwhelming bulk of the evidence for its existence, are a combination of hoaxes, misidentified animals (with the black bear, which not only looks like Bigfoot but whose territory is virtually the same as Bigfoot's, being the most likely suspect), or human imagination and point out that of the rest of the evidence, not a single item has been independently verified. A 2014 study conducted by geneticists at the University of Oxford and Lausanne's Cantonal Museum of Zoology (who are not cryptozoologists) looked at thirty samples of purported Bigfoot (and other ape-men) fur and found that twenty-nine came from known animals and one was human.

There are also a number of logical problems that cryptozoologists have been unable to explain to the satisfaction of scientists. Perhaps the most significant of these is the issue of breeding populations. In order for Bigfoot to have survived to the present, there must be a breeding population of other Bigfoots, and that population must be large enough to provide for genetic diversity.

Bigfoot's introduction to the world happened just as American tabloid journalism was developing. In 1957, just a year before Bigfoot first hit the presses, *The National Enquirer* underwent a revamp by its new owner, going from a broadsheet newspaper to a tabloid. With this, American tabloid journalism was born, and Bigfoot became a household name. By the end of the 1960s, interest in Bigfoot was waning, but the Patterson-Gimlin film, released in 1967, reignited public interest in the creature and moved it further out of the realm of science and into that of popular culture.

Bigfoot continues to thrive in popular culture. It is the subject of hundreds of movies, films, television shows, and podcasts and got an extra surge in popularity during the global Covid-19 pandemic when Bigfoot became an unofficial mascot for social distancing.

Bigfoot hunting expeditions, both informal and organized, are one of the ways that research into Bigfoot continues. There are a variety of organizations that sponsor research, host conventions, collect information on sightings, and act as hubs for the cryptozoology world, including the Bigfoot Field Researchers Organization, founded in 1995 and the world's largest organization dedicated to Bigfoot.

One of the most unusual theories to account for the origin of Bigfoot is the idea that Bigfoot is an extraterrestrial. In fact, there is a fringe part of the Bigfoot community that sees Bigfoot as a magical being that can turn invisible, communicate telepathically, and travel through both time and different dimensions. While these beliefs are rejected by cryptozoologists who see cryptids as (potentially) real beings, they do provide a ready explanation for why Bigfoot is so hard to find.

Bigfoot is America's, if not the world's, best-known wild man figure. If one of the functions of the wild man is to act as a kind of guardian of nature, it has become abundantly clear that it is us, humanity, that poses the threat—not monsters. This is especially in the context of Euro-American settler colonialism, in which Northern Europeans effectively replaced the humans already on this continent, mowing down forests and grasslands to make way for suburbs and Starbucks. It's not a coincidence that Bigfoot lives in one of America's last untamed forests, and that it was essentially brought into our world by loggers—men hired by the logging industry to destroy those forests. And just as this process of destruction is almost complete comes a mad rush by cryptozoologists and crypto-tourists to invade what remains of the places that Bigfoot once protected. If and when Bigfoot is finally "found," the process will be complete.

Bigfoot, as the most popular cryptid on the planet, is the subject of numerous songs from a variety of genres. Keeping with Bigfoot's hippy reputation, the songs are as unusual as they are numerous and include titles like "I got eaten by a Bigfoot" (Cool Parents, 2020), "Bigfoot was a Nazi" (The Anaconda Vampire Bats, 2019), "The Missing Link" (Ned Storm, 2021), "Bigfoot Exists" (Bloody Crying Twinks, 2019), and "The Bigfoot Howl" (Bran Reid, 2015).

See also: Almas, Yeren, Yowie

Further Reading:

Bindernagel, John A. 2010. *The Discovery of the Sasquatch*. Beachcomber Books.

Bord, Janet and Colin (2006). *Bigfoot Casebook*. Pine Winds Press.

Buhs, J. B. (2011). Tracking Bigfoot Through 1970s Children's Culture: How Mass Media, Consumerism, and the Culture of Preadolescence Shaped Wildman Lore. *Western Folklore*, 70(2), 195–218.

Buhs, Joshua Blu (2009). *Bigfoot: The Life and Times of a Legend*. University of Chicago Press.

Carpenter, Scott (2014). *The Bigfoot Field Journal*. Independently published.

Cartmill, Matt (2008). Bigfoot Exposed: An Anthropologist Examines America's Enduring Legend/Sasquatch: Legend Meets Science. *American Journal of Physical Anthropology*, 135(1), 118.

Coleman, Loren (2003). *Bigfoot!: The True Story of Apes in America*. Simon and Schuster.

Daegling, David J. (2004). *Bigfoot Exposed: An Anthropologist Examines America's Enduring Legend*. Altamira Press.

Green, John (2004). *The Best of Bigfoot/Sasquatch*. Hancock House Publishers.

Green, John (2006). *Sasquatch: The Apes Among Us*. Hancock House Publishers.

Krantz, Grover (1992). *Big Footprints*. Johnson Printing Company.

McLeod, Michael (2009). *Anatomy of a Beast: Obsession and Myth on the Trail of Bigfoot*. University of California Press.

Meldrum, J. (2006). *Sasquatch: Legend Meets Science*. Tom Doherty Associates, LLC.

Meldrum, J. (2013). *Sasquatch Field Guide*. Paradise Cay Publications, Inc.

Meldrum, J. (2016). *Sasquatch, Yeti, and Other Wildmen of the World. A Field Guide to Relict Hominoids*. Paradise Cay Publications.

Napier, J. R. (1973). *Bigfoot: The Sasquatch and Yeti in Myth and Reality*. E. P. Dutton.

Noel, C. (2019). *Midspeak: Tapping into Sasquatch and Science*. Independently published.

Rasmus, S. M. (2002). Repatriating Words: Local Knowledge in a Global Context. *American Indian Quarterly*, 26(2), 286–307.

Regal, B. (2011). *Searching for Sasquatch: Crackpots, Eggheads, and Cryptozoology*. Springer.

Shackley, M. (1983). *Still Living? Yeti, Sasquatch and the Neanderthal Enigma. 1986*. Thames and Hudson Inc.

Strain, Kathy Moskowitz. 2008. *Giants, Cannibals, & Monsters: Bigfoot in Native Culture*. Hancock House Publishers.

The Epic of Gilgamesh (1972). Penguin Books.

Wágner, Karel (2013). *Bigfoot Alias Sasquatch*. Independently published.

BUNYIP

Name: Bunyip

Alternative Names: Banip, Dongus, Kinepratia, Katenpai, Kyenprate, Mulyawonk, Tanggel, Tanutbun, Torrong, Tooroodun, Tunatpan

Related Cryptids: n/a

Locations: New South Wales and Victoria, Australia; lakes, billabongs, swamps, waterholes, and rivers

Most Recent Documented Sighting: 1965

The bunyip is one of Australia's indigenous mythological creatures. Like most native (i.e., nonintroduced) animals found in Australia, the bunyip is unique in that it doesn't resemble any other creature in the world. It is an aquatic, carnivorous mammal, known locally as a water spirit.

Australia, thanks to its geographic isolation and unique climactic features, is populated by animals that do not exist anywhere else on the planet. In fact, from 80 to 90 percent of all Australian mammals, reptiles, amphibians, and fish are endemic to the continent. Another result of this isolation has been the proliferation of more marsupials than exist anywhere else in the world. Marsupials—mammals that raise their immature young in pouches—are the dominant mammal in Australia, with bats, mice, and rats as the only native placental mammals. Finally, monotremes, mammals like the platypus that lay eggs rather than give birth to live infants, are also found in Australia.

Given how unique Australia's native animals are, it's not surprising that Australia's most famous monster is unique as well.

The bunyip has been described variously as looking like a seal, sea lion or otter, a crocodile, a sea star (starfish), or a dog. They are covered with thick black or brown fur (although some reports suggest that it was feathered). Some have described a creature with a long neck like an emu and a head like a horse with fangs or tusks, while others describe a creature with a short neck and a head like a dog. Bunyips are thought to be large, ranging from 5 to 15 feet long, and either have no tail (the dog-like short-necked bunyip) or a tail (the long-necked horse-like bunyip). It is important to note that descriptions of the bunyip as appearing like a dog or a horse must be relatively recent characterizations, as Australia's only canid, the dingo, arrived in Australia about 3,500 years ago, while the horse was introduced by Europeans in the late eighteenth century. On the other hand, crocodiles, emus, seals, sea lions, and sea stars are all native to Australia and most likely influenced the earliest descriptions of the animal. While otters do not exist in Australia, an otter-like water rodent called the rakali is indigenous to the continent and may have also shaped the appearance of the bunyip.

Taxonomically, the bunyip should be classified as either a marsupial or a monotreme. They are said to lay eggs like a monotreme, but descriptions of the animal resemble in many ways some of the ancient extinct marsupials of Australia, such as the herbivorous *Palorchestes*, an animal of the size of a horse with a nose like that of a tapir, *Zygomaturus trilobus*, a marsupial that looks like a giant wombat, *Diprotodon, a giant wombat*, or the carnivorous *Thylacoleo carnifex* or Marsupial Lion, an animal that looked like a big cat but is actually related to kangaroos, koalas, and wombats. For this reason, it is thought that the origin of the bunyip can be traced back to a time when these animals existed alongside of indigenous Australians. *Palorchestes* and *Diprotodon*, for example, went extinct about 11,000 years ago while the Marsupial Lion disappeared about 30,000 years ago. The first humans arrived in Australia about 60,000 years ago, so they would have lived alongside of these animals, and the memories of those animals may have merged with the beliefs about the bunyip.

Bunyips are water animals. They have been observed in swamps, rivers, billabongs (a local term for oxbow lakes), and lakes in southeastern Australia, and their presence is indicated by the large number of place names that reference the creature, such as the township of Bunyip, Bunyip River, the House of the Gentle Bunyip (an ecumenical Christian community), and Bangyeno banip, a local name for what the Europeans call the Avoca River.

Bunyips were described as having supernatural abilities, such as the ability to change water levels, hypnotize humans, and harm humans with their great roar. As carnivores, they were thought to eat eels and other aquatic creatures. Sometimes, however, they were known to eat people; one man said that his mother was killed by a bunyip at the Barwon River near Geelong, Victoria. A Boonwurrung man, for example, said that he was attacked by a bunyip and had the scars to prove it. They are described as nocturnal and rarely appear on dry land, preferring to stay under the water, and they lay their eggs in platypus nests. When on land, they either walk on two legs or on all fours. The most common origin story for the bunyip is that a man named Bunyip ate his totem animal and was punished by the Rainbow Serpent, an indigenous creator god, who turned him into an evil spirit.

The first locally produced image of the bunyip, known as the Bunyip of Challicum, was described for the first time in the mid-nineteenth century. According to George Henry Wathen, an English geologist who visited the Australian state of Victoria (just south of New South Wales) in 1850, he witnessed such an image, which he found carved in the earth in the vicinity of Fiery Creek in Victoria, near a large sheep ranch called Challicum Station. In an 1851 article published in his magazine *Australasian*, and the subsequent book he published in 1854, Wathen included his own hand-drawn rendering of the artwork, which shows a creature that looks somewhat like a chubby plesiosaur, an extinct aquatic reptile that lived until about 66 million years ago (and which have been found in Australia). Wathen described the creature being 28 feet long and looking a bit like an emu. According to Wathen, local legends tell of a bunyip that lived in a waterhole in the region, and after killing a local man (called a "blackfellow" by Wathen), the bunyip was killed with a spear, and afterward, other *Djab Wurrung people* cut an outline around the dead creature right into the earth, preserving its likeness.

Wathen was not the first European to report on the Chillicum bunyip. In the 1840s, the Commissioner for Crown Lands in the Wimmera, William Wright, mentioned the image to a friend and noted that the Aboriginal people would periodically recarve the image into the soil. Eventually, however, as European settlement to the area increased, pushing out the Aboriginal people, the image was no longer maintained, and it eventually disappeared altogether. The image was last reported in 1867, when a man named R. E. Johns retold the story of how the image appeared and included his own drawings of the image in his private notebooks.

While it had long been thought that there are no extent examples of the bunyip represented in indigenous Australian rock art since the disappearance of the Bunyip of Challicum, in 2016, a major discovery was made at the Grampians National Park, the most important site for

Aboriginal rock art in the state of Victoria. Here, during an expansion of the Grampians Peaks Trail, a park ranger named Kyle Hewitt found a previously unknown sandstone cave full of rock art—including four images of what look like bunyips. The existence of the cave was kept secret by park officials until 2019 in order to protect the art, and even today the public is not allowed in the cave to see it.

The presence of the bunyip images is linked to a story behind the most famous rock art in the vicinity—an image of the creator god Bunjil found in a cave called Bunjil Shelter. In the tale, Bunjil, who lived with his wife, children, and mother-in-law, threw his wife and children from a cliff and then caught them safely, but when he threw his mother-in-law off the cliff, he did not catch her and she broke into pieces and was then attacked by a bunyip. The mother-in-law, in order to protect herself, lured Bunjil to the waterhole where the bunyip was living and where the bunyip tore Bunjil apart. (He was later put back together by a bird using a double rainbow.) It may be that the bunyip cave images at Grampians are there to commemorate the fight between Bunjil and the bunyip.

Most Aboriginal peoples in southeastern Australia have their own tales about the bunyip, including, as in the Bunjil story, origin stories. One such tale comes from the Ngarrindjeri people of South Australia who explain how the bunyip (known by its local name the Mulyawonk) came to be. The story tells of a man who was very greedy, taking too many fish when he went fishing, and who was cursed to become a Mulyawonk—described by the Ngarrindjeri as half-human, half-fish—and sent to live in the river. This story, like so many stories still told today, includes not only the bunyip's origin (in most tales, he was once a man who was punished for some misdeed) but also a clear message for misbehaving children: behave properly or the Mulyawonk will get you.

Bunyip sightings, long known by the indigenous people of the area, started to be reported in print as early as 1845. While most white settlers dismissed these stories as the fabrications of superstitious natives, others claimed to have seen the creature themselves. The first such sighting by a European may have been that of mineralogist Joseph Charles Bailey in 1801, who said that he heard an animal bellowing in the Swan River in Western Australia. Another early sighting by Europeans was in 1822 when two men reported to a magistrate in Liverpool, New South Wales, that they saw a frightening snake-like creature, later called the Liverpool Monster. (The first time the name bunyip—or bahnyip as it was then written—was printed was in 1812 in the *Sydney Gazette*.) Because Australia, and its unusual animals, was so foreign to Europeans, many easily believed the local stories and reported them as fact. For example, botanist Richard Hanmer Bunbury wrote in 1846, "the question of the existence of an unknown animal in this country is at last set at rest; the beast exists."

The first written description of the animal, from an article titled "Wonderful Discovery of a New Animal," published in the July 2, 1845, edition of *The Geelong Advertiser and Squatters' Advocate*, described the creature as follows:

The Bunyip, then, is represented as uniting the characteristics of a bird and of an alligator. It has a head resembling an emu, with a long bill, at the extremity of which is a transverse projection on each side, with serrated edges like the bone of the stingray. Its body and legs partake of the nature of the alligator. The hind legs are remarkably thick and strong, and the fore legs are much longer, but still of great strength. The extremities are furnished with long claws, but the blacks say its usual method of killing its prey is by hugging it to death. When in the water it swims like a frog, and when on shore it walks on its hind legs with its head erect, in which position it measures twelve or thirteen feet in height. (Lloyd 1846)

This description was prompted by the discovery of a fossilized knee bone at Lake Colongulac, Victoria, which a Wathaurong man confirmed as a bunyip. (This fossil was later identified as *Thylacoleo carnifex*.) Other fossils thought to be bones of the bunyip include bones found in the Wellington Caves in New South Wales in 1830 and later identified as extinct marsupials Diprotodon and Nototherium and a skull found by a settler named Atholl Fletcher in 1846 at the Murrumbidgee River in New South Wales, which was later thought to be that of a fetal horse or camel (the skull disappeared before it could be properly identified). Besides these intriguing bones, many Europeans reported seeing the animals themselves, confirming for many the existence of bunyips and counteracting the belief that Aboriginal stories were just superstitious myths. Others told of killing or capturing bunyips, although those kills ended up being other, more mundane animals, such as a goat, a seal, and a bittern (a large marsh bird).

The first people to challenge the idea that the bunyip is real were, not surprisingly, Europeans, who have offered a variety of explanations for the sightings of the bunyip. Nineteenth-century colonial officer and amateur ethnologist Thomas Worsnop suggested that the bunyip stories are simply remnants of memories about real animals from the distant past, while geographer George Winsor Earl thought that the bunyip was really a dugong (a large marine mammal). In the 1930s, geographer Charles Fenner claimed that bunyip sightings were really elephant or leopard seals that traveled from the sea via rivers into Australia. Others suggested that it was an alligator (which is not found in Australia; they were probably referring to crocodiles.) In the 1950s, anthropologist Aldo Massola saw fur seals as the most likely explanation, based in part on the drawings by R. E. Johns, as well as on the fact that bunyips were said to roar, as seals do. Others have suggested the cassowary as the most probably source for the bunyip (even though they live in the north of Australia). Finally, many people feel that tales of the bunyip are simply boogeyman stories to frighten children away from dangerous waterways and to keep them from stealing the eggs of ducks and other water birds that inhabited the same waters as the bunyip.

While bunyip sightings were common in the nineteenth century, they began to decrease as European settlement increased. At the same time, a number of new uses of the term bunyip began to appear in Australian newspapers; it became a synonym for pretender, imposter, and false talk (humbug) and continues to be used as a slur today. The latest scientific interest in the bunyip came in 1890 when the Melbourne Zoological Gardens organized an expedition to find a bunyip in the Euroa swamp in Victoria. Even though most interest in the bunyip died with the end of the nineteenth century, a number of twentieth-century sightings have been reported, including one from the Lauriston Reservoir in Victoria in 1949 and one from the Nerang River in Queensland (just north of New South Wales) in 1965. Because the bunyip is so rare, relative to other cryptids around the world, it doesn't make its appearance in popular culture as often as others do. In addition, all of the appearances are Australia-specific. Bunyips are found in at least five children's books (most notably Jenny Wagner's 1973 book, *The Bunyip of Berkeley's Creek*), a children's song, a musical, and two Australian films. It's worth noting that the majority of these are media aimed at children, reinforcing the role that the bunyip has in Australian culture as a boogeyman intended to frighten children into behaving. There are also a handful of artworks that include or feature the bunyip, including one at the State Library Victoria, one in Mugildie, Queensland, one in Aireys Inlet, Victoria, and a coin-operated bunyip that emerges from the water in a cave on the banks of the Murray River in Murray Bridge, South Australia. With the rise in interest in cryptozoology around the world, the bunyip has found its way into international popular culture as well and can now be found in fantasy novels, videos games, and even the 2019 film, *Godzilla: King of the Monsters*. There is even a children's song called *The Bunyip*, released in 1977, which warns children:

> So you better come home quickly
> And you better hide very soon
> Or the Bunyip's going to get you
> In the Bunyip of moon.

See also: Lake Murray Monster, Yowie

Further Reading:

Barnard, E. (2012). *Capturing Time: Panoramas of Old Australia*. National Library Australia.

Clark, I. D. (2017). Bunyip, Bunjil and Mother-in-law Avoidance: New Insights Into the Interpretation of Bunjils Shelter, Victoria, Australia. *Rock Art Research: The Journal of the Australian Rock Art Research Association (AURA)*, 34(2), 189.

Clark, I. D. (2018). A Fascination With Bunyips: Bunbury, La Trobe, Wathen, and the Djab Wurrung People of Western Victoria. *Journal of the CJ La Trobe Society Inc.*, 17(1), 27.

Clarke, P. A. (2007). Indigenous Spirit and Ghost Folklore of "Settled" Australia. *Folklore*, 118(2), 141–61.

Holden, R., & Holden, N. (2001). *Bunyips: Australia's Folklore of Fear*. National Library Australia.

Lloyd, E. (1846). *A Visit to the Antipodes: With Some Reminiscences of a Sojourn in Australia (No. 22)*. Smith, Elder.

Minard, P. (2018). Making the 'Marsupial Lion': Bunyips, Networked Colonial Knowledge Production Between 1830–59 and the Description of Thylacoleo Carnifex. *Historical Records of Australian Science*, 29(2), 91–102.

Mulvane, J. (1994). The Namoi Bunyip. *Australian Aboriginal Studies*, 1, 36.

C

CADBOROSAURUS

Name: Cadborosaurus
Alternative Names: Caddie
Related Cryptids: Bownessie, Chessie, Loch Ness Monster
Location: Cadboro Bay, British Columbia, Canada
Most Recent Documented Sighting: 2019

Cadborosaurus, or Caddie for short, is the name given to the sea creature that lives in the waters of Cadboro Bay, just off the southern tip of Vancouver Island in British Columbia.

Caddie is, like many of the North American water creatures, a relatively recent discovery.

Like many other sea and lake creatures, there may have been stories about a legendary creature living in the depths of the Bay.

Caddie sightings first hit the news in 1933, which was the exact year that the Loch Ness Monster exploded onto the scene. In fact, it was just two months after Nessie became an international star that the first important sighting of Caddie occurred. But, as with other cryptids, supporters of Caddie suggest that it existed long before the 1930s and was a part of the folklore and mythology of First Nations peoples in British Columbia. In addition, it is said that from the late nineteenth century there were occasional reports by European colonists in the area about large sea creatures. For example, the first people to inhabit Victoria Island, the Manhousat, have a creature called the Hiyitl'iik, which is a sea serpent of some kind, but the descriptions that are available, and that have not already been linked to Caddie, do not seem to describe the same creature.

I think we can safely say that Caddie was "born" in 1933, which was not only the year that Nessie emerged but was also the year that *King Kong*, a movie about a giant ape that survived millions of years of evolution, was released.

The October 23, 1933, edition of the *Edmonton Journal*'s front page was dedicated to this exciting but terrifying new creature. The headline read, "Sea serpent seen again Saturday: Cadborosaurus cited by officers of ocean liner." Walter Prengle, the captain of the Santa Lucia, which was traveling from New York to Victoria, reported:

> My navigating officer called my attention to a big peculiarly shaped object about 300 feet away. At first we decided it was an upturned barge but on further observation, we started to be moving rapidly. It was inside only a minute or two when it dives beneath the surface of the water. We could only see what was probably the head of the serpent and it looked from the bridge of the ship to be about the size of my cabin. (*Edmonton Journal* 1933: 7)

On December 6, 1933, the *Capital Journal*, in Salem, Oregon, included a story headlined, "Sea serpent has head like a horse and pants like a dog, says witness" and included the following story, told first to a Victoria Island newspaper. Cyril B. Andrews of Pender Harbor, British Columbia, related that he and another young companion, Norman Georgesson, were duck hunting, and after shooting a duck, and paddling out to retrieve it, a giant serpent appeared beside their boat. Andrews wrote:

> I was still only ten feet away from it, with the duck right beside the thing, when to my horror it gulped the bird down its throat. It then looked at me, its mouth wide open, and I could plainly see its teeth and tongue, which were like those of a fish. When it closed its mouth, all the loose skin folded neatly at the corners while its breathing came in short, sharp pants, like a dog after a run.

> its coils rose at least 6 feet above me, gradually sinking under the water again. its head was like that of a horse but without ears or nostrils, and its eyes were in the front of the head which was flat. I would swear to the head being 3 feet long and 2 feet wide. its length when I first saw it lying in the bay was fully 40 feet long and from head to tail I would say it was all of that length. As it appeared in front of me its thickness was between 2 1/2 and 3 feet at the thickest part, gradually tapering to the tail. like a snake in color, it was a brownish gray, the skin smooth with no spikes or fins. (*Capital Journal* 1933)

That same year, *Victoria Daily Times* managing editor Archie H. Wills kicked off a contest inviting readers to submit possible names for the creature. The winning name submitted was Cadborosaurus, a combination of Cadboro and Plesiosaurs. Willis later said that it was the height of the Great Depression, and that one reason why he promoted the story was to bring a little bit of levity to a very dark time. As with a number of other American cryptids, it is often reporters or editors who not only report the story of these animals but also have probably played a major role in their acceptance in society and thus the sightings that occur.

Also in 1933, Jack Nord, who encountered Cadborosaurus near Oyster River, off the east coast of Vancouver Island, wrote about his encounter in a letter to the editor of the *Victoria Daily Times*:

> He was about 100 to 110 feet long. His body was about two and a half feet in diameter. His head was as large as a draft horse's, but it looked more like a camel's. He had fangs in his mouth, six to eight inches long. His eyes seemed to roll in their sockets, changing from a reddish color to green.

> He had whiskers under his jaw and a kind of mane from his forehead to the back of his head, looking like the teeth of a dragsaw. A fin on his back was raised to about three feet. From the water to the top of his head would be about seven feet. He was an ugly thing.

There were no super significant sightings during the 1940s, probably because of the war and the dislocations that it caused. Two important events did happen though, which contributed to the developing Caddie lore. In 1943, two fisherman claimed that they killed Caddie, causing quite a bit of outrage in the local community. Two weeks later, however, there was another sighting, and Caddie was alive again.

Three years later, a group of Vancouver men wanted to try to capture Caddie so that it could be featured in the upcoming sixtieth anniversary celebration for Vancouver. After the celebration, the men were going to sell it to Ringling Brothers' Circus, which at that time still had a sideshow for the display of freaks and other oddities.

In the 1950s, the sightings continued. On February 5, 1950, the Chief Justice of Saskatchewan's King's Bench, James T. Brown, had his own sighting. Chief Justice Brown's description of Caddie and the circumstances surrounding its appearance follow precisely the pattern of almost every other account.

> There was no question about the serpent—it was quite a sight. I'd think the creature was 35 to 40 feet long. It was like a monstrous snake. It certainly wasn't any of those sea animals we know, like a porpoise, sea lion and so on. I've seen them and know what they look like.
>
> Along about 3 p.m. Sunday, a clear sunny afternoon we were walking along by a Victoria beach. Mrs. Brown saw the monster first. By the time my daughter and I got our eyes sighted on the spot he had disappeared, but then he came up again about 150 yards from shore.
>
> His head, like a snake's, came out of the water four or five feet and straight up. Six or seven feet from the head one of his big coils showed clearly. The coil itself was six or seven feet long, fully a foot thick, perfectly round and dark in color. There must have been a great length of him under the water.
>
> He was swimming very fast for he came up 200 to 300 yards away from the spot where he went under each time. You couldn't follow his trail. We watched when he went under but couldn't spot any ripples.
>
> I got three good looks at him. On one occasion he came up almost right in front of us.

Caddie's main proponents are oceanographer Paul LeBlond and zoologist Edward Bousfield, who are convinced that Caddie is real and have published a number of papers on the subject. Bousfield, a researcher at the Royal British Columbia Museum, says there has been about one sighting per year on average for the last 100 years, and points out that people very rarely see giant squids, even though we absolutely know they exist. In a 1992 interview, he said:

> I'm convinced it exists. We have a mountain of evidence and all we lack is a current specimen. All attempts to track down the previous specimens have been fruitless because of the long passage of time. (Ferry 1992)

Bousfield based his conviction in part on the claim that since the Second World War, two skeletons and two carcasses of what appear to be Caddies have washed up on the shores of British Columbia and neighboring Washington state, although all four are now gone. In 1968, a 16-inch baby apparently was captured alive by a former whaling captain who put it in a bucket for the night on his ship—but took pity on it in the morning and released it.

The most convincing of these finds, to Bousfield and LeBlond, was a 10-feet-long juvenile carcass found in 1937 in the stomach of a sperm whale at a whaling station on off of Langara Island. But because none of the specimens—if they existed at all—survived, there was no way to study them. That changed in 1992 when three photos of that carcass, taken some time in the 1930s, were discovered in the archives of the Royal British Columbia Museum in Victoria. This gave Bousfield and LeBlond something to work with, and they were even able to find an eyewitness, Jim Wakelen, who was still alive in 1992 and who worked at the whaling station. Wakelen told the scientists that he and the others present all gawked at the body and concluded that it could not be any known species of fish or marine mammal, although the director of the museum, Francis Kermode, thought it was a fetal baleen whale.

LeBlond and Bousfield analyzed the photos, which show a dark creature with a serpentine body, a rectangular head, and a tail fin. Ultimately, the men concluded that what they were looking at was indeed a brand new species of animal, and a reptile at that. In particular, like so many other lake and sea creatures, they postulated that it could be a modern, surviving Plesiosaur. While most such monsters are described that way, Caddie had long been thought to be furry, which would suggest that she's a mammal. Some of the other features identified by witnesses are also not found on Plesiosaurs, such as ears or horns. In addition, only mammals with large stores of fat can survive in the very cold waters off of Victoria Island.

Today, Caddie remains a popular tourist draw, although sightings have slowed down considerably since their peak. According to the website Cadborosaurus.ca, which tracks sightings and has a large collection of photos, drawings, and archived newspaper articles, the last encounter was in May 2019 at Port Townsend, Washington.

See also: Bownessie, Chessie, Champ, Loch Ness Monster

Further Reading:

Bousfield, E. L., & LeBlond, P. H. (1992). Preliminary Studies on the Biology of a Large Marine Cryptid in Coastal Waters of British Columbia. *American Zoologist*, 32, 2A.

Bousfield, E. L., & LeBlond, P. H. (1995). An Account of Cadborosaurus Willsi, new Genus, new Species, a Large Aquatic Reptile from the Pacific Coast of North America. *Amphipacifica*, 1(supplement 1), 3–25.

Dash, M. (1993). The Dragons of Vancouver. *Fortean Times*, 70, 46–8.

Ferry, J. (1992). Sea Serpent Glides into Folklore of Canadians. *Los Angeles Times*, August 23.

Gardner, R. (1950). Caddy, King of the Coast: A sea Serpent That's as Real as the Flying Saucer and Just as Harmless Still Churns the Pacific for its Favored Fans. *Macleans*, June 15.

Naish, D. (2000). Where be Monsters? *Fortean Times*, 132, 40–4.

Naish, D. (2001). Sea Serpents, Seals, and Coelacanths: An Attempt at a Holistic Approach to the Identity of Large Aquatic Cryptids. *Fortean Studies*, 7, 75–94.

Nord, J. (1933). Letter to the Editor. *Victoria Daily Times*, October 11.

Paxton, C. G. M., & Naish, D. (2019). Did Nineteenth Century Marine Vertebrate Fossil Discoveries Influence sea Serpent Reports? *Earth Sciences History*, 38, 16–27.

Saggase, P. (2005). Cadborosaurus Willsi: Attributive Inquiry. *Bipedia*, 24, 5.

Sea Serpent has Head Like a Horse and Pants Like a dog, Says Witness (1933). *Capital Journal*, December 6.

Sea Serpent Seen Again Saturday: Cadborosaurus Cited by Officers of Ocean Liner (1933). *Edmonton Journal*, October 23.

CHAMP

Name: Champ

Alternative Names: Champie

Related Cryptids: Loch Ness Monster, Bownessie, Chessie

Location: Lake Champlain, United States and Canada

Most Recent Documented Sighting: 2019

Champ is the name of a lake monster thought to inhabit Lake Champlain, a large freshwater lake in upstate New York and that borders Vermont and Quebec. It is the sixth largest lake in the United States.

The French had already been in North America for almost a century by the time that Samuel de Champlain first arrived at the lake in 1609. Champlain was a fur trader who founded Quebec in what was then called New France.

Living in the area around the lake were Algonquin-speaking tribes including the Abenaki on the northern side of the lake and the Mohawk on the southern side. To the Algonquin Abenaki, the lake was called Petonbowk, and the St. Francis/Sokoki Abenaki People call it Bitawbagok. The Iroquois referred to the lake as Caniaderi Guarunte. In 1609, Champlain named the lake after himself.

Because physical evidence for the existence of cryptids is so hard to find, many cryptozoologists use indigenous myths and folktales as a form of evidence to help buttress the proposition that these creatures may be real. In the case of Champ, it is absolute true that the local tribes did (and still do today) have a belief in a great horned serpent, called Pita-Skog, which is an important spirit, representing darkness as well as power, and the counterpart to the thunderbird. Like the thunderbird, the great serpent is a manitou, a powerful guardian spirit. It lives in caves or caverns connected with lakes or within rocks.

Serpents—usually depicted with horns and a fish tail—can be seen in petroglyphs and burial mounds from the east coast to the Great Lakes. Serpents were also carved into ornaments and tools and were used as imagery for tattoos. These images, and the beliefs that underlie them, are harnessed into the argument that local peoples knew of a great monster in the lake.

The first sighting that we know of of the animal that would be known as Champ was in 1808 when one of the local papers simply announced, "Lake Champlain—A monster has lately made its appearance on the waters of the lake."

It was not until a decade later, in 1819, when a much more detailed account came out. The *Plattsburgh Republican* printed an article about a monster seen by a captain Crum at Bulwagga Bay. According to the paper:

> Captain Crum who witnessed the site relates that about 8 o'clock in the morning when pulling off the shore in a skow he discovered at a distance of not more than 200 yards an unusual undulation of the surface of the water which was followed by the appearance of a monster rearing its head more than 15 feet and moving with the most velocity to the south at the same time lashing with its tail two large sturgeon and a bill fish which appeared to be engaged in pursuit.

> After the consternation occasioned by such a terrible spectacle had subsided, captain Crum took a particular survey of the singular animal which he describes to be about 187 feet long, its head flat with three teeth, two in the under and one in the upper jaw, in shape similar to the seahorse—the color black with a star in the forehead and a belt of red around the neck. its body about the size of a hogshead with bunches on the back as large as a common potash barrel the eyes large and the color of peeled onion he continued to move with astonishing rapidity towards the shore for about a minute when suddenly started underwater and has not been seen, Although many fishing boats have been on the lookout. (*Plattsburgh Republican* 1899)

By the 1870s, people were reporting that their animals were going missing and suspected that the monster might be behind it. As the story got bigger and more sensational, promoter P. T. Barnum saw an opportunity and offered a $50,000 reward for anyone who could capture or kill the beast. This was an astounding amount of money—about $1.7 million today—so Barnum must have been pretty confident that there was no creature.

Champ is a relatively rare lake or sea monster in that documented sightings occurred prior to the twentieth century. Even though plesiosaurs fossils were turning up more and more regularly, the modern appearance of the sea serpent—big body, hump back, swan neck, horse-shaped head, and four flippers—had not yet gelled. The Loch Ness Monster was still little more than a rumor itself. So the nineteenth-century descriptions tended to vary, whereas after Nessie hit the news, the physical descriptions began to conform to a single type.

Sightings continued to occur, and with new developments in technology, photos, and much later videos, began to appear. By far the most well known is what's known as the Mansi photo, which is almost the equivalent of Bigfoot's Patterson-Gilman film.

On July 5, 1977, Sandra Mansi and her family were driving along lake Champlain when they stopped at a viewpoint to look over the lake, while the two children played in the water. Sandra saw something in the water that she couldn't understand, and her husband ran to the beach to get the kids out of the water. That's when she took the picture.

She said in a 2002 interview:

> I wasn't even scared, I'm just trying to figure out what I'm seeing. Then when Tony came over the field he saw it and started screaming, "Get the kids out of the water!'"

The photo is of something that resembles a plesiosaur-type monster: large humped body, long neck, and so on. The encounter happened in 1977 but it was four years later, in 1981, when she decided to come forward with her story.

Like the Patterson-Gimlin film, or the Zapruder film (the amateur footage shot of President Kennedy's assassination), a small number of scientists, and a much greater number of amateurs, have spent countless hours analyzing the photo, which some cryptozoologists consider to be the best photographic evidence of a lake creature anywhere in the world.

While cryptozoologists have largely accepted the accuracy of the photo, that is not the case with those outside of the community who have analyzed it, partly because there's no negative, the original picture is (now) almost fifty years old and has quite a bit of damage, Mansi does not remember where she took the photo, and, ultimately, it seems like no more than a piece of driftwood.

The photo has been analyzed by Benjamin Radford and Joe Nickell (2006) who concluded that whatever was in the picture was much smaller than witnesses reported. This is typical not just for cryptids but for anything that we might be watching from a distance. Oceanographer Paul LeBlond, who was a major advocate for Caddie, British Columbia's resident sea creature, also studied the photo and concluded that it was of a very large creature but also noted that his conclusion might be in error (1982).

None of the scientists who looked at the image thought it was a hoax. Rather, the consensus is that it's just a grainy photo of an object of some kind floating in the lake.

The most recent sighting was in 2019, when a member of the Champ Search Group, Katy Elizabeth, caught sight of the creature while on a cruise to search for it. She told the *Press Republican*:

> I saw two weird things moving on the sonar. I looked down at the display and said "what are they?" They were about 165 feet down. I took 65 pictures. I didn't look at them closely until the next morning. When I saw that head looking back at me, I started crying. I was shaking. I knew it was Champ. There were two animals.

> He looked annoyed. I think the sonar is very sensitive to their ears. It was amazing. There are protuberances on their heads, maybe for echolocation . . . I'm still working on what species it might have been.

It's pretty promising. I've sent the sonar images off to a analyzation expert I know, for optical analysis. I don't think it's a mammal species. We're dealing with a reptile. (McKinstry 2019)

Today, Champ enjoys its notoriety as well as, since 1986, a protected status thanks to laws passed by the New York and Vermont state legislature.

Plattsburgh folk musician Stan Ransom, who is known as the Connecticut Peddler, has written a song celebrating the mystery of the Lake Champlain Monster. It's called "Champ," and it's from his album, Songs of Lake Champlain. It is a celebratory song and emphasizes Champ's lovable nature, calling him "the king of the deep and the damp."

See also: Bownessie, Caddie, Chessie, Loch Ness Monster

Further Reading:

Clark, Jerome (1993). *Lake Monsters in Unexplained! 347 Strange Sightings. Incredible Occurrences, and Puzzling Physical Phenomena.* Gale Research Inc.

Kojo, Yasushi (1991). Some Ecological Notes on Reported Large, Unknown Animals in Lake Champlain. *Cryptozoology,* 10, 42–45.

Kurtz, Paul (1981). The Lake Champlain Monster Surfaces. *Skeptical Inquirer,* 6(1), 7–8.

LeBlond, Paul H. (1982). An Estimate of the Dimensions of the Lake Champlain Monster from the Length of Adjacent Wind Waves in the Mansi Photograph. *Cryptozoology,* I, 5–61.

McKinstry, L. (2019). *Possible Champ Sighting Near Westport.* Press-Republican.

Wilson, Fred (1981). "Champ" and the Mansi Photograph. *(Editorial) Pursuit,* 14(2), Whole 54, second Quarter.

Zarzynski, Joseph (1984). *Champ: Beyond the Legend Port Henry.* Bannister Publications.

CHESSIE

Name: Chessie

Alternative Names: n/a

Related Cryptids: Bessie, Bownessie, Champ, Loch Ness Monster

Location: Chesapeake Bay, Maryland

Most Recent Documented Sighting: 2014

Chessie is the name given to the sea serpent that lives in the Chesapeake Bay off the coast of Maryland.

Chessie is relatively unique in that it did not begin its life as a Native American myth, nor was it a product of the late Victorian focus on plesiosaurs, although countless articles and books suggest that there was one Victorian-era sighting in 1846, when a sailor named Captain Lawson spotted something unusual near the mouth of the Bay, but there is no evidence of such a sighting.

And while its story does include one element that is common to so many sea and lake serpents—the first possible sighting occurred in 1936, three years after the Loch Ness Monster became international news—Chessie's origin story really lies in the 1970s.

The Chesapeake Bay has been important to the humans living in its vicinity for more than 11,000 years. Native Americans who lived off of the bounty of the bay were Algonquin-speaking peoples, including the Powhatan, the Piscataway, and the Nanticoke. The first English colonists arrived in the sixteenth century, transforming the region entirely. As the United States grew, and especially with industrial growth, the bay became polluted, and by the early 1970s, it had gotten so polluted that oxygen levels dropped too low to support marine life. The situation as so dire that the newly formed environmental protection agency was asked to study the bay to determine how serious the problem was and to provide possible solutions. The study was completed in 1983, leading to a series of new programs aimed at cleaning up the bay and restoring the ecosystem's health.

It was in this environment that Chessie was born.

The year 1978 was the beginning, with a rumored twenty-five to thirty sightings in that year, although there is little to no documentation on most of those. The best known of the 1978 sightings was by Howard Smoot, who reported that they were looking at the Potomac River from their backyard and saw a large thing in the water. They watched it for about twenty minutes and even thought that it was traveling with two juveniles. He told the *Richmond Times*:

> It was really an awesome thing, frightening. It was a good 30-plus feet long and eight inches around and it had a head like a football. . . . I know what porpoises and turtles look like. But this thing was so unusual. I've never seen anything like it.

Smoot's first reaction was not to get a camera but to get his gun. He shot at the creatures but never saw them again.

The first good sighting of the creature was by Helen Jones in 1980, who said to the *Washington Post*:

> I was out crabbing. This great big thing come up out of the water. I could have reached out and touched it with my hand. It was about as round as a watermelon, more brownish than gray and had white spots on the hump. I told Officer Tesh, "Jack, you just missed it." He says, "Well I'll be doggone." (Brown 1982)

She also said:

> This great big thing come up out of the water. I could have reached out and touched it with my hand. It was about as round as a watermelon, more brownish than gray and had white spots on the hump. (Collins 1984)

In 1982 Robert and Karen Frew were enjoying an evening at their home on Kent Island when Robert saw something in the water and began to videotape and produced a three-minute-long color video.

This was at a time when owning a video camera was not that common and decades before we all began carrying tiny camera phones in our pockets. For the single most important evidence for the existence of Chessie, the video is surprisingly underwhelming. It does show something appearing to move slowly through the water, but what it is, or whether it is even an animal, is more difficult to answer. Robert was quoted as saying:

> When we came out of the Wye River, my wife said, "What's that over there?" I said that's a log. She said, "If that's a log, it's moving awfully fast." I don't know what it is. But it's here. (Collins 1984)

> A telephone pole that swims, like, not like a snake. There were four, five, six of us here—we all saw it. It went around the other side of the island, up in the rocks (to) a place called Clover Field, and a commercial artist there sketched it and it was exactly what we saw on the film. (May 1984)

Karen told the *Washington Post*:

> Chessie is part of the Maryland folklore. It probably was first sighted about 50 years ago, and other people have reported seeing it since. What we saw is not a run-of-the mill animal. I'd say it's similar to the Loch Ness Monster. (*Washington Post* 1982)

As we can see, the Frews were able to place their unusual encounter within a larger narrative in which the Loch Ness Monster provides the template for any new sighting or new creature.

The Frew video touched a nerve and sparked more sightings, as well as more publicity, which brought yet more sightings. In 1982, the same year that the Frews captured their video, the Maryland Department of Natural Resources Police formed what they called Chessie Patrol in order to collect evidence and keep an eye out for the creature.

Like the Mansi photo of Champ or the Patterson-Gimlin film of Bigfoot, both professionals and amateurs alike have studied the Frew video. The Enigma Project, a paranormal investigation group out of Baltimore, said that the video is authentic. Even the Smithsonian Institute, no less, weighed in on the video, saying in a statement in 1982:

> There was not enough visible evidence on the tape for a positive identification. The usual explanations of a partially submerged log, a string of birds or marching mammals, optical illusions, etc. seem inappropriate for the dark, elongated, animate object.

> The Chessie phenomenon differs in many ways from the typical sightings of marine animals. The front end is strongly angular, appearing and disappearing vertically instead of rolling above and below the surface as in most swimming animals.

Similarly, the object undulates in a vertical plane, according to eyewitnesses, rather than a horizontal plane as is normal swimming movement for elongated animals. The photographs and videotape are intriguing and identification of the object or objects in these films might be aided by some form of image enhancement. (*Richmond Times-Dispatch*)

What might the video actually show? And what might Chessie be?

Some people think it's a giant eel or snake, although neither of those animals grows longer than about 4 feet in the Chesapeake Bay, while others have suggested a turtle or even a misplaced manatee (occasionally a manatee from Florida will end up in waters as far north as Rhode Island; one such stray manatee was found in the Bay in 1994 and was named Chessie), while the Frews maintain that it was at least 30, if not 40 feet long. Another possibility is that giant South American snakes were accidentally released in the Bay, forming a colony of "serpents."

Chessie's real significance is not in its biological reality but in the way that it has been used to help create awareness about the pollution in Chesapeake Bay. It appeared at exactly the right time—when not only the Bay was at its unhealthiest but also when the national environmental movement was beginning, and in particular, when Chesapeake Bay become the focus of this movement, at least along the eastern coast. (In addition, Jaws came out a few years earlier, in 1975, creating a fear of the water that, for many, had not existed previously.) Its name and likeness were used in a number of local environmental campaigns. For example, in 1984, the US Fish and Wildlife Service got involved in efforts to clean up the bay and brought Chessie in as a mascot. One of their productions was a coloring book called *Chessie: A Chesapeake Bay Story*, released in 1986, featuring Chessie's likeness and a child-friendly poem about the damage to the Bay. In 1988, the director of the Fish & Wildlife Service at a congressional hearing on the Chesapeake Bay said:

The centerpiece of our public awareness program is "Chessie," the friendly Bay monster. Chessie was first introduced to the public in a story/coloring book developed by the service for use in elementary schools. Chessie has been enormously successful and recently received national recognition when the Service won a "Take Pride in America" award for its bay public awareness plan. A mascot-type costume of the legendary bay monster has been made for the Service and is now used in conjunction with our public affairs work. (United States. Congress. Senate. Committee on Environment and Public Works. Subcommittee on Environmental Protection. 1988)

This was no doubt the first time that a cryptid of any kind was discussed in Congress but demonstrates how critical Chessie was to the campaign. Of course, one might wonder about the campaign's emphasis on teaching children not to pollute, when it was the large industries surrounding the Bay that contributed the most to the pollution.

The latest sighting of Chessie was on April 5, 2014, when two young men were at the Magothy River and saw a 25–30-feet-long snake-like creature.

See also: Bessie, Champ, Bownessie, Loch Ness Monster

Further Reading:

Bay Monster (1982). *Washington Post*, July 12.
Brown, C. (1982). Creature Feature. *Washington Post*, July 16.
Cheezum, E. A. (2007). *Discovering Chessie: Waterfront, Regional Identity, and the Chesapeake Bay Sea Monster, 1960–2000*. Doctoral dissertation, University of South Carolina.
Chessie, the Chesapeake Bay Sea Monster (1980). *Richmond Times Dispatch*.
Mystery Creature Lurks in Baltimore County (2004). *WBAL TV*, July 27.
Okonowicz, E. (2012). *Monsters of Maryland: Mysterious Creatures in the Old Line State*. Stackpole Books.
United States Congress Senate. Committee on Environment and Public Works. Subcommittee on Environmental Protection (1988). *Effectiveness of Programs for the Protection of Chesapeake Bay* (Vol. 4).

CHUPACABRA

Name: Chupacabra

Alternative Names: Goat Sucker, Chupa

Related Cryptids: New Jersey Devil

Locations: Latin America and Southwestern United States

Most Recent Documented Sighting: May 17, 2019 (Houston, Texas)

The *Chupacabra* is a carnivorous canid found originally in Latin America. The word is a Spanish word meaning goat (*cabra*) and to suck (*chupar*), as chupacabras are thought to suck the blood of their victims, and goats, thanks to their ubiquity in much of the region, are a common victim. Besides livestock, they have also killed companion animals and have, according to some, attacked people on occasion.

The Chupacabra first emerged in popular culture on March 11, 1995, when a Puerto Rican rancher reported eight sheep found dead with puncture marks in their chest and no apparent blood in their bodies. But it wasn't until the killings began in and around the city of Canóvanas in August of that year that the panic set in. Multiple people began finding their animals dead and exsanguinated, leading to such a panic that the mayor of Canóvanas organized a number of hunting parties to find the predator, using a caged goat as bait. Hunting parties like this were unsuccessful, and the killings spread from Canóvanas, where about 150 animals died, to other parts of the island and ultimately claimed over a thousand chickens, rabbits, ducks, goats, sheep, cows, and horses, as well as cats and dogs. One resident in the town of Caguas even reported that the creature broke into a home and destroyed a teddy bear. The killings lasted from March 1995 through December 1995, when the first person, a man named Osvaldo Claudio Rosado, was attacked (and survived). The international attention that the killings garnered most likely led to the spread of the Chupacabra from Puerto Rico northward to other countries.

But the Chupacabra may also have its roots in the past. Puerto Rican villagers began reporting the unexplained deaths of small livestock in the 1970s. However, the term Chupacabra was not used prior to the 1990s. Instead, the killings in the 1970s were attributed to a creature by the name of *el Vampiro de Moca* (Moca Vampire), because many of the first deaths, which included cows, goats, chickens, geese, and a pig, happened in the town of Moca in early 1975. By the end of the killings, in the summer of 1975, hundreds of animals were killed throughout the island and drained of their blood. (There was also a rash of unexplained livestock killings in Texas in the same time period.) The killings were never solved, and exactly twenty years later in 1995, the Chupacabra killings began.

Unlike other cryptids, Chupacabra reports are typically not based on sightings of the animal itself. Instead, reports generally stem from someone finding dead animals, usually livestock, which appear to have been killed overnight and drained of their blood. Many reported that the animals had vampire-like punctures on their necks. Others found animals that had been killed but not eaten, which indicates to the witness that the killer was not a wolf or coyote, both of whom are thought (erroneously) to always eat their kills.

Even though most Chupacabra reports stem from the finding of dead animals, there have been multiple sightings of the animal over the years, and a number of people have captured or killed the animals, giving us a good idea of what they look like.

The Chupacabra is hairless, or at least has scraggly hair, and looks like a skinny, malformed canine. Many people say it walks on two feet, although it's more commonly seen walking on all fours, although usually with longer back legs than forelegs (giving it a kangaroo-like gait). Some have described the animal as looking like a demon, with a long, sometimes forked tongue. Others have described it as having an alien-like head, and in fact, Puerto Rico began experiencing UFO sightings in the 1970s, at the same time that the Moca Vampire appeared, which continued into the 1990s. In January 1995, the year that the Chupacabra killings began, a radio broadcaster named Orlando Morales saw a flying saucer while out camping in El Yunque rainforest with friends, and these sightings continued through April of that year; suspiciously, after the UFO sightings began, the government closed off El Yunque to locals without providing an explanation. Not coincidentally, many people think the Chupacabra originally came from El Yunque.

The Chupacabra has a terrible smell, which is sometimes reported as being like sulfur. (This may be linked to the widespread belief that hell smells like sulfur, and that the animal is a demon.) The eyes of the Chupacabra are red or black, and it often has spikes on its back or its head. The first physical description of the Chupacabra came in August 1995, when a Canóvanas resident named Madelyne Tolentino told the local paper that she saw a 4-feet-tall animal, spotted and hairy, standing upright on two legs, with an oval-shaped head and red or black eyes. Other early sightings were different, however. It was also reported by local Michael Negron to look like a scaly spiked dinosaur, while Luis Guadalupe described it as a flying demon. Even though all three reports made it into a 1996 *New York Times* article, Tolentino's description was the most widely distributed and most likely shaped many of the future sightings—at least in Puerto Rico, where the animal is more likely to be two legged. In the United States, on the other hand, chupacabras are more likely to be quadrupedal.

In December 1995, the last month of the killings in Puerto Rico, the first Chupacabra death was reported in the United States. In Klamath Falls, Oregon, a farmer reported that her cow was killed and mutilated, and that no blood was found around the animal. While this report was not from a state with a large Latino population (Latinos only made up 4 percent of the population of Oregon at that time), all the other reports in the 1990s were from Mexico as well as Florida and Texas—states with substantial Latino communities.

In some of these early cases, a dog-like creature was seen near the carcasses (Miami, March 1996), while in others, the bodies were found with punctures on the neck (South Texas, Chiapas, Mexico, and Miami, May 1996). One night in Miami in 1996, sixty-nine animals were killed in the Sweetwater neighborhood (home to the largest number of Nicaraguans in the United States).

As the stories continued, the descriptions of the Chupacabra became more elaborate: the creature had three toes on its feet and hands and spikes on its head (Juarez Mexico, May 1996), or it was a flying, bat-like animal (two locations in Sinaloa, Mexico, May 1996). As in Puerto Rico, locals in the Mexican state of Sinaloa began organizing into hunting parties to capture or kill the beast. Some of the reports at this time include claims that humans were attacked or killed, but no names of the victims have been reported.

The Chupacabra initially spread from Puerto Rico to Mexico, and from there, to Latin American communities in the southern and southwestern United States—especially Florida, New Mexico, Texas, and Arizona. In recent years, it has also been seen in other regions in North America as well as other Latin American countries like the Dominican Republic, Chile, Nicaragua, Honduras, Argentina, Ecuador, Costa Rica, and Brazil.

The Chupacabra is highly adaptable, living in both the tropical rain forests of Central and South America and the Caribbean, as well as the open plains and deserts of North America. They tend, however, to stay away from highly populated areas, preferring rural regions with fewer humans, fewer roads and highways, and more animals. They do not attack wildlife, focusing instead on domesticated animals with a clear preference for goats. It is unknown whether they need to have access to water or whether the blood that they drink meets their hydration needs. Unlike many North American cryptids, they are not found in swamps or wetlands.

In the United States, a number of chupacabras have been caught alive or killed. For example, in 2009, taxidermist Lynn Butler killed a Chupacabra that he found in his cousin's barn in Blanco, Texas, and had it stuffed. The creature was skinny, hairless, and with long legs, and while it was called a Chupacabra by the media that quickly sensationalized the story, it was most likely a coyote with sarcoptic mange—a disease that causes hair loss and thickened and crusty skin.

But the first Chupacabra to be captured was in Nicaragua in 2000, when a rancher killed one on his property that had been attacking his goats. After an analysis by the National Autonomous University of Nicaragua, it was determined that the animal was a dog with mange, although the rancher vigorously disputed that explanation, suggesting that the scientists switched the samples in order to conceal the truth.

For some reason, most of the Chupacabra carcasses have come out of Texas, where at least a half dozen chupacabras have been captured or killed, starting with the first in 2004.

One of the first live captures was in 2014 when a Ratcliffe, Texas couple named Jackie Stock and Arlen Parma caught a baby Chupacabra that they found in a tree and named Chupa. The couple kept it in a cage in their backyard, feeding it cat food, and it garnered a huge amount of media attention. It turns out that Chupa was a very sick raccoon, whom they had euthanized after a few days. Three years earlier, a Runway Bay, Texas, man named Tony Potter found a dead Chupacabra on the grounds of a golf course; that animal, too, turned out to be a raccoon.

The most recent live capture was not in Texas but in Oregon. In 2016, a Chupacabra was brought to an animal shelter in Eugene. It turned out to be a Patagonian mara, a large rodent from Argentina, which looks like a capybara. This is one of the only cases where the animal was not sick and still lives today—at the Oregon Zoo. Its name is Chupacabra.

Perhaps the most well known of all the Chupacabra specimens is what's called the Cuero Chupacabra, owned by Phylis Canion of Cuero, Texas. It is a skinny canid with thick grey skin and no hair. The animal was hit by a car in 2007 and brought to Canion, who maintained (and still maintains) that the creature is the Chupacabra that had been killing her chickens. Even after a sample of the animal's skin was sent for DNA analysis to Texas State University-San Marcos by the television show *Monster Quest*, with the results showing that her specimen was a coyote, Canion, who is a homeopathic doctor, rejects that explanation, telling reporters that her own DNA tests have shown that the animal is unknown to science. Canion had her Chupacabra stuffed and mounted and keeps it in her home, while she keeps the head in her freezer.

The most recent Chupacabra to be killed in Texas was in 2015 when a man named Philip Oliveira's dogs killed one at his farm in Rockdale. It turned out to be a mange-infected coyote.

In every other Chupacabra that has been tested, the results are similar: the animal is a dog, a coyote, or a coyote-dog or coyote-wolf hybrid with mange. The mange might also help explain why Chupacabras attack livestock rather than wildlife. Because the disease weakens the animals, they resort to attacking easier-to-kill animals like goats than their normal wild prey.

In the case of the animal kills, there have been a number of explanations for the ways that the animals have been killed. While many people think that predators do not kill and abandon their prey, the fact is that they often do. Known as surplus killing, many animals, including wolves, foxes, weasels, and coyotes, do sometimes kill many more animals than they need to eat; often they do so in order to return to the carcass later on to eat. In addition, feral dogs (and especially those in a pack) can and frequently do kill animals for fun, not intending to eat them at all. In fact, the very first killings attributed to the Chupacabra, in Canóvanas in 1995, were attributed to stray dogs according to the state veterinary office (although locals vigorously disputed that explanation).

Finally, to account for the lack of blood in many of the dead animals, many scientists have pointed to vampire bats, three species of which live throughout Central and South America, as the most likely culprit as they drink the blood of mammals at night. While vampire bats do not kill their prey, many do carry rabies, which can unintentionally kill those animals (or humans) that they bite. On the other hand, when necropsies have been performed on the dead animals, it has typically been found that they were not, in fact, exsanguinated. Even as far back as 1996, after the first rash of killings, Hector Garcia, director of veterinary services at the Agriculture Department's Veterinary Diagnostic Laboratory, found that the animals he dissected were full of blood. In addition, vampire bats and other blood suckers don't suck blood out of the jugular vein in the neck, like fictional vampires do. They will suck any part of the skin.

The Chupacabra owes much of its existence to the media, which has popularized and sensationalized the stories of both the unexplained animal deaths and the Chupacabra carcasses since the very first events in 1995. Unlike, for example, Bigfoot, which has had a long and busy life in American tabloid newspapers, the Chupacabra was and is featured in legitimate news— television programs, radio shows, newspapers, and more. It was featured almost continuously not only in the Puerto Rican newspapers, *El Nuevo Dia*, *El Vocero*, and the *Primera Hora*, but in international media as well. It was the international press coverage that allowed the Chupacabra to migrate from Puerto Rico to most of Latin America and much of the United States.

Outside of media reports of Chupacabra sightings and killings, the Chupacabra has been the subject of countless books and has been featured in a number of television shows and films, including those focused on cryptids like *Monster Quest*, *In Search of Monsters*, and *Monsters and Mysteries*, as well as other shows like the *X-Files*, *Grimm*, and *South Park*. It has also been featured in numerous fictional feature films, including *A Noite do Chupacabras* (2011), *Adventures Beyond: Chupacabra* (2001), *Blood of the Chupacabras* (2005), *Chupacabra* (2007), *Chupacabra Terror* (2005), *Chupacabra vs. the Alamo* (2013), *Chupacabra: Dark Seas* (2005), *El Chupacabra* (2003), *Goatsucker* (2009), *Guns of El Chupacabra* (1997), *Indigenous* (2014), *La Leyenda del Chupacabras* (2016), *Legend of the Chupacabra* (2000), *Mexican Werewolf in Texas* (2005), *Rise of the Chupacabras* (2003), *Scooby-Doo! and the Monster of Mexico* (2003), and *The Night of the Chupacabras* (2005).

There are also dozens of songs about the Chupacabra, more than this author has found for any other cryptids. Not surprisingly, many of these are from Latin America and are in Spanish. One of the most well known is called "Chupacabra" and is by Randy Rogers Band & La Maquinaria Nortena and is an example of Norteno music, which is Mexican-influenced music played on both sides of the border. Chupacabra, fittingly, is sung in both Spanish and English, and the chorus goes like this:

> Chu-chu-chupacabra
> Chupacabra gonna get you someday

> Why Latin America? And why a blood-sucking beast?

Livestock have been killed by wild predators ever since the Neolithic Revolution, when animals were first domesticated for food, starting at about 11,000 years ago. So why did the Chupacabra emerge as an explanation for these killings in Puerto Rico in the 1990s?

In cultures around the world, farmers and ranchers recognize the risk of wild predation on their farm animals. Even so, there are times when the animals are killed in a way that seems unusual or unexplainable to observers. At those times, a supernatural explanation is often sought, as it's a way to make sense of the unexplainable and to give some control back to those who have been victimized. Witchcraft accusations are often associated with these kinds of deaths. But attributing unexplainable livestock deaths to unknown creatures is also quite common.

In the case of the Chupacabra, there are other reasons for the unknown creature to be a blood sucker.

Before the Moca Vampire emerged in the 1970s, we can find references to vampires in pre-Columbian Mesoamerican mythology. Camazotz, for example, was a vampire bat god associated with death in the Veracruz and Mayan cultures on the Mesoamerican mainland. These beliefs may have traveled from southern Mexico to Puerto Rico prior to the Spanish conquest, as we now know that there was considerable trade and cultural exchange between the Mayans and the Taíno (the indigenous people of the Caribbean, including Puerto Rico). These beliefs may have persisted among the descendants of the Taíno who make up much of the contemporary population of Puerto Rico.

In addition, the Spanish who settled the island beginning in 1508 most likely brought vampire beliefs with them. For example, *Dip* was a demonic vampire dog in Catalan mythology while the *Guajona* was a blood-sucking witch in Cantabrian folklore, and in the Galician region of Spain, a blood-sucking witch called a *meiga xuxona* was a common belief. These beliefs may well have intermingled with the Taíno belief in the Camazotz and most likely survived in some form into the present.

Some scholars point to an explanation that moves from the supernatural to the economic. One theory (see, e.g., Derby 2005 and 2008) addresses Puerto Rico's history as an American colony and current status as a US territory. Since the United States gained control of Puerto Rico in 1898, the island has been subject not only to American military control but economic control as well. Most of the economy is dominated by American-owned agricultural plantations, whose products are exported to the United States to benefit American elites, leaving locals with little control over their economic and political futures.

In addition, the islanders have often been subject to other forms of exploitation at the hands of the United States. For example, in the 1950s, the inventor of the birth control pill tested it on 1,500 poor Puerto Rican women who were not informed of the risks posed by the drug. Many of the women developed devastating side effects and three died (the dosage given to the women was much higher than is found in birth control pills today). Before that time, the United States began a process of forced sterilization in both the United States and Puerto Rico, focusing on poor and "socially inadequate" women. This eugenics program was expanded, leading to the sterilization of one-third of Puerto Rican women by 1968, many of whom were not informed that the procedure was permanent. In this climate, it's not surprising that Puerto Ricans harbor a great deal of mistrust of the United States, which has translated into some of the origin myths surrounding the Chupacabra.

One common belief, for example, is that the Chupacabra was developed in an American biomedical laboratory on the island, and some of the animals escaped. Another belief is that the Chupacabra was created by NASA as part of a military experiment, and then either intentionally or unintentionally, some animals escaped or were released onto the island. This explanation dovetails with the UFO sightings in Puerto Rico and the fact that some people believe the Chupacabra is either an alien, the pet of aliens, or an alien-human hybrid. (Interestingly, the 1995 science-fiction film *Species*, about an alien-human hybrid, opens in Puerto Rico and was released just prior to the Tolentino sighting; Chupacabra expert and managing editor of *Skeptical Inquirer* Benjamin Radford (2011) interviewed Tolentino and discovered that she saw the film and suggests that she used the central character as the basis for her description of the creature.) Puerto Rican ufologist Jorge Martín (2001) suggested that the Chupacabra is an alien who was being studied at a US Department of Defense facility on the island of Vieques off of the east coast of Puerto Rico. While there is no proof that such a facility exists, it is true that Puerto Rico is host to multiple American military installations, all of which are closed to Puerto Ricans, so there is really no way to know what may be happening there or how many such places exist.

Variants of this belief include the idea that it was the FBI or the CIA that created the Chupacabra, and that the creature is an animal-human hybrid—perhaps a human-dog or human-monkey hybrid. These beliefs are not as outlandish as they might sound. Puerto Rico is home to large numbers of free-roaming rhesus and patas monkeys, which are not indigenous to the area and which escaped from the US-owned biomedical laboratories starting in the 1950s.

Other scholars have suggested that the Chupacabra is a metaphor for the United States in general and the way that its capitalistic and militaristic policies are sucking the blood of the island. Another suggestion notes that the Chupacabra's appearance in 1995 is contemporaneous with the arrival of HIV/AIDS in Puerto Rico, a disease that seems to suck the life out of its victims and which itself has been seen, in Puerto Rico and elsewhere, as a government-created disease intended to kill minorities.

In all these cases, it is clear that the secrecy of both the US government and the Puerto Rican government, combined with the distrust of the government by many islanders, is a contributor to the continued presence of the Chupacabra.

As more Chupacabra cases have been debunked with scientific evidence, reports have slowed down (although Chupacabras in Texas remain active to this day). Ironically, however, at the same time that they've slowed down in the Americas, they have spread across the world to new countries. In 2015, for example, a Chupacabra was captured in the Philippines and a video of the creature was shown on Facebook. (The animal was probably a Malaysian sun bear with mange.) In 2012, there was a Chupacabra sighting in Ukraine, followed by two in 2016. These animals were most likely foxes. In 2018, the Chupacabra arrived in India, with both dead animals and Chupacabra sightings reported by local people, and in 2019, the first sightings came in Pakistan.

At the time of this writing, a new case has emerged out of Mexico, which has prompted a great deal of concern. In March 2020, the body of a taxi driver named Melchor Anselmo Delgado was found in Valle de Bravo with deep wounds over his body. While it's most likely that the man was killed by a wild animal from a game ranch in the vicinity, many people began reporting that the killer was a Chupacabra.

See also: Beast of Bladenboro, New Jersey Devil

Further Reading:

Derby, L. (2008). Imperial Secrets: Vampires and Nationhood in Puerto Rico. *Past and Present*, 199(suppl_3), 290–312.

Derby, R. (2005). Vampiros del Imperio, o por qué el Chupacabras Acecha las Américas? In Salvatorre Ricardo (Ed.), *Culturas Imperiales: Experiencia y Representación en América, África y Asia*. Beatriz Viterbo Editora, 317–44.

Friedman, R. (1996). The Chupacabra Becomes a Recurring Legend. *The San Juan Star*. https://www.princeton .edu/~accion/chupa27.html.

Martín, J. (2001). *Vieques Poligono Del 3er. Tipo*. Cedicop.

Radford, B. (2011). *Tracking the Chupacabra: The Vampire Beast in Fact, Fiction, and Folklore*. UNM Press.

Strachan, A. E. (2003). *Chasing Chupacabras: Why People Would Rather Believe in a Bloodsucking Red-eyed Monster from Outer-space Than in a Pack of Hungry Dogs*. Doctoral dissertation, Massachusetts Institute of Technology.

D

DINGONEK

Name: Dingonek
Alternative Names: Luquata, Lukwata, Jungle Walrus, Ol-Umaima
Related Cryptids: None
Location: East Africa, specifically around Lake Victoria as well as the Maggori River in Kenya
Most Recent Documented Sighting: 1907

The Dingonek is an unusual African creature, said to live around Lake Victoria in Tanzania. It was thought to be a reptile of some sort because of its scaly skin and is most commonly represented as a pangolin-like creature.

The dingonek is, in some ways, Africa's most iconic monster. The history of this creature, from its first "discovery" by Europeans, illustrates European attitudes toward Africa during the final stages of European colonialism.

One of the most significant of the stories popularizing the creature was from 1918, when *Maclean's*, a well-known Canadian news magazine, published a story with the headline "Something About the Dingonek: A New Monster Discovered in Darkest Africa." This article set the tone for how this creature, and all other creatures found in or associated with sub-Saharan Africa, is discussed in the news media.

Terms like "Darkest Africa" or the "Dark Continent" represent the way in which Africa was seen to non-Africans during this period. Africa—its people, its animals, its land—was relatively unknown to most people outside of Africa, although of course Europe, Asia, and Africa had been linked for thousands of years through trade. But it was through European colonialism, largely driven by England, that Africa came to be known to outsiders. English explorers like Joseph Conrad, Henry Morton Stanley, Richard Burton, and David Livingstone wrote fantastical tales for their readers about the amazing but also frightening people, animals, places, and practices and were credited for "discovering" them. While these men did not actually discover anything that was not already known to Africans, or to those who had spent time there, the process of exploration and discovery, within the context of the last, most intensive stages of European imperialism, was marked by racism, violence, and exploitation.

While European countries—especially Portugal, England, Spain, and France—had long controlled much of the coastal areas of Africa, North Africa, and the southern tip of the continent, thanks to the Transatlantic Slave Trade, as well as trade in luxury goods like spices, ivory, and precious metals, the interior of the continent was not yet under direct European control. This would change starting in the nineteenth century as European nations began a dedicated land grab. There was so much European interest in controlling Africa that the leading imperialist nations got together in 1884 (at what would later be called the Berlin Conference or the Congo Conference) to determine how to best manage Africa and to ensure that there would not be fighting among the European powers scrambling for land. The result was the partitioning of the African continent, giving the most valuable areas to the largest European powers, and the ushering in of direct political control over the lives of the vast majority of Africans (prior to this time, European control in Africa was largely economic).

It was within this context that the notion of the Dark Continent emerged—the idea that Africa is an unknown, dangerous, and savage place, filled with people, plants, animals, and minerals that needed to be put under the control of civilized people. The great explorers of the era were central to this entire program of "civilization." Stanley himself used the term in two of his books, *Through the Dark Continent* (1878) and *In Darkest Africa* (1890). Not only did they name (using European names) all of the places, people, animals, and things that they saw, but that process of discovery directly resulted in those very resources being stripped from the continent.

At the same time that European superpowers were ensuring that they would be best positioned to exploit Africa's resources, they were also creating a master narrative to justify it. What Rudyard Kipling called "the white man's burden" referred to the idea that Europeans were obligated, by virtue of their imperial status, to civilize those savages that still remained on the planet. The narratives that the great explorers crafted about their adventures in Africa played into this, as the superstition, ignorance, and lack of sophistication of African natives were highlighted. So when an explorer like David Livingstone tells his readers that Africans believe in strange monsters, it helps to reinforce the impression that Africans *need* to be civilized. The discovery of the dingonek fits perfectly into this narrative and can't be understood without it.

The Maclean's article in 1918 would have been the first time that the word dingonek was seen by regular people who would not have had access to explorers' accounts of their travels. The article described the creature, made some guesses as to what it could be (perhaps a dinosaur relic or an unknown and unclassified reptile), but the bulk of the article was dedicated to firsthand reports of explorers and hunters who had either seen or heard about the creature.

Descriptions of the dingonek emphasize its unusual appearance; it was said to be from 15 to 18 feet in length, with scales all over its body. Most early accounts position the dingonek as a reptile, or perhaps an amphibian, because of the scales. The Maclean's article, in relying on the accounts of European explorers, reinforced the idea that Africa is dark, dangerous, and unknown, and that it is through Europeans, thanks to their civilized ways, that we can finally know Africa:

Mr. James Martin, one of the pioneers of Africa, at one time aide-de-camp to General Matthews (I think in 1880), who guided Joseph Thomas from Mombasa to the head of the Nile, and was, with the exception of Stanley, Speke, and Grant, one of the first white men to see the Victoria Nyanza Lake, asserts that a huge animal has been known in this water for many years. Mr. Martin has a greater knowledge of the natives dwelling on the banks of the Lake than any living man, and has sufficient experience to be able to extract the truth from their exaggerated accounts. (1918: 67)

Here we have an explorer, animal collector, and big game hunter who is being positioned as the best source for information about the people and animals of that continent. All other sources in the article are European or American, and virtually every description given in the article comes from a second- or third-hand report:

Mr. Bronson also tells us that the celebrated African naturalist, Mr. G. W. Hobley, C.M.G., who was at that time Senior Deputy Commissioner (and at whose residence in Nairobi Mr. Bronson was staying), informed him that certain tribes living on the north shore of the Lake, the Baganda, Wasoga, and Kavirondo, had from time immemorial sacrificed burnt offerings of cattle and sheep to a huge reptile of dreadful appearance living in the Lake, and whick they called the "luquata." From Mr. Hobley's description of this monster, gleaned from most careful inquiries among the native tribes referred to, there can be little doubt that the "luquata" and the dingonek are one and the same. (Ibid.)

Big game hunter John Alfred Jordan wrote of his own encounter with the creature in *Wide World Magazine* in 1917:

In 1905 I was making a trading and shooting expedition to the Loita Masai, near the border of Germany's late possessions in East Africa. I had to cross a river named the Magorc, a broad and rapid tributary of Lake Victoria Nyanza. . . . I should think I had been sitting there for about an hour when some of my Lumbwa came rushing back in a state of indescribable terror, all trying to tell me at the same time about some very strange and weird-looking animal they had come across asleep on the bank. From their account it seemed that the animal was a cross between a snake, a crocodile, and a leopard! Knowing the natives fairly well, I paid very little heed to their wild descriptions, but decided they had come across some rare beast that was unknown to them. I told them to return and see if it was still there; if so, one of them was to come back and fetch me, while the others were to keep watch in case it moved. After a period of about half an hour, a man returned to say that the monster was lying fully exposed on the water in midstream. I at once took my rifle and hurried through the forest with my boy to the place where the others were keeping watch. They pointed out the beast, and I got down the bank and stood at the water's edge. When I had taken up my position with great care, I glanced towards the animal, and saw a huge monster lying lengthwise in the centre of the stream, about thirty feet from where I was standing. I made careful observations for some minutes, and will endeavor to state what it appeared like. The beast measured from fifteen to eighteen feet in length. The massive head was shaped something like that of an otter; two large fangs descended from the upper jaw, resembling those of a walrus. The back of this strange beast was as broad as a hippo's, but scaled like an armadillo, and the light deflected on the scales gave it the appearance of being colored like a leopard. It had a broad tail, with which it lazily switched the water, this action apparently assisting it to remain stationary, heading up-stream in the extremely rapid current.

Jordan's account is unusual in that it is one of the only times that the writer actually saw the animal. He then discusses his attempt to kill it:

Before me lay a totally unknown monster which I should be the first to record; the thrill of possession was upon me. Taking careful aim, I fired at the head with a solid .303 cartridge. Then an extraordinary thing occurred. The beast turned and, facing the bank, leapt straight upwards into the air, standing, as it appeared to me, ten or twelve feet on end. What happened after that I do not know, for losing my nerve, I scrambled up the bank, and with the Lumbwa raced for about two hundred yards into the forest before I could pull myself together. There we stood, speaking in whispers, scared out of our lives and afraid to go back. At last, however, I regained my nerve and we returned, but no trace of the animal could we find. All over the bank, in the soft mud, the spoor of the beast was clearly impressed—huge imprints about the size of those of the hippopotamus, but bearing claws like those of a reptile. (Ibid.)

An entirely different account of Jordan's sighting was included in big game hunter Edgar Beecher Bronson's 1910 book, *In Closed Territory*.

During the first decade of the twentieth century, numerous reports came out authored by British colonial administrators, big game hunters, explorers and adventurers, and missionaries. Most were second- or third-hand reports, and from these we get our understanding of the creature. Another significant report comes from Charles William Hobley, a British colonial administrator in Kenya, who wrote the following account:

Major Toulson, a well-known settler on the plateau, saw one of these animals some time ago and his account is as follows: "It was getting dark when one of my boys came into my room and said that a leopard was close to the kitchen. I rushed out at once and saw a strange beast making off: it appeared to have long hair behind and it was rather low in front. I should say it stood about 18 in. to 20. in. at the shoulder; it appeared to be black, with a gait similar to that of a bear-a kind of shuffling walk. Unfortunately it was nearly dark at the time and I did not get a fair view of the head. Several Dutchmen had asked me a few days before what the strange animal was on the plateau; they said it was like a bear, but they had only seen it at dusk; it turned on their dogs and chased them off. They described it as a thick-set beast and it was making a peculiar moaning cry." (Hobley 1913)

Oddly, after a handful of reports in the first few years of the twentieth century, there have been no documented sightings of the creature since 1907. In 1978, cryptozoologist James Powell visited Kenya and was asked by Bernard Heuvelmans to research the dingonek, but other than some old stories told by very old people, Powell found nothing.

There have been a variety of explanations put forth to account for the dingonek. In the earliest days of its discovery, there was talk of it being a dinosaur relic or neodinosaur of some kind. The animal's scales made most people think it must be a reptile, even though by then the pangolin, a mammal with scales, was already known to Europeans. Similarly, it has been suggested that it is a crocodile of some kind. Only Bernard Heuvelmans thought it might be a mammal, but the mammal he suggested, the water lion, is another mystery creature with no known real-life counterparts. Today, the most likely candidate for the dingonek is that it is either an unknown species of pangolin or is simply the giant pangolin (Smutsia gigantea) that lives in Africa.

See also: Mamlambo, Mokele Mdembe

Further Reading:

Brantlinger, P. (1985). Victorians and Africans: The Genealogy of the Myth of the Dark Continent. *Critical Inquiry*, 12(1), 166–203.
Bronson, E. B. (1910). *In Closed Territory*. AC McClurg & Company.
Heuvelmans, B., & Garnett, R. (Trans.). (1958). *On the Track of Unknown Animals*. Rupert Hart-Davis.
Hobley, C. W. (1913). On Some Unidentified Beasts. *East African Geographical Review*, 3(6), 48–52.
Oswald, F. (1915). *Alone in the Sleeping-Sickness Country*. Kegan Paul, Trench, Trubner & Co.
Shuker, K. P. N. (1995). *In Search of Prehistoric Survivors*. Blandford.
Something About the Dingonek (1918). *Macleans*, January, 31, 3.
Stow, G. W., & Bleek, D. F. (1930). *Rock-paintings in South Africa*. Methuen & Co. Ltd.

DOBHAR-CHU

Name: Dobhar-Chu

Alternative Names: Omey Island Creature, Irish Water Hound, Irish Crocodile, King Otter; Dadharchu, Dhuragoo, Dorraghowor, Dobarcu

Related Cryptids: Steller's Sea Ape

Location: Northwest Ireland: Counties Galway, Mayo, Sligo, Wicklow

Most Recent Documented Sighting: 2003

The dobhar-chu is an aquatic creature that primarily lives in the waters of County Galway and neighboring counties. Its most recent sighting was in the marshes of Omey Island. The creature has also been seen in Glenade, in County Leitrim, and has also been associated with Lough Mask, and Lough Gowlan, all in County Galway. In County Wicklow, dobharchúnna or dobharchoin (the plural of dobhar-chu) have been seen in Lough Nahanagan, which means either "lake of the water monster" or "lake of the otters." They have also been seen in a number of loughs in County Mayo, such as Sraheens Lough. The name comes from the Gaelic *Dobhar*, which means water, and *chú*, which means hound. Dobhar-chu is also used, in Irish, to refer to otters (although today most Irish speakers use *uisce* or *madra uisce*—which also means water hound or water dog—to refer to these animals).

County Galway, on the far western shores of Ireland, has the largest population of Irish speakers in Ireland. Thus it makes sense that it continues to be home to a variety of creatures, many from pre-Christian Celtic times. In particular, County Galway has a variety of aquatic monsters besides the dobhar-chu, including an unnamed creature seen in the Ballynahinch River (1882) and others in Lough Derrylea (1888, 1961), Lough Fadda (1940s–1954), Lough Shanakeever (1945, 1954, 1963, 1982), Lough Dubh (1962), Lough Nahioon (1948, 1968, 1969), Lough Auna (late 1800s, 1980, 1985), Lough Pibrum (1974), Lough Claddaghduff (1956, 1968), and in Coole Lough, Lough Graney, and Lough Inagh.

These creatures, like the dobhar-chu, are distinctly Irish. While many countries with large bodies of water have a sea serpent living in them, most of which look the same around the world, the Irish lake (or lough) monsters are not serpents. Instead, they resemble eels (Ballynahinch River, Lough Claddaghduff, Lough Graney, Lough Fadda, Lough Nahioon), horses (Coole Lough, Clogheen, Lough Inagh, Lough Shanakeever), horned creatures (Lough Dubh, Lough Nahioon), or horse-eel hybrids (Lough Derrylea, Lough Auna). Other Irish counties have their share of water creatures as well, with water horses (kelpies), giant eels, and worms (péists) being the most common.

The dobhar-chu, however, is unique, even for Ireland. Ireland has relatively few native mammals, thanks to its long geographic isolation from the European mainland, and many of the larger animals that did once exist became extinct during the last Ice Age. This may be one explanation for why the most common Irish cryptids are worms and eels, both of which are native to the island and are found everywhere, and horses, which arrived in Ireland sometime after the end of the last Ice Age, were domesticated on the island by 2000 BCE, and played a major role in the culture of Bronze Age Ireland. Eels, in particular, have been an important food source and economic commodity in Ireland (as in England) since at least the Bronze Age and are steeped in local folklore.

The dobhar-chu is, however, most likely a Eurasian Otter, based on the descriptions of the creature. They are often described as being part canine and part water creature, and while Ireland is home to a variety of animals that may fit this description, such as the many seal varieties that are found on the coastlines, the otter fits the descriptions best. European otters are brown and cream, with short necks and a total body length of about 4 feet, including the tail. They live in streams, lakes, ponds, and other fresh water sources and sometimes can even be found living in coastal sea waters, as long as there is fresh water nearby. While many of these water sources are small—perhaps too small for such a large creature—some believers feel that as long as the dobhar-chu can move between bodies of water that their existence cannot be disproven.

The dobhar-chu is variously described as black, white and black, brown, or cream, and it is huge, ranging from 5 to 7 feet in length. The fur is sometimes described as slimy, and it offers the animals protective qualities. Like the otter, the dobhar-chu is a freshwater creature.

Another reason that the dobhar-chu is most likely an otter comes from a phrase heard by Irish folklorist Seán Ã h-Eochaidh: "the Dobharchú is the seventh cub of the common otter' (mada-uisge): the Dobhar-chú was thus a super otter."

Another possible source for the origin of the dobhar-chu is the sea mink (Neovison macrodon), an extinct animal that once lived off the coast of New England (and perhaps Nova Scotia) but was overhunted in the late nineteenth century to the point of extinction. The sea mink was much larger than other minks but was still much smaller than the 7-feet dobhar-chu. Another possible candidate for the dobhar-chu is the walking seal (Puijila darwini), an extinct seal that lived during the Miocene and looked more like an otter than a seal, given its lack of flippers; instead, it had feet and walked on the ground.

The dobhar-chu, unlike the otter, is thought to be the most dangerous predator in Ireland. As the island has very few native predators (the wolf went extinct there in the late eighteenth century and the red fox is hardly a threat to people), the dobhar-chu has been associated with attacks on humans for hundreds of years. In fact, not only does the creature indiscriminately and without warning attack people, but they also are thought to have a ravenous appetite for human flesh. The dobhar-chu is fast, both in the water where it lives and on dry land, and can travel long distances in search of food.

The earliest known written account of the creature is from 1684. Irish historian Roderick O'Flaherty, in his book *A Chorographical Description of West or H-Iar Connaught: Written AD 1684* (vol. 15), wrote an account of a man who was attacked while walking along the banks of Lough Mask, but before he was pulled under the water, he stabbed his attacker and escaped. The book also recounts a second story, this time of a man and his dog who were attacked but survived. O'Flaherty uses the term "Irish Crocodile" to describe the creature, as crocodiles (which are native to Africa, Asia, Australia, and the Americas) were known to Europeans as far back as the Middle Ages, although most Europeans (probably including O'Flaherty) did not know what they looked like. Two centuries later, another account of the dobhar-chu can be found in an 1896 article in the *Journal of the Royal Society of Antiquaries of Ireland*, which described it as a half-wolfdog and half-fish.

One of the most fascinating accounts of the serious threat that the dobhar-chu poses to humans is from the eighteenth century and is immortalized on a gravestone in Conwall Cemetery in Glendale (County Leitrim). The gravestone depicts a dobhar-chu with a knife sticking out of its neck and is found on the grave of a woman named Grace (or more likely Grainne) with a last name of McGlone, McGloighlin, Connolly, or Conalai. The carving depicts the dobhar-chu as a canid of some kind, with dog-like long legs and a puffy tail but with otter-like attributes such as tiny ears and a shortened snout.

The inscription on the tombstone is difficult to decipher, as it is heavily eroded, but tells of a woman named Grace, the wife of Terence (or *T'ruálach*) Mac or McLoghlin (Irish women at that time retained their maiden name after marriage), who lived in Creevelea and died on September 24, 1722. (There was, at one time, a second tombstone in the area that allegedly referred to the same incident.)

Locals tell the story of what happened to Grace/Grainne, and the story goes something like this. Grace was doing the washing at the lake and did not return home. Her husband, upon searching for his wife, found Grace's mutilated body at the edge of the lake alongside the dobhar-chu, which was still with her body (in some accounts asleep). Terence then stabbed the dobhar-chu in the neck, at which time the creature let out a whistle that alerted its mate, which then gave chase to Terence (and some say a neighbor). The story ends with the second animal being stabbed to death, just like the first. (It is said that both the creatures, plus Terence's horse, are buried in the neighboring County Sligo, near where the denouement occurred. It is also said that nothing will ever grow again on the land where the dobhar-chu's blood was spilled.)

This story is also told in a poem by an unknown author. The poem begins:

By Glenade lake tradition tells, two hundred years ago
A thrilling scene enacted was to which, as years unflow,
Old men and women still relate, and while relating dread,
Some demon of its kind may yet be found within its bed.

Later, the poet writes:

She, having gone to bathe, it seems, within the water clear,
And not having returned when she might, her husband, fraught with fear,
Hasting to where he her might find, when oh, to his surprise,
Her mangled form, still bleeding warm, lay stretched before his eyes.

Upon her bosom, snow white once, but now besmeared with gore,
The Dobharchú reposing was, his surfeiting being o'er.
Her bowels and entrails all around tinged with a reddish hue:
"'Oh, God,' he cried, 'tis hard to bear but what am I to do?"

The poem ends with the killing of the second creature, after a desperate chase on horseback:

Not long to wait, for nose on trail the scenting hound arrived
And through the horses with a plunge to force himself he tried,
And just as through the outermost horse he plunged his head and foremost part,
Mc Gloughlans dagger to the hilt lay buried in his heart. (National Folklore Collection 1937–9)

While there are other stories dating back centuries of attacks (to both humans and dogs) and deaths attributed to the dobhar-chu, this is the only case that is documented and indicates that at least the kin of the dead woman believed her death to be caused by the creature.

The dobhar-chu may be related to a number of other creatures, found both in Ireland and in other places. For example, the onchú, which also translates as water dog but looks like an enfield: a creature found in Irish heraldry with the body of a lion, the claws of an eagle, and the back legs and tail of a wolf. Like the enfield, the onchú was once used in heraldry.

More intriguingly, some cryptozoologists think that the dobhar-chu is related to the Loch Ness Monster—either as an immature version of Nessy or another relation. It was St. Columba, the Irish abbot, who is credited with establishing Christianity in Scotland, who saw the monster in 565, and whose account, found in the *Life of St. Columba*, was the first written description of the creature. Columba, after encountering the burial of a man killed by the creature, faced down the monster telling it to go back into the water. After this, it was said that Nessy's children traveled to Ireland to take revenge on the nation for Columba's actions. For some, these offspring were the dobhar-chu. Another possibility is that the dobhar-chu lives in Loch Gairloch, in Scotland, where an otter-like creature has been seen. For instance, the 1575 book, *The History of the Scots from Their First Origin* by Hector Boece, describes an encounter from 1510 between a group of hunters and a canid-like creature with goose feet, which resulted in the deaths of some of the men.

Other Loch Ness researchers believe that the Irish brought the Loch Ness Monster to America, where they live today by names like Champ, Ogopogo, or the Flathead Lake Monster. Some even feel that the dobhar-chu is in North America as well, as reports of underwater panthers or lynxes (known as *Mishipeshu* or *Mishibijiw* in Ojibwe) seen in Lake Superior could very well refer to a local variant of the dobhar-chu.

Sightings of the dobhar-chu have been rare in the twentieth century (and no sightings at all have occurred in the twenty-first century). One notable encounter was in 1968, when two men, John Cooney and Michael McNulty, saw a dobhar-chu run across the front of their car near Sraheens Lough in County Mayo. Others saw the creature around that time as well, reigniting the old stories. The most recent sighting was in 2003 when Irish artist Sean Corcoran and his wife saw a dobhar-chu in Omey Island. The couple was able to clearly see its webbed feet as it swam across Lough Fahy and heard it scream.

See also: Loch Ness Monster, Steller's Sea Ape

Further Reading:

Cunningham, G., & Coghlan, R. (2011). *The Mystery Animals of Ireland*. CFZ Press.

The Dobhar Cu (1937–1939). "The Schools' Collection, Volume 0189, Page 269–270" by Dúchas © National Folklore Collection, UCD is licensed under CC BY-NC 4.0.

Fennell, J. (2020). *Rough Beasts: The Monstrous in Irish Fiction, 1800–2000* (Vol. 82). Liverpool University Press.

O'Flaherty, R. (1846). *A Chorographical Description of West or H-Iar Connaught: Written AD 1684* (Vol. 15). For the Irish Archaeological Society.

Tohall, P. (1948). The Dobhar-Chú Tombstones of Glenade, Co. Leitrim (Cemeteries of Congbháil and Cill-Rúisc). *The Journal of the Royal Society of Antiquaries of Ireland*, 78(2), 127–9.

Wood-Martin, W. G. (1886). *The Lake Dwellings of Ireland: Or, Ancient Lacustrine Habitations of Erin, Commonly Called Crannogs*. Hodges, Figgis & Company.

E

EBU GOGO

Name: Ebu Gogo
Related Cryptids: Orang Pendek, Batatut, Rock Ape
Location: Indonesia
Most Recent Documented Sighting: Unknown

The ebu gogo is a small hominid creature that lives on the island of Flores in Indonesia. In the Nage language, ebu means grandmother and gogo means to eat anything. The ebu gogo is about 3 feet tall, with long hair and a pot belly. Their arms and fingers are very long, and while they do not speak the local language, they can mimic human voices.

Southeast Asia in general, and Indonesia in particular, has a large number of primate cryptids. Monkeys and apes live throughout Asia and often live lives in close proximity to humans. It shouldn't surprise us that we find so many "ape-men" in this region.

Indonesia is home to the only two Asian apes (the only apes outside of Africa), the orangutan, with three species in Indonesia, and the gibbon, with seven species in Indonesia. In addition, the island nation has a number of orangutan and gibbon-like animals, none of which has been confirmed by Western science. This includes the ape-like orang pendek and orang mawas, the human-like orang kardil, and the hantu pedek, a forest spirit or demon.

Indonesia is also well known by paleoanthropologists as an area where incredibly significant hominid fossils have been found. Java Man is one of the first examples of Homo erectus, an extinct hominid ancestor of ours, and was found on the island of Java in the late nineteenth century, confirming to some scholars that humans first evolved in Asia (although later fossil evidence out of Africa would change that conclusion). In addition, fossils from an extinct primate species called Gigantopithecus have been found throughout Asia, including in Indonesia. This species is not considered to be ancestral to humans but instead is classified as an extinct branch of the Ponginae subfamily, which includes orangutans and gibbons, rather than our own subfamily, the Homininae. Today, many cryptozoologists see Gigantopithecus, thanks to its large size, as either an ancestor to Bigfoot and other large-bodied hominoid cryptids or believe that Bigfoot and yeti (and perhaps other Asian ape-men) are actually modern, living examples of Gigantopithecus.

Even more significant were the finds made by anthropologists on the Indonesian island of Flores in 2003. Scientists found the fossil remains of nine individuals who have now been assigned the species name Homo floriensis—an extinct species of hominid, not ancestral to humans but most likely wiped out by modern humans when they arrived in Indonesia about 50,000 years ago. They are often referred to by the nickname "hobbit," which points to their diminutive size.

While neither the Homo erectus fossils nor the Homo floriensis fossils demonstrate that humans evolved in Asia, they do demonstrate that early hominids arrived in Southeast Asia as early as 1.6 million years ago. These proto-humans shared the islands with the ancestors to modern orangutans and gibbons.

But what if there were a creature alive today that is a descendant of or perhaps cousin to the hobbits of Flores Island? That is what some people think that the ebu gogo is.

The Nage, one of the indigenous peoples of the islands of Timor and Flores, claim that they once lived alongside of the ebu gogo, a group of small hairy human-like creatures, until they were killed by humans at some point in the past. They describe the ebu gogo as an animal and not, for example, a spirit. What makes the ebu gogo even more interesting is the fact that it existed, in the minds of the indigenous people of the region, long before the Homo floriensis fossils were discovered in 2003. Could the ebu gogo actually be relics of that population of Homo floriensis individuals? As with the other ape-like creatures in Indonesia, both scientifically known and unknown, the ebu gogo tries to maintain some distance between its own community and that of humans, but because it often raids human food caches, eating not just the food but also the plates, it is a nuisance. This explains why all, or most, of these creatures were wiped out by humans. (Another story told of the humans tolerating the crop raiding but fought back when an ebu gogo stole and ate a human baby.)

Even the paleoanthropologist who discovered the Flores fossils, Richard Roberts, does not dismiss out of hand the idea that Homo floriensis and ebu gogo may be the same species, and that some members of Homo floriensis may have survived into modernity. He recounted one of the many stories told to him by villagers, when the humans became fed up with the Ebu Gogo and tossed a burning bale of grass into the cave in which they lived. The creatures were able to escape and left the area, heading toward Liang Bua, where the floriensis fossils would be discovered. Roberts and his colleagues had heard these stories well before the discovery was made, indicating that local people must have known something about these small people who once lived on their island.

See also: Batatut, Orang Pendek, Rock Ape

Further Reading:

Burgkmair, H. *The Folk Zoology of Southeast Asian Wildmen.* The Newsletter of the International Institute for Asian Studies, no. 52.

Eggs, C. C., Large, S., & Shipping, F. (2004). Villagers Speak of the Small, Hairy Ebu Gogo. *Daily Telegraph,* November 18, 2004.

Forth, G. (2005). Hominids, Hairy Hominoids and the Science of Humanity. *Anthropology Today,* 21(3), 13–17.

Weerawardane, P. (2004). Ebu Gogo-the Little People of Flores. *SPAFA Journal (Old Series 1991-2013),* 14(3), 45–9.

Wong, K. (2005). The Littlest Human. *Scientific American,* 292(2), 56–65.

EL CUERO

Name: El Cuero

Alternative Names: Aquatic tiger, mantle, cloak, hide, Trelquehuecuve, cow hide

Related Cryptids: Nahuelito

Location: Lakes in the Chilean Andes

Most Recent Documented Sighting: 2019

El Cuero, or "the hide" or "cow hide" in Spanish, is a lake monster living primarily in Lake Lacar but can also be found in other glacial lakes in the Chilean Andes. It began its life as a *huecuve* or wekufe, a harmful spirit to the Mapuche of Chile and Argentina. It shares habitat with the Nahuelito, a lake serpent that lives in Lake Nahuel Huapi.

It is called el cuero because it looks like an animal hide that is in the process of drying; it also looks like a freshwater stingray (which do live in South America). It is hairless, usually white with brown or black spots, is without spines, fur, or feathers, and has a long sharp tail. It may or may not have claws around its edges, but it does have eyes on two stalks growing from its body and a proboscis that it uses to suck out the organs from its victims. El cuero can be as small as 2 feet across and as large as 5 feet.

El Cuero is related to a pre-Spanish Mapuche spirit called Invunche, which means "monster person" as well as "master of the hide," and is a ghastly creature that began life as a human baby, which was kidnapped by a witch; after years of ritual torture, the human turns into a beast that lives in the bottom of lakes, where it guards the lair of the witch. The invunche has a creature that does its bidding for it, like a witch's familiar, and is called the Trelquehuecuve, which is another term for El Cuero. Because the invunche cannot leave the bottom of the lake, when it needs to eat, the trelquehuecuve will lure young girls to the lake's edge and drag them in.

Cattle are extremely important animals in Chile, as in other former Spanish colonies. The Chilean folktale, the Magic Cow, illustrates that importance. It features of magic cow that is owned by a poor family and that tells its master to kill the cow so that the cow's parts can be helpful. After reluctantly doing so, the man finds that the cow's hide, hair, and eyes are magic and help the man out of his troubles. Each version of this tale is different, but each tale ends with the cow miraculously becoming whole again. One variant includes a witch who lives in a river and who drags people into the water where they drown, which is an element from the el cuero legend. Even without the water witch, who seems like a clear analog to the cuero, the legend of el cuero is still clearly linked to the idea of a magical cow hide.

The first time that el cuero showed up in print was in 1810, in Juan Ignacio Molina's *Essay on the Natural History of Chile*. Molina, a Jesuit priest, did not see the monster, but, based on the stories that he collected, he wrote:

The locals assure that in certain Chilean lakes there is an enormous fish or dragon, that they name Ghyryvilu, that is, Vulpangue or fox-snake, which, they say, is man-eating and for this reason they abstain from swimming in the water of those lakes.

But they are not in agreement the appearance that they give it: now they make it long, like a serpent with a fox head and now almost circular, like an extended bovine hide. If it was so, it would come to be species of Manta of a monstrous race. (Molina 1986: 233)

Missionaries and other Spanish officials had been in Chile and Argentina since the seventeenth century, but none had reported on the creature before this time, which may point to a relatively recent history for this creature.

El cuero is a dangerous beast that will attack both people and animals. It waits in the water for an unsuspecting victim to approach the shore and then, like a crocodile, will leap out of the lake to grab their victim and drag them back into the depths of the lake. Chileans will tell stories—always second-, third-, or fourthhand—about unsuspecting people who lost their lives to el cuero. Unexplained drownings are attributed to the cuero, which will engulf their victims in the folds of their skin and suck the blood from them.

El Cuero is similar to many other river creatures, both in South America and around the world, which function in part as a device for parents to teach their children to avoid dangerous waters. The fact that South America has so many is a testament to not only the large number of rivers on the continent but also the dangers that lie within them. South America has some of the most deadly animals in the world living in its rivers, lakes, and jungles, including the black caiman, the green anaconda, the Brazilian wandering spider, and the Amazonian giant centipede.

While el cuero began as a Mapuche spirit called Trelquehuecuve, it is now also thought of as a physical entity and has been incorporated into other areas of Chilean folklore, merging with Spanish beliefs. It can also possess people or animals, and, in some belief systems, it is where the souls of dead people go. El cuero is also known to have sex with cows; the babies produced by such a mating will be deformed.

Over the years, there have been multiple sightings of something that people have described as el cuero. There is also a 2014 photograph taken by a fisherman in Lake Nahuel Huapi as well as a number of stories of alleged deaths.

If el cuero is a real animal, it is most likely a stingray or else an invertebrate of some kind—perhaps a cephalopod, the animal class that includes the octopus. There are freshwater rays in northern Argentina, but they do not live further south, in Chile. However, there have been sightings of animals that looked like freshwater rays in the region, so it is not outside of the realm of possibility that the cuero is a ray. Others have put forth other suggestions, including jellyfish, giant squid, or that it may be a still-living form of an extinct species like the sea scorpion.

See also: Encantado, Nahuelito

Further Reading:

Aguirre, S. M. (2003). *Mitos de Chile*. Random House, Editorial Sudamericana Chilena.

Borges, J. L., & di Giovanni, N. T. (Trans.). (2002). *The Book of Imaginary Beings*. Vintage Classics, Random House.

Molina, M., & Jaramillo, R. (Trans.). (1986). *Ensayo sobre la Historia Natural de Chile*. Ediciones Maule, Santiago de Chile.

Soustelle, G., & Soustelle, J. (1938). *Folklore Chilien*. Paris: Institut International de Coopération Intellectuelle.

de Vidaurre, F. G. (1861). *Historia Geográfica, Natural y Civil del Reino de Chile* (Vol. 14). Impr. Ercilla.

EL HOMBRE CAIMÁN

Name: El Hombre Caimán

Related Cryptids: Encantado

Location: Colombia

Most Recent Documented Sighting: n/a

El Hombre Caimán, or the Alligator Man in English, is a legendary creature from the city of Plato in the Magdalena Department of Colombia.

The legend begins with a story about a fisherman named Saúl Montenegro. Saúl enjoyed spying on women bathing in the Magdalena River but did not want to get caught. So he paid a sorcerer to create two magic potions: one that would turn him into an alligator, so he could watch the women in anonymity, and one that would turn him back into a man. After using both potions successfully, Saúl enlisted the help of a friend to turn him back into a man, as handling the potions while in alligator form was difficult. Unfortunately, the friend became frightened at the look of Saúl in his alligator form and only managed to get a little bit of the second potion on Saúl's head before spilling the rest. The result was that Saúl was now permanently living in the body of an alligator but with a human torso and head. Because of the shame, he let the river carry him out to sea, startling the occasional fisherman who comes across the strange sight.

This is just one version of the story; as with other legends, the teller of the tale will usually embellish it with details specific to that teller. Other versions have our hero (or anti-hero), a storekeeper with no name, falling in love with a woman named Roque Lina, but the woman's father disapproves of the match and forbids his daughter from seeing him. In despair, the shopkeeper went into the river to search for his beloved, who often bathed nude, magically turning into an alligator. He and his beloved would spend time together in the river, until Roque's brother got suspicious of his sister. The result was that the alligator man took Roque underneath the surface, and neither have ever returned to land.

This second version of the story is strikingly similar to the Brazilian encantado, a dolphin-man shapeshifter who is known for dragging unwitting women into the watery depths with him.

As with the encantado, the story serves in part to warn men to keep an eye on their wives, lest El Hombre Caimán might steal them away. It also serves as a cautionary tale to the girls and young women of the town, to stay away from the river.

The legend itself is relatively new, only arising in 1940, when, according to the story, the Barranquilla newspaper, *El Heraldo*, printed a story about an odd animal that showed up in an oil camp, which was part alligator, part human.

Plato, where the story takes place, now celebrates their local celebrity with an annual festival as well as a number of statues and other depictions of el Hombre throughout the town. There is also a song called Se va el caimá, written by José María Peñaranda and first recorded in 1945, which tells the story of the alligator man. "Se volvió un hombre caimán," reads the lyrics, which translate to "he turned into an alligator man."

See also: Encantado

Further Reading:

O'Bryen, R. (2020). Untangling the Mangrove: Slow Violence and the Environmentalism of the Poor in the Colombian Caribbean. In L. Blackmore and L. Gomez (Eds.), *Liquid Ecologies in Latin American and Caribbean Art*. Routledge, 73–88.

ENCANTADO

Name: Encantado
Alternative Names: Boto Encantado
Related Cryptids: Merfolk, Selkies
Location: Brazil, Paraguay
Most Recent Documented Sighting: n/a

The encantado is a mythical river dolphin that lives in the Amazonian regions of Brazil, Bolivia, and Paraguay in South America. It is known as a helpful creature, as well as a trickster, making it very different from most cryptids around the world. Technically, an encantado can be any number of creatures, including snakes, turtles, and fish, by far the most common is the dolphin.

The word "encantado" means enchanted in both Spanish and Portuguese, referring to the magical nature of these creatures and to the realm from which they derive: the Encante. Encantados are shapeshifters and can switch between their human and dolphin forms at will. In their human forms, they dress in colorful, somewhat old-fashioned clothing and always wear a hat in order to disguise the blow hold on the top of their head.

The creature may derive in part from the moura encantada, or enchanted moura, a creature from Iberian folklore that, in its female form, brushes its long blonde hair while singing and can seduce men to do their bidding. In fact, in Brazil there is a female version of the encantado known as the bujeos colorados, and like the moura, in their human form, they are blonde. There is also a male version, the mouro encantado, which more closely resembles the encantado, although the dolphin form is unique to the South American encantado.

Encantados are tricksters. The trickster is one of the most common folklore characters in folklore from around the world. Tricksters are characters that frequently get into trouble but get out of it just as quickly through their quick wits and their ability to trick or deceive another animal (also generally an animal).

European and Asian trickster tales are derived from the satirical Northern European epic known as the *Roman de Renart*, in which a stupid bear or wolf is duped by a clever fox. The fox is almost always the clever animal in European tales, but as these stories migrated from Europe to Africa, and then to North America, the clever fox gave way to other species, such as the jackal, the coyote, or the rabbit. Trickster animals are found among most Native American tribes and include the spider, coyote, and raven. Tribes in the Plains and Great Lakes regions used the hare as their trickster animal; the Algonquin tribes' Great Hare Manabozho was a trickster rabbit. Africans in the Sudan and savannah country also see the hare as one of the most cunning animals, although the spider is the equivalent of the hare in the forest regions of Africa, probably because spiders are more common in forests than hares. Trickster spirits are also common among indigenous peoples in South America and might have arisen independently in the New World.

On the other hand, centuries of intermarrying between Amerindians and former African slaves certainly brought African beliefs into indigenous cultures. For centuries, enslaved men and women would escape Brazil's oppressive sugar plantations, establishing communities known as quilambos in the forests of the Amazon. Contemporary encantado stories, then, are a blend of African ideas about dolphins, tricksters, and shapeshifters with Amerindian ideas.

Tricksters, especially when found in cultures in which the people have very little political power, are clearly meant to be a commentary on inequality and how deception, intelligence, and humor can allow one to beat someone who is, on the surface, the obvious victor. Trickster characters understand that they are meant to lose but do not give up and, through their wits and trickery, are able to manipulate and even upstage those who seek to harm them. Tricksters are amoral—not clearly good or bad—but their amorality serves them well, allowing them to lie and trick others, in order for them to win.

Encantados are tricksters and partiers; they are also promiscuous and because they appear only as men in their human forms, their frequent sexual escapades with human women often result in illegitimate children. Like selkies and other shapeshifters, they can remain in their human guise permanently or semi-permanently if they choose to make a life exclusively with humans. They can also, like mermaids, kidnap humans to whom they are attracted and will often kidnap their own children to bring back to the land of Encante. On the other hand, they are also helpful and, when they choose, can help humans in a variety of ways.

Each of these characteristics can be found in the folklore and mythology of dolphins from other cultures. Dolphins are almost universally viewed as friendly, helpful, playful, and with a keen interest in humans. They are also highly sexual beings that have no problem initiating sexual contact with other species—including humans. These perceptions, which are rooted in both the reality of dolphin behavior and misinterpretations of dolphins—many people interpret the curved rostrum, or beak, of the dolphin as looking like they are smiling all of the time—lead to an exaggerated conception about dolphins and their links with humans. It is also what the

Figure 4 *Returning to the river, an encantado tosses its hat out of the ring. Copyright © 2023 Heidi Scheidl. All rights reserved.*

rapidly exploding industry of dolphin-assisted activities and swim with the dolphins centers use to bolster their claims that swimming with or interacting with dolphins is beneficial to humans (so far, the only evidence for this is anecdotal).

In Brazil, the encantado is linked with the legend of Boto Cor de Rosa, which tells of a dolphin that puts on beautiful clothing and a hat, takes on human guise, and seduces young women. One possible function of a legend like this is that it provides a form of cover for unmarried women who fall pregnant and whose children are known as *filho de boto*. In this legend, the dolphin can only take on his human form during the night; like Cinderella, at dawn the magical spell is broken and the dolphin returns to the river, leaving his paramour abandoned.

Because dolphins are not only seen to be friendly to humans, but because they are mammals—like us, they breathe air and give birth to live young, which they breastfeed—their existence seems to imply that humans too could live underwater. That's why dolphin-based cryptids are almost always shapeshifters or human-dolphin hybrids.

Encantados often will help fishermen with their catches and with navigating the waters of the Amazon in dangerous weather. This parallels a practice found in other parts of Brazil whereby real dolphins help fishermen to catch fish. Here, the dolphins are bottlenose dolphins rather than river dolphins, and they swim in the Pacific Ocean off of the coast of Brazil rather than in the Amazon and its tributaries. The fishermen there have developed a relationship with specific dolphins that chase fish toward the shore where the fishermen can catch them with their nets. This is an example of mutualism—a practice whereby two different species work together to achieve a mutual benefit. Aboriginals in Australia also engage in cooperative fishing with dolphins. The Australian and Brazilian cases are anomalies; usually fishermen view dolphins as competition.

Of all of the cryptids discussed in this book, encantados are in some ways the most unusual in that the magical characteristics attributed to them are not that different from most people's perceptions of dolphins. I would suggest that without this magical idea about dolphins, the encantado would not exist. It is the extraordinary characteristics of, and associated with, dolphins that allow for the supernatural version of the Encantado.

See also: Merfolk, Selkies

Further Reading:

Halloy, A., & Servais, V. (2014). Enchanting Gods and Dolphins: A Cross-cultural Analysis of Uncanny Encounters. *Ethos*, 42(4), 479–504.

Lockyer, C. (1990). Review of Incidents Involving Wild, Sociable Dolphins, Worldwide 18. In S. Leatherwood & R. R. Reeves (Eds.), *The Bottlenose Dolphin*. Academic Press, 337–53.

Mentz, S. (2012). "Half-Fish, Half-Flesh": Dolphins, the Ocean, and Early Modern Humans. In Jean E. Feerick & Vin Nardizzi (Eds.), *The Indistinct Human in Renaissance Literature*. Palgrave Macmillan, 29–46.

Roman, Joe. (2013). Fishing With Dolphins: An Astonishing Cooperative Venture in Which Every Species Wins but the Fish. *Slate Magazine*, January 31, slate.com/technology/2013/01/fishing-with-dolphins-symbiosis-between-humans-and-marine-mammals-to-catch-more-fish.html.

Slater, C. (1996). Breaking the Spell: Accounts of Encantados by Descendants of. In A. J. Arnold (Ed.), *Monsters, Tricksters, and Sacred Cows: Animal Tales and American Identities*. University of Virginia Press, 157–84.

F

FOUKE MONSTER

Name: Fouke Monster

Alternative Names: Boggy Creek Monster, Swamp Stalker, Southern Sasquatch

Related Cryptids: Bigfoot, Honey Island Swamp Monster

Location: The area surrounding Texarkana, Texas and Fouke, Arkansas

Most Recent Documented Sighting: 2021

The Boggy Creek Monster refers to a short period in 1971 when a handful of people were terrorized by a creature haunting the woods and roads where Texas and Arkansas meet. Called the Fouke Monster by local reporter Jim Powell, it is now mostly known by the name given to it in the 1972 film about the monster, *The Legend of Boggy Creek.*

While vague rumors of a wild man had existed in the past, there was no actual monster until the events of 1971 unfolded. A young couple named Bobby and Elizabeth Ford were attacked by something or someone in their Texarkana home on May 2, 1971. Mrs. Ford told a reporter with the *Texarkana Gazette* that she was asleep when:

> I saw the curtain moving on the front window and a hand sticking through the window. At first I thought it was a bear's paw but it didn't look like that. It had heavy hair all over it and it had claws. I could see its eyes. They looked like coals of fire real red. It didn't make any noise. Except you could hear it breathing.

Her husband Bobby continued:

> We shot several times at it then and then called Ernest Walraven, constable of Fouke. He brought us another shotgun and a stronger light. We waited on the porch and then saw the thing closer to the house. We shot again and thought we saw it fall. Bobby, Charles and myself started walking to where we saw it fall.

Soon after, however, things took a turn for the worse:

> I was walking the rungs of a ladder to get up on the porch when the thing grabbed me. I felt a hairy arm come over my shoulder and the next thing I knew we were on the ground. The only thing I could think about was to get out of there. The thing was breathing real hard and his eyes were about the size of a half dollar and real red. I finally broke away and ran around the house and through the front door. I don't know where he went. (Powell 1971a)

Bobby ended up at the hospital that night where he was treated for shock and some superficial scratches. After the attack, the Fords were so scared that they packed up their home and moved the very next day.

After the Fords' attack, other people in and around Texarkana began reporting that they had seen it too, although there was never another attack on a human. The next sighting came three weeks after the first attack, when three people driving home saw a large hairy, upright walking creature run across Highway 71 one night. Mrs. Woods told the *Texarkana Gazette*:

It was hunched over and running upright. It had long dark hair and looked real large. It didn't look too tall, but I guess that's because it was bent over. It was swinging its arms kind of like a monkey does. I though my eyes were playing tricks on me but there it was. My husband turned to me after it crossed the road and asked me if I saw it too. It was just unbelievable what we saw. I had been reading about the thing but thought it was just a hoax. Now I know it's true. It wasn't a bear.

Mr. Woods said:

It was really moving fast across the highway . . . faster than a man. I thought we were going to hit it. The thing didn't act like it even noticed us. It didn't look at the car. I looked like a giant monkey in a way. It had dark long hair and I would guess it would weigh well over 200 pounds. (Powell 1971b)

For the next three years, there continued to be occasional sightings of the beast, but eventually they died down and then dropped off completely.

The story, once it was picked up by the Associated Press, attracted cryptid hunters to Arkansas to look for the creature themselves. The attack and the subsequent media coverage happened just as Bigfoot was becoming a pop culture icon, so there were a lot of people who were interested in the case. This was especially true after the local radio station, KAAY, offered a $2,000 reward to anyone who could locate the beast.

Locals also began recalling earlier rumors about a hairy man in the area. Miller County Sheriff Leslie Greer was one person who remembered hearing a vague story about a tall, hairy, strange-looking man or animal in 1946, but it was only after the events of 1971 that he connected the old story to the modern case. The story got another bump when a local farmer named Willie Smith found a set of tracks from what looked like a creature with three toes (he later played himself in the 1985 sequel, *Boggy Creek II: And the Legend Continues*). That was the first physical evidence of the creature and gave it more authenticity. The modern story was also connected by some to two Civil War era accounts of a hairy creature, giving the story yet more weight.

What was behind the attack on the Fords and the subsequent (and perhaps prior) encounters? Experts feel that the footprint was most likely a hoax, as there are no three-toed primates anywhere in the world. But as to the attack and the eyewitness accounts? There has never been a single explanation that makes any sense, and to this day, no one knows what happened to the Fords.

It was the Fords' attack, and the hysteria that followed it, that drew a man named Charles Pierce to the story. It was Pierce, a television producer, actor, set designer, and commercial maker, who truly made the monster and put little Fouke, Arkansas (which had 506 citizens in 1970), on the map. Pierce had worked as a producer at a number of television stations in Louisiana, Arkansas, and Texas, before moving to Texarkana in 1969.

As soon as the story of the Fords' attack appeared in the local news, Pierce knew that he wanted to do something with it. He interviewed the Fords, as well as other residents on both sides of the Texas/Arkansas border, and found that other people had seen the creature as well.

He produced and directed a low-budget film called *The Legend of Boggy Creek*, hiring a colleague named Earl Smith to write it, based on the events of 1971. He sought funding for the film from L. W. Ledwell, who owned a company for whom Pierce produced commercials. Ledwell gave him $100,000, which covered the bulk of the $160,000 cost of filming.

The film was a mockumentary; in other words, it was shot as if it were a documentary, with interview footage with real community members, combined with dramatic recreations of the action, filmed using local people with no acting experience. In addition, Pierce took a great deal of artistic license with the story. The film was released in 1972, but because he could not find a distributor, he showed it himself in Texarkana's only movie theater, the Perot Theater. Eventually, he did get a distributor willing to take on the film, and the film became an instant cult classic. It was this film that created the legend of the Boggy Creek Monster and which also inspired future mockumentaries like the Blair Witch Project.

Pierce eventually (and reluctantly) made a sequel called *Boggy Creek II: And the Legend Continues* in 1985, which was not nearly as successful as the original and which Pierce himself—who also played the main character—hated. Before his film was made, however, another film called *Return to Boggy Creek* was released in 1977, and while it used the name of the monster, the film itself was entirely fictional. Two additional films were released in 2009 (originally called *The Skunk Ape Story*, it was renamed the *Legacy of Boggy Creek*) and 2010 (*Boggy Creek: The Legend Is True*) but Pierce had nothing to do with either film, and neither film was based on the original story.

Thanks to the film, as well as the lesser sequels, the area around Fouke and Texarkana became famous, and since 2013, the town of Fouke has hosted the Fouke Monster Festival.

Thanks in part to the promotional skills of Charles Pierce, the Boggy Creek Monster has always been a phenomenon of the media. So it should not surprise us that there are a number of songs dedicated to the creature. The Fouke Monster is a 1971 song by Billy Cole and the Fouke monsters, who describe themselves as Arkansas garage psychedelic rock band. The song tells the story of the monster, beginning with a simplified version of the Fords' story: "A man was sitting down watching tv when a hand came through the window."

See also: Bigfoot

Further Reading:

Blackburn, L. (2012). *The Beast of Boggy Creek: The True Story of the Fouke Monster*. Anomalist Books.

Crabtree, Julius E. (1974). *Smokey and The Fouke Monster*. Day's Creek Production Corp.

Powell, J. (1971a). Monster is Spotted by Texarkana Group. *Texarkana Gazette*, May 3.

Powell, J. (1971b). Hairy 'Monster' Hunted in Fouke Sector. *Texarkana Gazette*, May 3.

Thibodeau, S. (2001). The Fouke Monster 30 Years Later: Ex-journalists Recall Sifting Fact from Fouke Fiction After Sighting. *Texarkana Gazette*, June 24.

G

GROOTSLANG

Name: Grootslang

Alternative Names: Groot slang, Grote slang

Related Cryptids: Mamlambo

Location: The Richtersveld, South Africa

Most Recent Documented Sighting: 1959

The grootslang, or great snake in Afrikaans, is a giant snake rumored to live in south Africa—specifically in the Richtersveld, along the Orange River that separates South Africa from Namibia. It is not a traditional African myth; rather, it came with the Dutch Afrikaners who settled in South Africa in the eighteenth and nineteenth centuries.

The grootslang is sometimes described as a cross between a snake and an elephant; according to the origin story, they were originally created by the gods with snake and elephant characteristics, but when the gods realized that the creature they created was too powerful, with the cunning of a snake and the strength of an elephant, so they broke them into separate animals: snakes and elephants. Before that happened, however, a grootslang escaped and began to live and reproduce on earth.

They can grow up to 40 feet in length and measure up to 3 feet in diameter. Sometimes they are described as having diamonds in their eyes.

According to some, there are two types of grootslang: the forest creatures, which have long tails, scaly gray skin, and a row of spines down their back, and the cave dwellers, which are more snake-like, although with large tusks and ears like an elephant. The cave in which these grootslang live is known as the Bottomless Pit or the Wonder Hole and it is said to be filled with diamonds. Other stories do not differentiate between two types of grootslang; instead, they may live in the bottom of the river itself, in the Bottomless Pit, or even within a boulder. Some say they live underneath the Aughrabies Falls.

They can kill and eat large animals and are thought to kill cattle that make the mistake of drinking from the Orange River and can even eat elephants that come too close. There is even a story of an Englishman who traveled to South Africa in 1917 to look for the grootslang and who disappeared, allegedly killed by the creature. (I can find no evidence of this.)

The fact that the grootslang is connected to diamonds—the cave it lives in is filled with them, the river it lives in is the source of South Africa's first diamonds, and it has diamonds for eyes—speaks to the troubling history of diamond mining in South Africa. Since the mid-nineteenth century, when diamonds were first discovered on the banks of the Orange River, they have made white South Africans—and the entire nation of South Africa—rich and helped to kick off the apartheid regime.

In fact, the grootslang craves diamonds, and potential victims can save themselves from a terrible death by offering it diamonds. Its greed and lust for wealth can be seen as an allegory about white South Africa and its diamond lust.

There are other giant snakes in Africa, with different cultural groups having different beliefs; whether any of those are related to each other is unknown, but the Khoi bushmen have a belief in a koo-be-eng, a horned serpent, or perhaps crocodile, which lived in waterways. It may be that each of these creatures were combined into the newer, Afrikaner term, grootslang, with its newer characteristics, like the diamonds, which could not have come from pre-European myths.

As with other creatures, one of the problems with trying to sort out all of the grootslang stories is the fact that they come to us largely through the reports of colonial authorities, military men, explorers, and missionaries. Later, cryptozoologists like Bernard Heuvelmanns also began taking those second-, third-, and fourthhand accounts and weaving them together to create a master narrative.

Other than witness accounts, there is no physical evidence of the grootslang. If it does not exist, what could be the source of all of the stories? African rock pythons, which can grow up to 20 feet in length, can be found in South Africa, is one good possibility, as are crocodiles, or even giant fish.

See also: Mamlambo

Further Reading:

Cornell, F. C. (1920). *The Glamour of Prospecting.* T. Fisher Unwin Ltd.
Green, L. G. (1948). *Where Men Still Dream.* Standard Press Ltd.
Lombard, Jean (2004). Waterslangverhale in Afrikaans: die Relevansie van Mitisiteit. *Literator: Journal of Literary Criticism, Comparative Linguistics and Literary Studies,* 25(1), 113+.
Rose, C. (2000). *Giants, Monsters, and Dragons.* W. W. Norton and Co.

H

HONEY ISLAND SWAMP MONSTER

Name: Honey Island Swamp Monster
Alternative Names: Rugaru, Wookie, The Thing
Related Cryptids: Bigfoot, Fouke Monster, Skunk Ape
Location: Southeastern Louisiana and Southwestern Mississippi
Most Recent Documented Sighting: 2013

The Honey Island Swamp Monster is a hominoid creature that inhabits the swamps and other waterways of Louisiana and Mississippi. In particular, it is thought to occupy the Honey Island Swamp, a 250-square-mile swamp located at the border between southeastern Louisiana and southwestern Mississippi, sandwiched between the Old Pear River on the Louisiana side and the Pearl River on the Mississippi side.

The Honey Island Swamp Monster is described as very broad and tall, weighing at least 400 pounds, with grayish or reddish brown fur and yellow or orange eyes. Unlike other hominoid cryptids, this one leaves huge webbed footprints, clearly adapted to its watery habitat. It has either three or four toes. But while it is described as a hominoid, one of the creature's nicknames points to another type of creature: the werewolf. Rugarou comes from the French term for werewolf: loup garou—another frightening hybrid creature. This name also points to a source for the mythology, as the first Europeans to settle the region of Louisiana were Acadians, settlers of French Canada who, after their move to Louisiana, were known as Cajuns. These Cajuns brought their beliefs about werewolves with them to the New World, so it should not surprise us that they would use this term to refer to the mysterious creatures that they encountered in this frightening new land—even if those creatures looked more like ape-men than dog men.

The birth of the Honey Island Swamp Monster was in 1963 when a man named Harlan Ford, out hunting with his buddy Billy Mills in the swamp, had a face-to-face encounter with a large hairy bipedal creature. It wasn't until 1974, though, that Ford's story came out, after he was out in the swamp again and found some large, webbed footprints. He returned to the location and made plaster casts of those prints, and once the prints and Ford's story went out, the creature was born. Ford's granddaughter Dana Holyfield told a researcher that her grandfather had a third encounter as well; this time Ford and Mills were accompanied by their friend Jim Hartsong who said:

> I spotted that thing in the woods and I shot at it. I thought I got it, so I went into the woods to find it dead, but instead I saw big yellow looking eyes and whatever it was, was taller than me.

It growled at me so I shot at it again. I realized I only had one shot left, so I ran and jumped off the bluff. (Leary)

Since those early reports, the story of the Honey Island Swamp Monster continued to grow. Each new development added to the mystery, such as when zoologists from Louisiana State University were asked to look at the footprints, which were described as looking like a cross "between a primate and a large alligator." Scientists from the Louisiana Wildlife Commission as well as the Smithsonian Institute were also called in the early days. (Since the 1970s, however, it has been strongly suggested that the prints were created by someone—probably Ford himself—wearing a specially created shoe.) Another notable piece of evidence emerged in 1980 after Ford's death, when his widow purportedly found an old video taken by Ford of the creature.

Other forms of evidence that are thought to indicate the presence of the creature include screams, dead wild boars, disturbances in the foliage, and, of course, face-to-face sightings. Very rarely do witnesses report a foul odor, which is very common in other Bigfoot-type sightings.

While over the years a number of locals and tourists alike have seen or heard the creature, like some other local cryptids, the Honey Island Swamp Monster owes its continued existence primarily to one person. Dana Holyfield, the granddaughter of Harlan Ford, has devoted much of her life to proving her father's story and continuing to promote the legend of the Honey Island Swamp Monster with books, documentaries, and newspaper articles. Without Holyfield's persistence, it may be that the creature would not enjoy the popularity that it does today.

As with other creatures, cryptozoologists point to folklore from local tribes as offering support for the existence of the creature. And it is true that some local people—like people across North America and the rest of the world   have beliefs in a wild man of sorts who inhabited the swamps. The Choctaw, for instance, spoke of a big man known as hattak chito who lived in the swamps or river bottoms, while the Cherokee have creatures named "Nun Yunu Wi" (The Stone Man) and "Kecleh kudleh" (Hairy Savage). These creatures were often used as bedtime stories to warn children to keep away from the swamps.

There are a variety of theories to account for the presence of the Honey Island Swamp Monster. Like other cryptid hominids, one popular theory is that it is an extant surviving branch of Gigantopithecus, a giant extinct hominoid that primatologists think is ancestral to Asian great apes. Another theory is that it is a descendant of escaped circus monkeys apes. Perhaps many of the sightings are of local animals, such as black bears, panthers, and alligators.

One theory that is unique to the Honey Island Swamp Monster owes its existence to another population from the swamps of Louisiana—creoles. Creoles are those who are descended from the colonial inhabitants of Louisiana prior to it becoming an American state and who came from France as well as the French colonies in the Caribbean, most notably Haiti. These West Indian creoles brought voodoo with them to Louisiana, a syncretic religion based on West African Yoruba religion combined with elements of Catholicism. Practitioners of voodoo believe that a powerful boku, or sorcerer, can turn a person into a zombie: a being that is neither dead nor alive and that can be controlled by the boku, turning them into a form of supernatural slave. This belief, transplanted to the swamps of Louisiana, evolved into the idea that the swamp monster is akin to a zombie: a creation of a powerful boku. This makes the idea of encountering such a creature a terrifying prospect indeed.

Folklorists, on the other hand, suggest that what is important is not whether the creature is real but what purpose his existence serves. The Honey Island Swamp Monster legend is primarily used to teach children to obey their parents, lest the monster or boogeyman will get them. For the Cajuns who live in and around the Honey Island Swamp, the story of the Rougarou that harms children who wander into the swamp or do not listen to their parents is a core memory from their childhood.

In addition, as with other small communities that ended up with a cryptid in their midst, the monster today is the focus of a huge degree of commercialization. Today, the area around Slidell, Louisiana, in St. Tammany Parish is thick with references to the Honey Island Swamp Monster, and tourists can take a number of different boat tours dedicated to the monster.

The Honey Island Swamp Monster, like all good American monsters, has a number of folk songs dedicated to it. One such song is Honey Island Swamp Monster by John Farr Jr., and it describes the creature this way:

> He stood eight feet tall with long gray hair
> Flowing down from here to there
> He had four toes on his big webbed feet

See also: Bigfoot, Fouke Monster, Skunk Ape

Further Reading:

Holyfield, D. (1999). *Encounters With the Honey Island Swamp Monster*. Honey Island Books.
Leary, F. (2003). *The Honey Island Swamp Monster: The Development and Maintenance of a Folk and Commodified Belief Tradition*. Doctoral dissertation, Memorial University of Newfoundland.

I

ISSIE

Name: Issie
Alternative Names: Isshii, Ishii, Issie-kun
Related Cryptids: Bessie, Champ, Loch Ness Monster
Location: Japan
Most Recent Documented Sighting: 1991

Issie is the name given to the serpent that lives in Lake Ikeda, a lake on Kyushu Island in Kagoshima Prefecture in the southern end of the island chain. Its name, like that of most other lake monsters, is a shortened and cuteified version of Ikeda, just as Nessie is the nickname of the Loch Ness Monster. (But while most lake monsters are female, following in Nessie's example, Issie, or more properly, Issie-kun, is male.)

Lake Ikeda is a caldera lake, or a lake formed within the caldera, or whole in the ground formed from a volcanic eruption. That means that it is unconnected to any other water source. Because of its isolation, unique species of animals have developed there, including a giant eel measuring over 6 feet in length.

Unlike some other Japanese creatures, Issie is not a yokai, or an ancient Japanese spirit, but instead is a wholly new cultural phenomenon. The first recorded incidence of a creature living in Lake Ikeda was in September 1978 when the vacationing family of a man named Yutaka Kawaji saw a snake-like creature swimming across the lake. Family members described it as black, with two enormous humps, each measuring approximately 16 feet. Since then, countless people—both from within Japan and from other countries—have witnessed something unusual in the lake.

Also since then, an entire legend about Issie has developed. According to the story, Issie was once a white mare that lived on the shores of the lake with its foal, but a mean samurai kidnapped the foal. In anger, the mare threw itself into the lake, where it transformed into the beast that it is today.

In the months after the first encounter, Ibusuki, a city just a few kilometers away from the lake, offered a reward of 100,000 yen for anyone who could photograph the creature. While similar rewards have been offered for evidence of a creature's existence in other parts of the world, this is the first time (as far as this author knows) that such a reward was paid. Just a few months later came the second known sighting, and the first evidence, when a man named Toshiaki Matsuhara photographed the creature using a 16-mm camera.

The next best piece of evidence was in 1991, when someone took a video of the creature, which was then shown on the Japanese television show *World's Mysterious Phenomena*.

Figure 5 *Issie and Issie-kun. Copyright © 2023 Heidi Scheidl. All rights reserved.*

Issie is, like most lake monsters, considered to be of the long-necked plesiosaur variety. Most people who believe that lake monsters do exist claim that these creatures could be still-living members of the extinct genus Plesiosaurus, a genus that went extinct about 65 million years ago. What is harder to explain in the case of Issie is how it, or presumably members of its family, got into the lake to start with given its lack of connection to any other bodies of water.

For skeptics, the best explanation for the sightings is that people are mistaking a giant eel for a sea serpent. Of course the largest eels in Lake Ikeda are 5–6 feet long, and Issie has been described as being at least 30 feet long. But, as is the case with eyewitness identifications in criminal cases, our eyes often deceive us, showing us things that are not actually there.

As with other lake monsters, tourism authorities have capitalized on the Issie story to bring in visitors, and there are now Issie statues and other representations of the creature as well as a huge variety of merchandise that one can buy.

See also: Bessie, Champ, Loch Ness Monster

Further Reading:

Kimbrough, K., & Shirane, H. (Eds.). (2018). *Monsters, Animals, and Other Worlds: A Collection of Short Medieval Japanese Tales*. Columbia University Press.

Magin, U. (2016). Necessary Monsters: Claimed "Crypto-Creatures" Regarded as Genii Locii. *Time and Mind*, 9(3), 211–22.

Radford, B. (2006). *Lake Monster Mysteries: Investigating the World's Most Elusive Creatures*. University Press of Kentucky.

J

JERSEY DEVIL

Name: Jersey Devil
Alternative Names: Leeds Devil
Related Cryptids: Thunderbird
Location: The Pine Barrens of New Jersey
Most Recent Documented Sighting: 2015

The Jersey Devil is an unusual, and uniquely American, monster that haunts the Pine Barrens of New Jersey and is one of America's oldest cryptids. It is the official state demon of New Jersey.

The Pine Barrens, located along the coast of New Jersey just north of Atlantic City, is a temperate pine forest with a subtropical climate. In it are unique plant species and one very unique animal: The Jersey Devil. It is also said to be a location where members of the mafia bury their victims, and it has long been rumored that real estate tycoon and murderer Robert Durst buried his wife there.

The Jersey Devil has a much more detailed origin story than other cryptids do. As the story goes, it was the thirteenth child born to a witch named Mother Leeds in 1735, who cursed the baby, saying "O, let this one be a devil!"

The baby was born with the body of a deer, the head of a horse, the hooves of a goat, the wings of a bat, blood red eyes, and long, sharp claws. It immediately got up and flew out of the house via the chimney and ended up in the Pine Barrens where it still lives today. Whether or not you believe the story of a witch giving birth to a monstrous chimera, there really was a Leeds family living in New Jersey, who arrived there in 1677. In fact, before the Jersey Devil got its current name, it had been known as the Leeds Devil and was a very localized legend. With the change in name from the Leeds Devil to the Jersey Devil, however, it became a New Jersey phenomenon and is one of America's most well-known monsters. What is difficult with the Jersey Devil, as is the case with so many other cryptids, is separating out the older legends (which might also include beliefs of the local tribe, the Lenape) from the new and separating both of those from the exaggerations, hoaxes, and lies that often swirl around these creatures.

The Leeds family members most closely associated with the legend are Japhet and Deborah Leeds, who we know had twelve children and lived in what is now known as Leeds Point, which is part of the Pine Barrens. Monstrous births are certainly common in folklore and may have been a way to account for the occasional birth of a disabled or disfigured baby. Starting in about the sixteenth century, these births were interpreted as occurring because the mother, while pregnant, underwent some sort of traumatic experience, the results of which would be a monstrous child.

Historian Brian Regal, in his 2018 book, *Secret History of the Jersey Devil*, argues that it was a political rivalry between Benjamin Franklin and Daniel Leeds that resulted in a myth of monsters and witches being attached to the Leeds family name. Even with the dispute, why would Franklin associate his enemy with such a strange beast? It turns out that the Leeds family crest included a wyvern, a legendary creature with the body of a dragon and the wings of a bat.

By the early nineteenth century, the story had gelled, leading to stories about the devil, fears surrounding the devil, and, eventually, sightings. The legend was included in an 1859 article in the *Atlantic Monthly*, as well as, a few years later, the story found its way into an Indiana newspaper called the *Elkhart Sentinal*. By this time, the legend was already so well integrated into people's minds that sightings were already occurring. It was not until the twentieth century, however, that the story, with the new name, the Jersey Devil, made its first appearance in the printed press.

It was in 1909 when a rash of sightings of the devil occurred, which may or may not have been dreamt up by a Philadelphia huckster who created a Jersey Devil out of a dead kangaroo, some fake wings, and green paint and put it on display in Philadelphia for a small fee.

Because there is so much historical material available about the Leeds family and the history of the legend, most people know that the Devil is not real. Of course, the fact that it's a creature made up of at least five different species will convince most people that an animal like that cannot exist in nature. Even so, there are occasional sightings as well as the occasional new hoax, the most recent of which was a 2015 photo taken by a New Jersey man named David Black, which purported to be of the Devil.

Arguably New Jersey's most famous resident, Bruce Springsteen, released a song in 2008 about New Jersey's most famous monster, the Jersey Devil, in his album, *A Night with the Jersey Devil*, and explains how the Devil, born as a human as the thirteenth child on the thirteenth moon, was thrown into the river by his father, where he doesn't die, as was intended, but instead:

Come back kill six brothers and sisters, kill papa too
Sway down Mama, sway down low

See also: Thunderbird

Further Reading:

The Devil of Leeds (1887). *Elkhart Sentinel*, October 15, 8.

Gillespie, A. K. (2022). The Jersey Devil. *North American Monsters: A Contemporary Legend Casebook.* University Press of Colorado, 102–17.

McCloy, J. F., & Miller, R. (1976). *The Jersey Devil*. B B & A Publishers.

Regal, B. (2015). The Jersey Devil: A Political Animal. *New Jersey Studies: An Interdisciplinary Journal*, 1(1), 79–103.

Regal, B., & Esposito, F. J. (2018). *The Secret History of the Jersey Devil: How Quakers, Hucksters, and Benjamin Franklin Created a Monster*. JHU Press.

Ryan, A. V. (1958). The Jersey Devil. *New York Folklore*, 14(1), 55.

L

LAGARFLJÓT WORM

Name: Lagarfljót Worm
Alternative Names: Iceland Worm Monster, Water Snake of Lagarfljót
Related Cryptids: Mongolian Death Worm, Tatzelwurm
Location: Lagarfljót, Iceland,
Most Recent Documented Sighting: 2020

The Lagarfljót Worm is an enormous worm that lives in Lagarfljót, a 20-square-mile lake (technically it is a glacial river) in eastern Iceland near the town of Egilsstaoir. The worm was first mentioned in writing in 1345, in the Icelandic Annals, a set of documents chronicling the history of Iceland. Since then, it has made occasional appearances in print but never was as visible as, for example, the Loch Ness Monster, perhaps because of the isolated location of Lagarfljót.

It is long, perhaps as long as 200 feet. Descriptions of the worm vary, but it is mostly seen as a sea serpent, with humps that rise above the surface of the water but without the distinctive plesiosaur appearance so common in other lake creatures.

It has been described in similar ways to the Mongolian Death Worm that lives in the desert rather than the water but also spits venom from its mouth. In this sense, it also recalls the Indus Worm, a giant worm that Greek author Ctesias described as a 10-feet-long worm that lived in the mud along the banks of the Indus River. One of the notable similarities is that this worm, too, can produce and then spit a flammable oil, which could be used to set whole cities on fire.

Unlike a lot of more well-known cryptids, the Lagarfljót Worm seems very much like a local legend, and while its appearance and behavior does relate to those of other worms as well as other water serpents and snakes, it has not been collapsed into a broader category, erasing its local significance.

One Icelandic tale about the creature, called the Water Snake of Lagarfljót, explains the origin of the beast. It tells of a young girl who wanted a piece of gold to grow bigger. She was told to place it underneath a heath snake or heath worm, which she does, but when she goes to check on the gold the next day, the snake, rather than the gold, grew. She became frightened and threw the snake into the lake, where it grew to become enormous. Worse, it attacked people, even coming onto the shore of the lake to spit a poisonous substance at them. Eventually, two Lapps were hired to kill the snake, but instead, they tied the snake to the bottom of the lake, trapping it in order to keep it from hurting anyone.

Therefore the snake cannot harm anyone now, man or beast, but sometimes it happens that he thrusts a hump of his back up above the surface and whenever that is seen it is always thought a sign of dire events to come, for instance bad seasons, or a great shortage of grass. (Simpson 1972: 103)

The idea that snakes—or dragons, a closely related species—crave gold is an old idea and shows up in other Icelandic legends. Whether worm, lizard, or snake, the fears surrounding the Lagarfljót Worm can be related to attitudes and beliefs about these types of animals that slither.

Worms, for example, are not just associated with the earth but also with death and decomposition, as their presence in the soil has long been known to hasten the decomposition of corpses. The term "worm" has also often been used to refer to serpents with no limbs and no wings, so stories about great worms are often actually tales of dragons. This last point makes sense because dragons are also a feature of Icelandic lore, and the Lagarfljót Worm has no limbs.

In 2012, a sheep farmer named Hjörtur E. Kjerúlf who lives near the lake took a video of what looks like a snake-like creature casually gliding across the surface of the lake. He brought the video to his local television station, which aired it. The video went viral and attracted a massive amount of international attention. In a fairly short time, however, the video was debunked, not as a hoax but as a misunderstanding of how water moves around stationary objects and appears to make those objects move. However, a group called the Icelandic Truth Committee has deemed the video to be credible and claimed that the monster is real.

Kjerúlf's video generated publicity for the lake, for the monster, and for Iceland in general. The town council of Fljótsdalshérað, in East Iceland, offered to pay him a reward for finally catching the beast on camera. Multiple news agencies and television shows visited Lagarfljót in order to try to see the monster.

See also: Mongolian Death Worm, Tatzelwurm

Further Reading:

Lees, C. A., & Overing, G. R. (2018). Women and Water: Icelandic Tales and Anglo-Saxon Moorings. *GeoHumanities*, 4(1), 97–111.

McNamee, G. (Ed.). (2000). *The Serpent's Tale: Snakes in Folklore and Literature*. University of Georgia Press.

Pan, Yu-Yen, Nara, Masakazu, Löwemark, Ludvig, Miguez-Salas, Olmo, Gunnarson, Björn, Iizuka, Yoshiyuki, Chen, Tzu-Tung, & Dashtgard, Shahin E. (2021). The 20-million-year old Lair of an Ambush-Predatory Worm Preserved in Northeast Taiwan. *Scientific Reports*, 11(1), 1174.

Simpson, J. (1972). *Icelandic Folktales and Legends*. University of California.

Stewart, R. (2019). *Diction in the Description of Dragons in Icelandic Texts from c. 871 1600*. Master's thesis.

LIZARD MAN

Name: Lizard Man

Alternative Names: Lizard Man of Lee County, Lizard Man of South Carolina, Lizard Man of Scape Ore Swamp

Related Cryptids: Bunyip, Loveland Frogman

Locations: Lee County, South Carolina

Most Recent Documented Sighting: Unknown

Lizard Man is a small-town American cryptid, found only within one county in South Carolina.

Unlike other American cryptids, the Lizard Man has no associated Native American lore that can be used to provide a history for the legend. Instead, it is an entirely new—and very recent—phenomenon.

The Lizard Man was born in July 1988 when the sheriff in Lee County, South Carolina, received a phone call from a citizen from a small town called Browntown about a car that had been vandalized the previous night. When the sheriff began investigating the report, he began hearing stories about a 7-feet-tall green monster with glowing red eyes, scaly skin, and long hands with three bony fingers. That would end up with the name Lizard Man. One seventeen-year-old, Christopher Davis, even took a polygraph test to prove that he saw this creature attack his car while he was stopped by the side of the road to change a flat tire. It continued to chase his car after he drove away, attacking it as he drove. It did not take long before local residents formed an armed posse to hunt down the creature. It also did not take long before all of the elements of the lore emerged; because the first two encounters involved vehicles, locals quickly came to understand that the creature is attracted to chrome.

The Lizard Man story quickly went from local news to national and then international, with newspapers and television shows—including *Good Morning America*—covering the story. Bishopville, the city at the center of the reports, became known internationally. This pattern—local person or persons experience a frightening encounter with a monstrous being, which attracts local and then national and international coverage, and which spurs more sightings, until finally the encounter is commercialized—is familiar to those who follow cryptozoological stories in the news media. But the saga of the Lizard Man went from unknown local monster to popular culture phenomenon almost immediately. In fact, it was just a week after the first news report on the Lizard Man that a local sports equipment store was selling T-shirts and hats, which read "Lee County Lizard Patrol."

The 1980s was a good era for swamp monsters, with multiple comic books and movies coming out about the DC character Swamp Thing. But just as quickly as the story emerged and went viral—at the peak of the excitement, local radio station WCOS offered a million dollar reward for anyone who could catch the creature—it died down with no more sightings. All told, it was a matter of weeks from first encounter to last encounter. One reason for the short lifespan of the Lizard Man was the concern, shared by many in town, that Bishopville had become the subject of ridicule. It took another twenty years—enough time for the humiliation to pass—for the Lizard Man to get his second wind and for Bishopville to finally embrace their monster.

In 2015, a local woman took a photograph that was alleged to be of the Lizard Man, and there were rumors that it appeared during the solar eclipse of 2017. But for the most part, the Lizard Man is one of America's most elusive cryptids, appearing every few years to attack a vehicle, only to vanish once again into the swamp.

See also: Altamaha-ha, Bunyip, Loveland Frogman

Further Reading:

Blackburn, L. (2013). *Lizard Man: The True Story of the Bishopville Monster*. Anomalist Books.

LOCH NESS MONSTER

Name: Loch Ness Monster
Alternative Names: Nessie
Related Cryptids: Bessie, Champ
Location: Loch Ness, Scotland
Most Recent Documented Sighting: 2022

The Loch Ness Monster is Great Britain's most famous cryptid and is second only to Bigfoot in terms of worldwide popularity. It is a sea serpent, of the plesiosaur type.

It lives in Loch Ness, one of Scotland's 30,000 freshwater lochs, or lakes, and one of the largest, located in the Scottish highlands. It is about 21 square miles in size and 800 feet deep at its deepest.

The Loch Ness Monster, or Nessie as it is often called (the creature is gendered female), is an enormous beast with a huge body, a long, swan-like neck, and a small head. It is a reptile, which means that it breathes air, although the infrequency of sightings cast some doubt on this idea, as an air breathing species would have to come up for air multiple times per day. It has two/one sets of flippers and often a ridge of fins down the back.

While many cryptids began their careers as folktales, myths, or legends, it appears as though the Loch Ness Monster is entirely a modern creation, with all of the early sightings occurring in the 1920s and 1930s, although these sightings built on a preexisting collection of sea serpent myths.

In 1933, London visitors George Spicer and his wife were driving along the shore of Loch Ness on their way to Inverness when they saw something that caught their attention. Spicer later wrote to the *Inverness Courier* with his account, which is typical for other witness reports of the time:

> I saw the nearest approach to a dragon or a prehistoric animal that I have ever seen in my life. It crossed my road about fifty yards ahead and appeared to be carrying a small lamb or animal of some kind. It seemed to have a long neck which moved up and down, in the manner of a scenic railway, and the body was fairly big, with a high back. (Loxton and Prothero 2013: 130)

This letter kicked off a frenzy around Loch Ness, which became inundated by reporters, explorers, and naturalists from as far as the United States.

By the time Spicer's letter came out in the local paper, and before the story spread around the world, there had already been rumors of a monster lurking in the depths of the loch. In fact, some say the legend goes all the way back to Saint Columba, an Irish monk who lived in the sixth century and met a creature in the River Ness; Columba made the sign of the cross at the beast and said the words, "Go no further. Do not touch the man. Go back at once," which caused it to disappear into the Loch. This account was included in *Vita Columba* (The Life of Columba), published in the seventh century by the abbot of Iona.

Given how recently sightings of, and the legend of, the Loch Ness Monster emerged, why are so many of the witness descriptions similar? Each witness has seen essentially the same creature, with the swan-like neck and humps on its back.

For as long as people have sailed the ocean there have been reports of dangerous monsters whose home is the deepest, darkest oceans and lakes. Cultures that depend on the water for their livelihood have more stories than land-locked cultures. These stories help provide a sense of control and meaning to fishermen, whalers, explorers, and sailors and help explain the dangerous and often unexpected occurrences at sea.

With the Age of Exploration, starting in the fifteenth century, and throughout the waves of colonization that followed, sightings picked up with the increase in ocean traffic. The nineteenth century was a high water point for sea serpent stories, which came out frequently in newspapers around the world. By the time George Spicer saw Nessie, most people had a well-developed understanding of what sea monsters look like and a bit about the dangers they posed.

In addition, Arthur Conan Doyle's *The Lost World* was published in 1912, which told a story about a journey to the Amazon region in South America, where the explorers encounter dinosaurs and other animals that have long been extinct. It was wildly successful and popularized the idea of the "evolutionary holdover," which is so useful to cryptozoologists.

And just months before George Spicer's experience, the film *King Kong* came out. The film is about a giant ape that is also some sort of evolutionary relic and certainly contributed to the ideas circulating in society at that time about evolution (the Scopes Monkey Trial, where an American science teacher was prosecuted for teaching evolution, occurred in 1925), monsters, and nature.

In 1975, the Loch Ness Monster was written up in the journal *Nature* (Rines and Scott 1975), albeit not in the main journal, whose articles are peer reviewed by scientists, but in the Comment and Opinion section. The authors (Rines was at the time head of the Academy of Applied Sciences in Boston while Scott was an amateur naturalist) provided the creature with a proper Linnaean, or binomial, name, Nessiteras rhombopteryx, which means Ness Monster with diamond fins. This was done, in part, not only to legitimize the creature, if it ever did turn out to be real, but also to protect it legally if it were ever found. (It was pointed out later that Nessiteras rhombopteryx was an anagram for "monster hoax by Sir Peter S.")

By far the most popular theory to account for the existence of the Loch Ness Monster, or for that many other water serpents, is that they are evolutionary holdovers from an extinct species. In particular, virtually every cryptozoologist agrees that Nessie must be a Plesiosaur, an extinct reptile (not dinosaur) that disappeared from the fossil record some 66 million years ago, along with the dinosaurs with which they have been associated.

While there had been a handful of plesiosaur fossils (but not a complete or even partial skeleton) found prior to the nineteenth century, but without an evolutionary understanding, what these fossils represented was debated among professional and amateur scientists.

In 1821, these fossils were given a new genus, Plesiosaurus, which roughly translates to almost-reptile or almost-crocodile. Even then, and in the subsequent decades when more and more complete fossils were found, the framework within which these creatures were understood was biblical. In fact, the word "fossil" means "things that are dug up" and not, for example, "things that are dead" or "things that went extinct." In the days before paleontology, these finds were found by amateurs and kept in private collections.

By the seventeenth century, most fossil hunters knew that the fossils were remnants of animals that had disappeared, but there was still no knowledge of how or why this occurred, nor any notion of geologic time. It was not until the early decades of the nineteenth century that the field of paleontology was created, with the specific purpose of studying the remains of animals that were now extinct. The word "dinosaur" did not even exist until 1842.

With the publication of Darwin's *Origin of Species* in 1859, there was now a theoretical paradigm to help explain all of the fossils sitting in private collections. This attracted a whole new population of collectors and hunters, and newer and larger, more complete, fossils began to be unearthed, starting with the first virtually complete Plesiosaur skeleton found by Mary Anning in Dorset, England, in 1823.

As the nineteenth century passed, paleontology continued to grow, and more dinosaurs as well as plesiosaur fossils were found, adding to a growing data set about life on this planet. These fossils ended up with a number of different names, and amateurs and professionals argued about which fossils belonged in which category and whether or not there were two main types of Plesiosaur—a long-necked variety and a short-necked variety.

Scientists outside of the cryptozoological community have challenged the idea that the Loch Ness Monster, if it exists, is a Plesiosaur; while the reconstructed skeletons resemble representations of the monster, those superficial similarities do not take into account some of the morphological features of the Plesiosaur, which would make it incompatible with the life of Nessie and the environment of Loch Ness.

In addition, as with the other supposed evolutionary relics (most specifically, Bigfoot-type creatures), scientists dispute the idea that random members of a species could survive, virtually unchanged, for millions of years after the rest of that species went extinct. The Plesiosaurs died out as a result of the Cretaceous–Paleogene extinction event, which wiped out three quarters of all life on the planet, including almost every single large animal. It was this event that paved the way for mammals.

For the Loch Ness Monster in particular, the loch itself is only about 10,000 years old, which is certainly incompatible with the age of the Plesiosaurs. In addition, while big, it is certainly not large enough to contain a breeding population of creatures, nor is it warm enough to host what must be a cold-blooded reptile.

Some Nessie scholars posited instead that Nessie could be a product of parallel or convergent evolution. Dolphins and sharks are good examples of animals with very different evolutionary histories, but that have independent developed similar adaptations, because they live in similar conditions. Here, the various sea serpents around the world all look like plesiosaurs because there is something particular about that particular set of adaptations that works well in big bodies of water.

The nineteenth century, which roughly coincided with the era of Queen Victoria in England, where most of the Plesiosaurs were found and where paleontology as a field developed, was marked by a number of social changes, including a new scientific literacy among the middle classes and, by the end of the century, a wholesale change in the people engaged in scientific pursuits. The wealthy amateur aristocrat who collected materials and published articles in scientific journals, by the end of the nineteenth century, were replaced by professional, university-trained scholars.

Even so, the focus around Nessie as well as other cryptids that began to appear during this era was on the idea that members of ancient, extinct species could survive into the present day as essentially living fossils.

The Victorian era was progressive, in the sense that Industrialism was in full force and new technologies and new machines were, it seemed, coming out every day. That is one of the reasons that Prince Albert, Queen Victoria's husband, organized the Great Exhibition of the Works of Industry of All Nations, also known as the Great Exhibition, to showcase the world's (but especially Great Britain's) technological achievements.

But it was also an era focused on the domestic, on childrearing, and on nostalgia. Earlier historical periods and events became romanticized in this era, perhaps as a counterpoint to the new and unsettling changes rocking society. That's why the myth of King Arthur was resurrected in this era, and the Celtic warrior queen Boudica was reimagined as a modern British heroine.

The Loch Ness Monster fit right into this reevaluation of history, as it can at one point be a monster, while at another, it is a symbol of Scottish nationalism, and at a different point, it is a scientific specimen.

But while the idea of Nessie may have been born in the Victorian era of dinosaur collectors, it actually came to be in the early twentieth century, as rumors and reports came together along with a new popular scientific understanding. Letters to the editor in both local Scottish papers and in the international press brought scientific discussions and debates into ordinary people's homes. For the first time, the level of education, the type of press coverage and access, and a new popular scientific literacy helped give these stories a context, helping to create the modern monster in the process.

Skeptics explain Nessie sightings as examples of our eyes seeing things that are not really there. Boat wakes, waves, catfish, seals, and floating logs are examples of occurrences that can appear like a large creature moving through the water. In addition, there is no question that images of sea serpents are so ubiquitous that it is difficult to imagine a water creature that does NOT look like a Plesiosaur—but especially in Great Britain and especially during the era of regular fossil discoveries.

Evidence for the existence of the monster is limited to witness sightings and the occasional photograph or video. The most famous image of the monster by far is what is known as the surgeon's photo, because it was allegedly taken by a British surgeon named Colonel Robert Wilson in April 1934. For most of the twentieth century, that photo was thought to be a genuine depiction of Nessie, until the photo was exposed as a hoax in 1994. There are no known physical artifacts associated with the creature.

There is, however, a song called *Loch Ness* (2005) by English heavy metal band Judas Priest, which describes the creature as having "a beastly head of onyx, With eyes set coals of fire" and tells us that its "leathered hide glides glistening" through the murky darkness.

Today, the Loch Ness Monster continues to be the subject of scientific inquiry, tourism, and fantasy. One reason for its continued popularity may be the very modernity, or postmodernity, that we are living in right now. It seems as though the entire planet is mapped, every species has been identified, and the mysteries and magic of the past are gone. The Loch Ness Monster allows us to once again live in a world of mystery, danger, and magic.

See also: Bessie, Champ

Further Reading:

Bauer, H. H. (1987). Society and Scientific Anomalies: Common Knowledge About the Loch Ness Monster. *Journal of Scientific Exploration*, 1(1), 51–74.

Bauer, H. H. (2002). The Case for the Loch Ness Monster: The Scientific Evidence. *Journal of Scientific Exploration*, 16(2), 225–46.

Jylkka, K. (2018). "Witness the Plesiosaurus": Geological Traces and the Loch Ness Monster Narrative. *Configurations*, 26(2), 207–34.

Kallen, S. A. (2008). *The Loch Ness Monster*. Capstone.

Loxton, D. (2004). The Loch Ness Monster. *Skeptic (Altadena, CA)*, 11(1), 96B.

Parsons, E. C. M. (2004). Sea Monsters and Mermaids in Scottish Folklore: Can These Tales Give us Information on the Historic Occurrence of Marine Animals in Scotland? *Anthrozoös*, 17(1), 73–80.

Piippo, M. (2020). Loch Ness Monster and Her Impact on Culture. INSPIRE Student Research and Engagement Conference, 16. https://scholarworks.uni.edu/csbsresearchconf/2020/all/16.

Rines, R. H., & Dougherty, F. M. (2003). Proof Positive-Loch Ness Was An Ancient Arm Of The Sea. *Journal of Scientific Exploration*, 17(2), 317–23.

Scott, P., & Rines, R. (1975). Naming the Loch Ness Monster. *Nature*, 258(5535), 466–8.

LOVELAND FROGMAN

Name: Loveland Frogman

Alternative Names: Loveland Frog, Frogman

Related Cryptids: Bunyip, Lizard Man

Locations: Cincinnati, Ohio

Most Recent Documented Sighting: 2016

The Loveland Frog is a frog-human hybrid that lives in Loveland, Ohio, a suburb of Cincinnati. It is the only known frog cryptid in the world, which is odd, given their importance as a folkloric animal.

The Loveland Frog was first spotted in 1955 by a traveling salesman who saw three humanoid figures, each with frog faces, webbed hands and feet, and thick, leathery skin. He reported that one of the frogs had a wand that produced sparks, scaring him off. Loveland has a small river running through it called the Little Miami River. It's here that the Frogman is thought to live.

The frogs were not spotted again until 1972, perhaps because they spend much of their time in water. That year, a Loveland police officer named Ray Shockey spotted the creature on the road next to the river while driving and almost hit it before it returned to the river. Two weeks later, a second officer named Mark Mathews spotted the creature in the same area (although this time with a tail) and shot at it (some reports say the animal was killed, which the officer denies); while the officer claimed that the animal he shot was the Frogman, he later (perhaps out of embarrassment) said it wasn't bipedal or 4 feet tall, and that was actually an iguana (which are not native to Ohio).

Another few decades passed until the next report of the Frogman. In 2016, a Loveland man named Sam Jacobs was playing Pokémon Go at Lake Isabella (also in Loveland, close to the river) and spotted the Frogman. Jacobs took a number of photos of the creature as well as a video, which was uploaded to YouTube and shows on the local Fox affiliate television station.

The video, which was taken at night, shows only a dark creature with very large, very bright eyes. As with the reports from the 1950s and 1970s, this frog was 3–4 feet tall and walked on its hind legs like a person.

Jacobs told the local television station:

> We saw a huge frog near the water. Not in the game, this was an actual giant frog. Then the thing stood up and walked on its hind legs. I realize this sounds crazy but I swear on my grandmother's grave this is the truth. Not sure if it was a frogman or just a giant frog. Either way, I've never seen anything like it.

Frogs are important animals in folklore for a number of reasons. Because frogs are amphibians, they live in watery areas and are both associated with rainfall and the fertility of the fields and are sometimes thought to be linked to creation itself.

Frogs are also known for their transformative abilities: after all, the frog begins life as a tadpole and only later becomes an actual frog. Frogs are also liminal creatures: as amphibians, they spend part of their lives on dry land but part of their lives in the water. This makes the idea of a frog-human hybrid seem a bit less outlandish.

That's why frogs are so frequently found in stories about the transformation from human to animal or animal to human. For example, in one of the most famous of these stories, "The Frog Prince," a human who was cursed to take on the appearance of a frog tricks a princess into marrying him, and only later in the tale does the frog revert back to his original, human form. Another element of these stories is the appearance of the frog (or toad): famously ugly, the frog repulses his bride by his appearance, which of course only conceals a handsome man underneath.

Frogs are also both different from us—uncannily so—and like us in some ways. Their voices can sometimes sound human, which is why hearing a group of frogs or toads croaking makes one think of a human council of some kind.

Today, there is an annual triathlon held in Loveland called the Loveland Frogman Race, which consists of a 5-mile boat race, an 8-mile bike race, and a 5-kilometer foot race. The race takes place alongside the Miami River, the home of the Frogman, with the boating part of the race taking place in the river. There was also a musical produced in 2014 called *Hot Damn! It's the Loveland Frog!* And like any good American cryptid, there are a handful of songs about it as well. Fangs and Twang, a roots rock trio, wrote a song called *Loveland Frogman* (2017), which tells of the original 1995 sighting by the traveling salesman and which tells the story from the perspective of multiple characters, including state Trooper Dan, who notes:

> he hopped up and took me by surprise
> with his big bug eyes and a tongue for Catching Flies

See also: Bunyip, Lizard Man

Further Reading:

Are the Legends True? Man Claims he Spotted Fabled Loveland Frogman: Legend of Humanoid Frog Lives on. (2016). *KWLT5*, August 4.

Thay, E. (2001). *Ghost Stories of Ohio*. Ghost House Books.

Zipes, Jack (2008). What Makes a Repulsive Frog So Appealing: Memetics and Fairy Tales. *Journal of Folklore Research*, 45(2), 109–43.

M

MAMLAMBO

Name: Mamlambo
Alternative Names: Abantu bomlambo, brain sucker
Related Cryptids: Encantado, Mermaid
Locations: The Western Cape of South Africa
Most Recent Documented Sighting: 1997

The Mamlambo is a South African goddess or spirit. The name is a Xhosa (Bushman) word meaning mother of the river, and she is most associated with the Mzintlava River.

She is primarily described as a snake or serpent, but she is a shapeshifter and can shapeshift into a mermaid, where she uses her feminine wiles and her sexuality to seduce men, sometimes killing them, but she can also bring great wealth. In her snake form, she is approximately 60 feet in length, and she has a snake neck, a horse head, and a crocodile torso. She glows at night, and her eyes glow as well, hypnotizing those who gaze into them. In her river form, she is a guardian of the river.

Stories of the Mamlambo started to filter into the media in the 1990s, when villagers in the area surrounding Mount Ayliff began reporting that they saw a creature in the river. Allegedly nine people lost their lives in 1997 to the Mamlambo, who, after pulling a victim into the water, will eat their faces and brains. According to police who investigated the deaths, they were natural deaths and in some cases their bodies had been mutilated due to animal activity.

In Africa, people have a largely positive view of snakes, and they play an important role in the myths and folklore of many African groups. In some cultures they are the incarnation of ancestors, in others they signify immortality, fertility, or protection. The Xhosa believe that their ancestors now live as river spirits like Mamlambo.

A newer, and darker, understanding of the Mamlambo has arisen in recent years. Here, Mamlambo also refers to a snake whose power can be bought from a traditional sorcerer, or sangoma, in order to bring good luck and fortune through engaging in a ritual known as ukuthwala.

Ukuthwala, in Xhosa, refers to the practice of kidnapping a girl in order to marry her without her parents' consent. It also refers to the ritual that uses the malambo in order to generate wealth. Implicit in the ritual use of the term is the idea that Mamlambo requires great sacrifice and will often require that the client put his personal morals aside in order to give her what she wants.

After paying the sangoma, and by following the instructions given by the sangoma, the believer will see their fortunes grow. But the Mamlambo, which is cared for by the sangoma for as long as the client continues to pay, can be dangerous and can kill. While she can grant wealth, there is a price to pay, and that price continues to increase over time and can involve animal sacrifice and murder. In particular, the magic that the Mamlambo offers for generating wealth is most affective when the client offers up the one thing that is most important to them: a child or other family member.

Other countries in southern Africa have similar wealth-giving spirits, such as the Malawian njoka, the chikwambo of Zimbabwe, the chitapo or nakamwale of Zambi, or Mami Wata of West Africa.

Because the Mamlambo is a sexual being, another result of the ukuthwala is that the client will often have to have sex with the Mamlambo, harming his or her relationships with their spouse. For instance, anthropologist Felicity Wood collected a story from one of her informants about a man who was very rich, thanks to his relationship with a Mamlambo. His wife recounted catching her husband in the act of having a sexual relationship with a Mamlambo in her human guise:

> One evening, I came in without knocking. I caught them by surprise. What a lovely lady at the table candle lit, with golden hair and blue eyes. Then she dived into the water. My husband's bald head was running sweat. (Wood 2008: 97)

Some anthropologists see the Mamlambo as a particularly modern being, in that most people who engage the practices of a Mamlambo do so because they want money. It is that greed that lies at the heart of the danger associated with her and her ritual. Eventually, in order to achieve great wealth, one must put aside everything and everyone else who once mattered to them. The fact that sometimes the Mamlambo is represented as a white woman, or wearing Western clothes, reinforces the idea that the Mamlambo's focus on money is largely connected with the West.

See also: Encantado, Merfolk

Further Reading:

Hazel, R. (2019). *Snakes, People, and Spirits, Volume One: Traditional Eastern Africa in its Broader Context* (Vol. 1). Cambridge Scholars Publishing.
Maseko, B. (1984). Mamlambo. *Kunapipi*, 6(3), 13.
Mnensa, M. (2010). Mamlambo's Helping Hand. *Journal of Pan African Studies*, 4(2), 249–50.
Wood, F. (2008a). Aspects of the Wealth-Giving Mamlamgo. *Southern African Journal for Folklore Studies*, 18(2), 96–109.
Wood, F. (2008b). The Mermaid Woman in the 21st Century: Oral Narratives Concerning the Wealth-Giving Mermaid Woman, the Mamlambo, in Their Contemporary South African Context. *International Journal of the Humanities*, 6(8), 71–90.
Wood, F., & Lewis, M. (2007). *The Extraordinary Khotso: Millionaire Medicine man from Lusikisiki*. Jacana Media.

MAPINGUARY

Name: Mapinguary

Alternative Names: Mapinguari, juma, kida harara, segamai

Related Cryptids: Encantado, Chupacabra

Locations: The Amazonian Rainforest of Brazil and Venezuela

Most Recent Documented Sighting: 2014

The mapinguary is a giant beast that lives in the Amazonian rainforest in Brazil and Venezuela. The name comes from the Tupi-Guarani language and means "thing with a crooked foot." In Portuguese, the national language of Brazil, it is macaco-preguiça gigante, which means giant sloth monkey.

For a lot of monsters around the world, there is no one physical description or set of behavioral characteristics. Part of the reason for that is the different realms in which monsters reside: they can live in folktales, in myths, in urban legends, and they can live as physical beings who can be seen. Sometimes the folkloric or mythic characteristics will not be found in descriptions of creatures taken in witness reports, and vice versa. Belief systems and folk traditions are dynamic and flexible; they can take in material from new sources and can change as conditions change. This is certainly the case with the mapinguary, a creature with roots in Amerindian belief systems, which have been shaped by Spanish colonists and settlers and which have been impacted by cryptozoological beliefs and practices from outside of the area.

The first descriptions of the mapinguary, as recounted by Europeans, were about a humanoid or anthropoid (ape-like) creature of some kind. In more recent years, a newer belief emerged of a one-eyed humanoid monster with a mouth on its stomach—the single eye was most likely a Portuguese introduction. And at some point, descriptions began to emerge of the mapinguary as a giant, hairy sloth, while the Portuguese called it the rubber monkey, to refer to the fact that its long hair repels bullets. Other accounts have said that it was the size of a dog while others said a horse. Still others have described an animal that looks more like a crocodile than a monkey or a sloth. In most cases, the animal has large claws like those of an armadillo. Biologist David Oren (1993 and 2001) collected dozens of witness accounts, which he put together to form a description of a large, strong animal, each quadrupedal or bipedal, with long red, brown, or black fur, backward-facing feet with four toes, and a simian face. Witnesses have also reported a strong smell associated with the creature.

It may also be that there are different unknown animals that witnesses are seeing and that cryptozoologists have combined into one named creature. For example, the kida harara is a similar creature to the mapinguary, but the descriptions and stories of the two overlap so much so that it appears that they are the same. There is evidence for this: sloth-like monsters tend to be seen in the West, while monkey-like monsters are more common in the East. In recent years, it has been described as "the bigfoot of Brazil," which suggests that non-Amazonian concepts have been influencing descriptions of this creature. Cryptozoologists Bernard Heuvelmans and Ivan Sanderson thought that it was a new species of primate, but most people who believe that the mapinguary is real think that it is a relic giant sloth.

In particular, the megatherium is a genus of ground sloths from South America that went extinct only around 12,000 years ago. That means that not only did these sloths, which included species as large as elephants, live alongside of humans, who first arrived in South America around 18,000 years ago, but they may have been driven to extinction by them as well. Even if there are no giant ground sloths still living today, the fact that they coexisted for a few thousand years with humans may mean that the tribes living in the Amazon today may still retain cultural memories of these animals, which have informed their belief in the mapinguary.

The first printed reference to the mapinguary was in the nineteenth century, and since then, there have been dozens of reported sightings or audio accounts—the mapinguary has a low roar and a high-pitched cry—and a number of accounts of mapinguaries being killed. Other than these accounts, biologist David Oren has collected casts of purported mapinguary tracks, an audio recording, a photo of a tree with claw marks, and some feces and hair samples. In addition, three hunters told Oren that they captured mapinguaries, but that they could not keep them because they smelled too bad. Unfortunately for Oren, who is perhaps the mapinguary's greatest advocate, he has so far been unable to substantiate any of the accounts that he collected. His position regarding the mapinguary is that it is most likely a still-living survival of the giant ground sloth (megalonychid), which shares the "backward" feet (inward-turned in actuality) and reddish hair of so many witness sightings.

The folktale, *Mapinguari: One-Eyed Ogre*, tells of a hunter who wanted to go hunting, but because it was Sunday, his wife told him to stay home. His response was "No domingo também se come. One must also eat on Sundays." The hunter and his friend heard screaming and when they went to investigate the source, they came across a beast:

> when it came closer, they saw that it was an animal, a black-haired, ape-like creature with a turtle 's shell and one big green eye in the middle of its forehead. The men were terrified. The hunter started to shoot, but the bullets could not penetrate the beast's shell.

The creature began tearing the hunter apart, while the second man watched "in horror as the animal tore apart his friend. As it gnawed his friend's arm, it said, 'No domingo também se come. One must also eat on Sundays'" (Galeano 2009: 39–40).

See also: Chupacabra, Encantado

Further Reading:

Galeano, J. C., & Morgan, R. (2009). *Folktales of the Amazon*. Libraries Unlimited.

Hoefle, S. W. (2009). Enchanted (and Disenchanted) Amazônia: Environmental Ethics and Cultural Identity in Northern Brazil. *Ethics Place and Environment (Ethics, Place & Environment (Merged with Philosophy and Geography))*, 12(1), 107–30.

Oren, D. C. (1993). *Did Ground Sloths Survive to Recent Times in the Amazon Region?* Departamento de Zoologia do Museu Paraense Emílio Goeldi.

Oren, D. C. (2001). Does the Endangered Xenarthran Fauna of Amazônia Include Remnant Ground Sloths?. *Edentata*, 4, 2–5.

Velden, F. F. V. (2016). Reality, Science and Fantasy in the Controversies About the Mapinguari in Southwestern Amazonia. *Boletim do Museu Paraense Emílio Goeldi. Ciências Humanas*, 11, 209–24.

MERFOLK

Name: Merfolk (plural)

Alternative Names: Mermaid, Merman (singular gendered), Merrow (Irish)

Related Cryptids: Feejee Mermaid, Siren

Locations: Oceans around the world but especially cultures with strong fishing and seafaring traditions

Most Recent Documented Sighting: 2012

Merfolk is the gender-neutral, plural, term for human-fish hybrids (mere is the old English word for sea). Mermaids, the most well-known variant, are female water creatures whose upper body takes the form of a woman and whose lower body comes from the tail of a fish. Mermen are male mermaids; they also have the upper body of a human and the lower body of a fish tail.

Historically, human-fish hybrids existed in a variety of cultures. For example, the Canaanite goddess Atargatis was portrayed with a fish body and human head, and, according to legend, Alexander the Great's sister was turned into a mermaid, and she could either cause calm weather for sailors or rough weather. There was also a fish-human god named Era or Oannes in ancient Babylonia, the merman Triton from Greek mythology. Mermaids and mermen are most common in cultures where fishing is an important aspect of the economy and culture.

Unlike most other cryptids, merfolk are found throughout much of the world, and most are not named.

Merfolk are gendered, which is also rare in the world of cryptids. While there have been sightings of female Bigfoots, it is rare for a cryptid to have both male and female forms. Mermen are often more violent and dangerous than mermaids, but they, like some mermaids, can warn friendly humans of upcoming storms and other disasters. Merrow refers to both mermaids and mermen in Ireland. The Norwegian tale, *The Grateful Merman*, tells the story of a group of men who were fishing and encountered a strange man who appeared in the water, calling out

"Huttetu! I'm freezing!" One of the men threw a mitten to the man, who disappeared back into the water. Later that night, after going to bed, the man had a visitor, who said to him, "Hey there, Mitten Man, who gave the glove to me, there's lightning to the north and thunder in the sea!" (Christiansen and Iversen 1964: 54).

While mermaids are often beautiful (especially in the European tradition), the Irish merfolk are ugly creatures; like many other merfolk, both males and females can shapeshift into humans. A Scottish version of the mermaid is known as the *mhorag*; she only comes out of the water when a member of her family is about to die. Mermaids in many cultures can have offspring with human men, producing children that are sometimes part human/part mermaid—webbed feet or hands are a common trait of such offspring.

There is no definitive "skin color" for merfolk; in European and Euro-American traditions, they look like Europeans. But elsewhere in the world, they have a variety of physical features as well as skin tones. What merfolk should look like became an issue in 2019 when Disney announced that they were producing a new, live action version of the 1989 film, *The Little Mermaid*, and had cast singer Halle Bailey in the role of Ariel, the lead mermaid. Because Bailey is African American, the casting choice led to outrage on the part of some white Americans, who claimed that mermaids can only be white. Some even tried to use science to justify their positions, claiming that because mermaids live underwater, where there is little exposure to sunlight, their skin should be white. In fact, it is thanks to the popularity of *The Little Mermaid* that so many of us have a perception today that mermaids are Caucasian.

Other parts of merfolk anatomy are less clear. For example, while merfolk must have lungs, because their upper body is human and they breathe when on land, they must also have hidden gills in order to breathe underwater. In addition, merpeople should have some sort of swim bladder to allow them to stay submerged in the ocean, and no one knows how they reproduce, or if they even have genitalia.

In terms of diets, mermaids and mermen are most commonly described as eating fish and other ocean life plus seaweed and other plants. It is unknown what mermaid teeth are like (although they would appear to be human), a factor that helps scientists determine the diet of other animals. It is sometimes thought that they eat humans, but, while the ancient Greek sirens did in fact eat people, it is rare for most merfolk to do so. Instead, merfolk may be prey for larger marine animals like whales and sharks. (In fact, in the nineteenth century, some fishermen in Iceland caught a shark and found, inside of its stomach, the remains of a merman of some kind.)

Mermaids are often seen by humans sitting on rocks in the sea. Because they are often portrayed as not just beautiful but also vain, they are often seen brushing their long hair. Much of the folklore surrounding mermaids has them using their beauty, and their beautiful voice, to entice and seduce men—often fishermen—sometimes causing their death. (The Siren is a related creature—they are beautiful females, sometimes with wings, who lure sailors to their deaths.)

Mermaids are not always bad, however. They often marry mortal men and can bring them helpful gifts, like cures for illness. Both mermaids and mermen often warn sailors of upcoming storms.

Much of what we know about merfolk come from folktales. In the Swedish tale, "A Handout for the Merman," a farmer's son and a farm hand found a merman who washed ashore on the beach. The merman asked for some money, but the farmer's son said no, while the farm hand gave him what he had. The farmer's son, from then on, was slow-witted, while the farm hand became quite successful, demonstrating the value of being polite to a merman.

In the Norwegian tale, "The Grateful Merman," a group of fishermen were out fishing and saw a man jump out of the water, telling the men, "I'm freezing!" One of the fishermen gave the man his mittens, upon which he sank back into the sea. Later that night, while he was asleep, the man who gave the strange man his mittens received a visitor, who told him that there was a storm coming from the north. He then told the other fishermen, since they had not tied up their boats, so they went to the shore and tied the boats up, just before the storm hit. Their boats were saved while many other boats were lost. In this tale, the strange man was a merman, but he did not actually look like one, demonstrating the ability of merfolk to appear human.

In the Irish tale, "The Child from the Sea," a fisherman was out fishing and had caught what he thought was a very big fish. Instead of a fish, however, he pulled in a boy who he took home. Once the boy was at home with the fisherman, though, he would not eat or drink and hid under the bed. A priest, whom the fisherman asked for advice, told him to bring the boy back out to the sea, exactly where he found him. When he arrived at the spot where he found the boy, the boy jumped out of the boat with a laugh and swam away, never to be seen again. As in the previous story, the child was not clearly a mermaid based on his appearance, but his behavior gave him away.

Scotland also has stories of merfolk. In particular, the Blue Men of the Minch are a group of mermen who threaten sailors and fisherman. In many of the tales of the Blue Men, the mermen will challenge a ship captain to a rhyming contest; if the captain loses, the ship and all her men will be destroyed.

Merfolk, known as *Rusalkas*, are found in the Slavic countries. Rusalkas are not human-fish hybrids, however; they are the spirits of dead women who died violent or distressing deaths—especially drowning—and who live in rivers and lakes.

Japan has a few types of mermaids, none of which are beautiful or seductive like European mermaids. The *Ningyo* is a grotesque creature, half-man, half-fish, with a scaly body and claws for hands. Some mermaids in Japan have no arms at all—just a torso, head, and tail, while others can transform into humans. There is also the *kappa*, which is a smaller water spirit that inhabits lakes and rivers. One of the most well known of the Japanese sea creature is known as *Amabie*, which was first documented in 1846 and has been described as being green, with fins and, unusually, three legs and a beak. The first man to see Amabie reported that the creature told him that Japan would be blessed with a good harvest, and that a pandemic would arrive in

Japan. The only way to stop the pandemic, according to the creature, was to draw an image of it and share it with as many people as possible. After the woodblock print was included in the local paper, the pandemic did not arrive. Interestingly, belief in Amabie has resurfaced in 2020 thanks to the Covid-19 pandemic. As of this writing, Japanese people are resharing images of Amabie, producing products like face masks and sushi with her likeness, painting her image on vehicles, and dressing up their pets as Amabie.

Japanese mermaids may have originally come from China as a great many cultural traditions in Japan arrived by way of Chinese migrants starting in the fifth century BCE; the creatures in both countries are said to cry tears of pearls. Mermaid sightings were once common in Japan—so common that fishermen often reported even catching mermaids. From the eighteenth century through the twentieth century, mermaid carcasses began appearing in Japanese sideshow carnivals—these were creatures made by fishermen of pieces of taxidermied monkeys and fish. A few still survive today, in museums and temples throughout Japan. One set of mermaid remains, which are said to date back to 1222, are held in a temple in Fukuoka.

Merpeople are also known in the Middle East, although here they do not look like fish; instead, they look like normal people who simply live under the water. The story "Abdullah the Fisherman and Abdullah the Merman," from *One Thousand and One Nights*, tells of a fisherman who accidentally caught a merman and then learns to breathe underwater from him. In the Slavic countries, mermaids per se do not exist; instead, *Rusalkas*, which are spirits of the dead who did not die peacefully, live in lakes and rivers.

Many African cultures have a long tradition of half-human, half-fish (or serpent) water spirits, such as Yamaya, the mother goddess of the ocean; Oshun, a goddess of freshwater rivers and lakes; and Mami Wata, a female water spirit that also migrated to the New World with African slaves. In fact, at the Cango Caves in the Klein Karoo region of South Africa, the rock paintings there (which are probably about 2,000 years old) appear to depict a number of creatures with a humanoid upper body and a fish lower body. This region of South Africa was once under the sea, so the people who painted them, the ancestors of the modern San people, would have lived in a very different environment from today, so it should not surprise us that these people would have seen, and depicted, sea creatures in their art.

Merfolk or related water creatures also were found in Polynesia, which makes sense given how important the ocean is to Polynesian people. For instance, the Cook Islands held a belief in Avatea, a half-man, half-fish, and Hawaii is home to water spirits known as *moʻo*. One Hawaiian folktale tells the story of a moʻo named Hina and her battle against her evil rival moʻo, Mokuna. Hina is also a popular figure in the folklore of New Zealand's indigenous people, the Maori. In one Maori tale, Hina is a beautiful woman (not a water spirit) who fell in love with a man she saw swimming in the ocean. Tuna, the man, told Hina that they could only meet at the beach and only at night. It turns out that Tuna was a moʻo during the day but at night he transformed into a human—an extremely popular motif found in similar tales around the world.

Merfolk can be seen wherever people have a deep reliance on the sea for their way of living.

In recent years, mermaid sightings have decreased as fishing as a lifestyle has become increasingly rare but there are plenty of documented sightings that go back centuries. Christopher Columbus, for example, saw three mermaids on Hispaniola (the Caribbean island that is occupied by the countries of Haiti and the Dominican Republic) in 1493 but was disappointed by their lack of beauty (he wrote that they had masculine faces). Captain John Smith (one of the founders of the first permanent English settlement in North America, Jamestown) saw a mermaid in 1614 and reported that her beauty was such that he began to fall in love with her. Other early reports involve either a live or dead capture, as in the 1737 capture of a dead merman in Spain or the 1775 capture of a dead mermaid in the Holy Land, which was then exhibited throughout Europe (and was probably made of, in part, a shark).

Some of the better-known cases include a group of Japanese soldiers stationed in Indonesia during the Second World War who often encountered merfolk. Called by the native Indonesians *Orang Ikan* (human-fish), these were not the beautiful mermaids of northern European lore. Instead, they were ugly creatures, described by one witness, a Sergeant Horiba, as follows: "Roughly 4-foot 9-inches tall, pinkish skin, human-looking face and limbs, spikes along its head, and a mouth like a carp."

A more stereotypically beautiful version of a mermaid was seen by a group of tourists on an island in British Columbia in 1967. One man, George Harrison of Sioux City, Iowa, even photographed the creature, and the *Daily Colonist*, the local paper, reprinted his photo the day after the sighting. The mermaid was topless and had long silver hair. A man named Charles White, who ran an ocean attraction called Undersea Gardens in Newport, Oregon, offered $25,000 to anyone who could capture the mermaid. White would have displayed her at his aquarium and discussed paying her a salary plus room and board. Mermaids have also been seen in recent years in Hawaii, when in 1998 a diver named Jeff Leicher photographed a mermaid, in Israel, where the government offered a million dollar reward for any documentation of the mermaid that had been seen by numerous people over several months in 2009 in the town of Kiryat Yam, and in Zimbabwe, where, in 2012, a group of workers building a dam were scared off the job site by a dead mermaid (known as *Njuzu*), which washed ashore at Lake Mutirikwi. Many African cultures have a long tradition of water spirits, such as Yamaya, the mother goddess of the ocean; Oshun, a goddess of freshwater rivers and lakes; and Mami Wata, a female water spirit that also migrated to the New World with African slaves.

In recent years, mermaids have been spotted throughout South Asia. In 2005, a dead mermaid washed up in Chennai, India (where they are called *Kadal Kanni*), after the Indian Ocean earthquake and tsunami. In 2014, a mermaid was spotted in Karachi, Pakistan (where they are called *Jalpari*), and then made its way to Porbandar, India.

Merfolk are extremely well represented in the popular culture of a variety of seafaring cultures. From folktales about merfolk to films, it is easy to find stories about merfolk (mostly mermaids) that are romantic, frightening, dramatic, or even comedic. Some of the most well-known films include *Aquaman* (the rare film about a merman), *Aquamarine, A Mermaid's Tale, Fishtales, Little Mermaid* (based on the 1837 fairy tale by Hans Christian Andersen), *Mermaids, Pirates of the Caribbean: On Stranger Tides, Scales, The Mermaid, The Secret of Roan Inish*, and *Splash*. Many of these films feature beautiful mermaids who fall in love with human men and who are forced to give up their "fish side" as a consequence of joining the world of humans (as in both *Splash* and *The Little Mermaid*).

One of the most interesting results of the popularity of the 1989 animated film, *The Little Mermaid*, is how it has spurred a strong interest in and identification with mermaids within the queer community. The fact that mermaids are hybrid creatures, halfway between fish and humans, resonates with many gays and lesbians but especially with trans people. (In addition, it is well known among the LGBTQ community that Hans Christian Andersen, the author of the original fairy tale on which the film was based, was gay and wrote the story after being rejected in love by another man.)

One of the most interesting films, or series of films, in recent years to feature merfolk were the Animal Planet mockumentaries *Mermaids: The Body Found* and its sequel, *Mermaids: The New Evidence*. Both films, which aired in 2012 and 2013, begin with the premise that mermaids are not only real, but that the United States National Oceanographic and Atmospheric Administration (NOAA) not only knows of their existence but also has been engaged in a massive coverup of the evidence. Even though Animal Planet included a small disclaimer at the end of both films, many people watching the shows thought that they were real. (The second film, *Mermaids: The New Evidence*, was, at the time, the highest watched show in Animal Planet's history.) After massive public outrage, NOAA ended up releasing a press release stating that mermaids are not real.

In fact, the idea of a mermaid marrying a human male is extremely popular in merfolk lore, especially in the British Isles and Iceland. These stories often involve a motif found in the tales of other hybrid humans: the mermaid is often held captive by the husband, who is able to control her as long as he has her (fish) skin. If she finds it, she will often swim away, abandoning him forever. These stories indicate that such marriages between man and mermaid are often not consensual. For instance, in the Irish tale, "The Lady of Gollerus," a man named Dick sees a mermaid and quickly decides he must have her:

> But what was his astonishment at beholding, just at the foot of that rock, a beautiful young creature combing her hair, which was of a sea-green color; and now the salt water shining on it, appeared, in the morning light, like melted butter upon cabbage.

> Dick guessed at once that she was a merrow, although he had never seen one before, for he spied the *cohuleen driuth*, or little enchanted cap, which the sea people use for diving down into the ocean, lying upon the strand near her; and he had heard that if once he could possess himself of the cap, she would lose the power of going away into the water; so he seized it with all speed, and she, hearing the noise, turned her head about as natural as any Christian.

When the merrow saw that her little diving cap was gone, the salt tears—doubly salt, no doubt, from her—came trickling down her cheeks, and she began a low mournful cry with just the tender voice of a newborn infant. Dick, although he knew well enough what she was crying for, determined to keep the cohuleen druith, let her cry never so much, to see what luck would come out of it. (Croker & Croker 1862: 3–13)

Dick is eventually able to stop the mermaid from crying, by assuring her that he will not eat her. Instead, he proposes to marry her. After they marry, she bears him three children, and one day she finds her enchanted cap and decides to return to the sea to visit her parents. Even though she only planned to visit for a short while, upon reaching the sea, she forgot all about her human family and never returned to the shore again.

While the above tale features a magical cap that binds the mermaid to her husband, in many other stories, especially when they feature selkies rather than mermaids, it is the wife's skin that keeps her human. In most cases, one of the children finds the skin, but occasionally, as in "The Lady of Gollerus," the wife herself finds it. In some versions of the tale, like "The Silkie Wife" from the Shetland Islands, it turns out that the mermaid or selkie was already married to one of her own kind in the sea, and she makes her escape in order to reunite with her first husband.

Could mermaids exist? The question applies to other sea creatures as well, as humans have never explored the vast majority of this planet's oceans, so it is possible that there are many varieties of unknown species living in the deep waters. According to ecologist Charles Paxton, there may be as many as fifty large ocean species that have not yet been discovered. On the other hand, it's likely that many reports are simply sightings of other water creatures like dolphins (known around the world) and manatees, also known as sea cows. Manatees are found in the Gulf of Mexico, the Caribbean, the Amazon basin, and West Africa. Christopher Columbus, for example, most likely saw manatees when he arrived in the West Indies, a species that would have been unknown to most Europeans at the time. (Dugongs, a close relative of the manatee that live in the Pacific and Indian oceans, are another creature for whom mermaids may be mistaken.)

Another hypothesis that has been put forth to demonstrate the existence of mermaids is the Aquatic Ape Hypothesis. This theory, developed by marine biologist Alister Hardy and popularized by writer Elaine Morgan, claims that humans evolved from a primate ancestor that was primarily aquatic. Because humans are hairless, have a layer of subcutaneous fat, and have webbed fingers (all of which are associated with marine mammals), this has led some to feel that humans must have had an aquatic past. Most scientists view this theory as pseudoscience, however.

Early European scientists considered mermaids to be real and worked on categorizing them into the various taxonomies of nature that were being developed in the seventeenth and eighteenth centuries. For instance, Linnaeus included mermaids in his groundbreaking *Systema Naturae* (1740) and classified mermaids as "paradoxa" along with other hybrids and unusual creatures like the satyr. Artedi, another eighteenth-century naturalist, considered mermaids to belong to the same family as whales. More recently, oceanographer Karl Banse published a facetious account of mermaid biology in the journal *Limnology and Oceanography* (1990). In it, Banse discusses the three varieties of merpeople (*Sirena sirena*, who live in the Mediterranean, *Sirena indica*, who live in the Caribbean, and *Sirena erythraea*, who live in the Red, Arabian, and Indonesian seas), the diet (human flesh), reproduction (one birth at a time), and what happened to them (they went extinct thanks to an explosion of the jellyfish population). It's notable that Banse chose *Sirena* as the order to which mermaids belong as the term comes from the Greek Siren and is the order to which manatees, dugongs, and the extinct Steller's sea cow belong.

There are, actually, real mermaids. Florida, in fact, has hosted a mermaid show at Weeki Wachee Springs State Park since 1947, where beautiful women in mermaid costumes perform for paying audiences. (They have an underwater breathing hose that allows them to remain underwater for their thirty-minute shows.) The current show at Weeki Wachee is a performance of *The Little Mermaid*. There have also been mermaid shows in Las Vegas, Great Falls, Montana, Myrtle Beach, South Carolina, Denver, Colorado, and Sacramento, California. Mermaids also perform at the Coney Island Mermaid Parade, an annual festival held on Coney Island every summer. In addition, besides the professional mermaids that work at the mermaid shows, there is now a worldwide community of amateur or hobby mermaids, which has emerged since the 1990s. These men and women make and wear often elaborate mermaid costumes, which they wear to swim, lounge, and attend mermaid conventions. These mermaids can be found around the world and have a surprisingly large presence in Israel.

See also: Feejee Mermaid, Siren

Further Reading:

Banse, K. (1990). Mermaids-their Biology, Culture. And demise 1. *Limnology and Oceanography*, 35(1), 148–53.

Christiansen, R. (Ed.). (1964). *Folktales of Norway*. University of Chicago Press.

Croker, T. C., & Croker, T. F. D. (1862). *Fairy Legends and Traditions of the South of Ireland*. William Tegg.

Curtin, J. (1895). *Tales of the Fairies and of the Ghost World: Collected from Oral Tradition in South-west Munster*. David Nutt in the Strand.

MOEHAU

Name: Moehau

Alternative Names: Maero, Matau, Tuuhourangi, Taongina, Moehau Man, Rapuwai

Related Cryptids: Bigfoot, Yowie

Location: Moehau mountain range on the Coromandel Peninsula of the North Island
Most Recent Documented Sighting: 1972

In the folklore and mythology of the Maori, the indigenous people of New Zealand, the moehau is a wild man that lives in the Moehau mountain range on the Coromandel Peninsula of the North Island. They once lived in other places as well, but this is the area most associated with the moehau, as both the mountain range and the range's highest peak share the creature's name.

They are described as man-beasts, which are neither fully human nor fully animal. They are tall and covered in hair, with a simian face. They are aggressive and will kill and eat both animals and people. Like wild men or ape-men in other places, they will throw rocks at people to make them leave their presence. They have long fingers ending in long claws, but they are also thought to use stone tools.

The moehau is just one of a number of supernatural figures, or iwi-atua, in Maori. These creatures or spirits live in the forests and are referred to by different names throughout the islands, although there is, as with other creatures in other places, some confusion over whether these are really the same creature or different creatures altogether. For instance, the Maeroero is either a hairy wild man or ape-man, or sometimes it is described as something akin to a fairy. In a collection of Maori folktales from 1918, comes a story about the Maeroero:

> The Maeroero which lived in the Owaka forest was a fearsome creature. Two knobs in the Ratanui Range are called Puku and Miki after two sisters who were married to Te Waka-tau-puka, an uncle of Tu-hawaiki (and incidentally an uncle of the narrator also). One of these women wandered into the bush where she killed a *kakaruai* (robin), and the Maeroero pounced out and carried her and the dead bird away. She came back about a week later but was unable to relate her experiences owing to fright and collapse. Her friends made an *umu* (oven) and covered it with clay upon which the woman was laid. This act of *tao-whakamoe* was done to remove the spell and avert evil. It shifted the *tapu* off her and made her an ordinary woman again. (Beatie 1918)

With the settlement of New Zealand by Europeans in the nineteenth century, settlers began hearing stories about Maori gods and other supernatural beings, including the moehau. It was not too long before those same settlers were reporting their own sightings and blaming the moehau for unexplained killings.

Other than witness sightings, there are a number of cases of animal and human deaths that have been linked to the moehau, including two human victims, a man and a woman, killed in 1882. In addition, footprints—of which there are many—form another important source of information about the moehau. The first recorded set of enormous footprints was discovered in 1903 in the Karangahake Gorge.

What are people seeing when they have an encounter with a moehau?

Could a population of orangutans have sailed or swam from Indonesia to New Zealand and then evolved there into a new species? While even crazier things have happened—the ancestors of New World monkeys, for example, are understood to have sailed on natural rafts from Africa all the way to South America some 40 million years ago.

Another story, not necessarily any more credible, is that a ship carrying a gorilla was moored off the coast in 1924 and the gorilla escaped.

What makes the existence of the moehau as a flesh-and-blood animal unlikely is the fact that New Zealand, like Australia, has no endemic land mammals, much less any primates, so there are no actual animals that could be mistaken for the moehau.

After the 1920s, sightings of the moehau dropped to almost nothing. The 1950s had one sighting, which was covered in the *Taranaki Daily News* on February 5, 1952. The article opened like this:

Persistent reports from Coromandel Peninsula say that a strange hairy creature thought by some to be a gorilla lurks at the back of the Waiaro, in the wild bush country of the Moehau Range. When Dr. Roy Norman of Waikawau, and Mr. Douglas Taiwahana of North Auckland, were pig hunting in the area, they said they caught a fleeting glimpse of a hairy man or possible a gorilla running along a bush track. Mr. F. W. Wenzlick of Amadeo Bay, said tonight that about 30 years ago a ship was lying off Waiaro Bay which had a young gorilla as mascot. The animal left the ship and got ashore. (1952)

This marks the first time that the "escaped gorilla" would show up in print, forming a part of the legend of the moehau. Mr. F. W. Wenzlick, the source of the gorilla story, was known to be a prankster and a storyteller, so the entire story could have been made up by Wenzlick. The reporter also interviewed the director of the Auckland Zoo, Robert Roach, who pointed out that an escaped gorilla living in New Zealand was highly unlikely, although he did suggest that a better possibility might be a baboon. Roach pointed out, however, that great apes and monkeys make their nests in trees, and not in caves, like some have suggested for the moehau.

There were two known moehau sightings in the 1960s and 1970s, the era when Bigfoot became an international celebrity. While it is difficult to know whether or how much Bigfoot might have influenced the later sightings, it seems clear that whatever the Maori moehau was, it is most likely a very different creature today. Bigfoot lore has crept into New Zealand and, like it has in so many places around the world, inserted itself into moehau lore.

As with other creatures around the world, there are far fewer sightings of the moehau today. It may be that these mythic and folkloric creatures cannot survive in modern society. One thing that does tend to ensure a creature's survival is becoming incorporated into cryptozoology; the more that a creature is embraced by the cryptozoological community, the longer a life it seems to have. On the other hand, once a creature gains the attention of outside experts or hunters, then it begins to lose its connections to the original myths that created it.

But the reason that the moehau, like so many similar creatures, seems to have disappeared, could be very simple. New Zealand was, before the people who would become the Maori arrived in the fourteenth century, almost completely covered in forest. The Maori cut down or burned down about half of the forest, and with the arrival of Europeans, the forest cover was halved again. Today, less than a quarter of New Zealand's ancient forests remain, which means that the moehau has far less habitat than it used to.

See also: Bigfoot, Yowie

Further reading:

Beattie, H. (1918). Traditions and Legends Collected from the Natives of Murihiku. (Southland, New Zealand.) Part XI. *The Journal of the Polynesian Society*, 27(3), 107.
Cowan, J. (1925). *Fairy Folk Tales of the Maori*. Whitcombe & Tombs Limited.
McCoy, N. (2005). *New Zealand Mysteries: Secrets, Spooks, Conspiracies and con Artists*. Whitcouls.
Strange Hairy Creature Reported on the East Coast Believed by Some to be a Gorilla (1952). *The Taranaki Daily News*, February 5, Press Assoc. Auckland, NZ.

MOHA MOHA

Name: Moha Moha

Alternative Names: Moha Moha of Sandy Cape

Related Cryptids: Mapinguary

Location: Great Barrier Reef off of coast of Queensland

Most Recent Documented Sighting: 1964

The moha moha is a sea creature that lives in the Great Barrier Reef off the coast of Queensland, Australia. It is sometimes called the Moha Moha of Sandy Cape, because most of the sightings have been on or near the Sandy Cape and what used to be called Great Sandy Island (now Fraser Island).

It has been described as both a sea serpent with the classic Plesiosaur form (long serpentine neck, dome-shaped back, small head), but it has also been described as a turtle or something with a hard shell. It has short, stumpy legs like those of a crocodile.

It is often repeated that Captain James Cook described a moha moha, or a similar creature, circling the *HMS Endeavor* while on his first journey to Australia in May 1770, but there seems to be no evidence of this. Joseph Banks, a naturalist aboard the *Endeavor*, did write in his journal on May 20, 1770, of a grampus (which may have referred either to a dolphin or whale), but that animal was known at the time, and Banks mentioned it by name. It is this grampus sighting that is cited by cryptozoologists as the first report of a moha moha, even though it is clear that Banks was describing a known animal rather than a monster.

It would not be for another 120 years that the idea of a monster living off of the Queensland coast was first reported. A teacher and naturalist named Shirley Lovell, living on Great Sandy Island near Sandy Bay, was walking on the beach with some companions when she saw a large sea serpent, which she identified as a moha moha, based on what she knew about a monster known by the local populations.

After her sighting, Lovell began a correspondence with William Saville-Kent, the assistant curator at the Natural History Museum in London, who was writing a book on the ecology of the Great Barrier Reef. She ended up sending him a package with testimony from the other witnesses who were on the beach that day, a very detailed description of what she saw, and some sketches of the monster, and signed it on behalf of the other witnesses who said they saw the monster that day.

Saville-Kent's discussion of Lovell's sighting was printed in the *Maryborough Chronicle* in 1894 and not just included Lovell's description but also referenced the Butchulla people, the traditional owners of Fraser Island (known to the Butchulla as K'gari). The article was largely tongue in cheek, referring to "the sea serpent tribe" and discussing the creature's potential use in turtle soup. Saville-Kent also came up with a cheeky binomial name for the moha moha:

> With reference to its obviously-combined chelonian and saurian peculiarities (cf. infra), coupled with a fitting acknowledgment of its discoverer, it is here distinguished as the Great Barrier sea-serpent, Chelosauria Lovelli [turtle dinosaur discovered by Lovell].

Saville-Kent writes:

> As related by Miss Lovell, the Moha-Moha, according to the natives, possesses feet like an alligator, and is, in such cases, referable to the tortoise and terrapin, and not to the turtle, section of the chalonians. The mouth armature, represented in Miss Lovell's sketch by distinct dentition, is, moreover, remarkably saurian in the aspect. The one anomaly in the sea-serpent's morphology is its tail, which is delineated as distinctly forked, and with bony rays, as in an ordinary fish.

Lovell herself said this:

> I was while walking on the Sandy Island beach admiring the stillness of the sea, it being a dead calm, when my eye caught sight of the head and neck of a creature I had never seen before. I went to the edge of the water and saw a huge animal, lying at full length, which was not at all disturbed by my close proximity to it, enabling me to observe the glossy skin of the head and neck, smooth and shiny as satin. Its great mouth was wide open all the time it was out of the water. In about a quarter of an hour or so it put its head and neck slowly into the sea closing its jaws as it did so. I then saw what a long neck it had, as it moved round in a half circle, and also perceived that the head and neck were moving under a carapace. When

the head was pointing out to sea it rose up, putting a long wedge-shaped fish-like tail out of the water over the dry shore, parallel to myself, and not more than five feet from me, not touching the sand, but elevated. I could have stood under the flukes of its tail.

. . . the great dome shaped carapace, dull slate-grey, was standing quite five feet high, and so hid its long neck and head from my view, which before it rose I could see as a long shadow in the water. The carapace was smooth and without marks of any sort.

The fish-like part of the tail was as glossy and shiny as the head and neck, but of a beautiful silver-grey, shading to white, with either markings or large scales, each bordered with a ridge of white, but if scales, not like those of a fish in position, as the fishes' scales lie horizontally, whilst the Moha's, if scales, lie perpendicularly, each the size of a man's thumbnail. It had a thick fleshy fin near the end about three feet from the flukes and like them, chocolate-brown. The flukes were semi-transparent—I could see the sun shine through them, showing all the bones very forked. One of the girls asked me if a shark had bitten a piece out of its tail, and the other one wanted to know if I thought it was an alligator. The fish-like part was quite twelve feet long. (1893: 2–3)

Lovell also says that there had been, prior to her sighting, nine separate events where someone else had seen the creature, including someone who she called "the black-boy" who saw it a week before she did. Two months later, in June 1891, she saw it again. Lovell received a lot of ridicule for her claims, not only from mainstream scientists like William Saville-Kent but also from cryptozoologists like Bernard Heuvelmans who dismissed Lovell and the moha moha as works of fiction.

The next documented sighting would not occur for decades; it was in 1964 that a fisherman named Jacob Lack found the badly decomposed carcass of what ended up being described as the moha moha. A story about the discovery, accompanied by photos and a sketch of the creature, was published in Brisbane's *Courier Mail* on March 8, 1964.

What is, or was, the moha moha? As with most cryptids, a variety of explanations have been offered, some mundane and some quite fabulous, for the sightings. It could be a giant sea turtle or a giant fish. Perhaps it was a turtle caught up with detritus from the sea, which made it look like a combination turtle and plesiosaur; botanist Robert France has suggested that this explanation may cover lots of sea serpent sightings around the world.

See also: Mapinguary

Further Reading:

France, R. L. (2016). Historicity of sea Turtles Misidentified as sea Monsters: A Case for the Early Entanglement of Marine Chelonians in pre-plastic Fishing Nets and Maritime Debris. *Coriolis: Interdisciplinary Journal of Maritime Studies*, 6, 1–24.

France, R. L. (2017). *Imaginary Sea Monsters and Real Environmental Threats from International Review of Environmental History* (Vol. 3). Edited by James Beattie. Canberra: The Australian National University, Australia retrieved from ANU press on the June 24, 2019.

Heuvelmans, B. (1968). *In the Wake of the Sea-Serpents*; trans. Richard Garnett. Hill & Wang.

Saville-Kent, W. (1893). *The Great Barrier Reef of Australia*. W. H. Allen & Co..

The Moha-Moha (Chelo-Sauria Lovelli). A Sandy Cape Curiosity (1894). Maryborough Chronicle, September 22, 2–3.

MOKELE-MBEMBE

Name: Mokele-mbembe

Alternative Names: Sanki, *'mbulu-em'bembe* or *m'kuoo-m'bemboo*

Related Cryptids: Mamlambo

Location: Congo River Basin, Republic of Congo, Zimbabwe, and Cameroon

Most Recent Documented Sighting: Unknown

The Mokele-mbembe is a sauropod dinosaur that is thought to live in the Congo River Basin in Central Africa. In particular, it has been identified by cryptozoologists as being most likely to belong to the Apatosaurus genus.

Sauropods are one of the most well-known dinosaur groupings; next to the iconic Tyrannosaurus Rex, the Sauropod—with its enormous body, long slender neck, and tiny head—is the dinosaur that most children think of when they think of dinosaurs. Sauropods were among the most widespread of all dinosaurs in terms of distribution; fossil sauropods have been found on every continent—including Antarctica. Sauropod dinosaurs—like all terrestrial and amphibious dinosaurs—went extinct about 65 million years ago, but many cryptozoologists feel that some have survived into the present era.

The term "mokele-mbembe" is a Lingala word that means "one who stops the flow of rivers," which refers both to the habitat and its enormous size. And while the creature has been known to local people for some unknown amount of time, it was not until 1909 that the rest of the world heard about it, when animal collector and big game hunter Carl Hagenbeck described it in his autobiography. He wrote:

Some years ago I received reports from two quite distinct sources of the existence of an immense and wholly unknown animal said to inhabit the interior of Rhodesia . . . The natives it seemed had told both my informants that in the depth of the great swamps there dwelt a huge monster, half elephant, half dragon . . . this however is not the only evidence for the existence of the animal it is now several decades ago since [naturalist Joseph] Menges who is of course perfectly reliable, heard a precisely similar story from the Negroes and still more remarkable on the walls of certain caverns in central Africa there are to be

Figure 6 *Parting the river, mokele-mbembe bathes. Copyright © 2023 Heidi Scheidl. All rights reserved.*

found actual drawings of the strange creature. From what I have heard of the animal it seems to me that it can only be some kind of dinosaur seemingly akin to the brontosaurus. (1909: 96)

While Hagenbeck never saw the creature, and only heard of it through secondhand stories, his description—and in particular, the comparison to a Brontosaurus, which by this time was already the archetypal sauropod—would shape our understanding of the Mokele-mbembe for over a century to come.

The earliest possible written account comes from the late eighteenth century, from French missionary Liévin-Bonaventure Proyart, in his *Histoire de Loango, Kakongo et Autres Royaumes d'Afrique*. His account, which like all other European accounts is second- or thirdhand, tells of a monstrous animal:

> the marks of the claws were noted on the ground, and these formed a print about three feet in circumference. The arrangement of the impressions indicated that the animal was walking, not running; the distance between the footprints measured seven to eight feet. (1776)

Sauropod fossils had been collected by amateur naturalists for hundreds of years, but it was only in the nineteenth century that they were identified as belonging to a group of extinct reptile species. By the time that Hagenbeck was in Africa (he was in Zimbabwe at the time, which was then called Rhodesia), the sauropod was well known among scientists and the scientifically literate and provided the perfect template in which to place indigenous stories of the great monster.

The mokele-mbembe is a good example of the colonial, or neocolonial, nature of cryptozoology. While cryptozoologists eagerly collect the stories and myths about legendary creatures from indigenous people, it is only the actual "discovery" of such a creature by a Western cryptozoologist that matters. If and when a Western scientist can prove the existence of the mokele-mbembe, it will confirm what many people already think of Africa—a primitive, backward continent where prehistoric creatures still roam.

If there is no extant species of dinosaur living in the Congo basin, then what could the witness reports be describing? Some people may have seen a black rhinoceros, which used to live in the area and is critically endangered. Early descriptions of the creature noted either a single, large tooth or some kind of horn or spines, making the rhino a good candidate for the creature. If the rhino is the source for at least some of the sightings, it explains why some locals have told cryptozoologists that they think the monster is now dead. The African softshell turtle, which is thought to reach 15 feet in length and has an unusually long neck, has also been offered as a possible species that has been misidentified.

After the German defeat in the First World War, Cameroon was taken from Germany and given to the British and the French. Shortly afterward, French linguistic anthropologist Pierre Alexandre attempted to discover the roots of the word mokele-mbembe and was told by at least some of his informants that it was a giant crocodile. A couple of decades later, in 1959, a chief described the creature as a water elephant, and it has since been suggested that an elephant swimming with its trunk lifted out of the water may look like a sauropod.

The mokele-mbembe has been the subject of a number of international expeditions and one formed by Congolese biologist Marcellin Agnagna in 1983, led by cryptozoologists, documentary film crews, and others with an interest in so-called living dinosaurs. The first of these expeditions was in 1913 and was led by Germans explorers and military men, as at that time the region of the Congo was a colonial possession of Germany. The 1913 Likuala-Kongo

Expedition, like all of those that would follow, was hampered by war as well as the difficulties of making such a journey.

Over the next few decades, further reports would come out of Africa about giant lake or swamp creatures, including from areas well outside of the Congo River Basin, indicating that either the creature had expanded its territory or else there were other mysterious giant animals hiding in other parts of Africa.

Other than witness sightings, there is very little physical evidence to support the claims of mokele-mbembe believers. There have been some inconclusive photos, a number of footprints and scratch marks, an unusual audio recording made by Herman Regusters, and, in 1959, a mokele-mbembe was allegedly killed and eaten by some Bangombe men at Lake Tele in Congo. By the time that news of the encounter got out, all of the men involved had supposedly died. A man named Mateka Pascal, who heard the story of the killing, told the story this way:

> After the animal had entered the lake, the pygmies blocked off its waterway by constructing a barricade of large stakes across it. When the mokele-mbembe tried to return to its moliba [waterway], it was trapped by the barricade and killed with spears. Some of the stakes used to construct the trap were large tree trunks, and are still there. The pygmies cut up the animal and ate it. All who ate of it died. (Powell 1981)

As with so many mokele-mbembe stories, there is a great deal of confusion around this one; some think that the story actually happened in the 1930s, not the 1950s, and involved two creatures rather than one.

The mokele-mbembe is, like all sauropods, an herbivore, but that does not mean that it does not incite fear; it is thought that while it won't eat a person, it can trample them to death. There are multiple accounts told by expedition guides, explorers, and other Europeans of the native "superstitions" regarding the creature; one such belief is that to talk about the monster is bad luck and could even bring death. Certainly the story about the pygmy hunters dying after eating a mokele-mbembe would serve as a warning to not eat the creature.

In the late twentieth century, cryptozoologists with an interest in the mokele-mbembe were joined by Young Earth Creationists, who believe that finding a living dinosaur, or "neodinosaur," like the mokele-mbembe or the Loch Ness Monster will disprove evolution, show that dinosaurs and humans lived at the same time, and demonstrate that the earth is just a few thousand years old. For instance, cryptozoologist and Young Earth Creationist Roy Mackel has suggested that the mokele-mbembe is actually the Behemoth from the Book of Job. In addition, some cryptozoologists are followers of the theory, first put forth by German archaeologist Robert Koldewey in 1918, that the sirrush or mushussu, the legendary dragon-like creature from Babylon, was a living dinosaur—and for some, that dinosaur is the mokele-mbembe.

See also: Loch Ness Monster

Further Reading:

Emmer, R. (2010). *Mokele-mbembe: Fact or Fiction?* Infobase Publishing.

Guimont, E. (2019). Hunting Dinosaurs in Central Africa. *Contingent Magazine*.

Loxton, D. (2012). Mokele Mbembe! *Skeptic (Altadena, CA)*, 17(3), 65A.

Mackal, R. P. (1987). *A Living Dinosaur?: In Search of Mokele-Mbembe*. Brill Archive.

Nugent, R. (2016). *Drums Along the Congo: On the Trail of Mokele-Mbembe, the Last Living Dinosaur*. Open Road Media.

Powell, J. (1981). On the Trail of the Mokele-Mbembe: A Zoological Mystery. *Explorers Journal*, 59(2), 84–90.

Proyart, L. B. (1776). *Histoire de Loango, Kakongo, et autres royaumes d'Afrique: rédigée d'après le mémoires des préfets apostoliques de la mission françoise; enrichie d'une carte utile aux navigateurs: dédiée a Monsieur.* éditeur non Identifié.

Regusters, H. A. (1982). *Mokele-Mbembe: An Investigation into Rumors Concerning a Strange Animal in the Republic of the Congo, 1981*. Munger Africana Library Notes, Issue 64. https://authors.library.caltech.edu /25708/1/MALN_64.pdf.

MONGOLIAN DEATH WORM

Name: Mongolian Death Worm

Alternative Names: Olgoï-Khorkhoï, Allghoi Khorkhoi, Allergorhai Horhai

Related Cryptids: Colovia, Lagarfljót Worm, Minhocão, Tatzelwurm

Location: Mongolia

Most Recent Documented Sighting: Unknown

The Mongolian Death Worm is a creature that lives underneath the sands of the Gobi Desert, a vast desert made up of over a half million square miles in southern Mongolia and northern China. It is not well known outside of Mongolia, probably because so few tourists travel to the region. Unlike most cryptids, the Mongolian Death Worm has never been photographed or filmed. In addition, no remains have ever been found.

According to the Mongol herders who travel with their animals through the Gobi Desert, the worm is able to kill both animals and people by spitting yellow venom or acid from their mouth. Some stories also claim that they can spit electricity—enough to kill a cow or a man. In addition, some people claim that one can die simply by touching it or by walking over the ground under which it lies. According to cryptozoologist Ivan Meckerle, who organized three expeditions to Mongolia to find the worm, it does not produce its own venom. Instead, Meckerle offered the theory that the venom comes from the animal eating the red goyo plant (*Cynomorium songaricum*), a plant with a wide variety of medicinal benefits. While there are rumors of deaths resulting from the worm, there is no documented record of an attack on a person.

In many ways, descriptions of the Mongolian Death Worm recall descriptions of the ancient mythical worm, the Indus Worm. Described by the Greek physician and writer Ctesias as a 10-feet-long worm that lived in the mud along the banks of the Indus River, the worm emerged from the mud at night when it would stalk and kill large animals like horses, cows, and camels. It was described by another Greek writer, Philostratus, as being white. Most intriguingly, the Indus Worm produced a flammable oil, which could be used to set whole cities on fire. It is unknown whether reports of the Indus Worm would have ever made it as far as Mongolia.

Called *Olgoï-Khorkhoï* in the Mongolian language, which means "large intestine worm," the worm is blood red, with a segmented body like other worms, a huge open beak full of sharp teeth, and ranges from 1 to 3 feet in length. Like other animals with neither arms nor legs, the worm moves by sliding back and forth with their body. One local legend says that the worm lays its eggs in the intestines of camels, giving the worm its distinctive red color.

Even though it looks like an intestinal worm, the Mongolian Death Worm is probably no worm. Most worms need moist conditions and could not survive in the dry environment of the Gobi Desert (however, two recently discovered species of worms that do live in the Gobi Desert, *Eisenia nordenskioldi mongol* and *Eisenia nordenskioldi onon*, are examples of worms that can tolerate dry and hot conditions). It may be a snake—perhaps a type of boa constrictor known as *Eryx tataricus*, or tartar sand boas (although these snakes do not live in this area). Another possibility is that it is an unknown type of *amphisbaenia*, or a legless lizard. Unlike snakes, amphisbaenia (or worm lizards) are segmented, so they look much more like the death worm. They are also built for burrowing into the sand. Other candidates for the worm include those species of snakes that live in the desert, including two species of pit viper, both of which are venomous (and one, the Central Asian Pit Viper, *Gloydius intermedius*, can sometimes appear red). And while no worm or snake is known to spit electricity at its victims, an animal moving through the desert sand can certainly produce a charge of electricity.

Giant worms do exist. In fact, the largest known earthworm is *Microchaetus rappi*, or the African giant earthworm, which ranges from 4.5 feet in length to an astonishing 22 feet. No such worms are known to live in this part of the world, however. The nearest giant worm to the Gobi Desert is *Amynthas mekongianus*, also known as the Mekong giant earthworm. This worm is found in Southeast Asia in the vicinity of the Mekong River and can reach 10 feet in length.

It is thought that Mongolian Death Worms live underneath the sand of the Gobi Desert, only coming to the surface during the hottest months of June and July; they hibernate for the rest of the year. They are attracted to the color yellow. Much of their diet is made up of the small mammals called jerboa that live there, but occasionally they may kill much larger prey, such as camels, cattle, or people.

The first written description of the worm was in 1922 when the prime minister of Mongolia, Sodnomyn Damdinbazar, described it to naturalist Roy Chapman Andrews (and reportedly asked Andrews to find it) who was in Mongolia to search for dinosaur fossils. Andrews wrote up his account of that trip first in a 1922 article in *Asia Magazine* and later in his 1926 book, *On the Trail of Ancient Man: A Narrative of the Field Work of the Central Asiatic Expeditions*. Andrews's work was the first time that the Mongolian Death Worm was described in English: "It is shaped like a sausage about two feet long, has no head nor legs and is so poisonous that merely to touch it means instant death." After finding no evidence of the creature, Andrews wrote:

> If the faith in its existence was not so strong and widespread among the Mongolians and if everyone did not describe the animal exactly the same way, I would believe it to be an idle myth. I hope the next explorers have better luck then we had.

Czech cryptozoologist Ivan Mackerle is the next Westerner to demonstrate an interest in the Mongolian Death Worm, traveling to Mongolia in 1990 (and again in 1992 and 2004) to find evidence of its existence after hearing a story from a Mongolian student. (He had to wait until 1990 and the fall of Communism for his first trip as the communist Mongolian government rarely allowed outside researchers into the area.) After breaking down the resistance to answering his questions with alcohol, Mackerle was able to elicit some stories about the worm:

> We were told it has a dark-red color, like blood or salami and that it is difficult to tell its head from its tail because it has no visible eyes, nostrils or mouth. The creature also moves in odd ways, either it rolls around or it squirms sideways, sweeping its way about.

Mackerle also gathered one of the only stories of a human death attributed to the worm, triggered by the creature's interest in the color yellow:

> The story of a yellow box having enticed the evil worm right inside a yurta. A little boy was playing in the yurta, and he went into his yellow box to pull out a toy. But he touched the worm, hidden inside, and he was killed on the spot. When the parents returned, all they saw was the wavy trail from the yurta. They realised what had happened and followed that trail in order to avenge their little son, but the Allghoi khorkhoi killed them too.

He published his accounts of his journeys in 1992 and 1993, but it was not until the first English translation of one of his articles appeared in 1992 that much of the Western world first found out about the Mongolian Death Worm. In fact, other than the brief description of the worm by Andrews in 1922, virtually every single report on the worm's existence, appearance, or behavior comes from Mackerle's work, at least until the 2005 Center for Fortean Zoology team's trip to Mongolia.

On his second trip, Mackerle reported that he was told by a shaman that the creature is supernatural. The shaman called it the Demon of the Desert and counseled Mackerle to stay away; he received similar advice from a Buddhist monk. Ultimately, Mackerle, who created a device, inspired by the 1984 film *Dune*, that would thump the sand to draw the worm out, never found any evidence of the creature and concluded that it was a myth. (One of the problems that Mackerle encountered was that people were afraid to talk to him about the monster, for fear that just mentioning its name could bring evil on them.)

Additional teams of cryptozoologists have since visited Mongolia in order to find the worm. Cryptozoologist Richard Freeman of the Center for Fortean Zoology led one such team in 2005.

They spent four weeks in the desert, looking for evidence of the worm's existence as well as collecting witness reports. As was the case with the Mackerle expeditions, as well as Andrews's trip in 1922, all of the witness statements collected by this group were second- or third-hand reports. Freeman concluded that the animal is most likely a skink. The most recent expedition to hunt for the Mongolian Death Worm was led by a journalist named David Ferrier in 2009, but this trip, again, ended with no sighting or proof.

Whether worm, lizard, or snake, the fears surrounding the Mongolian Death Worm can be related to attitudes and beliefs about these types of animals.

Worms, for example, are not just associated with the earth but also with death and decomposition, as their presence in the soil has long been known to hasten the decomposition of corpses. The term "worm" has also often been used to refer to serpents with no limbs and no wings, so stories about great worms are often actually tales of dragons.

Snakes are also animals to be feared in much of the world. People are afraid of and fascinated by snakes—even nonhuman primates share this same fear, making it one of the near-universals of our kind. Snakes have a variety of characteristics that make them important animals in folklore and myth: their sudden, odd movements, their flickering tongue, the fixed eyes, their violent way of feeding themselves, and so on. All of these physical and behavioral characteristics add up to making the snake one of the most feared, but also revered, animals on the planet.

Because snakes shed their skin, they are associated with rebirth, and their skins are often seen to have their own power. Many of the ancient Mesoamerican religions revered the snake, and the gods Coatlicue, Tlaloc, Quetzalcoatl, and Q'uq'umatz were linked to snakes in imagery. Many Native American tribes also had snake gods or goddesses, such as Situlili (for the Hopi and Zuni), Unktehi (for the Lakota), and Awanyu (for the Pueblo). In China, snakes, sometimes known as "small dragons," were also revered. The mythological figures Fu Xi and Nü Wa were snake-human hybrids, and some of the ethnic tribes that live in the remote region of Fujian once wore snake tattoos as a sign of their importance. Mongolian mythology, too, has snake gods like Aq Yilan, the King of Snakes.

The Mongolian Death Worm, unlike better-known cryptids, is not well represented in popular culture. Perhaps it is because it is such a local creature and perhaps it is because it lives in a region of the world that is not regularly visited by tourists, but the worm has only been featured in a single film: *Mongolian Death Worm*, a science-fiction film released in 2010 and aired on the SyFy channel. The creatures in the *Tremors* series of movies, called Graboids, also resemble Mongolian Death Worms, and perhaps inspired the films, and the sandworms (known as *shai-hulud*) in *Dune* may have been inspired by the Mongolian Death Worm.

The Mongolian Death Worm is a small part of J. R. R. Tolkien's *The Hobbit* (1937). In the very first, unpublished manuscript draft, Bilbo demonstrates that he is brave enough to face down the dragon Smaug by announcing that he would walk to "the Great Desert of Gobi and fight the Wild Wire worms of the Chinese." It seems clear that the "wire worms" (which might mean "were-worms" or human-worm hybrids) "of the Chinese" must refer to the Mongolian Death Worm, given the reference to the Gobi Desert. In the published book, the phrase was changed; Bilbo said, "Tell me what you want done, and I will try it, if I have to walk from here to the East of East and fight the wild Were-worms in the Last Desert."

See also: Lagarfljót Worm, Tatzelwurm

Further Reading:

Andrews, R. C. (1926). *On the Trail of Ancient Man: A Narrative of the Field Work of the Central Asiatic Expeditions*. Putnam.
Chao, D. (1979). The Snake in Chinese Belief. *Folklore*, 90(2), 193–203.
Mackerle, I. (2001). *Mongolské Záhady [Mongolian Mystery]* (in Czech) (1st ed.). Ivo Železný.
McNamee, G. (Ed.). (2000). *The Serpent's Tale: Snakes in Folklore and Literature*. University of Georgia Press.
Sax, B. (2001). *The Mythical Zoo: An Encyclopedia of Animals in World Myth, Legend, and Literature*. Abc-Clio.
Shuker, K. (1996). *The Unexplained: An Illustrated Guide to the World's Natural and Paranormal Mysteries*. Barnes & Noble Books.

MOTHMAN

Name: Mothman

Alternative Names: Mason County Monster

Related Cryptids: Devil Bird, Flatwoods Monster, Thunderbird

Location: Point Pleasant, West Virginia

Most Recent Documented Sighting: 2016 (Point Pleasant); 2019 (Chicago)

The Mothman is a highly localized, quite unique cryptid. Found only in the vicinity of Point Pleasant, West Virginia, it nevertheless has an outsized reputation among cryptids, being one of the most well known of all such monsters internationally.

The Mothman is a large, black, humanoid creature with glowing red eyes and large wings. It does not actually look like a moth, and its wings are really the only insect-like feature of this creature.

Unlike many other cryptids, the Mothman's history is well documented, and we know the precise date when the creature was first seen. On November 12, 1966, five grave diggers in Clendenin, West Virginia (about an hour and a half from Point Pleasant), saw a large flying figure pass over them, followed in short order by another sighting just outside of Point Pleasant, at the West Virginia Ordnance Works, an abandoned munitions storage facility and military bunkers from the Second World War. This facility, surrounded by over 3,000 acres of forested land, known as the TNT area to locals, ended up being the site of a number of Mothman sightings, perhaps because of its out-of-the-way location and perhaps because young people from the area had long used the property as a Lovers Lane. In fact, it was two young married couples making out in the TNT area who saw the Mothman on the evening of November 15, 1966, and whose account of seeing this large black monster eating a dead German Shepherd would kick off the Mothman panic. The teenagers told the local police that after they saw it, it began chasing them, flying after their car as they drove away. This story was featured in the *Point Pleasant Register*, with the headline, "Man-Sized Bird . . . Creature . . . Something" (the account was also published in the *Columbus Dispatch* and the *Athens Register*), and from there, the sightings multiplied and the legend of the Mothman began to take shape.

One of the teenagers, Linda Scarberry, described what happened:

All at once [Steve Mallette] yelled for us to look at that thing in the road. I looked up and saw it go round the old Power house. It didn't run but wobbled like it couldn't keep its balance. Its wings were spread just a little. We sat there a few seconds then [Roger] took off. I kept yelling for him to hurry. We didn't even stop for the curves. We got out on Route 66 and was coming down the road and that thing was sitting on the second hill when you come into the 1st bad curves. As soon as our lights hit it, it was gone. It spread its wings a little and went straight up into the air. When we got to the armory, it was flying over our car. We were doing between 100 and 105 mph down that straight stretch and that thing was just gliding back and forth over the back end of the car . . . To me it just looks like a man with wings. It has a body shape form with (It was a dirty gray color) wings on its back that come around it. It has muscular legs like a man and fiery-red eyes that glow when the lights hit it . . . I couldn't see its head or arms. I don't know if the eyes are even in a head.

For the next few weeks, the TNT area saw hundreds of visitors who arrived at the spot to see if they could see the monster (known at this time as the Mason County Monster) for themselves. Over the next year, dozens more people reported seeing the creature, often while they were driving at night, and almost all of the reports were the same: a large, hulking, hairy black figure with glowing red eyes and bat-like wings. The creature's head, such as it was, sat right on the body, with no real neck and a steeply sloping forehead, which gave the monster a primitive appearance.

Just three days after the sighting at the TNT area, a wildlife biologist at West Virginia University, Robert Smith, suggested that the animal that the witnesses saw may have been a Greater Sandhill Crane. (Sandhill cranes can be as large as 5 feet tall with a wingspan over 6 feet, making them good candidates for such a large creature. In addition, cranes have a small area of red, featherless flesh around their eyes, which may explain the red eyes. Of course, some birds' eyes also glow red at night, a condition called eyeshine.) Over the years, other birds like Barn Owls, Barred Owls, or Great Horned Owls have been put forward as possible candidates for the creature (owls are good candidates because their heads seem to connect directly to their bodies), while Mason County Sheriff George Johnson thought that it might be a shitepoke, a type of heron. In fact, before the monster was given the name Mothman (which was a play on Batman, from the television show that started to air that year), some people described it as a large bird of some kind. In addition, the TNT area, which was the site of the most well-known encounter, is surrounded by the Clinton F. McClintic Wildlife Management Area, which is host to many species of animals, including a number of birds.

As more sightings were reported, the legend started to expand, as witnesses told of mysterious happenings either before or after seeing the Mothman. Typically, witnesses spoke of bad things happening after their encounter, leading to the idea that the appearance of the Mothman acts as a kind of omen, bringing bad luck or tragedy. Some people reported coming down with conjunctivitis or pink eye after seeing it. Others talked about other strange occurrences, such as mysterious hang-up calls or visits by "men in black." As time went on, the stories started to resemble each other more closely as witness accounts become colored by media stories.

But it was not until a year later, on December 15, 1967, that many people feel that the curse of the Mothman was realized. That day, the Silver Bridge, the main bridge over the Ohio River connecting Point Pleasant to Gallipolis, Ohio, collapsed during the evening rush hour, killing forty-six people and seriously injuring an additional nine. While structural engineers determined that the collapse was caused by a failed eyebar and the increasing weight of vehicles (when the bridge was built in 1928, the average vehicle weighed less than half of the average weight of a vehicle in 1967), many locals attributed the disaster to the presence of the Mothman in the previous months, solidifying the idea that the Mothman is an omen of ill fortune. In fact, some eyewitnesses actually saw it standing on one of the bridge towers. The collapse of the Silver Bridge marked the last time (for a while) that the Mothman was seen, but the legend did not end.

Once the link between the Mothman and tragedy was fixed in the minds of the public, thanks in no small part to Keel's book and movie, the Mothman began to appear at other natural or human-caused disasters. For instance, the Mothman was reportedly seen in 1986 in Chernobyl right before the nuclear disaster and in Moscow in 1999 just before a series of apartments was bombed by Chechen rebels, killing over 300. The monster was also seen in New York City just before the planes struck the towers on September 11, 2001.

The idea that the Mothman is a portent of doom is found in a handful of other cryptids as well, such as the Devil Bird, a Sri Lankan cryptid known locally a Ulama, whose shrieks indicate that something terrible will happen (like an Irish banshee). Even though the Mothman is not actually a moth, there is one way that the Mothman is connected with moths. In English folklore, a moth—especially a white moth—can either be a messenger of the dead or a warning of an imminent death. They may also be the embodiment of an ancestor. In fairy lore, moths are connected to witches, while the related, but more extravagant, butterfly is associated with fairies. It is also worth pointing out that Mothra, a Japanese kaiju, or monster, first appeared to American audiences in 1961, when the film *Mothra* was released and then in three more films before the first Mothman sighting.

The Mothman legend received a huge jump in publicity after ufologist John Keel wrote *The Mothman Prophecies* in 1975, which connected the Mothman sightings to UFOs and which was made into a film of the same name in 2002 starring Richard Gere and Debra Messing. Besides *The Mothman Prophecies*, the Mothman has been the subject of a number of documentaries and books. In addition, there is an entire cottage industry in Mothman merchandise: stuffed animals, clothing, figurines, and even scented candles.

There are even at least two songs about the Mothman. One is by the Paranormal Song Warrior (2011) and describes the creature like this: "well he's 7 feet tall with eyes of red." The song serves as a warning about the Mothman's prophetic qualities and points directly to the Silver Bridge collapse:

He tried to warn everybody yes he did
about how they were in danger from a broken bridge

The past few years have seen a resurgence of Mothman sightings but this time in Chicago, rather than West Virginia. Since 2011, a number of Chicagoans have reported seeing a large, human-size figure in the skies above the city. Dubbed the Chicago Mothman by local media, it has been described as black with huge wings and red glowing eyes. The creature was spotted over four dozen times in 2017 alone, the year with the most activity, but so far hasn't brought any terrible happenings to the city. The latest report of the Chicago Mothman dates to November 26, 2019, when a truck driver spotted a large upright bird person with outstretched wings at the O'Hare Airport. According to Manuel Navarette of the UFO Clearinghouse, the witness was from Mexico and recalled seeing a similar creature as a teenager. He told Navarette that this happened about a week before the 1985 Mexico City earthquake, which killed over 5,000 people.

That same week, the Mothman may have also returned to Point Pleasant. On November 20 of that year, a man photographed what looks to be a man with wings flying over State Route 2. Local television station WCHS included one of the pictures on the next day's news. Some skeptics have suggested that the photos are a hoax and were produced and released to coincide with the fiftieth anniversary of the original sightings.

Point Pleasant, like other towns with their own cryptid, has benefited from the presence of the Mothman. The town has an annual Mothman Festival, held every September (canceled for the first time in 2020 because of the Covid-19 pandemic), a Mothman Museum, and a life-size statue of the Mothman in the center of town.

The Mothman sightings happened during the height of the Cold War, during a period when Americans were nervous about nuclear technology, Russian spies, and the threat of war. This was also the Space Age, an era marked by its focus on technological progress and the space race; it would only be three more years before Americans sent a man to the moon. Science-fiction films that featured aliens from outer space and animals that were turned monstrous thanks to modern science were popular at the box office. This period was also known for the rapidly

Figure 7 *Returning home after a long night, Mothman ensures its surveillance cameras have not been disturbed. Copyright © 2023 Heidi Scheidl. All rights reserved.*

increasing numbers of UFO sightings; in fact, 1965, the year before the Mothman sightings began, saw more UFO reports than any year previous to that time.

It has been suggested that author and ufologist John Keel influenced the witness reports; it may be that his certainty that the Mothman was a type of "ultraterrestrial" (creatures from another dimension that can shapeshift and appear when they like) combined with his belief in and popularization of the concept of "men in black" (secret government agents involved in a UFO coverup or, as Keel saw them, ultraterrestrials themselves) shaped the discourse surrounding witness reports of the Mothman.

Ultimately, the Mothman's continued existence in legend and popular culture may come down to people's need to exercise some control over their lives and to explain away unfortunate events. Having a creature like the Mothman, to which one can ascribe some of the worst human disasters, allows us to make sense of the world around us, offering meaning when it seems like all there is is chaos.

See also: Flatwoods Monster

Further Reading:

Coleman, L. (2001). *Mothman and Other Curious Encounters*. Cosimo, Inc.
Keel, J. A. (2002). *The Mothman Prophecies*. Macmillan.
Laycock, J. (2008). Mothman: Monster, Disaster, and Community. *Fieldwork in Religion*, 3(1), 70.
Sergent, D., & Wamsley, J. (2002). *Mothman: The Facts Behind the Legend*. Marks Phillips Pub.

N

NAHUELITO

Name: Nahuelito
Alternative Names: Patagonian Plesiosaur
Related Cryptids: Loch Ness Monster
Location: Nahuel Huapi Lake, Argentina
Most Recent Documented Sighting: June 2022

The Nahuelito is a lake creature and the largest of South America's lake creatures. It lives in Nahuel Huapi Lake, a large glacial lake in Patagonia Argentina. It is also known as the Patagonian plesiosaur. The name Nahuelito means little jaguar or puma in the Mapuche language but was only given to the creature in the 1980s.

It (unlike a lot of other more well-known cryptids, Nahuelito is not gendered male or female) is typically described as being anywhere from 10 to 20 feet long, with two humps and the typical long neck associated with many sea serpents. It is dark, either a black or dark gray, or perhaps a dark green, and its skin is described as leathery.

As with so many other cryptids, it is reported in virtually every discussion of the Nahuelito that local people have told stories about the creature for thousands of years. Unfortunately this is probably not the case. While the Spanish first arrived in Argentina in the mid-sixteenth century, initially focusing their conquest on the capital of the Inca Empire, there are no accounts by any Spanish conquistador, missionary, or settler regarding the creature, even though the Spanish were well known for intensively documenting their excursions.

Supposedly legends about the creature were told prior to the Spanish conquest but the first report that we have comes from Dr. Clemente Onelli, director of the Buenos Aires Zoo, who did not himself see the creature but was allegedly informed of its existence by local people. We don't have another report until 1910, when another European, George Garrett, saw something that he described as about 20 feet long, rising about 6 feet out of the water. Garrett later said that he spoke to a number of residents of the lakeside town of San Carlos de Bariloche who told him that yes, such a creature exists, but no interviews—at least in English—have been conducted with local residents to confirm his account. (Allegedly an Argentinian newspaper conducted a survey of Bariloche residents and found that half believe that the Nahuelito exists, but this author has not been able to confirm that.) Garrett's story made it into print in 1921 when he was interviewed by the *Toronto Globe*, triggering a new wave of interest in Nahuelito and other lake monsters. In fact, it was right after Garrett's story, headlined "*Local man lays claim to having caught sight of gigantic plesiosaur*," emerged in the international press that the Buenos Aires Zoo sponsored the first organized expedition to find the creature.

It's not until 1897, at the tail end of the Victorian era, an era where interest in the paranormal, especially among the middle and upper classes, was at an all-time high. Spiritualism and magic were popular beliefs and practices during this era, and it shouldn't surprise us to learn that cryptozoology, although not yet a named science, began to emerge here. This was also the time of the amateur naturalist, as scientific disciplines like biology or zoology were not yet fully professionalized, so those with an interest in nature, and the funds to pursue such an interest, could develop a career as a naturalist. It was during this era that the modern understanding of the sea serpent was born.

Sea serpents like Nahuelito or the most famous of all sea serpents, the Loch Ness Monster or Nessie, began to appear in news stories throughout the nineteenth century, but those stories became more common as the century progressed. In particular, it was the discovery of the first *Plesiosaurus* fossils, found in England in 1821, combined with the publication of Darwin's *On The Origin of Species* in 1859, which together provided both the appearance of and explanation for the modern sea serpent. According to the most popular theory accounting for the existence of lake or ocean serpents, creatures like Nahuelito or Nessie are not new or undiscovered at all. Rather, they are evolutionary holdovers—members of the *Plesiosaurus* genus of dinosaurs whose members went extinct about 65 million years ago, but a handful survived and can be found in waterways around the world today. In fact, three plesiosaur skeletons were found in the years between 1998 and 2001 in northern Patagonia. (One problem with this theory is the fact that Nahuel Huapi Lake was formed only about 2½ million years ago, about 64 million years after the plesiosaurs went extinct.) This theory got a significant push after the publication of Arthur Conan Doyle's *The Lost World* in 1912. *The Lost World* tells the story of an expedition to South America where the explorers discover that prehistoric, long-extinct animals survived there. This would become a popular trope in science-fiction films and television shows starting in the 1950s and helps to support the theory that members of species that are long extinct can still be found today.

Another explanation for the existence of Nahuelito is that it is a genetic anomaly created by nuclear experiments gone awry in the 1950s on the island of Huemul in the middle of Lake Nahuel Huapi. In 1949, Argentinian president Juan Peron worked with a number of German scientists who emigrated to Argentina after the Second World War to develop a nuclear reactor, but by 1955, the project was shut down as a colossal and expensive failure. While this explanation recalls one of the most significant theories to account for the chupacabra, another Latin American cryptid, and indicates a deep distrust of the government, it doesn't make factual sense in this case given the timeline. Even if there were no sightings of the creature until the late nineteenth century, it is still much too early to fit the nuclear disaster theory.

Other explanations for the creature fall into the "misidentification" category. As with other lake creatures, it is easy to see a log or other natural debris and mistake it for a living animal. Nahuelito may be a submarine (another theory that reflects a distrust of the government and/or the military) or may even be sheep, pigs, deer, or otters swimming across the water.

The Mapuche are the indigenous people who live in south-central Chile and southwestern Argentina, and while there are no English-language records attesting to an ancient belief among the Mapuche in Nahuelito, the Mapuche's traditional religion, like that of many indigenous people, envisions a world in which humans and animals share both the living world and the supernatural world. In addition, snakes of all kinds figure prominently in Mapuche religion as well as in the beliefs of other South American groups. South America, and especially the Amazonian region, has 3,600 snake species with many over 6, 10, and even 17 feet long. It shouldn't surprise us that snakes would figure into the mythology and folklore of people in the area. The Mapuche creation myth includes a flood narrative, but unlike the Christian version, the Mapuche myth features two serpents, one that controls the land (Trentren Vilu) and the other that controls the water (Caicai Vilu); when the water serpent tried to take the land from the land serpent, the result was a great flood that wiped out much of humanity.

One mythic creature that is well represented in Mapuche myth is the colo colo, a rat-like creature that can drain the life force out of its human victims. The colo colo is said to have hatched from a snake egg, and some descriptions feature the body of a snake with the head of a rat. Finally, the peuchen is a shapeshifter that has a snake-like form but can transform into any other animal and can, like the colo colo, suck the life out of human or animal victims. Other than the connection with the serpent, there seems to be no evidence of Nahuelito existing as part of Mapuche beliefs.

A final Mapuche belief that may be connected to Nahuelito is the Cuero. The word itself means leather in Spanish (while the Mapuche call it Threquelhuecuvu, which means both leather/hide and bad spirit) and describes a creature that looks like a large cow hide and that lives in all bodies of water, with a preference for smaller lakes. This creature was first described by a European in the eighteenth century, and while it appeared very differently from the other mythic creatures, it behaved in a similar manner to the cola cola and the peuchen in that, using its mouth that sits underneath its body, it sucks the life out of its victims. Obviously, the best living candidate for the cuero is some type of ray, with its large, leather-like body with a mouth hidden underneath, although no ray lives in the waters of Patagonia.

After the 1922 press coverage incited international interest in the creature, no other sightings were reported until 1938, at a different (but nearby) lake, followed by a decades-long period with no sightings at all. The 1970s, when cryptozoology jumped into the popular culture, saw the next sightings, which led to the first time that the name Nahuelito was used by local reporter Carlos Bustos. Throughout the next decades, more sightings occurred, and the first photograph of the creature was published in the Diario Rio Negro in 1986, while the first purported video of Nahuelito was released in 1993. Unlike Nessie, which is regularly spotted by tourists and locals alike, Nahuelito only makes an appearance every couple of years, although one sighting, after being reported in the press, tends to generate additional clusters of sightings.

See also: Loch Ness Monster

Further Reading:

Coleman, L., & Huyghe, P. (2003). *The Field Guide to Lake Monsters, Sea Serpents and Other Mystery Denizens of the Deep*. Jeremy P. Tarcher/Putnam.

Gasparini, Z., Salgado, L., & Casadío, S. (2003). Maastrichtian Plesiosaurs from Northern Patagonia. *Cretaceous Research*, 24(2), 157–70.

Picasso, F., (1998). South American Monsters and Mystery Animals. *Strange Magazine*, 20(12), 28–35.

NANDI BEAR

Name: Nandi Bear

Alternative Names: Chemosit, Kerit, Koddoelo, Ngoloko, Duba, Nkampit

Related Cryptids: Beast of Exmoor

Locations: East Africa; specifically Kenya and Uganda

Most Recent Documented Sighting: 1998

The Nandi bear is a mysterious, dangerous animal from Swahili folklore, which is also considered to be a real animal. The Nandi bear was named by paleontologist Geoffrey Williams, the first European to encounter it, and the first to describe it. He named it after one of the indigenous groups in Kenya, the Nandi, and he called it a bear because he thought it looked like one, even though there are no bears known in Africa. The Nandi, however, call it a kerit, while other groups use the term chemosit.

The Nandi bear is large, about the size and shape of a lion, with a sloping back and high shoulders, and has long reddish or brown fur, a long snout, tiny ears, and no tail. The Nandi bear was usually seen walking on all fours, although some witnesses did report that they saw it standing on its hind legs. According to the tracks that have been left by the creature, it has five toes—like a bear, rather than a lion or a dog.

Other than witness sightings, beginning in 1905, and paw tracks, there have been a number of alleged Nandi bears that were shot, some of which were sent to museums, but none remain today, and the only photographs taken of one have been lost as well. The first one, described as a lynx-like creature was shot in 1936, with the skin and skull being sent to the British Museum; others were allegedly sent to other museums, but all have been lost. Some people also think that an animal living in a private menagerie in Yorkshire in the 1930s, described as looking like a cross between a hyena and a bear, was a Nandi bear but there is no way to know that today. There were no photos of this creature, unfortunately. The other major evidence for the beast was the remains of animals—or people—that it had killed. For instance, one report came in 1919 when a farmer found over four dozen goats and sheep, all with their brains ripped out of their heads. This is a typical report, triggered by the discovery of mutilated animal remains. The Nandi is also said to kill people; locals say that it does so by scalping them. The most significant of those was a six-year-old girl who was killed, and her head crushed in, in 1925.

The first recorded sighting came from Geoffrey Williams in 1905, who wrote the following about his encounter:

We had been camped . . . near the Mataye and were marching towards the Sirgoit Rock when we saw the beast . . . I saw a large animal sitting up on its haunches no more than 30 yards away. Its attitude was just that of a bear at the "Zoo" asking for buns, and I should say it must have been nearly 5 feet high . . . before we had time to do anything it dropped forward and shambled away towards the Sirgoit with what my cousin always describes as a sort of sideways canter. I snatched my rifle and took a snapshot at it as it was disappearing among the rocks, and, though I missed it, it stopped and turned its head round to look at us . . . In size it was, I should say, larger than the bear that lives in the pit at the "Zoo" and it was quite as heavily built. The fore quarters were very thickly furred, as were all four legs, but the hind quarters were comparatively speaking smooth or bare . . . the head was long and pointed and exactly like that of a bear . . . I have not a very clear recollection of the ears beyond the fact that they were small, and the tail, if any, was very small and practically unnoticeable. The color was dark. (Williams 1912)

Over the years, the sightings began to be less frequent; after the 1930s, they dropped significantly, and by the 1950s, there were only a few sightings per decade. The last known sighting was in 1998, by a couple who described it as an enormous, shaggy hyena.

There have been a number of interpretations for the Nandi bear. In the 1920s, Paleontologist Charles Andrews offered the idea that it may be a surviving member of the Chalicothere clade, a group of three-toed ungulates that went extinct approximately 12,000 years ago—which means that they lived alongside of humans. (Related living species include the rhinoceros, the horse, and the tapir.) A decade later, paleoanthropologist Louis Leakey said the same thing. The problem with the Chalicothere theory is that as far as we know, all members of this group were herbivores, while the Nandi bear is a vicious predator.

More recently, the consensus has been that the Nandi bear is simply a misidentified primate; there are twenty-three monkey species living in Kenya today, including the giant baboon, and while there are no apes living in East Africa, chimpanzees live just over the border in Tanzania, and fossil evidence shows that great apes had lived in the area about 8 million years ago.

The Nandi bear could also be a misidentified hyena; hyenas are common in East Africa, as are honey badgers, another animal that has been offered as a candidate for the bear. Hyenas, and the spotted hyena in particular, may be the best candidate for at least some of the sightings. Hyenas will often crush the skulls of their victims, which is how the Nandi bear kills. In addition, in 1960, the manager of a Kenyan tea plantation named Angus Hutton shot and killed a Nandi bear, which ended up in Nairobi's Coryndon Museum, where it was labeled "giant forest hyenas" before it eventually disappeared. But before it reached the museum, Hutton photographed the carcass and sent the slides, along with the skeleton, to Louis Leakey, who told Hutton that it was clearly a long-haired brown hyena, or what is called the brown hyena today. One of the features that stood out to Hutton also convinced him that it was a hyena: he described the genitals of the animal he shot this way: "The sexual organs were huge and absolutely astounding. The animal appeared to be both male and female at the same time" (Hutton 2009). Cryptozoologist Karl Shuker also thinks that the Nandi bear is a hyena, but an unknown variety, or a contemporary representative of the extinct giant short-faced hyena. It is probably the case that different people have seen different animals, from hunting dogs to hyenas to aardvarks to honey badgers.

Another possibility to account for the human killings is that they were caused by witches; a more mundane explanation is that they were killed by other people, but the Nandi bear is used as a cover for murder.

One of the problems for identifying creatures alleged to live in Africa is that the vast majority of what we know about these animals comes second-, third-, or fourthhand, through the stories told to missionaries, colonial authorities, explorers, and others from outside of the continent. As more reports of more creatures begin emerging, they are collected by cryptozoologists, who combine different reports from different locations to create a master narrative, which may or may not actually exist on the ground. So the Nandi bear, which is only a bear because it was named by a European, eventually swallowed up other similar-sounding creatures, like the Magdi Railway Animal and the shivuverre. And while most reports of the Nandi bear came from the areas around Kapsabet and Kapsowar, some cryptozoologists claim that they have been seen in Uganda, from Mount Elgon, as well as from Rwanda, demonstrating the ways that cryptids can "creep" into new areas as the stories spread.

Cryptozoologist George Eberhart, looking at the various descriptions of the Nandi bear, suggested that there are two versions, one that looks more like a hyena and one that looks like a baboon. This is a common cryptozoological practice: when faced with different, and even conflicting, descriptions of a creature, believers often suggest that there are subspecies that account for those differences.

The other thing that seems to happen, in particular with African monsters, is that sightings follow a predictable pattern. The pattern seems to be that the first reports come out of Africa during the first stage of colonialism, usually in the nineteenth century. These were taken by Europeans as part of the process of colonial exploration and exploitation. By the first decades of the twentieth century, these reports were circulating in the anthropological literature and were attracting biologists, would-be cryptozoologists, and others with an interest in discovering a new animal. By the end of the twentieth century, in virtually every case, the sightings had slowed to a trickle or disappeared entirely. It is almost as if the process of colonial exploration and exploitation causes these creatures to disappear from the lives of Africans, just as they enter the imagination of people from outside of the continent.

See also: Zanzibar leopard

Further Reading:

Hutton, A. (2009). Legendary Nandi Bear Unveiled. *Old Africa*, 25, October/November.
Percival, A. B. (1914). The Chemosit. *East African Geographical Review*, 4(8), 127–8.
Pickford, M. (1975). Another African Chalicothere. *Nature*, 253(5487), 85.
Williams, G. (1912). An Unknown Animal on the Uasingishu. *Journal of the East Africa and Uganda Natural History Society*, 4(5), 123–5.

O

ORANG PENDEK

Name: Orang Pendek
Alternative Names: Sedapa, Hantu Pedek, Gugu
Related Cryptids: Barmanou, Batutut
Locations: Sumatra, Indonesia
Most Recent Documented Sighting: Unknown

The orang pendek is Indonesia's version of a wild man, relic hominid, or ape-man. It lives on the Indonesian island of Sumatra.

The ancient rainforests of Sumatra are home to some of the most critically endangered animal species in the world, including the Sumatran and Tapanuli orangutans—two of three known species of orangutan (the third being the Bornean orangutan, found on the island of Borneo) in the world. Orangutans are more elusive than other great apes (besides the orangutan, all other great apes are native to Africa), in part because they are solitary, rather than gregarious, and in part because they spend most of their time in trees. First described by Europeans in the seventeenth century, the orangutan—the word means "man/person of the forest" in Malay—was seen by both foreigners and locals to be, if not a full person, a quasi-person—one with similar ways of seeing and engaging in the world.

The orang pendek, on the other hand, is thought to be an as-yet-undiscovered species or subspecies of hominoid, or perhaps hominid. Because the forests of Sumatra are so dense, and what we know of orangutans tells us how shy and elusive they are, it makes sense that many people think there is yet another species of hominoid living in those dark forests. When Europeans first heard about the creature, they did not use the term orang pendek; instead they used the term googoo or gugu, which is how William Marsden described the animal in his 1783 travel guide, *The History of Sumatra*.

While the orangutans on the island live primarily in the north, the orang pendek is thought to live in the west of the island, making it less likely that locals have misidentified orangutans for orang pendek. Kerinci Seblat National Park is a national park in West Sumatra, established to help preserve the plant and animal species within the area. It is one location where the orang pendek—which means, in Malay, short person—is thought to live.

The orang pendek is described as a short, bipedal creature, covered with reddish or tan-colored hair, and powerfully built. Like orangutans, they leave their forest home to raid crops and other foods grown or kept by the Sumatran people; they are thought to favor wild ginger and rattan and eat insects that they pull from old logs.

Indonesia is not only host to Asia's only great ape, but it also was the home of a population of hominids called Homo floriensis. Fossil remains of these individuals were found on the Indonesian island of Flores and indicate that a short, human-like species lived on that island as recently as 50,000 years ago—indicating that these proto-humans shared the island with anatomically modern humans for at least 10,000 years. While the orang pendek is described as more ape-like than human, there is another mystery species on Sumatra, which is thought to be more human than ape. That is the orang kardil, which also dwells in the deep forests, only emerging to steal food or cause mischief. A related creature is the hantu pedek, or short ghost, which is a forest spirit or demon, while the orang mawas is a very tall ape-man.

Finally Indonesia alongside Brazil, Colombia, and Madagascar are thought to be the most likely countries where newly discovered plan and animal species might be located. It is for all of these reasons that some cryptozoologists think that the orang pendek offers perhaps the best chance for a newly discovered primate species. Westerners and Indonesians alike have had encounters with the creature, but so far, no physical evidence has ever been linked to an unknown primate species living on Sumatra. One researcher, Jeremy Holden, who first saw the beast when visiting Sumatra as a tourist in 1994, even got a three-year grant from Fauna and Flora International in 1995 to return to Indonesia to find evidence of the creature alongside fellow researcher Debbie Martyr. (Holden described the creature he saw in 1994 as follows: "bipedal, upright, travertine, pale yellowish hair, quite short blocking hair.") That project failed to uncover any hard evidence of the orang pendek, as did a second expedition, funded by National Geographic, which ran from 2005 to 2008. The most recent expedition was led by Adam Davies in 2011, but it too failed to bring back concrete evidence.

Besides witness sightings, by both Indonesian locals and foreign visitors, the only evidence collected by researchers thus far—including hair samples, footprints, and a few photos—has been inconclusive or has pointed to known species. For example, a number of the footprint evidence of the orang pendek has been ruled as coming from sun bears. One of the most interesting claims about the orang pendek is that when it walks, its feet are turned backward. This is explained as one way that the creature maintains its anonymity and keeps cryptid hunters away.

One of the best described early sightings by a European was in 1923 when Dutch explorer Jacob Van Herwaarden caught sight of a strange creature, called a sedapa by locals, when in the forest hunting wild boar. He described what he saw in the journal *Tropical Nature* in 1924:

The sedapa was also hairy on the front of its body; the color there was a little lighter than on the back. The very dark hair on its head fell to just below the shoulder blades or even almost to the waist. It was fairly thick and very shaggy. The lower part of its face seemed to end in more of a point than a man's; this brown face was almost hairless, whilst its forehead seemed to be high rather than low. Its eyebrows were frankly moving; they were of the darkest color, very lively, and like human eyes. The nose was broad with fairly large nostrils, but in no way clumsy . . . Its lips were quite ordinary, but the width of its mouth was strikingly wide when open. Its canines showed clearly from time to time as its mouth twitched nervously. They seemed fairly large to me; at all events they were more developed than a man's. The incisors were regular. The color of the teeth was yellowish-white. Its chin was somewhat receding. For a moment, during a quick movement, I was able to see its right ear, which was exactly like a little human ear. Its hands were slightly hairy on the back. Had it been standing, its arms would have reached to a little above its knees; they were therefore long, but its legs seemed to me rather short. I did not see its feet, but I did see some toes which were shaped in a very normal manner. The specimen was of the female sex and about five feet high. There was nothing repulsive or ugly about its face, nor was it at all ape-like. (Reprinted in Heuvelmanns 1958: 133)

The first decades of the twentieth century were a boom time for sightings and descriptions of the orang pendek, thanks to Dutch expansion during this period. After Indonesian independence in 1945, sightings and other witness accounts dropped sharply—especially after an orang pendek corpse that was discovered in 1923 turned out to be a hoax.

One theory to account for the beliefs in the orang pendek suggests that perhaps the orang pendek is not a relic hominid, wild man, or ape-man but instead is simply a different species of orangutan, perhaps one that once lived on the southern end of Sumatra (while the known orangutan species on the island are found in the north). It was only in 2013 that one of Sumatra's two species of orangutans—the Tapanuli orangutan—was identified for the first time as a separate species. Perhaps there is another species of orangutan—or perhaps a gibbon, a smaller ape with three species on Sumatra—more secretive than the others, which is the source of the sightings?

See also: Barmanou, Batutut

Further Reading:

Cribb, R. (2009). Nature Conservation and Cultural Preservation in Convergence: Orang Pendek and Papuans in Colonial Indonesia. In Stella Borg Barthet (Ed.), *A Sea for Encounters: Essays Towards a Postcolonial Commonwealth*. Editions Rodopi B.V., 221–42.

Cribb, R., Gilbert, H., & Tiffin, H. (2014). *Wild Man from Borneo*. University of Hawaii Press.

Forth, G. (2014). Gugu. Evidence from Folk Zoological Nomenclature and Classification for a Mystery Primate in Southern Sumatra. *Anthropos*, 109(1), 149–60.

Freeman, R. (2004). In Search of Orang-Pendek. *Fortean Times*.

Heuvelmans, B. (1958). *On the Track of Unknown Animals*. Rupert Hart-Davis.

Van Herwaarden, J. (1924). Een Ontmoeting met een Aapmensch. *De Tropische Natuur*, 13, 103–6.

OZARK HOWLER

Name: Ozark Howler

Alternative Names: Nightshade Bear, Ozark Black Howler, Devil Cat, Hoo Hoo

Related Cryptids: Beast of Exmoor

Locations: Ozark region of the United States (Arkansas, Missouri)

Most Recent Documented Sighting: 2015

The Ozark Howler is a large feline that is said to haunt the Ozark Mountains of northern Arkansas, southern Missouri, and eastern Oklahoma. The name Ozark Howler refers to both the habitat of the animal and the sound that it makes, which has been described as either guttural and low or high pitched; in either case, it is always very unsettling to the listener.

The Ozarks were first settled by Native Americans as early as 14,000 years ago. By the time that Europeans arrived, the Osage and the Quapaw lived in the western side, in and near to Oklahoma. The first Euro-American settlers to arrive were farmers who came in the early to mid-nineteenth century from Tennessee, Kentucky, and North and South Carolina. Those first Europeans came to this country originally from Great Britain. They brought their beliefs with them—including beliefs in ghosts, spirits, and monsters. They also may have brought a belief in what are now called Alien Big Cats (ABCs), which are phantom cats that appear out of nowhere throughout Britain but which are probably escaped big cats as well as some misidentified house cats. Another extremely common folk belief on the British Isles is the Black Dog. While most people who describe the Howler see them as more feline than canine, the characteristics of the Black Dog (a large, black animal with glowing red eyes that appears suddenly, often as a portent of bad things to come) seem to have been grafted onto the feline sightings in the Ozarks. Interestingly, Arkansas has a second feline cryptid. The Heber Springs Water Panther is a bipedal cat-like creature with a terrible howl. Heber Springs is located about 150 miles from the Ozarks, so it may be that the legend traveled from one area to the other.

The written story of the Ozark Howler began in 2005, when people began seeing what looked to be huge cats. But it may be that people have been seeing big cats in the area for as long as people have been there. It is often repeated that the sightings began in the 1950s, but this author has been unable to find any corroboration.

Sometimes they were described as simply large cats like pumas or panthers, but some saw them as more demonic: accounts include glowing red eyes and devil horns. They can be as large as a bear (and black bears do live in the southern Ozarks), with dark, sometimes shaggy fur. Because the Ozark Howler only emerged into popular culture in the twenty-first century, many of the sightings are accompanied by photographic or video evidence. Over the past twenty years, that evidence has been uploaded to YouTube and aired on local television shows (as well as the national shows devoted to cryptozoology). This has allowed people from all over to see the animals and to make their own judgments about what it is that they are seeing. But it is the howl that is the most distinctive about the creature, and those who have heard it tend to be quite affected by it.

What is the Ozark Howler? There have not been any native big cats in Arkansas for years, as they were all (allegedly) killed off through hunting. The last time a Florida Panther was seen was in the 1920s, and the last puma was seen in 1975. While the Ozark Howler could be a remnant of either of those populations, it is more likely that it is an escaped big cat, probably from a private home. In fact, the Arkansas Game and Fish Commission gets about 100 calls per year with mountain lion sightings. There's no way to know how many big cats are kept as pets in the United States, but the International Fund for Animals estimates that there may be as many as 10,000 wild cats living in homes throughout the United States. And the Arkansas Game and Fish Commission conducted a study in 2002 and found that there were approximately 150 cougars kept as pets in Arkansas.

One possibility is that the Ozark Howler is an elaborate hoax. Cryptozoologist Loren Coleman, in a 2011 interview for the film, *Chasing Discovery*, has said that a college student began planting stories on the internet beginning in about 1998, including fake folklore, and that it was those fake stories that essentially created the monster. It may also be that it is a combination of both real sightings of real big cats and false lore about a beast that does not exist.

Some of the materials created by this still unnamed hoaxter still exist on the internet, including an entire website called Ozark Howler Network, which is allegedly the website of an organization dedicated to finding the Howler, but that does not actually exist. The website is well put together, with carefully chosen pieces of fiction mixed with fact with an intent to create a long history of Ozark Howler lore. There is even a book called *Tales of the Ozark Howler* that can be purchased on Amazon; the Amazon description says it was originally published in 1936, and that soon after, the author, Saul Ashton, died. The description goes on to say that Hawthorne Cornelius got permission from Ashton's family to reissue the book, which was published in 2019.

There is even an alleged song called *Ozark Howler* that, according to the Ozark Howler Network, was released in 1927 as part of something called the Ozark Songbook. If this were legitimate, that would place the origins of the creature much earlier, giving it more authority. The song compares the Ozark Howler to a number of other, familiar animals, like the dog ("I'd sooner say it's a giant frog"), the cat ("I never seen a kitty with horns like that"), and the bear ("a long tale like that you've seen nowhere"). The song ends with this refrain:

Oh Ozark Howler, just stay away.
Oh Ozark Howler, don't come around today.

See also: Beast of Exmoor

Further Reading:

Big Cats Caught on Camera in Arkansas (2009). *4029 TV*, May 18.

Carroll, C. M. (2021). *Missouri Ozarks Legends & Lore*. Arcadia Publishing.

P

POPE LICK MONSTER

Name: Pope Lick Monster
Alternative Names: Pope Lick Goatman, Goatman
Related Cryptids: Jersey Devil, Mothman
Location: Kentucky
Most Recent Documented Sighting: 2016

The Pope Lick Monster is a monster that lives in the area around the Pope Lick Creek outside of Louisville, Kentucky. In particular, it lives underneath the trestle bridge called Pope Lick Trestle, a rail bridge or trestle operated by the Norfolk Southern Railroad.

The Pope Lick Monster is one of the very few cryptids in the world that is not just thought to kill humans; it has been linked to the deaths of dozens of men, women, and children since its construction in the late nineteenth century. For that reason, the lore surrounding this creature is darker and more frightening than most other monsters.

The Pope Lick Monster is quite similar to the Mothman of West Virginia in that both are creatures that are linked to death, and there are very real, documented deaths that have occurred in association with these legends. But they are also similar in that they are both linked to a physical structure: a bridge.

Bridges are a site of religious and folkloric significance. Bridges are often thought to connect two different worlds: usually the land of the living with the otherworld, or the land of the dead. In the myths of many cultures, these spiritually significant bridges are often guarded by a creature; Cerberus, for example, is the three-headed dog that guards the entrance to Hades in Greek mythology. So the idea that a bridge might have a supernatural being associated with it, and one that often determines the fate of the traveler who wants to cross it, should not surprise us. In addition, in the world of the living, bridges are important as well—they connect different localities with each other, giving people the opportunity to cross bodies of water. But bridges are fallible; they collapse, sometimes without warning, and can kill people.

In 1957, without warning, the Silver Bridge linking West Virginia to Ohio over the Ohio River collapsed, killing forty-six motorists, and, thanks to the stories of a mysterious Mothman that was seen before the collapse, the legend of the Mothman was born. The Pope Lick Trestle Bridge, first constructed in the late nineteenth century and suspended over 100 feet above the river, is also associated with tragedy, although there have been no mass tragedies on this bridge. Instead, there have been dozens of deaths associated with it, and with each new death or accident, the legend of the Pope Lick Monster grows.

The most recent death on the bridge was in 2019, when fifteen-year-old Savanna Bright lost her life when she and a friend were taking pictures on the bridge and were struck by a train that arrived too quickly for the girls to escape. Savanna died and her friend Kaylee was hit, fell off the bridge, and survived. And while most people agree that Savanna lost her life when she was struck by a train, her death, like every other tragedy associated with the bridge, only adds to the legend. (The bridge is almost 800 feet long and is suspended 100 feet in the air. It takes a train from five to seven minutes to pass over the trestle, meaning that that is how long someone needs to hang from it to survive.)

Others who died on the bridge found themselves there in the first place because of the legend of the Pope Lick Monster. Roquel Bain, for example, a 26-year-old woman from Dayton, Ohio, traveled to the bridge in 2016 with her boyfriend to investigate stories about the monster. Like so many of the victims, Roquel did not see or hear the train until it was too late and was killed. Her boyfriend survived by hanging from the edge of the bridge until the train passed overhead. It may be that some of the deaths occur because the age and condition of the bridge may signal to visitors that it is no longer in service; in fact, there are as many as twenty-five freight trains per day that cross those tracks.

The Pope Lick Monster, or Goatman, is a goat-human hybrid, although it is often described as having sheep-like characteristics as well. It is bipedal, and like the satyr of classical mythology, it walks on two goat legs; the torso, arms, and head are human.

Unlike most American cryptids, there are no Native American myths or legends that support the existence of the Pope Lick Monster. Instead, its origins may be similar to those of urban legends: the stories may have begun as a cautionary tale for youngsters. It may have begun as a warning unconnected to the bridge, which would give it its name, and only became associated with the Pope Lick Trestle after one of its tragedies. One of the many legends associated with the monster tells of a creature that was part of a traveling circus or carnival freak show and which escaped into the woods outside of Louisville after the train transporting the circus derailed. While there is no evidence of a train carrying a circus or carnival derailing in the area, a train—carrying Christmas toys—did fall from the trestle in 1909, but there were no deaths, nor was there a goatman that survived the accident. This incident, reported in the December 19, 1909, edition of *The Courier-Journal*, was also the first time that the trestle had been mentioned in print, but the monster was not included in the article.

It makes sense that a dangerous bridge would have a legend associated with it, which can not only explain the large number of tragedies but can also be used to warn young people away from the site (although the legend most likely has encouraged, rather than discouraged, visitors to the bridge). What makes less sense is why the monster is a goat.

In the West, the goat carries a heavy symbolic load. The Greek half-man, half-goat god Pan, god of shepherds and flocks, along with the satyr and the faun (goat-like nature spirits), was probably an early inspiration for the later Christian image of the Devil as a half-man/half-goat.

Pan was also associated with sexuality and was often depicted with a giant erect penis. In the New Testament, goats represent the damned, while sheep represent the saved. By the Middle Ages, Christians associated goats with lust, the demonic, and evil. Goats are typically gendered male and often are said to represent uncontrolled male sexuality. Medieval European depictions of the goat represented it as the Devil, and goats were thought to be witches' familiars and to have sex with witches. Isidore of Seville wrote that the goat was "a lascivious animal; it likes to butt heads and is always ready to mate. Because of its lust its eyes are slanted. The nature of goats is so hot that their blood can dissolve diamonds."

The fact that the monster associated with countless deaths on an old rickety bridge is a goat only makes sense within this context and helps explain why a goat-like creature is associated with a place of death. In addition, the fact that it has been primarily young people, drawn to the bridge because of the lore, who have died there makes the stories even more compelling.

It is said that the goatman lures its victims to the bridge via hypnosis. This idea is in line with the idea of the goat as a smooth, dangerous, seductor of women. And the reality is that the monster does in fact lure its victims up onto the trellis where they meet their end. The devil, too, is thought to be seductive, quick witted, and manipulative. One story tells of a farmer who struck a deal with the devil, who demanded that the farmer sacrifice goats to him in exchange for supernatural power.

Whether or not one believes that there is a half-man, half-goat that lives underneath a trestle bridge in Kentucky and lures teenagers to their deaths, the reality is that this is in fact what is happening. After the 1988 film *The Legend of the Pope Lick Monster* was released, a new wave of monster hunters visited the bridge, resulting in new deaths.

As unusual a creature as the Pope Lick Monster is, it is not the only goatman in America. There are at least two others: the Lake Worth Monster (or Goatman) and the Goatman of Maryland/ Goatman of Prince George's County. The Lake Worth Monster was a goat-human hybrid creature seen by teenagers at Lake Worth, outside of the city of Fort Worth, in the summer of 1969, but which had largely disappeared by the time school started in the fall. Neither goatman had been rumored to kill people, although Lake Worth's goatman once threw a tire at some teenagers. Maryland's creature was also a half-human, half-goat, which was said to live in the woods of Prince George's County in Maryland. The sightings began in 1971 with the discovery of a handful of dead dogs and turned into a full-blown legend. Like Lake Worth's goatman as well as the Pope Lick goatman, Prince George's County's Goatman is most well known among teenagers.

See also: Mothman

Further Reading:

Crouch, J. N. (2021). *Goatman: Flesh or Folklore?* Createspace.

Fee, C. R., & Webb, J. B. (Eds.). (2016). *American Myths, Legends, and Tall Tales: An Encyclopedia of American Folklore [3 Volumes]: An Encyclopedia of American Folklore (3 Volumes)*. ABC-Clio.

S

SKUNK APE

Name: Skunk Ape
Alternative Names: Skunk Ape, Myakka Skunk Ape, Louisiana Bigfoot, Florida Bigfoot,
Swamp Ape, The Everglades Skunk Ape, Swamp Cabbage Man, Swampsquatch
Related Cryptids: Bigfoot, Fouke Monster, Honey Island Monster
Location: Southeastern United States, especially Florida
Most Recent Documented Sighting: Unknown

The skunk ape is Florida's version of Bigfoot. More precisely, while Bigfoot is known to live in the redwood forests of the Pacific Northwest, the skunk ape, which lives in the swamps of Florida, is more closely related to the other ape-men of the southeastern United States, like Louisiana's Honey Island Monster.

Like the other hominoid cryptids of North America, the skunk ape is a large bipedal ape-man. It is covered in reddish brown fur, stands from 5 to 8 feet tall, and is called the skunk ape because of the foul smell that it emits. While many cryptids are said to give off a bad smell, often like sulfur or rotten eggs, the skunk ape is uniquely described as smelling like a skunk. It lives primarily in the region surrounding Big Cypress National Preserve as well as Everglades National Park, although there have been sightings as far south as Key Largo in the Florida Keys.

Some indigenous tribes in the southeast of what would become the United States did share a belief in a large hairy creature, known as esti capcaki (or tall man) to the Seminole; stories would pass from native peoples to Europeans. It was not until the nineteenth century that the skunk ape showed up in print. It was in 1818 when a newspaper in Apalachicola, Florida, reported on a hairy bipedal creature that was causing mischief. It took well over another century for the monster to make another appearance, when a number of sightings occurred in the 1940s. Because these sightings took place in Bardin, Florida, the monster came to be known as the Bardin Booger.

Sightings began to increase in the 1950s, at a time when Bigfoot was developing its own reputation, which would then shape the legends of other hominoid cryptids around the world. As with other cryptids, but especially those in countries with a robust popular press, it is the news reports of the creature that generate new sightings, new media reports, and additional sightings. The 1970s were the peak of skunk ape sightings, a period that coincides with the apex of tabloid journalism in the United States—journalism that was centered in south Florida, where the National Enquire was headquartered until 2014 and where the Weekly World News is still located. In addition, Palm Beach County was experiencing a major growth spurt, with new developments overtaking Florida's natural spaces, creating more opportunities for human-animal conflict. This also created more opportunities for monster sightings.

One could easily argue that 1977 was the year in which the interest in the skunk ape peaked; one of the best sightings of the skunk ape occurred that year when the Stoeckman family of Key Largo, Florida, saw what they described as an 8-feet-tall hairy man hanging around their yard. The skunk ape returned a number of times, causing the family to flee for the duration of the visits. Mr. Stoeckman told the local newspaper, "It had a huge head and shoulders, long fur all over, and he stank like a dirty wet dog. The noise he made was a high-pitched wailing." The sightings were so terrifying that Stoeckman and a number of other men in the community formed a posse to hunt down and kill the creature.

Also that year, the Florida legislature voted on (but did not pass) a bill that would have prohibited the hunting, killing, or capturing of "anthropoids or humanoid animals." And finally, south Florida is the perfect location for a mysterious creature, given its placement at the western point of the Bermuda Triangle, an area in the Atlantic Ocean where odd events are thought to occur and which was also popularized in the 1970s.

Over the years, skunk ape sightings have continued to occur, although without the frequency of the 1970s. Many reports involve domestic animals either chasing or getting chased by one of the creatures. One Florida man in particular, Dave Shealy, who has probably seen the skunk ape more times since his first encounter as a child in 1974 than anyone else, has been collecting reports and evidence of sightings at what he calls the Skunk Ape Research Center, which he founded in 1999.

Is there really a large hominoid living in the forests and swamps of Florida? And if not, what explains these sightings? Some of the sightings could be of other species of animal, such as the black bear or black panther, both of whom live in south Florida. Florida has also been home to, over the years, multiple facilities that bred and sold monkeys and apes for scientific research as well as for other uses. Both monkeys and apes have escaped from those facilities, forming wild colonies of African animals living in Florida forests and swamps. Any of these animals can also serve as the basis for either individual sightings or the legend itself. There are also countless roadside zoos, as well as an unknown number of private owners of nonhuman primates, and animals have escaped from all of these places. Finally, over the past few decades, a number of primate sanctuaries have opened in Florida, taking advantage of that state's climate in order to care for apes and monkeys retired from research or entertainment. When you take into account the surprisingly large number of facilities housing monkeys and apes in Florida, the idea that there might be one or more mysterious primates living in the Florida Everglades begins to seem a lot more likely. In fact, one of the more significant pieces of evidence regarding the skunk ape was a pair of photos taken by an anonymous Sarasota woman in 2000, known as the Myakka photos because of their proximity to the Myakka River State Park. She sent those photos to the Sarasota County Florida sheriff's department and wrote in the accompanying letter that she wondered whether the creature might be an orangutan. It has since been suggested that it was in fact an orangutan in the photos.

Other than individual sightings, there are also a number of photos and some grainy film footage purported to be of the skunk ape. One video was taken in 2000 by Dave Shealy of the Skunk Ape Research Center and a second by Mike Falconer in 2013. There have also been a number of hoaxes, including one well-known hoax in 2013, when a young man dressed in a gorilla suit was spotted by dozens of tourists in Myakka River State Park.

Most people—and certainly all of the scientists who have weighed in on the matter—agree that there is no unknown species of ape-man living in Florida. The evidence is just too shaky, and there are too many hoaxes. There is also really only one person who is dedicated to trying to find the skunk ape—Dave Shealy. There is no question that without Shealy's work—the articles, field guides, television appearances, and other promotional activities associated with Shealy's research center, not to mention all of the evidence that he has personally collected—the skunk ape might have faded into history the way that a number of legends popular in the 1970s have. Besides Shealy, Stacy Brown, a Florida man who took video footage in 2012 of a creature Brown is calling the skunk ape, is perhaps the second most dedicated skunk ape believer. After Brown's footage (known as the Torreya footage) ended up on the television show, *Finding Bigfoot*, Brown filmed his own documentary on the creature, called *The Skunk Ape Lives*, released in 2020.

Skunk ape sightings have also been reported in Georgia and Alabama, although Florida is by far the most popular area.

See also: Bigfoot, Fouke Monster, Honey Island Swamp Monster

Further Reading:

Desjarlais, J. (2020). *The Florida Skunk Ape: A Complete History* [self-published].
Jenkins, G. (2010). *Chronicles of the Strange and Uncanny in Florida*. Pineapple Press Inc.

T

TATZELWURM

Name: Tatzelwurm

Alternative Names: Stollenwurm, Stollwurm, Bergstutz, Praatzelwurm, arassas, Daazlwurm, Praazlwurm, Bergstutz, Stutzn, Springwurm

Related Cryptids: Lagarfljót worm, Mongolian Death Worm

Location: The Alpine regions of Switzerland, Austria, France, and Italy

Most Recent Documented Sighting: 2009

The Tatzelwurm, or Stollenworm in Switzerland, is a giant worm-like creature that lives in the Alpine countries of Europe: Austria, Switzerland, Italy, and France. The name means "clawed worm" in German, referring to its clawed toes, while other names refer to the worm's ability to jump, to tunnel, or to its similarity to a tree stump.

It is one of the world's more unusual creatures; unlike the Mongolian Death Worm or Iceland's Lagarfljót worm, both of which are giant serpent-like creatures, the Tatzelwurm is a hybrid creature, made up of the body of a snake or worm with the head of a cat. Sometimes the creature is described as having no legs; alternatively, it has been spotted with two and sometimes four legs. Like dragons, the Tatzelwurm is thought to be able to spit venom from its mouth, making it quite dangerous to encounter. Whether the worm has hair, scales, a crest running down its back, or other features is debatable as witness sightings differ.

It ranges from 2 to 6 feet in length, and, depending on the number of legs the witness saw, it either slithers, drags, or walk-crawls to move. Its legs are unusually short and stumpy, and the feet have three toes with a claw on each. Its face looks like that of a cat, with large eyes and ears. Unlike a cat, however, it is not cute. It hibernates in the winter and lives in the crevices and caves of mountains.

Italian sightings of the creature differ significantly from those found in the German-speaking countries. Instead, some Italians have reported seeing a bipedal lizard man.

The Tatzelwurm is aggressive, attacking and killing livestock and, occasionally, humans. They can also kill without meaning to; it is said that a single drop of Tatzelwurm blood will kill anyone, man or beast, that it touches. That is how Heinrich von Winkelried, a fourteenth-century Swiss man, died; after stabbing a Tatzelwurm to death with his sword, a single drop of the beast's blood fell on him and killed him instantly.

The worm has been known in the German-speaking countries bordering the Alps since at least the nineteenth century and may be related to much more ancient beliefs surrounding dragons. For example, in a sixteenth-century chronicle written by pastor Johannes Stumpf,

Figure 8 *A sleepy Tatzelwurm in Kolowrathhöhle. Copyright © 2023 Heidi Scheidl. All rights reserved.*

Stumpf described two kinds of dragons—the "track," which referred to a conventional dragon with wings that can fly, and the lintwurm or lindwurm, a giant worm or perhaps crocodile, living in forests and water ways. Lindwurms are magical beings, can either be good or bad, and sometimes have legs and, confusingly, wings. If the Tatzelwurm is basically a more modern version of a lindwurm, it suggests that people of the region have feared giant worms for hundreds of years. There is even a northern European fairy tale called King Lindwurm or Prince Lindwurm, which tells of a pair of twins born to a king; one is handsome while the other was cursed to be a lindwurm.

But why does the Tatzelwurm have the face of a cat? No one seems to know.

While most people do not believe in the Tatzelwurm anymore, seeing it more as a figure of local legend, there were a handful of sightings in northern Italy in 2009. One person said it was smaller than an iguana, while another described it as looking like a lizard with a giant tale or a scaly kangaroo.

What is the creature that people saw? Some scientists have pointed toward eels and in particular to the conger, an eel that can be as long as 6 feet. Lungfish are another possibility for a misidentified species. Finally, giant salamanders are another option.

See also: Lagarfljót worm, Mongolian Death Worm

Further Reading:

Pohanka, R. (2013). *Tatzelwurm und Donauweibchen: Österreichs Naturgeister und Sagengestalten*. Amalthea Signum Verlag.

THUNDERBIRD

Name: Thunderbird
Alternative Names: n/a
Related Cryptids: Sarimanok
Location: North America
Most Recent Documented Sighting: 2010

The thunderbird is a mythical bird common to a number of Native American tribes but especially to Algonquin-speaking people. It is the most important of the sky spirits and is often used to signify strength, bravery, and military accomplishments. Similar North American mythical birds include the Panola of the Penobscot people, the Rain bird of the Hopi and the Zuni, the Ikii of the Anishinabe, the chequa of the Potawatomi, and the Huhuk of the Pawnee.

In the Algonquin cultures of Northeast America (the United States and Canada), as in many indigenous cultures, there is a belief in an animating spirit or life force that is present in all or most things. For the Algonquin-speaking peoples, that spirit is known as a manitou. Manitou can be good—those associated with the earth and the sky—or bad—those associated with the underworld and bad weather. Thunderbirds are the creation of good manitous.

The thunderbird is a thunder god and inhabits the form of an eagle (occasionally it is depicted or described as a bird-man hybrid, but typically it is the eagle, a symbol of bravery and warfare). Depictions of the thunderbird tend to be relatively stylized and easily recognizable: they tend to be angular, either triangle- or X-shaped, with the wings spread out and the head pointing downward, as if the bird is descending very quickly from the sky. It is often difficult to distinguish between artistic depictions of thunderbirds and those of eagles, however. One of the most well-known depictions of the thunderbird to reach Europe was the portrait of Mahican chief Etow Oh Koam, who visited England with three chiefs from the Iroquois Confederacy, who were requesting that England join with them to fight France in the French and Indian wars. The chief had four thunderbirds tattooed on his face, and his portrait, painted by Dutch portraitist John Verelst, represented the first time that many English people had seen a tattoo, a thunderbird, or even a Native American.

Among a number of Plains tribes, there are four different thunderbirds, called Wakinyan, the Lakota word for thunder, one associated with each of the directions. The Brule Sioux tale called Wakinyan Tanka, or the Great Thunderbird, as recounted by John Fire Lame Deer, a Sioux medicine man, opens like this:

> Wakinyan Tanka, the great thunderbird, lives in his tipi on top of a high mountain in the sacred Paha Sapa, the Black Hills. The whites call it Harney Peak, but I don't think he lives there anymore since the wasichu, the whites, have made these hills into a vast disneyland. No, I think the thunder beings have retreated to the farthest ends of the earth, where the sun goes down, where there are no tourists and hot dog stands. (Erdoes and Ortiz 2013: 218–19)

Here, the narrator points toward the displacement of native traditions and beliefs in favor of modern, Euro-American traditions, and in fact we have seen the idea of the thunderbird has now been appropriated by non-natives, especially in Pennsylvania where most contemporary sightings take place.

The thunderbird has magical powers, such as the ability to create thunder by beating its wings, to shoot lightning from its eyes, and to create wind by the speed at which it flies. In Algonquin folklore, the thunderbird is often contrasted with the Great Horned Serpent, a mythical being associated with a number of Native American tribes but mostly in the southeastern United States. Thunderbirds have been featured in the art of many Native American cultures, including pictographs and petroglyphs, many of which date back thousands of years. For example, there is a prominent petroglyph of a thunderbird in Washington state park in eastern Missouri, and these petroglyphs have been dated to between 3,000 and 4,000 years old. At Bighorn Basin in Wyoming, there are multiple bird petroglyphs, which may represent thunderbirds but may also represent eagles, as the bird petroglyphs at Bighorn Basin have been found near eagles' nests.

Thunderbirds have also played a role in the ritual practices of many indigenous North Americans. The skin and feathers of eagles and other large birds have been found at a wide variety of archaeological sites representing older native cultures, and while some of these may represent the birds from which they are taken, others offer evidence of the (symbolic) inclusion of thunderbirds in ritual.

Thunderbirds are now seen by many non-native people as cryptids—mysterious, secretive, and hidden animals that may actually exist in real life. Cryptozoologists who specialize in cross-cultural comparisons have noted the appearance of other large bird creatures in the myths and legends of people around the world, so it is clear that there is something significant about large predatory birds that make them excellent symbols for a wide variety of human concerns. But just because there are thunderbird-like birds in other cultures does not necessarily mean that the thunderbird can be seen or treated as a local variant of a wider phenomenon. To this author, removing mythic creatures from the cultures from which they came and looking for commonalities between and among them carries the risk of eliminating the specificities of that cultural context and turning a creature with a very important set of meanings into something very different. Thunderbird imagery today is found in advertising for a wide variety of goods, thunderbirds serve as sports mascots, and their images are used in logos for companies everywhere.

In addition, as the thunderbird moved into cryptozoology, it also became a subject of cryptozoological inquiry. One theory that is popular among cryptozoologists is the idea, found in discourses surrounding other cryptids like Bigfoot or the Loch Ness Monster, that thunderbirds are a contemporary remnant of pterosaurs, the first flying vertebrates, which went extinct some 60 million years ago. The alternative to that approach is one that has developed in some corners of cryptozoology where the field is used as a kind of cover for Creationism. In this approach, thunderbirds were indeed pterosaurs, but they lived recently enough that they coexisted in North America with native peoples. Here, the timeline of how long the earth has existed is radically shortened, from about 4½ billion years to closer to 6,000 years. The idea is that if pterosaurs lived alongside humans, they could not have existed more than 10,000 years ago, which shortens the time frame of all life on earth, making it consistent with Creationist theory.

Another possible extinct creature that could be linked with the thunderbird is the teratorn, an extinct family of huge birds (related to modern vultures) with a wingspan of up to 12 feet. Unlike the pterosaurs, which disappeared over 60 million years ago, members of the Teratornithidae family only went extinct about 11,000 years ago, probably thanks to overhunting by Native Americans.

The folklore of indigenous people can often be interpreted in a way that either whitewashes or eliminates the cultural context, or that serves another, often political, purpose. The thunderbird has experienced both of these. First, skeptics and those who have little respect for Native American religious beliefs simply say that the entirety of the thunderbird is a myth, with no relationship to reality. Second, cryptozoologists remove the thunderbird from its cultural and spiritual context and turn them into exemplars of another creature, which means removing all of the details that make it specific to their historical and cultural setting. And third, creationists use indigenous stories and myths, which typically look toward a mythic history in which humans, animals, and gods and spirits may interact, in order to support their belief in creationism.

Now that the thunderbird has entered the realm of cryptozoologists, there have been a number of sightings of thunderbirds or large birds described later as thunderbirds. There was a major encounter in 1977 in Illinois when a boy was attacked by two giant birds, one of whom carried the boy for 30 feet until his mother intervened. They have been seen in recent years in Pennsylvania (2010, 2012, 2013) as well as Alaska (2018). Pennsylvania in particular seems to be a hotspot for thunderbird sightings, including a series of sightings over a period of several weeks.

See also: Gamayun

Further Reading:

Erdoes, R., & Ortiz, A. (2013). *American Indian Myths and Legends*. Pantheon.
Métraux, A. (1944). South American Thunderbirds. *The Journal of American Folklore*, 57(224), 132–5.
Stephany, T. J. (2007). *The Great Thunderbird: Source of the American Indian Symbol*. http://timothystephany .com/papers/Article-Thunderbird_rev09b.pdf..

THYLACINE

Name: Thylacine
Alternative Names: Tasmanian Tiger, Tassie
Related Cryptids: Beast of Exmoor
Location: Tasmania and Southern Australia
Most Recent Documented Sighting: 2021

The thylacine (*Thylacinus cynocephalus*) was a carnivorous marsupial, which was native to the island of Tasmania and went extinct in 1936 when the last known thylacine died at a zoo in Hobart. Nicknamed Tasmanian Tigers, even though the thylacine is more closely related to dogs than cats, they were first spotted by Europeans in 1642. The Tasmanian Tiger name came from the fact that the animals were striped like a tiger. The animal's Latin name, *Thylacinus cynocephalus*, means "dog-headed pouched dog." The thylacine is not a true cryptid, because we know that they once lived. But the many purported sightings of the animal since its supposed extinction make the thylacine a creature of importance to cryptozoologists.

They were first described scientifically in 1805 by the Lieutenant Governor of Tasmania, William Patterson, in the *Sydney Gazette and New South Wales Advertiser*:

An animal of a truly singular and nouvel description was killed by dogs the 30th of March . . . it must be considered of a species hitherto unknown, and certainly the only powerful and terrific of the carnivorous and voracious tribe yet discovered on any part of New Holland or its adjacent islands. It is very evident this animal is destructive, and lives entirely on animal foods; as on dissection his stomach was found filled with a quantity of kangaroo . . . The form of the animal is that of the hyoena, at the same time strongly reminding the observer of the appearance of a low wolf. The lips do not appear to conceal the tusks. (Smith 1982: 237–8)

Figure 9 *Deaccessioned thylacine. Copyright © 2023 Heidi Scheidl. All rights reserved.*

Thylacines were about the size of a coyote. They were yellowish brown in color, measured about 40–50 inches long, not counting their tail, weighed about 40 pounds, and had short legs, which means they most likely stalked their prey (probably small marsupials) rather than chasing it down like wolves. They had the long snout and facial features as well as the foot structure and claws, of a canine, combined with the stripes of a tiger. Their tail was distinctive in that it was oddly stiff—somewhat like a kangaroo. While they were quadrupedal, they could also hop like kangaroos. Mothers kept their young in a rear-facing pouch beneath their bellies, and, unusually, males also had a pouch.

Behaviorally, thylacines were nocturnal or perhaps crepuscular. Unfortunately, even though they did not go extinct until the twentieth century, they were never subject to any real behavioral research, so what scientists understand about thylacines is part speculation. While Europeans blamed them for killing sheep, it is probable that thylacines did not prey on (or rarely preyed on) livestock, both because they were notoriously shy around humans and because they were most likely not strong enough (unlike dingos) to bring down large animals like sheep.

Thylacines were once were found on the mainland of Australia, Tasmania, and were found as far north as the island of New Guinea. We know that they arrived in Australia at least 30 million years ago, thanks to a collection of fossils that were found in Queensland in the 1990s, including a perfectly preserved full skeleton from an individual who lived 17 million years ago. Thylacines are pictured in much of Australian rock art, and it may be that some indigenous tribes once hunted them for food. It is thought that the thylacine disappeared from the mainland about 2,000 years ago, thanks to competition from dingos and, perhaps, later from domesticated dogs. But the thylacine was still living on Tasmania when the first Europeans arrived in the early seventeenth century. Indigenous Tasmanians lived alongside of thylacines for about 30,000 years until Europeans arrived on the island in the seventeenth century. It took them just 300 years to eliminate the species, which was officially declared in 1986 (fifty years after the last known animal died).

Animal studies scholar Carol Freeman argues that one of the main reasons that the Tasmanian Tiger disappeared has to do with how the animal was seen and represented within Australia. Starting in the nineteenth century when the English founded a colony on Tasmania (then called Van Diemen's Land), thylacines were portrayed as dangerous vermin, thanks to their supposed tendency to attack the sheep and other livestock that the colonists brought with them to the island. (In one now infamous photo that was used to justify the eradication of the thylacine, an animal is photographed with a chicken in its mouth. The photo was staged, and both the thylacine and the chicken were actually dead.) Ultimately, the animals were systematically hunted to extinction, starting in the 1830s when the government of Tasmania offered cash bounties to anyone who killed one—one pound per head. The last wild thylacine was shot in 1933, and after that, the last (known) remaining thylacine, named Benjamin, was captured and placed in the Beaumaris Zoo in Hobart where the animal lived alone until it died in 1936. (The date of Benjamin's death, September 7, is now known as National Threatened Species Day in Australia.) At the time, the death of Benjamin was not a major news story because no one at the time realized that it was, most likely, the last living survivor of its species, nor had there been any attempts to breed Benjamin (which was most likely female, even though during its lifetime it was thought to be male) with the other remaining captive thylacines.

Besides the government eradication campaign lodged against the thylacine, its extinction was also enabled by the spread of European colonists across the island of Tasmania and the resulting habitat destruction.

What makes the story of the Tasmanian Tiger more than just a sad commentary on the ignorance and violence of human beings toward animals that they do not understand is what has happened since the thylacine disappeared. Perhaps because of a sense of collective guilt over the anthropogenic extinction of this unique animal, and perhaps because it disappeared less than 100 years ago, Tasmanians and foreigners alike have been reporting sightings of the thylacine for the last few years.

Proponents of the theory that thylacines still exist formed the Thylacine Awareness Group of Australia in 2014 and compile thylacine sightings in order to prove the animal's continued existence. As outlandish as this sounds, almost half of the island of Tasmania is undeveloped land, so proponents of the theory that the thylacine is still alive say that they could simply be well hidden. There have also been, according to the Thylacine Awareness Group, thousands of reported sightings of the thylacine on the mainland of Australia—where they have supposedly been extinct for thousands of years.

Government officials are taking these reports seriously, and, in 2019, the Department of Primary Industries, Parks, Water and Environment released a document compiling the reports they received of thylacines from 2016 to 2019. (Prior to that time, the Department of Conservation and Land Management compiled reports of thylacine sightings on the mainland and found over 200 such reports from 1936 to 1988.) In 2016, wildlife scientist Hans Naarding saw what he believed to be a thylacine while working in the Togari/Arthur River region on Tasmania's western side. He said:

> I saw the creature for three minutes, which is one hell of a long time. It stood absolutely still and every part of him was clearly visible. It was a fully-grown male wearing a fine (sandy-coloured) coat which was in good condition. I counted twelve black stripes over its back. It had a massive angular head with small rounded ears. The tail was very slender, but very thick at the butt, quite unlike the tail implant of a dog . . . It just stood there staring into the distance—he didn't seem to notice me or the driving rain. (Healy and Cropper 1994: 17–18)

Some of the witnesses reported seeing just footprints, but other people claim to have seen one or more thylacines themselves. Most witnesses saw a striped big cat crossing the road in front of them while driving at night (thylacines were nocturnal), but occasionally the witness was able to see the animal more clearly. One account from 2018 describes the animal as follows:

> It didn't really make sense to me as being a typical cat, location wise, behaviour and the way it walked, it was obvious it wasn't a fox although it was the size of a big fox, not fluffy and hairy like a fox, the way it was walking across the road was by keeping its body gliding at the same height and not hopping/walking typical of a fox, it wasn't a sneaky walk of a fox hunting or crouched down to pounce on prey, that's why I thought at the time it could be a cat , although it didn't make sense to be a cat, it was way to [sic] big to [sic] high from the ground and the body proportions were quite wide (stomach to back/the girth). I noticed the creature had markings on the body, these markings were black stripes on the back side of the body, the fur on the creature was dark brown. (Department of Primary Industries, Parks, Water and Environment 2019)

The last report provided by the Department was from July 2019 and was regarding a footprint found on Trestle Mountain. The Thylacine Awareness Group of Australia collects not only reported sightings from the public but also hosts on their website the photos and videos taken by witnesses. These images can be compared to the photos and video footage taken of the last thylacines in captivity, helping cryptozoologists to determine the possible validity of them. One of the most well known of such photos is of an animal colloquially called the Ozenkadnook tiger. The picture, taken by a Victorian woman named Rilla Martin in 1964, depicts a large quadrupedal animal with thylacine-like stripes. The shape of the animal is not consistent with what we know of the thylacine, however, and the photo has been called a hoax by a number of critics.

Today, there are approximately 100 taxidermied thylacines held in a number of museums. Until definitive proof arrives of the thylacine's continued existence, most scientists say that the animal is extinct. Thylacine lovers, however, still hold out hope that some small number of the species may still be lurking in the unexplored interior of Tasmania, and that, perhaps, the species can be resurrected through cloning.

In 2021, during the second year of the Covid-19 pandemic, there was a rush of new thylacine sightings, including a new series of photos and a video that was released in February 2021 by the Thylacine Awareness Group. Neil Waters, the group's president, claimed that the animals depicted in the images included two adult thylacines, accompanied by juveniles. These latest images, according to experts, did not depict thylacines, however; instead, it was probably a family of pademelons, a wallaby-like marsupial.

The thylacine is important not only to animal lovers in Australia who mourn the extinction of one of their native species but also to cryptozoologists in general. If it can be proved that the thylacine still lives, eighty years after the last known individual died, then that means that other creatures could also still be discovered or rediscovered.

See also: Beast of Exmoor, Bunyip

Further Reading:

Black, G. F., & Thomas, N. W. (1903). *Examples of Printed Folk-Lore Concerning the Orkney and Shetland Islands*. London. https://archive.org/details/examplesprinted00thomgoog.

Department of Primary Industries, Parks, Water and Environment (2019). *Thylacine Sighting Reports*, September 1, 2016 to September 19, 2019, https://dpipwe.tas.gov.au/Documents/RTI%20025%20-%202019 -20.pdf (Accessed October 8, 2020).

Freeman, C. (2010). *Paper Tiger: A Visual History of the Thylacine*. Brill.

Healy, T., & Cropper, P. (1994). *Out of the Shadows: Mystery Animals of Australia*. Ironbark.

Letnic, M., Fillios, M., & Crowther, M. S. (2012). Could Direct Killing by Larger Dingoes Have Caused the Extinction of the Thylacine from Mainland Australia? *PLoS One*, 7(5), e34877.

Paddle, R. (2002). *The Last Tasmanian Tiger: The History and Extinction of the Thylacine*. Cambridge University Press.

W

WENDIGO

Name: Wendigo
Alternative Names: Atchen, Chenoo, Wetiko, Wiindigoo, Weendigo, Windego, Wiindgoo, Windgo, Windago, Windiga, Wendego, Windago, Widjigo, Wiijigoo, Wijigo, Weejigo, Widjigò, Wintigo, Wentigo, Wehndigo, Wentiko, Windgoe, Wītikō, Wintsigo
Related Cryptids: n/a
Location: Ontario and Quebec, Canada; Great Lakes, Great Plains, and Eastern States
Most Recent Documented Sighting: n/a

The wendigo is a manitou, or spirit, in the folklore and mythology of Algonquin-speaking First Nations (Canada) and Native American (US) tribes. It is primarily an evil spirit, although it can also bring luck or opportunities.

The Algonquin-speaking tribes of North America are located in the Great Lakes region of the United States and Canada, the Great Plains, and the eastern forests. They include the Cree, the Ojibway, the Shawnee, the Kickapoo, the Abanaiki, and the Mahican tribes, to name just a few.

The wendigo is one of many spirits in the religious worldview of Algonquin-speaking tribes. It is primarily known as a cannibal: constantly hungry, constantly seeking food, and willing to murder humans to get it. What makes the wendigo so dangerous is that it can influence the behavior of humans whom it has possessed. But the most frightening thing about the wendigo is what, or who, it eats. The wendigo feels an overpowering, insatiable hunger that can only be (partially) satisfied through eating humans. And a human who is possessed by a wendigo will be a cannibal, and humans can actually turn into wendigos through experiencing prolonged hunger. The manifestation of that starvation is becoming a wendigo. Psychiatrists have even coined a term—wendigo psychosis—which refers to a state of psychosis caused by starvation.

When the wendigo is described, it tends to be described as a very tall being with an appearance that is monstrous. In popular depictions of the creature in Western media, it is often depicted with antlers or as a human-animal hybrid. Because the wendigo is a spirit rather than a physical being, most of the physical descriptions that we have of it come from nonindigenous people. But of all of the descriptions, the most salient feature is the gauntness of the wendigo. In every depiction, it is so thin that its hunger is a physical characteristic. In his book on the manitous of the Ojibway, Basil Johnston described the wendigo as:

> gaunt to the point of emaciation, its desiccated skin pulled tightly over its bones. With its bones pushing out over its skin, its complexion the ash gray of death, and its eyes pushed back deep into the sockets, the Wendigo looked like a gaunt skeleton recently disinterred from the

grave. What lips it had were tattered and bloody . . . Unclean and suffering from suppurations of the flesh, the Wendigo gave off a strange and eerie odor of decay and decomposition, of death and corruption. (Johnston 1995)

The taboo against cannibalism is one of the very few cultural universals, according to anthropologists. Where it is found, it occurs in a ritual or warfare context; all other instances are strictly forbidden. Historically, the only time that we see cannibalism outside of a ritual context tends to be during times of starvation. The original settlers of Jamestown, Virginia, who suffered through disease and starvation in the winter of 1609, the Donner Party, a group of California-bound settlers stuck in the Sierra Nevada mountains during the winter of 1846–7, and the Uruguayan rugby team that crashed in the Andes in 1972 are examples of starvation-induced cannibalism. One of the functions of the wendigo belief may be that it reinforces the taboo against eating human flesh—even during times of famine. Many tribes once performed a ceremonial dance known as wiindigookaanzhimowin, as another way of educating the community about the taboo.

Because the Algonquin tribes live in the far north, where winters are long and extreme, starvation is a very real threat, as is the threat of cannibalism when conditions are too harsh. This may explain why there are no similar wendigo beliefs in areas where resources are more plentiful or where the weather is kinder.

As Europeans began to settle in North America, some settlers, explorers, and traders began to hear stories of the wendigo, incorporating aspects of the wendigo myth into their own stories. For example, in New France (what would later become Quebec), the wendigo beliefs became appended to French werewolf, or loup-garou beliefs.

One of the first written accounts of the wendigo came in 1661, when a report by Jesuit missionaries related to their experiences in New France included the following passage on the phenomenon of what would later be called wendigo psychosis:

Those poor men (according to the report given us) were seized with an ailment unknown to us, but not very unusual among the people we were seeking. They are afflicted with neither lunacy, hypochondria, nor frenzy; but have a combination of all these species of disease, which affects their imaginations and causes them a more than canine hunger. This makes them so ravenous for human flesh that they pounce upon women, children, and even upon men, like veritable werewolves, and devour them voraciously, without being able to appease or glut their appetite— ever seeking fresh prey, and the more greedily the more they eat. This ailment attacked our deputies; and, as death is the sole remedy among those simple people for checking such acts of murder, they were slain in order to stay the course of their madness. (Thwaites 1901)

It is interesting to note that it was not just indigenous people who were affected by this strange disease; instead, members of the Jesuits' own party succumbed to the disease and were killed to stop them from killing others. Wendigo psychosis is more than just eating human beings to survive; it refers to an almost inhuman level of starvation. If it exists (and there is some debate about that), it is an example of a culture-bound illness: a disease or other disorder that is specific to a particular cultural setting.

The practice by cryptozoologists of incorporating the folklore and mythology of indigenous peoples into cryptozoological accounts is problematic in many instances, but in the case of the wendigo, it is even more troubling. Because the wendigo is not, according to Algonquin mythology, a physical being. Instead, it is a condition, a curse, or even an indication of a lack of harmony within an individual or community.

While the wendigo predates European arrival in the New World, the wendigo is in many ways a figure that only makes sense within the context of European colonialism. With the arrival of the first Europeans in the seventeenth century, and with the massive expansion across the American continent in the nineteenth century, disease, starvation, genocide, and dislocation arrived along with them. Starvation was just one symptom of the pain caused by the arrival of Europeans to the Americas, a people who seem to embody the worst qualities of the wendigo: an insatiable hunger for land, for wealth, for property, and for status. European colonialism is inherently consumptive: it seeks out and consumes the resources—plant, animal, land, mineral, and even people—for itself, leaving very little for the people and animals who were here first. They perfectly embody the wendigo spirit in terms of its hunger, its greed, and its destructiveness. As Ojibwe writer Bezhigobinesikwe Elaine Fleming wrote in her retelling of the wendigo story:

> Over the years, the Ojibwe experienced many traumas. That is the way of the Wiindigo. A story is told of the Wiindigo, running amok amongst our people and killing them. There had been thousands of Ojibwe and many villages before the Wiindigo came. The Wiindigo was killing everyone, so an Ojibwe man challenged Wiindigo to a race. If the Ojibwe man won, the Wiindigo would leave. They raced, and the Ojibwe man lost. After that, the Wiindigo continued killing our people. (Fleming 2017: 51)

It should not surprise us to hear that wendigo attacks reached a fever pitch in the late nineteenth century, the era when Native American and First Nations people were most threatened. The wendigo then is both a manitou and a metaphor for the destructive nature of colonialism. This makes the appropriation of the wendigo and its incorporation into contemporary American horror especially problematic.

See also: Chupacabra, Thunderbird

Further Reading:

Colombo, J. R. (1982). *Windigo, an Anthology of Fact and Fantastic Fiction: An Anthology of Fact and Fantastic Fiction*. University of Nebraska Press.
Fleming, B. E. (2017). The Ojibwe Who Slew the Wiindigo. *Tribal College*, 28(3), 51.

Howard, A. J. (2021). *Wild man, Cannibal, Trickster: The Wendigo in Literature and Media*. Doctoral dissertation, University of Leeds.

Johnston, B. (1995). *The Manitous: The Spiritual World of the Ojibway*. Harper Perennial.

Jusiak, K. (2015). The Embodiment of the Taboo: The Images of Wendigo in Literature and Their Rendition in Modern Media. Doctoral dissertation, bachelor's thesis, Adam Mickiewicz University in Poznań.

Kolan, M., Leis, K., Baska, A., Kazik, J., & Gałązka, P. (2019). Wendigo Psychosis. *Current Problems of Psychiatry*, 20(3), 213–16.

Landrum, C. (2011). Shape-shifters, Ghosts, and Residual Power: An Examination of Northern Plains Spiritual Beliefs, Location, Objects, and Spiritual Colonialism. In C. E. Boyd & C. P. Thrush (Eds.), *Phantom Past, Indigenous Presence: Native Ghosts in North American Culture and History*. University of Nebraska Press, 255–79.

Thwaites, R. G. (Ed.). (1901). *The Jesuit Relations and Allied Documents: Travels and Explorations of the Jesuit Missionaries in New France, 1610–1791; the Original French, Latin, and Italian Texts, with English Translations and Notes* (Vol. 73). Burrows Bros. Company.

Turner, D. H. (1977). Windigo Mythology and the Analysis of Cree Social Structure. *Anthropologica*, 19(1), 63–73.

Y

YEREN

Name: Yeren

Alternative Names: Chinese Wildman, The Wildman of Shennongjia, Man-Monkey, Man Bear

Related Cryptids: Almas, Bigfoot, Yeti, Yowy

Location: China

Most Recent Documented Sighting: 1992

The yeren is a wild man or ape-man from China and is often seen as not just the Far Eastern analog to North America's Bigfoot but is also sometimes considered to be its direct ancestor.

The yeren lives in China's most remote mountains and forests and has primarily been seen in the Hubei province on the eastern edge of China, where the mountainous caves and dense forests offer some protection from those who might harass them. They try to avoid people, who they sometimes encounter when they raid villagers' homes for food. Sometimes they will also kidnap and rape women and forcibly taking women for their wives.

The fur of the yeren is often described as reddish colored, similar to an orangutan (and some Europeans). It is fully bipedal, which means that if the Gigantopithecus origin story is true, the yeren then evolved bipedalism independently from humans.

Wild men or hairy men have been a part of Chinese folklore for thousands of years. Because China has had a written script for so long, there is a long history of written accounts of forest spirits or beings. For example, a Shan gui is a mountain ghost that looked like a man and was first included in a written report in the third century BCE, while a maomin refers to hairy people and dates to the same general period . The feifei is another hairy creature first recorded in the third century as is the xingxing. In subsequent centuries, reports of other hairy creatures called maoren and knu emerged into the written record. None of these creatures, however, look (in artistic representations) like a giant ape-man, and the literary descriptions often do not track with images.

Chinese literature has mentioned hairy men since at least the Tang dynasty (618–907 CE), but they did not enter the broader discussion around hairy men around the world until the 1950s when Bigfoot became internationally known. Coincidentally, it was in 1955 that Chinese scientists began to search for the remains of any Gigantopithecus fossils (the species of extinct ape most closely connected to Bigfoot lore today), finding the first such fossils in the field in Guangxi province in 1956. With the Cultural Revolution instigated by Chairman Mao in 1966 came a push to rid the country of the so-called Four Olds, which referred to traditional customs, beliefs, and practices. Yeren beliefs, deemed superstitious by the state, then went underground, only to reemerge after Mao's death in 1976.

With the official end of Maoism in China came a new interest in the yeren, both because the need to quash "superstition" no longer existed and Chinese scientists finally had access to literature from the left: both scholarly and popular. The Chinese Academy of Sciences was the first official body to investigate these witness accounts and to collect footprints, hairs, and other possible evidence. Even though the stigma associated with folk beliefs had largely disappeared, it is still the case that proving that the yeren is not a superstitious belief, but a real live biological creature, would go far in terms of elevating the position of China as an international leader in scientific discoveries.

In addition, with Bigfoot hunts on the rise in the United States, the idea of finding the first living ape-man became a sort of competition between China, Russia, and the United States. In America as well, starting in the 1950s, some cryptozoologists like Ivan Sanderson argued that Bigfoot needed to be found—before the Chinese found their version. As it became clear that Bigfoot hunters were not part of the scientific mainstream in the United States, and that it was more of a fringe pursuit, there was less of an interest on the part of Chinese scientists to research the yeren. Global politics have always played a role in how we understand cryptids, as colonialism has shaped almost every understanding that we have of beings from outside of the European context.

One of the most popular theories to account for the existence of the yeren (as well as Bigfoot) is that it is an evolutionary relic that has managed to survive millions of years after other such ancient hominoids, or large-bodied apes, disappeared. In particular, it is often thought that it is an extent member of the species known as Gigantopithecus, which lived in southern China for over 2 million years. The fossils assigned to this species were dated to between about 2.6 million years and 300,000 years, when it was thought to go extinct.

Paleoanthropologists consider it to be a potential ancestor to the modern orangutan, Asia's only great ape, and not an ancestor to humans (albeit a distant relative). Even though only teeth and molars have been recovered so far, scientists have estimated that Gigantopithecus may have been as large as 12 feet high, weighing up to about 600 pounds, and lived in subtropical forests in the south of China—the area with which yeren is associated.

For much of the time when Gigantopithecus lived, Homo erectus, an archaic human, also lived in China and, toward the end of that time, it may be that late Homo erectus—as represented by Peking Man, a fossil skull that has been dated to about 780,000 years ago—caused the extinction of Gigantopithecus. But while the size and hairiness of Gigantopithecus makes it an attractive candidate for an ancestor to the yeren, Gigantopithecus was an ape. It was quadrupedal, walking on all fours for much of the time, although virtually every single reconstruction of this animal depicts it as standing fully upright. This is one of the reasons why so many people think that not only was Gigantopithecus bipedal but was also closely related to or ancestral to humans. Putting aside the difficulty of imagining that a breeding population of Gigantopithecus survived for 350,000 years without leaving a single bit of trace evidence, this creature would have had to independently develop bipedalism after all fossils of it disappeared from the fossil record, in order to become a wild man or ape-man.

The evolutionary relic theory is particularly useful in a Chinese context, because it plays into a debate that has been raging in biological anthropology for many years. While most paleoanthropologists agree that all human life originated in Africa, and that populations of anatomically modern humans left Africa starting about 100,000 years ago and, by about 50,000 years ago, eventually replaced the populations of Homo erectus that had been living in Asia and Europe. This approach, known as the Out of Africa model, means that physical differences between modern human populations all emerged after proto-humans had been replaced by anatomically modern humans. The alternative approach, known as the Multiregional model and supported by many Chinese scientists, argues that modern humans evolved separately in Africa, Europe, and Asia, which would mean that so-called racial differences are extremely ancient—as old as 2 million years. Today, most scientists favor a modified Out of Africa model where anatomically modern humans did leave Africa, replacing other archaic humans, but may have also interbred with them, thus creating regional differences between Europe, Asia, and Africa. It is the Multiregional model that is most consistent with the idea that the yeren is not a different variant of Bigfoot but is actually an entirely different creature, specific to China.

The second theory to account for the yeren is that it's simply a shy, elusive animal that has successfully concealed its existence for thousands of years—perhaps an as-of-yet unknown species of orangutan. And finally, one explanation is that every sighting of a yeren is simply a misidentification of a living animal—perhaps a monkey or bear. Besides the notoriously incorrect nature of eyewitness accounts, most sightings of the yeren (as with Bigfoot) occur in a dense forest environment where it is difficult to distinguish details.

One interesting idea is that hairy man legends refer to Europeans. For centuries, there was little contact between the East and the West, other than through trade exchanges along the Silk Road. In the Medieval era, there was more contact between East and West, with a large number of Europeans living in China. This did not last, but in the sixteenth century, the Portuguese established a colony on Macau, opening up more contact. It could be that sporadic contact with Europeans from the Middle Ages through to the modern era generated stories about hairy men, as the Chinese recognized not only that Europeans were much hairier than them, with often full beards on their faces, but also that hairiness (combined with European manners) was interpreted as a sign of savagery. During the Opium Wars of the nineteenth century, this belief was intensified as the Chinese fought, and lost, two wars over Britain's opium trade in China. Depictions of Europeans as hairy, animalistic men were common in Chinese newspapers of the time, and terms like "red-haired barbarian" were used to refer to the Dutch, while the Portuguese were thought to be inhuman tall. In addition, beards—popular with European men at the time—were associated with barbarians as well as the demonic.

Another possibility is that yeren sightings, when made by the Han, members of China's ethnic majority, could have been, at least some time, triggered by the sight of one of China's many minority groups. Chinese scientists have also offered the idea that perhaps since these ethnic groups have "survived" while maintaining their "primitive" habits, that might mean that the yeren have as well.

While there was once a great deal of scientific interest in the yeren, especially in China starting in the 1970s, most scientists today have concluded that the yeren is not an animal. Even among cryptozoologists, there is less consensus now than there was in the past. None of the hair samples and footprints that have been pointed to as evidence of the yeren's existence have been validated, nor has there ever been any convincing photos or videos.

See also: Bigfoot, Orang Pendek, Yowie

Further Reading:

Debenat, Jean-Paul (2014). *The Asian Wild Man*. Translated by Paul LeBlond. Hancock House.

Dikötter, F. (1998). Hairy Barbarians, Furry Primates, and Wild men: Medical Science and Cultural Representations of Hair in China. In G. Obeyesekere (Ed.), *Hair: Its Power and Meaning in Asian Cultures*. State University of New York Press, 51–74.

Forth, G. (2008). *Images of the Wildman in Southeast Asia: An Anthropological Perspective*. Routledge.

Meldrum, J., & Guoxing, Z. (2012). Footprint Evidence of the Chinese Yeren. *The Relict Hominoid Inquiry*, 1, 57–66.

Peng, Z. (2000). The Image of the "Red-Haired Barbarian" in Chinese Official and Popular Discourse. In H. Meng & S. Hirakawa (Eds.), *Images of Westerners in Chinese and Japanese Literature*. Brill, 17–23.

Schmalzer, S. (2009). *The People's Peking Man*. University of Chicago Press.

Smith, O. D. (2021). The Wildman of China: The Search for the Yeren. SINO-PLATONIC PAPERS Number 309: 1–20.

YETI

Name: Yeti

Alternate Names: Abominable Snowman, Snowman

Related Cryptids: Batatut, Bigfoot, Yeren, Yowie

Location: Himalayas of Tibet and Nepal

Last documented sighting: 2019

The yeti, more commonly known as the Abominable Snowman, is a cryptohominid that lives in the highest elevations in the Himalayas of Tibet, Nepal, and India.

Yeti is a Tibetan word that refers to a mountain-dwelling bear, which perhaps points toward how at least some local people saw the creature. Other names that refer to similar beings include the dzu-teh, a Nepali word that refers not only to the Himalayan brown bear but may also refer to the yeti, bun manchi, which is a Nepali word that means jungle man; migoi, a Tibetan word for wild man; and michê, a Tibetan word that means man-bear. In Chinese, the word is Xueren, which means "snow man," while the Tibetan word metoh-kangmi refers both snowman and man-bear.

In Tibet, there are thought to be three types of yeti: the smallest version is the Ran Shim Bombo, at only 3 to 5 feet tall and with reddish brown fur; the Chuti, which is intermediate and is about 8 feet tall; and the black-furred Nyalmo, the largest of the yeti, which is 15 feet tall. The Sherpas say that the yeti lives primarily in the tundra above 15,000 feet, and all known footprints were observed in the snow. Most sightings come from the western end of the Himalayas.

Asia has a wide variety of such beliefs, from the Russian Chuchuna and Almas to the Chinese yeren to the Batutut of Vietnam. They share similarities to each other and to other wild man stories around the world but differ as well, drawing from local conditions. While these beliefs are most likely quite ancient, predating even Hinduism, they probably blended with similar beliefs from neighboring cultures.

Like Bigfoot, its North American counterpart, the yeti is a combination of local (i.e., Tibetan, Nepali, and Sherpa) folklore, which has been grafted onto European and Euro-American lore, specifically as it relates to Bigfoot and Bigfoot-like creatures, known as crypto-hominids. It's also important to point out that the yeti, like a number of cryptids, is also the product of colonialism. The "discovery" of the yeti was enabled by the fact that the British were deeply involved in the cultures of the area; they had controlled India since 1858 but by this time, the Indian independence movement was gaining momentum. At the same time, Russia and China, and to a lesser extent Germany, were also competing with the English for access to the highest mountain in the world.

The yeti came to the attention of Westerners with the first European expedition to Mount Everest in 1921, led by Englishman Charles Howard-Bury. Howard-Bury later wrote that while on the mountain, his group came across some tracks in the snow, which one of the Sherpa guides told him belonged to a wild man. An English journalist, Henry Newman, interviewed Howard-Bury and other members of the team, where he learned about the metoh-kangmi, which he translated as the Abominable Snowman.

In the nineteenth century, isolated reports of an ape-like creature did appear, such as an 1832 account published in the *Journal of the Asiatic Society of Bengal*, but these were not linked with other accounts, nor did the term yeti show up in European writing. Another nineteenth-century report came from *Among the Himalayas*, a travel guide published in 1899, which referred to a large ape-like creature that left huge footprints. Neither of these accounts spurred any further interest in the beast.

After Howard-Bury's expedition, and Newman's article about the expedition, including the term Abominable Snowman, sightings became more frequent. One reason for the jump in sightings certainly had to do with Mount Everest; while Howard-Bury's team did not make it to the summit, that trek paved the way for future expeditions, which brought more foreigners to the mountain. In total, there were three expeditions to the Himalayas in the 1920s, five in the 1930s, and, after the end of the Second World War, and especially after the first successful summit in 1953 by Edmund Hillary and Tenzing Norgay (who themselves reported seeing large footprints in the snow), foreigners would continue to be drawn to Mount Everest, where Abominable Snowman lore would continue to develop. With each new expedition came new opportunities for climbers to either have a sighting themselves or to hear stories from Sherpas as well as other climbers.

It was the 1950s, after Hillary and Norgay's ascent, that sightings really multiplied, and descriptions and photos of giant footprints taken by climbers began to circulate in the international press. Starting in the late 1950s, foreigners like explorer Tom Slick, followed by cryptozoologists like Ivan Sanderson, began traveling to the area specifically to investigate yeti stories for themselves, opening up cryptozoology in Asia.

In 1954, explorers brought some hair samples, which allegedly came from a yeti scalp taken from a Buddhist monastery in Pangboche, back to England, where they were subject to analysis by an anthropologist named Frederic Wood Jones who, while unable to definitely identify the source, thought it most likely came from an ungulate. Along with the alleged scalp, the monastery also had in its possession a desiccated hand, which was also said to belong to a yeti. A piece of the hand, known as the Pangboche Hand, was then stolen by a member of one of Tom Slick's expeditions to Nepal in 1959 and was, as the rumor goes, smuggled to England by American actor James Stewart. Even Edmund Hillary, the first European to climb Everest back in 1956, caught yeti fever, traveling back to Nepal in 1960 to look for more evidence of the creature.

The remains of the Pangboche Hand have been subjected, over the last fifty years, to a number of tests to determine its origin. British primatologist William Charles Osman Hill thought that it might be from a Neanderthal, while American anthropologist George Agogino, who kept a finger, thought it was like a human. Finally, in 2011, it was subjected to a DNA analysis with the result being that it came from a modern human being.

Further expeditions to the Himalayas followed in the decades after the Abominable Snowman was named, bringing back stories, photos of footprints, and further hair samples. As scientific tools for analysis have improved, and the results of these analyses are disseminated, it has become clear that most of the physical evidence for the existence of the yeti does not in fact point to an unknown hominid but instead to known animals like the Himalayan brown bear, the Tibetan blue bear, the Asiatic black bear, or the Himalayan goral, an ungulate. It is the Asiatic black bear in particular that makes the best candidates for the yeti, as they can walk upright, and, because of the shape and attitude of the claws, their hind prints can look like those of a hominid rather than a bear. They are also found on the western side of the mountain range, while the Himalayan brown bear, for example, is located primarily on the east side, where no sightings have occurred.

Finally, in 2017, conservationist Daniel Taylor published a meta-analysis of all of the yeti materials collected until that time, including photographs and casts of footprints, hair samples, and more. Taylor concluded that the Asiatic black bear is in fact the yeti.

The yeti is a product of local lore—from Nepal, Tibet, India, China, and Bhutan—that has been combined with Bigfoot lore from the Americas and Almas lore from Russia. It was shaped initially by English colonialism, but, after the end of the Second World War when interest in both Bigfoot and yeti exploded, it also became a product of the Cold War. During this time, Russian and American cryptid hunters both worked together, but also competed, to scientifically prove the existence of one of these creatures. It was the hunt for the yeti in particular that kicked off this competition, but that also allowed for cooperation between Western and Russian scientists.

Figure 10 *Self-assured and composed: Self portrait of an adolescent Nyalmo yeti. Copyright © 2023 Heidi Scheidl. All rights reserved.*

In both Russia and China, cryptozoology (and hominology, the search for unknown hominids) was influenced by international politics, with both state governments sponsoring research into the Almas and yeren, respectively. In the United States, on the other hand, where cryptozoology was never accepted by either the scientific community or the government, cryptozoologists work on their own. But beginning with yeti research in the 1950s, a number of scientists and amateurs from these countries began organizing joint expeditions to the Himalayas, including archaeologists, climbers, botanists, zoologists, and other scientists from China, the United States, and the Soviet Union—at the height of the Cold War.

The last alleged sighting of a yeti, or evidence of a yeti, was in 2019 when the Indian Army shared pictures of yeti footprints taken by Indian mountaineers at the Makalu Base Camp in Nepal, on the Army's Twitter account, to much international ridicule.

See also: Almas, Bigfoot, Yeren, Yowie

Further Reading:

Loxton, D., & Prothero, D. R. (2013). *Abominable Science: Origins of the Yeti, Nessie, and Other Famous Cryptids*. Columbia University Press.

Messner, R. (2001). *My Quest for the Yeti: Confronting the Himalayas' Deepest Mystery*. Macmillan.

Sykes, B. (2016). *Bigfoot, Yeti, and the Last Neanderthal: A Geneticist's Search for Modern Apemen*. Red Wheel Weiser.

Sykes, B. C., Mullis, R. A., Hagenmuller, C., Melton, T. W., & Sartori, M. (2014). Genetic Analysis of Hair Samples Attributed to Yeti, Bigfoot and Other Anomalous Primates. *Proceedings of the Royal Society B: Biological Sciences*, 281(1789), 20140161.

Taylor, D. C. (2018). *Yeti: The Ecology of a Mystery*. Oxford University Press.

Ward, M. (1997). Everest 1951: The Footprints Attributed to the Yeti-myth and Reality. *Wilderness and Environmental Medicine*, 8, 29–32.

YOWIE

Name: Yowie

Alternate Names: Quinkin, Joogabinna, Ghindaring, jurrawarra, myngawin, puttikan, d oolaga, gulaga and thoolagal, yaroma, noocoonah, wawee, pangkarlangu, jimbra, tjangar a, yahoo, Australian ape

Related Cryptids: Batatut, Bigfoot, Yeren, Yeti

Location: Eastern Australia

Last documented sighting: 2022

The yowie is an ape-man from Australia. Known as Australia's Bigfoot, yowie is one of the world's most well-known ape-men, next to Bigfoot and yeti. Yowie began as a figure of Australian indigenous myth but is today one of Australia's best-known and best-loved creatures. Like all ape-men, the yowie is a large, powerfully built, hairy man beast, with large, distinctive footprints.

The first time that the term yowie was used in print was in 1875, when it made an appearance in Reverend William Ridley's guidebook to Australia, *Kámilarói and Other Australian Languages.* Ridley wrote the creature's name as "Yō-wī" and called it a spirit, rather than a physical being. These early written reports are confusing and often contradictory, pointing toward the difficulty that Europeans had in understanding Australian religious concepts and beings as well as the fact that Aboriginal beliefs differ widely across the continent. One point of dissent is the origin of the yowie and whether it is related to, or is the same as, the yahoo.

The word yahoo first came to European attention with the 1726 publication of Jonathan Swift's *Gulliver's Travels.* Swift describes yahoos as a race or tribe of unpleasant, smelly, hairy men:

> The fore-feet of the yahoo differed from my <u>hands</u> in nothing else, but the length of the <u>nails</u>, the coarseness and brownness of the palms, and the hairiness on the backs. [. . .]
>
> The sorrel nag [. . .] brought out of the yahoo's kennel a piece of ass's flesh, but it smelt so offensively that I turned from it with loathing; he then threw it to the yahoo, by whom it was greedily devoured. [. . .] As to those filthy yahoos, although there were few greater lovers of mankind, at that time, than myself; yet I confess, I never saw any sensitive being so detestable on all accounts; and the more I came near them, the more hateful they grew, while I stayed in that country. (Swift 1726)

It has been argued that the yahoo of *Gulliver's Travels* was inspired by stories about the North American Sasquatch that made it from the New World back to Europe (Argue 2018), while others suggest that it makes more sense that Swift was inspired by stories of hairy men from Australia, newly settled by the English, and with a belief in an ape-like figure.

However, it may be that the yahoo was never an Aboriginal term at all but arrived in Australia after the publication of *Gulliver's Travels* (Joyner 1984). Joyner points out that it is not until 1842 that the term yahoo—to refer to a being or spirit from Australian folklore—showed up in print and argues that yahoo is instead an English word used in the past to refer to orangutans, a creature seen initially as a sort of wild man or hairy man. Joyner points to two descriptions from the first two decades of the nineteenth century of yahoos being displayed in English traveling menageries, an early version of the zoo and freak show, and in both cases, the term refers to the at-that-time-still-unknown orangutan. If Joyner is right, the term yahoo has nothing to do with Australia, and we should look elsewhere for the origins of the yowie. That doesn't, however, mean that there are no indigenous hairy men in Aboriginal cultures; there are numerous terms specific to different Australian languages that express some sort of wild man or ape-man.

It is also worth pointing out that misidentifications of Australian flora and fauna were incredibly common during the first centuries of English settlement on the island. No other place on the planet has such a unique collection of animals—especially marsupials—so the English confusion over what is a real animal, and what is an element of folklore or myth, was very real.

As articles began to emerge in the English-speaking press about Australia, references to the "Australian ape" or members of "the monkey tribe" began to make an appearance. Was there an unknown primate species living in Australia or were these sightings and rumors simple misidentifications of native animals such as koalas? Nineteenth-century naturalist Henry James McCooey described his own encounter with the Australian ape:

A few days ago I saw one of these strange animals in an unfrequented locality on the coast between Bateman's Bay and Ulladulla. My attention was attracted to it by the cries of a number of small birds which were pursuing and darting at it. When I first beheld the animal it was standing on its hind legs, partly upright, looking up at the birds above it in the bushes, blinking its eyes and distorting its visage and making a low chattering kind of noise. Being above the animal on a slight elevation and distant from it less than a chain, I had ample opportunity of noting its size and general appearance.

He described the creature as follows:

I should think that if it were standing perfectly upright it would be nearly 5ft high. It was tailless and covered with very long black hair, which was of a dirty red or snuff-color about the throat and breast. Its eyes, which were small and restless, were partly hidden by matted hair that covered its head. The length of the fore legs or arms seemed to be strikingly out of proportion with the rest of its body, but in all other respects its build seemed to be fairly proportional. It would probably weigh about 8 stone. (McCooey 1882)

In his article, McCooey also referred to "yahoo" as the term used by the "bushmen" to describe the creature, indicating that, if the term really was an invention by Jonathan Swift, it had by that time infiltrated local languages.

As with other cryptids, there are surprisingly few written accounts of yowie encounters. But those accounts that do exist serve as the basis for the "truthiness" of the yowie and are repeated over and over to give the stories legitimacy. There is also very little in the way of physical evidence. One piece of physical evidence dates to October of 1912, when a rancher named Mr. Summerell noticed some unusual foot and hand prints, prints that were not human but were not recognizable either. Summerell took plaster casts of the prints, which he shipped to a geologist named Edgeworth David for analysis, who suggested that they may have been faked. Another notable piece of evidence was an alleged carcass, purported to be of a yowie killed in 1893 by Arthur Marrin and which shared—according to the report of the one man who saw it—similar hand morphology to Summerell's plaster casts.

While it is clear that many Aboriginal peoples do have a belief in a wild man or hairy man, either as a spirit or a physical or quasi-physical being, the contemporary ideas surrounding yowie—that it is the Australian variant of a "type" known as Bigfoot—are a relatively recent phenomenon, dating to the 1970s when Bigfoot was gaining traction internationally. Here, yowie is linked to Swift's yahoo, which by then had been incorporated into the Australian stories such that it takes on a truthful, ahistorical quality. Were any of the indigenous forms of this creature thought to be real, or are they denizens of the Dreamtime? It is also important to point out that the yowie or yahoo is not the only Aboriginal creature that is described as human-like. The junjudees, for example, is a small, rather than large, anthropoidal figure with supernatural powers, while the dulagal or doolagarl is another hairy man but this time with glowing red eyes, a long forehead, no neck, and a curious way of walking sideways.

Since the 1970s, there have been dozens of encounters with the yowie. These range from finding a dead domestic animal, to hearing the calls of an unknown animal late at night, to actual first-person sightings. These sightings were primarily located in New South Wales and Queensland, with a few sightings scattered throughout the Northern Territory, but the area around Springbrook in Queensland is the most popular area in the country for encounters. Yowiesightings.com, a website maintained by photographer John Wilson, collects sightings and evidence accounts from the public and has logged multiple encounters in 2022, the most recent of which described the creature, seen in the area around Brooweena, Queensland, as follows:

> The dark-haired figure was incredibly large and didn't seem to be having any problem navigating the swiftly flowing water according to the witness. He [the witness] got a glimpse of the "enormity" of the creature when it heaved itself from the water onto a bank before disappearing into the bush and trees.

Another source of yowie information is the Australian Yowie Research Centre, founded by yowie enthusiast Dean Harrison, with thousands of alleged sightings.

Today, as with well-known cryptids in other parts of the world, the yowie has become one of Australia's pet creatures. It, like the bunyip, is now a central part of contemporary Australian lore, whether or not it actually exists in reality.

See also: Bigfoot, Yeren, Yeti

Further Reading:

Argue, D. (2018). Does the Yahoo in Gulliver's Travels Represent an Eighteenth Century Description of the Sasquatch? *The Relict Hominoid Inquiry*, 7, 97–106.

Hawkins, J., Ryan, J. S., & Adams, P. (2007). The Folklore of Awe: Elements and Influences Involved in the Construction of Tales Concerning Strange Creatures and Phenomena Arising in the Australian Environment and Culture. Unpublished thesis. https://rune.une.edu.au/web/bitstream/1959.11/6442/2/open/SOURCE03.pdf.

Joyner, G. (2012). *Monster, Myth or Lost Marsupial? - The Search for the Australian Gorilla in the Jungles of History, Science and Language*. Hayes and Thomas.

Joyner, G. C. (1977). *The Hairy Man of South Eastern Australia*. Published by the author.

Joyner, G. C. (1980). *More Historical Evidence for the Yahoo, Hairy Man, Wild Man or Australian "Gorilla"*. National Library of Australia, MS 3889.

Joyner, G. C. (1984). The Orang-utan in England: An Explanation for the use of Yahoo as a Name for the Australian Hairy man. *Cryptozoology: Interdisciplinary Journal of the International Society of Cryptozoology*, 3, 55–7.

Joyner, G. C. (2003). Scientific Reaction to Evidence for the Yahoo or "Australian ape", 1882–1912. *Journal of the Royal Australian Historical Society*, 89(2), 162–78.

Laurance, B. (2013). *Yetis, Yowies and Dinosaur Trees: Amazing Finds in the Hunt for Living Legends*. The Conversation.

Ridley, W. (1875). *Kamilaroi, and Other Australian Languages*. T. Richards, Government printer.

Roman, C. (2019). Indigenous Beliefs About Little People. *Ab-Original: Journal of Indigenous Studies and First Nations and First Peoples' Cultures*, 3(1), 124–9.

Ryan, J. S. (2002). *The Necessary Other, or "When One Needs a Monster": The Return of the Australian Yowie*. Australian Folklore.

Swift, Jonathan (1726). *Reprinted as Gulliver's Travels into Several Remote Nations of the World*. Lee & Shepard, 1876.

Varner, G. R. (2007). *Creatures in the Mist: Little People, Wild men and Spirit Beings Around the World: A Study in Comparative Mythology*. Algora Publishing.

Extinct, Invented, or Mythical Creatures Similar to Cryptids

AL-MI'RAJ

Al-mi'raj is a horned rabbit known in the Arabian world. It was first described in the "Marvels of Things Created and Miraculous Aspects of Things Existing" (*'Ajā'ib al-makhlūqāt wa-gharā'ib al-mawjūdāt*) by Zakariya Ibn Muhammad al-Qazwini, a Persian geographer who lived in the thirteenth century. The term "al-mi'raj" means the (al) mi'raj, which refers to the elevation of the prophet Mohammed to meet God.

Known as the unicorn rabbit, al-mi'raj is related to the jackalope, a North America horned rabbit. But while the jackalope has a set of horns akin to a deer or antelope, the al-mi'raj only has a single, black horn, like a unicorn. It has yellow fur and either has black spots or stripes. They are territorial, carnivorous, and can be quite vicious when defending their territory; they will attack prey with their horn and will then devour them.

Beliefs in the existence of al-mi'raj, like the jackalope, can be explained in part by the fact that rabbits can be infected with a virus known as Shope papilloma virus; this is a virus that causes horn-like growths to appear on the heads of a number of species of rabbits and hares. By itself, the virus is not fatal, but if the horns grow too big, they can impact the animal's ability to feed itself or evade prey. In addition, it can cause cancer in the host animal.

Al-mir'aj lives, according to legend, on the island of Jezîrat al-Tennyn, or Island of the Dragons, a mythical island in the Indian Ocean. The Christian name of the island, Antillia, derives from the Moorish conquest of the Iberian Peninsula, and according to Christian legend, a group of bishops escaping the Muslim conquerors escaped to Antillia. But it's the Arab island, and Arab legend, that describes the al-mir'aj. In this telling, the islanders of Jezîrat al-Tennyn gave Alexander the Great an al-mir'aj as a thank you after he killed the serpent that had been terrorizing them.

Unicorn-like creatures of all kinds are frequently found in Medieval Islamic art. For instance, the karkadann is a rhinoceros-like creature with a large horn on its head; the Persian word for rhinoceros is kargadan, indicating that this creature was most likely a rhino. Griffins and sphinxes also show up in Islamic art, as well as a unicorn-like creature from China known as a qiln. Unicorn horns were highly coveted as they were thought to be able to protect a person against misfortune and can also detect poison and help with impotence.

See also: Jackalope, Wolpertinger

Further Reading:

Ettinghausen, R. (1950). *The Unicorn.* Studies in Muslim Iconography, Freer Gallery of Art Occasional Papers Vol. 1, No. 3, Washington.

Kato, S., Miyamoto, H., Takahashi, M., & Kamahora, J. (1963). Shope Fibroma and Rabbit Myxoma Viruses. II Pathogenesis of Fibromas in Domestic Rabbits. *Biken Journal*, 6, 135–43.

Zabihi, M., Salim-Zadeh, M. J., & Farrokhfar, F. (2020). A Comparative Study on Characterization of Imaginary-Synthetic Beings in The Miniatures of the Wonders of Creation, by Zakariya al-Qazwini, Schools of Painting in the Ilkhanid and Mughal Eras. *Negareh Journal*, 15(55), 35–47.

BILI APE

The Bili ape, also known as the Bondo mystery ape, was thought to be an ape-man or wild man living in the forests of the Democratic Republic of the Congo (DRC). Today, it is recognized as a subspecies of the chimpanzee, named by scientists Pan troglodytes schweinfurthii, or the eastern chimpanzee.

The Bili ape was thought to be a new species of ape that was "discovered" living near the village of Bili in the north of the DRC. The first evidence of this new species came in 1908 when a handful of what looked to be gorilla skulls were found outside of Bili. However, DNA testing of some of these animals indicated that they were no new species. Rather, they are a subspecies of the chimpanzee, known as the eastern chimpanzee, and one that had been known, not just to Africans but also to scientists, since 1872. (Primatologist Colin Groves, however, has suggested that the eastern chimpanzee is too broad a category for the Congo chimpanzees, which have larger heads and longer limbs than the other eastern chimps, and recommends that it be divided, creating a fifth subspecies.)

What were thought to be gorilla skulls were first collected by a Belgian army officer near the town of Bili in 1898 (Belgium at that time controlled what was then called the Belgian Congo). These were sent to the Trevuren Museum in Brussels where, in 1927, the museum curator, Henri Schoutenden, named them as a new subspecies of gorilla: *Gorilla gorilla uellensis*.

In 1996, a Swiss photographer living in Kenya named Karl Ammann visited Bili in order to photograph one of these mysterious gorillas, which had still not been seen by a Westerner, even though they had been named in 1927. While there, he collected photographs, cast footprints, fecal samples, and a skull and then later returned in 2000 to follow up on his 1996 trip. Ammann and the scientists he brought with him did not find the still elusive gorilla but did find what looked like chimpanzee nests. Another expedition was mounted in 2001, which was also unsuccessful.

Ammann made another trip in 2003, where one of his team members, psychologist Shelly Williams, reported that she had seen four of them, and that they were most likely a brand new species of bipedal ape-men. That same year was the year that hairs taken from nests were subject to a mitochondrial DNA analysis, which revealed that the creatures that Ammann had been searching for since 1996 were simply eastern chimpanzees, which by that time had been studied by none other than Jane Goodall. In 2006, primatologist Cleve Hicks brought a team of researchers back to the DRC and they were able to, for the first time, observe a troop, and Hicks confirmed that they were chimpanzees in terms of their physiology and their behavior, confirming the DNA analysis from three years prior. In 2004, he also visited the nearby region of Bondo where additional chimps were living. This designation was cemented when feces samples that Hicks brought back were also tested and found to be from the eastern chimpanzee.

Eastern chimpanzees, like the other three subspecies (Nigeria-Cameroon chimpanzee, western chimpanzee, and central chimpanzee), are endangered, thanks to migration, war, development, bushmeat, and the capture and sale of chimpanzees for pets. For the eastern chimpanzees, it is estimated that there are perhaps 180,000–256,000 animals.

Some cryptozoologists have taken the "discovery" of this creature as proof that new species—even large species like apes—can still be discovered, which means that there is hope for all of the other mystery apes that mainstream primatologists and other scientists shun. Others still think that the Bondo ape might be out there, either as *Gorilla gorilla uellensis* or another species.

See also: Deloy's Ape

Further Reading:

Burton, A. (2013). Gone Fishing. *Frontiers in Ecology and the Environment*, 11(9), 516.

Hofreiter, M., Siedel, H., Van Neer, W., & Vigilant, L. (2003). Mitochondrial DNA Sequence From an Enigmatic Gorilla Population (Gorilla Gorilla Uellensis). *American Journal of Physical Anthropology: The Official Publication of the American Association of Physical Anthropologists*, 121(4), 361–8.

Meldrum, J. (2012). Adaptive Radiations, Bushy Evolutionary Trees, and Relict Hominoids. *Relict Hominoid Inquiry*, 1, 51–6.

BLACK DOG

Dogs—and especially black dogs—are seen as the embodiment of the devil in European folklore, a belief that can be traced back to classical times. In particular, the appearance of a large black dog (often with piercing red eyes) has long been thought of as both a bad omen (meaning someone will most likely die soon) and the appearance of the devil himself.

The black dog is a common feature in folklore from the British Isles but is also found throughout Scandinavia, where they possibly originated. Black dog tales usually feature a lonely traveler walking along a country road, often at night, when he or she encounters the unexpected and alarming appearance of a large black dog (often with piercing red eyes). Sometimes the dog appears in other locations, but the idea is the same—the dog is demonic.

In the Swedish tale *The Devil as a Black Dog*, a person encounters a dog that seems normal but turns out to be a terrifying encounter with the devil himself. One variant goes like this:

> At a dance at someone's house right here in the parish, I myself, and several others, saw a big black dog with flames coming out of its mouth. it was prowling around, back and forth among the dancers. The fiddler got a glimpse of it too; and he threw down his fiddle and never played again. The dog disappeared through a crack in the window, and we all went home. (Lindow 1978: 147)

This tale is interesting because it does not end with a death or disaster, which is common in black dog tales. Instead, it is an almost mundane encounter but clearly fraught with the potential of danger.

In England, there are countless stories about black dogs and the terror that they bring. Different localities have regional differences in terms of the dog's name (the Devil's Dandy in Cornwall, the Gurt dog in Somerset, Guytrash in West Yorkshire, the Mauthe Doog on the Isle of Man, Shuck in Norfolk, Skriker or Trash in Lancashire, and the Yeth hound of Devon), with more sightings and more tales found in East Anglia and Yorkshire than any other region. Folklorist Peter Jennings (2014) suggests that this is because this area of the country was settled by Vikings and other Norse explorers, who may have brought their beliefs about the role that dogs played in guarding the underworld. (They may have also brought with them the practice of burying companion dogs alongside of their human owners so that the dog could both lead his master to the next world and provide companionship for him while there. Not only was this burial practice common throughout Scandinavia, but dogs have also been found in human graves in Viking settlements along the eastern coast of England.)

Interestingly, passage to the underworld, even when accompanied by a dog, was not assured in Scandinavian myth. In order to gain access, the deceased must provide something to the dog (i.e., the sop to Cerberus), or the deceased is judged by his treatment of dogs during his own lifetime. The idea that the dog–human relationship is ideally a reciprocal one, in which both partners benefit, can be seen here, although what is less common is the idea that ill treatment on the part of the human can result in the dog, that most loyal of beasts, blocking someone from Valhalla. Among Native American cultures, which also see dogs as guides to the underworld, travelers must also make a gift of food to the dogs; otherwise, their passage will be denied.

Besides regional differences in names, England's black dog also appears differently in different regions. In all cases, the dog is huge, black, with shaggy (sometimes curly, sometimes straight) hair and glowing red eyes. It is variously described as tall and thin, it sometimes has just one eye, and its fur is so dark that it stands out against the night sky.

A Shetland Island folktale called *The Black Dog* moves from the typical black dog lore and turns it into a witch:

> A witch, desirous of injuring a neighbor, changed herself into a black dog and made her way into the neighbor's ben-end-o'-the-hoose, where she would certainly have created serious disturbance if an old man in the family had not recognized her by a peculiar formation of the eyelids, which, it seems, she could not discard from her canine appearance.

Seizing the tongs, the worthy patriarch brought them down upon the black dog's back with might and main. "Tak' doo yon, Minnie Merran" (the witch's name), he cried, "an bear doo da weight o' dis auld airm as lang as doo leeves."

> The dog ran howling and limping out of the house, and when next the witch was seen, she who hitherto had walked upright and with the dignity of a Norna, leant upon a stick, and had a hump upon her back. She said she had fallen from a height, and was afraid her spine was broken. But folk called it "the mark o' auld Jockie's taings." (Black 1903: 53)

The color black, at least in Europe, has long been associated with death, mourning, nighttime, and evil, which helps explain why demonic beasts (both canine and feline) are often black. In recent years, there has also been a healthy debate over whether black dogs face a harder time getting adopted in American animal shelters—a phenomenon known as black dog syndrome. While the debate is still ongoing as to how serious the problem is, some scholars feel that the negative associations of the color black may in fact be at fault.

These sightings, which often took place in cemeteries or locations where violence had occurred, were well-known portents of ill tidings to come, most commonly a (human) death. Cemeteries are particularly potent locations for sightings; the sight of stray dogs consuming the corpses of plague victims during the Black Death of the fourteenth and seventeenth centuries must have been a common, and unpleasant, one, and this memory may have fed into black dog lore. (In addition, dogs' scavenging abilities—including the fact that stray dogs can and do eat human corpses—are one of the key reasons that dogs were attracted to humans in the first place.) Black dogs often haunt prisons, another place associated with death and suffering; the black dog of Newgate Prison terrorized the inmates from the Middle Ages until 1904 when it was torn down. It was especially active on the nights before an execution was to be held.

Another location where black dog sightings were commonly encountered was intersections, as crossroads of any kind are, going back to the classical civilizations, known to be spiritually powerful. Crossroads are often seen as liminal spaces where spirits may gather and where the borders between the worlds can be porous. That is one reason why for centuries, the English buried the corpses of executed killers and victims of suicide at crossroads. Finally, bridges are another location associated with black dog sightings; bridges are metaphorically associated with connecting two different realms: clearly, they mark the boundary between water and land, but metaphorically, they divide the sacred and the profane. Bridges are also used to represent crossings of all kinds; it is no surprise that the relatively recent belief in the Rainbow Bridge imagines a bridge connecting this world, where we live with our companion animals, to a sort of heaven where we are reunited with our dead pets. While black dog tales no doubt predate Christianity, with the arrival of Christianity in the British Isles, the specter of the black dog has become associated with the Devil. Interestingly, even though the black dog is found at crossroads, bridges, and other liminal border spaces, it cannot itself cross parish boundaries and must always remain in its home parish.

The idea of a dog—man's best friend, after all—being associated with the devil seems strange to us. But historically, there are a great many cultures that believed that dogs either lived in the underworld or were responsible for guiding humans to the underworld after death.

Dogs are associated with the underworld, and death, in a wide variety of cultures, perhaps because they are expected to be our companions in the afterlife, as well as in this life. In Greek and Roman mythology, Cerberus, the three-headed dog, guarded the gates of the underworld, while in Norse mythology, Garm, a giant dog, watches over the land of the dead, and Fenrir, a monstrous wolf, was to kill the god Odin in the final days. In the ancient Zoroastrian religion, dogs were intermediaries between the profane and the sacred realms and were especially important in rituals surrounding death. When a person died, dogs were brought in to witness the body, they played a role in the funeral, and after death, the soul was accompanied to the afterlife by two dogs. And in ancient Egypt, Anubis, a dog or jackal-headed god, was god of the dead. These beliefs, alongside the ancient Greek idea that dogs brought bad luck, may have led to the idea of a black dog being the embodiment of the devil in Christian Europe.

Because black dogs were such an important folk belief, not just to the English but also to the English transplants who settled the New World, it should not surprise us to learn that there are multiple folk songs about the black dog or about the devil in black dog guise. One of the more interesting of such songs is *Hellhound on My Trail*, made famous by blues singer Robert Johnson in 1937. One line, repeated throughout the song, reads:

There's a hellhound on my trail, hellhound on my trail
Hellhound on my trail

The song was written and originally performed during the darkest parts of the Jim Crow era when African Americans were not only subjected to racism of all kinds but also when African American men could be lynched for any slight—but especially one that is interpreted as threatening the virtue of white women. It has since been interpreted as an anti-lynching song, with the hellhound standing in for the white man, often called a white devil. It also refers to the notion popular in southern churches in the past of hellhounds chasing down sinners. References to hellhounds chasing people are found in other old blues songs as well, such as Devil Blues, from 1927 ("Hellhounds start to chase me man, I was a running fool, My ankles caught on fire, couldn't keep my puppies cool"), and Howling Wolf Blues No. 3 in 1931 ("I take time when I'm prowlin', an' wipe my tracks out with my tail . . . Get home and get blue an' start howlin', an' the hellhound on my trail"). Finally, the fact that dogs were used to track down and terrorize escaped slaves lends the hellhound concept another layer of significance to African Americans.

See also: Cerberus

Further Reading:

Berezkin, Y. (2005). "The Black Dog at the River of Tears": Some Amerindian Representations of the Passage to the Land of the Dead and Their Eurasian Roots. In Andy Byford (Trans.), *Forum for Anthropology and Culture* (Vol. 2), 130–70.

Black, G. F., & Thomas, N. W. (1903). *Examples of Printed Folk-Lore Concerning the Orkney and Shetland Islands.* London. https://archive.org/details/examplesprinted00thomgoog.

Brown, T. (1958). The Black Dog. *Folklore*, 69(3), 175–92.

Harte, J. (2011). Shock! The Black Dog of Bungay: A Case Study in Local Folklore. *Folklore*, 122(3), 347–8.

Lindow, J. (1978). *Swedish Legends and Folktales.* University of California Press.

Rudkin, E. H. (1938). The Black Dog. *Folklore*, 49(2), 111–31.

Thurston, Mary Elizabeth. *The Lost History of the Canine Race.* Andrews McMeel Publishing, 1996.

Witcutt, W. P. (1942). The Black Dog. *Folklore*, 53(3), 167–8.

Woods, B. A. (1954). The Devil in Dog Form. *Western Folklore*, 13(4), 229–35.

Zmarzlinski, A. (2020). The Black Dog: Origins and Symbolic Characteristics of the Spectral Canine. *Cultural Analysis*, 18(2), 35–73.

CERBERUS

Cerberus, also known as the hound of Hades, is the three-headed dog that, in Greek mythology, guards the gates of the underworld; those who want to pass to the next world must give it a gift (what has become known as a "sop to Cerberus" and which was often baklava) to distract it.

Cerberus was born to two serpent gods, Echidna and Typhon, so besides its three heads (in some depictions it has more than three heads, but three is the typical number and represent the past, the present, and the future), its tail takes on the form of a snake and in many depictions there are snakes protruding from its body. It ate raw flesh, had glowing red eyes and black fur, and, according to Horace, had three tongues as well. Its saliva was toxic. Cerberus's story is most well known from the story of its capture by Heracles (later known as Hercules), which was told by a number of Greek authors and which features a story in which Heracles is forced to perform a number of acts, or "labours," in order to atone for the sin of killing his wife and children. The eleventh of these labours is the order to capture Cerberus. The Greek Anthology includes the following description of Heracles's labours:

First, in Nemea he slew the might lion. Secondly, in Lerna he destroyed the many-necked hydra. Thirdly, after this he killed the Erymanthean boar. Next, in the fourth place, he captured the hind with the golden horns. Fifthly, he chased away the Stymphalian birds. Sixthly, he won the Amazon's bright girdle. Seventhly, he cleaned out the abundant dung of Augeas. Eighthly, he drove away from Crete the fire-breathing bull. Ninthly, he carried off from Thrace the horses of Diomede. Tenthly, he brought from Erythea the oxen of Geryon. Eleventhly, he led up from Hadesthe dog Cerberus. Twelfthly, he brought to Greece the golden apples. In the thirteenth place he had this terrible labour: in one night he lay with fifty maidens. (*The Greek Anthology*, 1917: 208–9)

Why was Cerberus a dog? Dogs are associated with the underworld, and death, in a wide variety of cultures. Dogs, more than any other animal, act as guardians to the next world; they may guard the gate that separates this world from the next, or perhaps the bridge separating the worlds. In addition, one of dog's most enduring functions is that of loyal companion; think of Argo, Odysseus's faithful dog, that, after twenty years of waiting for its master to return from war, immediately died after wagging its tail: "But Argos passed into the darkness of death, now that he had fulfilled his destiny of faith and seen his master once more after twenty years" (Book 17, lines 290–327).

We expect our dogs to accompany us throughout our lives; it makes sense that we might expect them to accompany us to the next life as well. While other animals—as well as a variety of spiritual entities—can act as psychopomps (the Greek term for entities that escort the souls of the dead to the afterlife), no animal fulfills this purpose better than the dog.

In ancient Egypt, Anubis, a dog or jackal-headed god, was god of the dead and was known to guard cemeteries as well as to accompany the dead on their journey to the underworld. Called "the dog that swallows millions," Anubis, unlike other Egyptian gods, had no temple dedicated to it. Instead, it haunted places of death, suffering, and fear. Anubis, like Cerberus, was also responsible for judging the life of those who died.

In Norse mythology, Garm, a giant dog with fur stained with the blood of the dead, lives on the end of a chain in a cave at the mouth of Hel. All of these beliefs may stem from India, where Yama, the Hindu god of death, owns a pair of dogs named Sharvara (associated with Canis Major) and Syama (Canis Minor), which are responsible for guarding the bridge that connects this world to the netherworld. In the ancient Zoroastrian religion, many of these beliefs come together in rituals surrounding death. When a person died, dogs were brought in to witness the body, they played a symbolic role in the funeral, and after death, the deceased human's soul was accompanied to the afterlife by two dogs.

These beliefs and practices were found in the New World as well. Many of the cultures of ancient Mesoamerica, like the Olmec, Toltec, Maya, and Aztecs, saw the hairless dog as the guardian of the dead who accompanied them to the underworld; for this reason, mummified dogs were buried in the tombs of the deceased throughout the region. Even today, small dogs are thought to ward off ailments in parts of Central America. Some Native American tribes hold the belief that the Milky Way is a path to Heaven, with a pair of dogs guarding the bridge that lies at the fork of the Milky Way, a belief that is strikingly reminiscent of the Hindu gods Sharvara and Syama.

In general, cultures that believe that an animal guards the souls of the dead, or accompanies them to the afterlife, will revere the specific animal. Sometimes that means refraining from killing them, as with Nepalese Hindus, who worship dogs at an annual festival called Kukur Puja, and sometimes it means sacrificing them, as with the hairless dog of pre-Columbian Mesoamerica. But in the Eurasian context, it meant the transformation of the dog that guards the border through which the dead must pass into the afterworld into one that lives in this world and whose presence signals an imminent death: the black dog.

See also: Black Dog

Further Reading:

Berezkin, Y. (2005). "The Black Dog at the River of Tears": Some Amerindian Representations of the Passage to the Land of the Dead and Their Eurasian Roots. In Andy Byford (Trans.), *Forum for Anthropology and Culture* (Vol. 2), 130–70.
Bloomfield, M. (1905). *Cerberus, the Dog of Hades: The History of an Idea*. Open Court Publishing Company.
Gow, A. S. F., & Page, D. L. (Eds.). (1965). *The Greek Anthology: Hellenistic Epigrams* (Vol. 2). CUP Archive.
The Greek Anthology, Volume III: Book 9: The Declamatory Epigrams. Translated by W. R. Paton. Loeb Classical Library 84. Harvard University Press, 1917. https://www.loebclassics.com/view/greek_anthology_16/1918/pb_LCL086.209.xml (Accessed September 20, 2022).
Grey, S. F. (2018). Cosmology, Psychopomps, and Afterlife in Homer's Odyssey. In R. Mattila, S. Ito, & S. Fink (Eds.), *Imagining the Afterlife in the Ancient World*. Springer VS, 101–16.
Wilkosz, I. (2019). Aztec Dogs: Myths and Ritual Practice. In R. Mattila, S. Ito, & S. Fink (Eds.), *Animals and Their Relation to Gods, Humans and Things in the Ancient World*. Springer VS, 367–87.

CHAMROSH

Chamrosh is a mythical bird-like creature from ancient Persian and Mesopotamian mythology. It is a hybrid in that it has the body of a dog and the head, wings, and tail feathers of a bird— specifically an eagle—and is sometimes referred to as Cynogriffin, reflecting its resemblance to the griffin, another bird-dog hybrid. During Chamrosh's time, there were a number of other hybrid bird creatures in the ancient Near East, including the Jewish bird Ziz (lion-bird), the phoenix of Arabia, the Old Testament Cockatrice (dragon-rooster), the Greek sphinx (human-lion-falcon), griffin (lion-eagle), hippalectryon (horse-rooster), the Assyrian lammasu (lion-eagle), the Sumerian Anzu (human-bird), the Islamic Burāq (donkey-mule-bird), Simurgh (dog-bird), the Cretan Hippalectryon (horse-rooster), and the Egyptian hieracosphinx (lionhawak). Other cultures had similar creatures, including India (Sharabha which is a lion-bird) and pre-Columbian Mesoamerica (the feathered serpent, which is a bird-serpent hybrid).

Chamrosh was created by the Zoroastrian creator god Ahura Mazdā, along with his cousin Amrosh, who is also known as Simurgh. (It may be that Chamrosh and Amrosh/Simurgh were once the same creature but their myths may have continued to evolve and develop over time). Chamrosh lived at the base of the Harvisptokhm tree (also called the soma tree in some versions) on the top of Mount Alborz, the highest mountain in Iran, located in the north of the country, and, every three years, Amrosh would shake the tree branches, dropping the seeds to the ground, where Chamrosh would gather them and distribute them around the world. In this sense, Chamrosh was considered to be the guardian of Persian land. Stories of Chamrosh are found in a number of ancient Persian texts, such as the Avesta and the Rivayats. The Avesta, for example, a major Zoroastrian text, tells of Chamrosh's role in helping to ward off invaders, while in the *Shahnameh*, Chamrosh, or perhaps Simurgh, helped the Persian king Zal gain his throne.

Why birds? Why are so many of these creatures, especially those that lived in the classical world, birds? Birds were an extremely important part of divination rituals in the cultures of the ancient Middle East. Divining the future through birds is known as ornithomanteia and is a common form of early scientific practice. Birds share a long evolutionary history with humans, and while wild, many species of birds have been intertwined with human culture for thousands of years. In addition, birds can fly, making them ideal candidates for creatures that can interface between this world and the next world or the world of spirits. One belief, for example, was that after a human death, their soul would reincarnate into the body of a bird.

Birds also famously demonstrate agency; many divination rituals involving birds allow the bird to fly off in any direction they choose; what they choose is then seen as a sign from the gods, which must be interpreted by diviners in order to understand the message. These practices are at least as old as the Mesopotamian culture and might go back at least 5,000 years. In particular, political and military leaders in many ancient cultures—but especially in the Greek and Roman worlds—would not consider going to war or making any other momentous decision without the aid of divination. For all of these reasons, birds are an extremely common motif in not just the art of the ancient world but particularly Islamic and pre-Islamic Arabian art.

See also: Gamayun, Siren

Further Reading:

The Bundahishn (2019). Dalcassian Publishing Company.
Mynott, J. (2018). *Birds in the Ancient World: Winged Words*. Oxford University Press.

DELOYS' APE

De Loys' ape, or *Ameranthropoides loysi,* was an alleged new ape species found in South America. It is either a terrible misidentification of a known animal or else it was a hoax perpetrated by French anthropologist George Alexis Montandon, with or without the participation of the man who found the creature, Swiss geologist Louis Francois Fernand Hector de Loys.

In 1920 (or perhaps a few years earlier; stories differ), de Loys was in Venezuela on an oil survey expedition. While in nearby Colombia near the Tarra River, he photographed what he claimed to be an unknown primate species, and specifically, an ape. As he later explained it, he and his crew were in the jungle and saw two bipedal monkey-like creatures approach the men in a threatening fashion; one of the men shot them, killing one, the female, while the other disappeared back into the jungle.

When the men returned to Europe, de Loys brought back the dead female's body as well as a photograph he had taken of it. In the photo, a tall thin creature is shown sitting upright on a wooden box, with a stick under the chin propping up the animal. Because the body later disappeared, this photo remains the only piece of evidence from the encounter.

It was not until a few years later that French anthropologist George Alexis Montandon saw the photo and concluded, based on the animal's size—it looked to be at least 4 feet tall—lack of tail, hominoid dental structure, and upright gait, that it could not be a New World monkey but must be a hominoid or an ape. And since there are no apes that are native to the New World, Montandon postulated that the photo represented a new, unknown species of South American ape.

Montandan persuaded de Loys to go public with his discovery, and in 1929, he published a piece in the *Illustrated London News,* while Montandan announced the find, which he named *Ameranthropoides loysi,* in the *Journal de la Societe des Americanistes.*

By the late 1920s, physical anthropologists were already familiar with the New World monkeys, so they were immediately suspicious of Montandan's claims. Many thought that the photo looked an awful lot like a spider monkey, specifically a white bellied spider monkey (Ateles belzebuth), including what had been interpreted as a large penis in the picture but what could also have been the clitoris of the female spider monkey, which grow to the size of a penis.

To back up the men's claims, Montandan used indigenous beliefs about a variety of spirits local to the tribes in the region as well as stories about locals who had been attacked by mysterious animals.

While there is no evidence of an ape living in South America, and most scientists have concluded that de Loys's ape is just a spider monkey without a tail (or with one that was hidden in the photo), it is unclear whether the entire episode was a hoax or an accidental misidentification.

De Loys may not have had anything to gain by his discovery, but Montandan did, and further, as an anthropologist he would have recognized the incredible significance of finding an ape in South America. In addition, Montandan, like a number of scientists at the time, believed in the polygenetic theory of human evolution, which claims that the modern "races" of people evolved separately from each other, perhaps as long ago as 2 million years, from separate populations of Homo erectus or perhaps archaic Homo sapiens. If there were an ape native to South America, this could be proof of this theory and would show that native people from South America evolved on that continent. This theory, rejected by all but the most fringe of scientists, would, if proven, demonstrate that race as a biological concept is real (most scientists now recognize that it is a social concept more than anything else), and that the world's "races" were created millions of years ago.

Whether the whole episode was a hoax, or whether de Loy and/or Montandan genuinely thought that de Loys had discovered a new species of ape, the fact remains that the creature in the picture has no tail. It could be hidden in the picture, but if it was, de Loys still would have seen it, and he was clear in his accounts that neither creature had a tail. If it did not have a tail, and was indeed a spider monkey as most people believe today, then that tail was removed somehow—with or without de Loys's knowledge. If it were with his knowledge, that means that it was definitely a hoax and that de Loys was in on it.

There is good evidence to support this. In 1962, Enrique Tejera, who spent some time with de Loys on the expedition, wrote a letter to the newspaper *Diario el Universal*, in which he claimed that the photo was of a monkey given to de Loy, who was a prankster, by his coworkers, and that someone in the group amputated the animal's tail. After the monkey died of an unknown cause, Tejera wrote, de Loys took the photograph that has become the iconic photo of de Loys's ape.

Today, there is virtually no one who believes in the reality of an undiscovered ape in the Americas. Even Ivan Sanderson, one of the fathers of cryptozoology and a man who believed in the legitimacy of a number of troubling finds, called this a hoax.

See also: Great Mammoth Hoax

Further Reading:

Ashley-Montagu, F. M. (1929). The Discovery of a New Anthropoid Ape in South America? *The Scientific Monthly*, 29(3), 275–9.

Newton, M. (2005). *De Loys's Ape. Encyclopedia of Cryptozoology: A Global Guide*. McFarland & Company, Inc.

Urbani, B., & Viloria, Á. L. (2008). *Ameranthropoides Loysi Montandon 1929: The History of a Primatological Fraud*. LibrosEnRed.

DINOSAUR MAN

Dinosaur man not only refers to a number of creatures from science fiction but also refers to the idea that there may be a humanoid dinosaur, either who lived in the past or who could potentially live in the present.

In 1982, paleontologist Dale Russell suggested that if Stenonychosaurus, a dinosaur for which he himself found the first skull, had not gone extinct, that it may have eventually evolved a cranial capacity that rivals the size of humans. The Stenonychosaurus had a brain case approximately six times the size of other dinosaurs, and, given what Russell assumed was a base rate for the increase in brain size compared to body size, he suggested that of all of the dinosaurs, the Stenonychosaurus had the best chance of evolving into an intelligent being.

In addition, these dinosaurs had a number of features found in primitive primates, which later developed into some of the primate order's most salient characteristics. The Stenonychosaurus had forward-facing eyes, like primates, which means it would have had binocular vision, like we have. It also had hands that could hold and manipulate objects and a finger that was semi-opposed. And it was bipedal. Russell's "dinosauroid," the name he gave to his modern dinosaur, has been heavily criticized by other scientists who saw the dinosauroid as far too anthropomorphic with its upright gait, prehensile hands, and forward-facing binocular vision.

Russell commissioned artist Ron Seguin to create a sculpture of what his dinosauroid may look like. It does not look like a dinosaur at all; instead, it looks like a twentieth-century version of a Hollywood alien. It is fully bipedal, with a humanoid head with a high forehead, articulated hands capable of holding tools, and fully human body structure including long legs. It is short, about 4 feet, the size of our earliest ancestors but also the size of a typical Hollywood alien. (According to Darren Naish, Russell also had a strong interest in aliens, which might explain the dinosauroid's appearance.) Apparently, Russell felt that the human body type is the most probable or predictable evolutionary end for a big-brained creature. The only "dinosaur" element in the sculpture is the missing genitals; Russell thought that, like birds, they would be internal—even though the rest of the body is humanoid.

This intense anthropomorphism demonstrates why paleontologists—for whom a large flightless bird would be a better evolutionary outcome for the Stenonychosaurus—would be put off by Russell's creature. In addition, Russell was a practicing Catholic. Being a Catholic is not necessarily inconsistent with science and the theory of evolution, but Russell's own beliefs may have shaped his idea that humans are in some sense the pinnacle of evolution. While progress or directionality is not considered to be a part of evolutionary theory by mainstream scientists, it is clear that Russell did hold that belief, which explains why the dinosauroid looks like a human rather than a dinosaur—or any other creature.

The original sculpture now lives at the Canadian Museum of Nature while replicas can be found in other museums.

But it is precisely those human-like characteristics that make the dinosaur man so interesting—especially to those outside of paleontology. Dinosaur men, or sapient dinosaurs, are imagined to be not just intelligent dinosaurs. The word "sapient" means wise, but it also means human-like. And we have already seen that Russell thought that the human shape was the natural or inevitable end point of evolution. So whether Dr. Russell intended to or not, his thought experiment about a modern intelligent dinosaur has created a space for the development in recent years of much more far-fetched speculation about humanoid dinosaurs or reptiles.

One of the most far-out examples of this is the modern reptilian conspiracy theory. This theory, which was first postulated by conspiracy theorist David Icke, claims that there is a race of shapeshifting reptilian creatures from another dimension that have been reproducing with humans for hundreds of thousands of years, and that one group of alien-human hybrids is currently controlling the world. Icke's beliefs have been picked up and incorporated into other conspiracies. During the presidency of Donald Trump, the QAnon conspiracy emerged, which suggested that there is a vast network of Democratic-controlled cannibalistic pedophiles who control the media and politics and began spreading through right-wing networks in the United States and to a lesser extent abroad. QAnon supporters have adopted some of Icke's theories into their own, including the reptilian conspiracy, and the idea that powerful families and individuals are Satanists who drink blood and eat babies. According to Public Policy Polling, 4 percent of American voters in 2012 believed in the reptilian conspiracy theory and the idea that there are lizard people walking around us.

See also: Flatwoods Monster, Lizard Man

Further Reading:

Lewis, T., & Kahn, R. (2005). The Reptoid Hypothesis: Utopian and Dystopian Representational Motifs in David Icke's Alien Conspiracy Theory. *Utopian Studies*, 16(1), 45–74.

Naish, D., & Tattersdill, W. (2021). Art, Anatomy, and the Stars: Russell and Séguin's Dinosauroid1. *Canadian Journal of Earth Sciences*, 58(9), 968–79.

Russell, D. A.; Séguin, R. (1982). Reconstruction of the Small Cretaceous Theropod Stenonychosaurus Inequalis and a Hypothetical Dinosauroid. *Syllogeus*, 37, 1–43.

Varricchio, D. J., Hogan, J. D., & Freimuth, W. J. (2021). Revisiting Russell's Troodontid: Autecology, Physiology, and Speculative Tool use. *Canadian Journal of Earth Sciences*, 58(9), 796–811.

ELWETRITSCH

The elwetritsch is a creature said to live in the Pfalz region (now part of the state of Rheinland-Pfalz) of Germany, but it can sometimes be found in other regions in southern Germany. It is an invented hybrid creature, with the body of a squirrel, the wings of a bird, and the head of a rabbit, or more properly a jackalope, since it has horns. One of a large number of invented creatures, such as the German wolpertinger and Rasselbock, the Swedish skvader, and the American Coney Island sea rabbit, the elwetritsch is a popular tourist attraction.

It is a bird-like creature, with the body of a bird and the antlers of a deer. Even though the elwetritsch is a bird, it is closely related to the horned rabbits found in a number of cultures, including Germany, because of the antlers. It is thought by some that, just as the wolpertinger, the al-mir'aj, and the jackalope may have been inspired by sights of rabbits with the shope papilloma virus, which creates horn-like structures on the heads of infected creatures, this may be the root of the elwetritsch or at least may be at the root of the horns.

It does not fly and is typically depicted as a shy but comical creature, often resembling the dodo. It is almost always gendered female and is often shown with breasts. According to the legend, it is the product of breeding chickens and other fowl with goblins or elves and lives in the forest, and particularly in willow trees.

The elwetritsch was most likely invented by a man named Gus Espenschied, who in the early 1980s set up organized hunting expeditions to find the creature. At the same time, the oldest organization to promote the creature is the Elwetrittche-Club in Landau, Germany, which formed in 1982.

See also: Skvader, Wolpertinger

EMELA-NTOUKA

The emela-ntouka is a Congolese swamp creature that is thought to live in the Likoula swamp. It is similar in description and lore to the mokele-mbembe. It, or a creature very similar to it, has also been found in Zambia, Zimbabwe, and Cameroon and goes by the names of Chipekwe, Irizima, *Aseka-moke*, *Njago-gunda*, and *Ngamba-namae*.

Emela-ntouka means killer of elephants. It has been described as a large beast with a single horn or tooth—similar to the rhinoceros, which may be the source of the stories. The horn is the creature's weapon, and it is known to kill elephants by goring them with its horn. Unfortunately, as with the much better-known mokele-mbembe, virtually all of the reports of this creature are second-, third-, or fourth-hand accounts taken by colonial authorities, explorers, or missionaries, and by the time those stories were collected, the sightings were quite old.

The creature is as large as an elephant and has variously been described as rhinoceros-like or like a hippopotamus. Like the mokele-mbembe, and virtually every other lake or swamp monster, it is an herbivore as well as solitary and territorial.

One of the first written accounts of the monster comes from 1919 when British expat C. G. James, now living in Zambia, wrote a letter to the *London Daily Mail* in which he discussed a rumored monster living in Lake Bangweulu called "chipekwe." Other explorers told of similar stories. There is also one story, that has been retold a variety of times, about some native people who killed one; this story is virtually identical to the monster killing story of the mokele-mbembe.

Because the cryptozoological interpretation of the emele-ntouka is that it is a relic dinosaur, just like the mokele-mbembe, creationists have a serious stake in seeing it move from cryptid, rumor, or extinct creature to still-living dinosaur. Young earth creationists understand that the discovery of a living dinosaur can be used to disprove the theory of evolution and to prove that the Bible's account of the creation of the planet, and all of its inhabitants, is the correct one.

Cryptozoologists who believe that the emela-ntouka is a dinosaur point primarily to the ceratopsian suborder, which includes the triceratops.

See also: Mokele-mbembe

Further Reading:

Mackal, R. P. (1987). *A Living Dinosaur?: In Search of Mokele-Mbembe*. Brill Archive.

FEEJEE MERMAID

The Feejee mermaid was a popular freak show attraction during the nineteenth through the twentieth centuries, which purported to be a mummified mermaid from "Feejee" (Fiji).

Freak shows in the eighteenth century featured people who were physically or intellectually disabled or were suffering from a disfiguring disease, people from non-Western countries (i.e., "native people"), people who modified their bodies to make them appear freakish (through tattoos, piercings, and the like), and novelty acts, like sword swallowers and fire eaters. Besides these people, unusual animals (again, those with disfigurements were popular) and hoaxes were also commonly found at freak shows. A hoax—also known as a gaffe—was something entirely artificial or a person purporting to be something that they were not. For example, circus showman P. T. Barnum displayed an attraction called "What Is It?," which was supposedly a very unusual creature but was in fact two men—one who was born with very short legs and one who was mentally retarded and also possessed a sharply sloping forehead.

In the mid-nineteenth century, freaks were brought together by entrepreneurs such as P. T. Barnum into sideshows, which featured multiple attractions at once and which traveled with circuses, carnivals, and dime museums.

In July 1842, Levi Lyman, a showman (who called himself Dr. Griffin, a naturalist from England), brought the first Feejee mermaid—supposedly a mermaid caught in the waters surrounding Fiji—to New York City, where it was put on display on Broadway, alongside other exotic attractions such as an orangutan and a ventriloquist. Later, Barnum (who was behind the hoax in the first place) displayed the mermaid at his dime museum, the American Museum, then sent it on tour through the American South, and, after its return, shared it with Kimball who continued to display it in Boston when it was not in New York. In the handbills created by Barnum advertising the shows, the mermaid was depicted as a beautiful woman. In real life, however, it was a dry, withered thing, made probably from the head and upper body of a taxidermied monkey, with the tail of a fish sewn on. It had been leased from another showman, Moses Kimball, who had been displaying it in Boston.

While some observers must have believed that the Feejee mermaid was real, it was clear to others that it was not. John Timbs, writing a few years after Barnum's mermaid began making the rounds, wrote:

> Less than half a century ago, a pretended Mermaid was one of the sights of a London season; to see which credulous persons rushed to pay half-crowns and shillings with a readiness which seemed to rebuke the record. (Timbs 33)

The mermaid's history goes back well before American carnival and circus men, however. The Japanese have long-held beliefs about mermaids, known as human fish (*ningyo*) or fish human (*gyojin*), but unlike the Western mermaid—depicted as lovely and seductive females—Japanese mermaids were usually more ape-like and were certainly not beautiful. In Japanese sideshows in the eighteenth and nineteenth centuries, mermaids made by fishermen of the taxidermied bodies of fish and monkeys were often displayed. It was most likely such a Japanese mermaid, known for being made with the highest-quality craftsmanship, that made its way to the United States and eventually into Barnum's hands, after having been shown in Europe as early as 1822. From Europe, it made its way to America via Dutch merchants who sold it to an American sailor named Samuel Barrett Eades, who then sold it to Moses Kimball in Boston. This is how Barnum described his mermaid:

> The animal was an ugly, dried-up, black looking, and diminutive specimen, about 3 feet long. Its mouth was open, its tail turned over, and its arms thrown up, giving it the appearance of having died in great agony. (Harris 1981: 63)

Barnum's mermaid is thought to have either been destroyed in a fire at the American Museum in 1865 or at Kimball's Boston Museum in 1880, but there are a number of specimens that can still be found on display in Japan, as well as in other countries, today.

See also: Merfolk

Further Reading:

Bondeson, J. (1999). *The Feejee Mermaid and Other Essays in Natural and Unnatural History*. Cornell University Press.

Harris, N. (1981). *Humbug: The art of PT Barnum*. University of Chicago Press.
Levi, S. (1977). C. P.T. Barnum and the Feejee Mermaid. *Western Folklore*, 36(2), 151.
Nickell, J. (2005). *Secrets of the Sideshows*. University Press of Kentucky.
Timbs, J. (1869). *Eccentricities of the Animal Creation*. Seeley, Jackson and Halliday.

FLATWOODS MONSTER

The Flatwoods monster, or the Braxton County monster (Braxxie for short), is one of the most unusual of all of the cryptids; it is thought to be some kind of alien. The Flatwoods monster is also, like the Fresno nightcrawler or the Pope Lick Goatman, a hyper local creature, which is associated with a very specific place—Flatwoods, West Virginia, in Braxton County.

The story dates to 1952, an era when UFO sightings in the United States were in the media almost every week, when Americans could go to the movie theater and watch any of the dozens of alien invasion movies and when the term "flying saucer" entered the lexicon. A few months earlier, *LIFE Magazine* had a cover story that asked, "HAVE WE VISITORS FROM SPACE?" In addition, the Cold War was just heating up; three years before, Russia successfully tested its first nuclear bomb.

On the evening of September 12, 1952, three boys, Ed and Freddy May, who were thirteen and twelve, and ten-year-old Tommy Hyer, saw a light stream across the sky and crash into a nearby hill while playing at the Flatwoods Elementary School. The boys ran home, got the Mays' mother, Kathleen May, who called Eugene Lemon, a seventeen-year-old who was in the National Guard, and a neighborhood dog named Rickie, and went to see what happened. On their way up the hill, the party smelled what they would later describe as the smell of rotten eggs, and once they got to the site, they came face to face with a tall, thin, alien-like creature with long arms ending in sharp claws and a large, red, spade-shaped head with huge shining eyes. It glided toward the crowd, letting out a loud shriek. While they did not find wreckage of a flying saucer, there was what looked like evidence of a crash or something burning; it turned out to be motor oil that leaked from a truck.

The story hit the local news the next day and quickly went international, attracting attention from cryptozoologists like Loren Coleman as well as those with an interest in UFOs. Law enforcement took the report seriously, and the site was investigated by both the Braxton County Sheriff's office and the National Guard, and, allegedly, the US Air Force. Mrs. May and Eugene Lemon went on the news and presented a drawing made by a sketch artist, and all of the witnesses have spoken to the media countless times.

What was the Flatwoods monster? It is unclear what the boys and Mrs. May saw that evening in 1952. Some of the stories have changed over the years, perhaps because of time but perhaps also because of a fear of ridicule. It could have been as mundane as an owl—barn owls, which live in the area and have heart-shaped faces, are a possibility. But it is most likely the case that what they saw in the sky was a meteor; it had been seen in the sky overhead by other witnesses.

Most of the people involved in 1952 are now dead, but the May brothers are still alive. In fact, both brothers appeared in a 2018 documentary on the monster, and both stick by their story. Fred May, in his late seventies, says in the documentary, "As far as for myself, it doesn't matter to me whether people believe, or don't believe."

Like a lot of other towns with famous monsters, Flatwoods has embraced their monster, and images of the creature can be seen throughout the area as well as signs proclaiming "Home of the Green Monster." There is an annual Flatwoods Monster Fest and a Flatwoods Monster Museum.

See also: Fresno Nightcrawler, Mothman

Further Reading:

Coleman, Christopher K. (2011). *Dixie Spirits: True Tales of the Strange and Supernatural in the South*. New York: Fall River Press Feschino, Frank C. 2004. *The Braxton County Monster*. Quarrier Press.

Elliott, D. M. (2021). *West Virginia Urban Legends and Their Impact on Cultures Both Local and Abroad*. Bowling Green State University.

Living, V. (2012). *Monsters of West Virginia: Mysterious Creatures in the Mountain State*. Stackpole Books.

FRESNO NIGHTCRAWLER

The Fresno nightcrawler, which is also known as the Fresno alien, ghost pants, or walking pants, is an unusual cryptid from Fresno, California.

It is a rare humanoid cryptid; it has no animal characteristics whatsoever but instead looks like a pair of big white pants, without arms, a torso, or a head. It is about 2–4 feet tall. Video footage taken by witnesses also may show that the legs are partially webbed.

It is both a hyperlocal creature, in that it is primarily associated with just one place, Fresno, a small city in California's Central Valley, and it derives entirely from a single event. Although there have been a few alleged sightings since then, it is the first Fresno sighting that has come to define the creature.

The Fresno nightcrawler is also one of the rare cryptids that is only known through video footage. Both the first, 2010 sighting that created the creature and a second sighting from 2011 were captured on video.

In November 2007 or 2008, a man named Jose (no last name has ever been given, and it is said that he has since died) woke up to the sound of barking dogs and saw on the CCTV monitor hooked up to his outdoor camera two creatures walking across his front lawn. Since that time, not only has the witness died, but the video footage has also been lost; all that is left is a two-minute recording of a television playing the original (alleged) footage. But the information about the monster reached Victor Camacho, a ufologist, who helped to publicize it, ultimately resulting in the television show, *Fact or Faked*, investigating the video in 2010. (The results of that investigation, as well as subsequent ones, are inconclusive.)

In 2011, after *Fact or Faked* aired, the second sighting occurred, this time in Yosemite National Park, about a three-hour drive north from Fresno. This one was also caught on a security camera and, just like Jose's video, captured two creatures that looked like nightcrawlers. In fact, the stories behind both videos are similar as well; Jose's story explains that he had security cameras set up outside of his house because he had been recently robbed; the Yosemite story is the same: staff had put up cameras because they had recently been robbed.

While it is difficult to explain how the original footage was created, or what is depicted, we do know that there have been hoaxes of the Fresno nightcrawler since Jose's footage first came out. YouTuber Captain Disillusion created a video of a nightcrawler in 2012 by filming himself and digitally erasing the top part of his body.

Are there other humanoid creatures like the Fresno nightcrawler out there?

In 2014, a couple driving near in Highland County, Ohio, saw a tall thin armless humanoid creature, which was immediately dubbed the Carmel Area Creature. Was it a type of Fresno nightcrawler? Even further from Fresno was the 2017 Polish sighting of a creature that looked— it was again captured in video footage—an awful lot like the Fresno nightcrawler.

What could the nightcrawler be? The video footage—especially the 2010 footage—clearly shows what looks like a pair of white pants "walking" down the street, so it's difficult to imagine that it could have been a misidentified animal.

See also: Flatwoods Monster, Loveland Frogman, Mothman

GAMAYUN

The gamayun, sometimes known as huma, is one of a number of bird-human hybrid creatures found in myths around the world. The gamayun is a figure of Slavic folklore, with the body of a bird and the head of a woman, like the harpy, the siren, and the sirin, other bird-bodied, female-headed creatures.

Birds are often gendered in folklore and myth. This may be partly due to the fact that many bird species are sexually dimorphic: they display obvious physical differences between males and females of the species. This may have translated into their roles as symbols and metaphors and certainly is reflected in how many people think about and represent birds: predatory birds like hawks and eagles are coded as masculine, while songbirds are almost universally seen as female. In some cultures, water birds are classified as female while birds that fly (but are not drawn to water) are male; this is the case in many African cultures and reflects the long-held symbolic association between women and water and also the fact that sky gods tend to be male. Birds also are associated with fertility, another strongly gendered characteristic, as well as death.

Slavic mythology in particular is riddled with bird-women. Besides gamayun, alkonost, rarog, stratim, and sirin are all creatures with bird bodies and human heads and may all derive from Greco-Roman beliefs in similar beings. In particular, the siren, which we know primarily through Greek literature and poetry but which itself may be pre-Greek in origin, provides a good model for the Slavic and Russian bird creatures.

Sirens are beautiful creatures with a human female head and the body of a bird and, like another famous sea creature, the mermaid, lure sailors with their beautiful songs (which is where we got the term "siren song") and alluring faces to their deaths. While some sirens were represented as fish-women, providing a stronger link to mermaids, most include at least the legs, if not the body and wings, of a bird.

The gamayun is also a prophetic bird. This puts the gamayun into the category of birds used in divination, or birds that are thought to be prophetic, like chamrosh, a Zoroastrian bird god. And because birds also signify the creation of life, gamayun has the power to understand the secrets of life, which she imparts through her song. Unfortunately, like the siren's song, the song of the gamayun can lure men to give up their lives and follow it forever. "Its prophecies are available to a selected group of people, and its appearance can cause deadly elements" (Shuklin 2001). Other prophetic birds in Russia include real birds like crows and owls, both of which foretell sad events. But gamayun sits at the crossroads of many of these beliefs; it can lure men to their deaths; foretell upcoming events; signal an imminent death; and impart the wisdom of the universe, which, as with Eve in the Garden of Eden, can be dangerous in and of itself.

See also: Merfolk, Siren

Further Reading:

Dederen, J. M., & Mokakabye, J. (2018). Negotiating Womanhood: The Bird Metaphor in Southern African Folklore and Rites of Passage. *Tydskrif vir Letterkunde*, 55(2), 91–103.

Кузнецова, О. (2021). Birds' Eden: Birds of Paradise in Early Modern Russian Culture. *Acta Universitatis Lodziensis. Folia Litteraria Rossica*, 1(14), 9–16.

THE GREAT MAMMOTH HOAX

The great mammoth hoax refers to a hoax perpetrated at the turn of the twentieth century about what was alleged to be the last living wooly mammoth. (The wooly mammoth lived during the Pleistocene, which began about 2½ million years ago, and went extinct between 14,000 and 10,000 years ago, thanks to either hunting, climate change, or a combination of the two.)

The story came out in an article published in the October 1899 issue of *McClure's Magazine* called "The Killing of the Mammoth." In it, the writer, Henry Tukeman, told how he, along with a Native American guide he hired, killed the last remaining mammoth in Alaska and later sold the bones to a naturalist in San Francisco. At the end of the article, Tukeman wrote that the bones were now at the Smithsonian Institute in Washington, DC. While the story was intended to be fictional and was marked as fiction in the magazine's table of contents, readers were nonetheless fooled by the story and thought that it was real. Many readers were outraged at the killing of an animal that most people thought was extinct and wrote to the magazine (as well as the Smithsonian) to express their feelings. The magazine was forced to print a statement in the next issue, assuring its readers that the story was fictional.

While the 1899 story was not, in the truest sense of the word, a hoax, since no intent to mislead the public was involved, since the publication of the story, there have been a number of other reported sightings of live wooly mammoths, which clearly were intended to mislead. For example, in 2012, a YouTube video circulated, which purported to show a mammoth crossing a Russian river, even though the man who shot the footage, Ludovic Petho, maintained that there were no mammoths in his original video, and that the video was doctored after he made it. Even so, there is clearly an interest among many people in seeing once-extinct animals come back to life, à la *Jurassic Park*.

See also: Thylacine Chupacabra

Further Reading:

Besse, Nancy L. (1980). The Great Mammoth Hoax. *Alaska Journal*, 10(4), 10–16.

HODAG

The hodag is a creature that lives in the woods of Northern Minnesota. Like Babe the Blue Ox, the hodag is not just a uniquely American creature but is a product of the logging industry of the nineteenth century, and particularly, of Minnesota. It is also a hoax, with no known legend or sightings before the first written report appeared.

While the first Europeans to visit Minnesota were primarily interested in fur trapping, by the nineteenth century when Minnesota became a territory of the United States, logging, especially in the white pine forests of the northeastern part of the state, became an especially important economic activity. Because Minnesota has so many rivers, the lumber was easily transported south, helping Minnesota grow.

It was in these pine forests that the legend of the hodag emerged. The first written account of the hodag was published in 1893, and it is that account that has given the hodag its appearance, behavior, and of course the name. According to this first report, the hodag doesn't look like any other cryptid in the world. It has the body and head of a dragon, a huge mouth full of sharp teeth, and the short stocky legs of a dachshund. It also smelled like "buzzard meat and skunk perfume," and Shepard described how the creature emerged from the burnt remains of an ox—the most significant animal at any logging camp and the source of the Babe the Blue Ox legend. Shepard said that because the oxen used in the camps experienced so much abuse from the loggers, it created demons that emerged from the oxen and that is how the hodag was created. Its name comes from lumberjack lingo for some of the tools used by loggers: grub hoes and maddoxes.

This account (which was accompanied by a photo taken by Shepard of the beast) was written by a timber cruiser named Eugene Simeon Shepard, who described how it killed his hunting dogs, and, after he and his companions shot the creature, which did not kill it, they exploded the beast with dynamite. Shepard had talked about the creature before, but it wasn't until his account was published in the local newspaper, and then spread to other papers, that the legend of the hodag solidified. In 1896, three years after Shepard's first article came out, he published another article in which he claimed to capture a live hodag using chloroform, which he exhibited at the Oneida County fair and which, according to reports at the time, was made out of wood and untanned animal hides. Shepard was able to leverage his story, and various examples of the beast, into a modest living.

As with Babe the Blue Ox and its companion Paul Bunyon, the Hodag emerged from the logging camps of the north. Logging camps offer a great opportunity for the telling of legends, as the men who worked in logging lived and worked in the camps, isolated from friends and family and from urban life. In addition, these particular stories emerged at the exact time that logging was ending, as commercial logging had depleted many of North America's forests. In this sense, both creatures represent a nostalgic look at an industry that was once central to this nation's economy but which was rapidly disappearing. In addition, Shepard, who, besides being a logger, was an opportunist who sought out new ways to make money, saw the hodag as the key to not just making money for himself but also for reviving the economy of northern Minnesota in the face of the death of the timber industry.

Since the hodag's creation at the end of the nineteenth century, the town of Rhinelander, Minnesota, has become the center of all things hodag. The town has multiple statues of the beast, the local high school's mascot is the hodag, a number of businesses include Hodag in their name, and Rhinelander hosts an annual music festival named after it, the Hodag Country Festival. And even though the hodag has now entered the folklore of American cryptids, most people who are interested in or have claimed to see it do not actually believe it is real.

The hodag, as an American folk tradition, has an American folk song to match. This one is by Rob Lefty Letvinchuck and was released in 2011. Called *Hodag*, it gives the history of the beast, its physical description ("two ivory horns on a head like a frog" combined with "needle like claws and razor sharp teeth"), but also warns listeners who visit the woods at night to bring with them a 12 pack of beer and suggests:

get that thang intoxicated

with the alcohol in your tears

See also: Skvader

Further Reading:

Edgar, M. (1940). Imaginary Animals of Northern Minnesota. *Minnesota History*, 21(4), 353–6.

Kearney, L. S. (1928). *The Hodag and Other Tales of the Logging Camps.* LS Kearney.

Kortenhof, K. D. (2006). *Long Live the Hodag!: The Life and Legacy of Eugene Simeon Shepard, 1854–1923.* Hodag Press.

Neville, S. (2020). Midwestern Strange: Hunting Monsters, Martians, and the Weird in Flyover Country by BJ Hollars. *Indiana Magazine of History*, 116(1), 87–8.

JACKALOPE

The jackalope is a mythical North American creature, which is made up of a jackrabbit with the horns of an antelope or deer; sometimes the jackalope also has a pheasant's tail.

The American jackalope was popularized in the 1930s by two American hunters who created a taxidermy animal made out of a jackrabbit with deer antlers and began selling them. It is now a common feature of the American west, found on postcards, posters, in stuffed animals, and, in its taxidermied form, in bars and other tourist locations throughout the western and plains states.

According to legend, the jackalope, now extinct or almost extinct, was first seen in 1829 in Douglas, Wyoming; the town now has a large statue of a jackalope in the town center. Jackalopes are said to be aggressive, fighting (with its antlers) with other jackalopes for territory, and supposedly have a great talent for mimicry, being able to mimic human voices. Jackalopes, like rabbits and hares, are also known for their fertility and sexuality, and as such, jackalope milk is said to have aphrodisiacal qualities; they are also sometimes called "horny rabbits," because of both their horns and their sexuality.

Jackalopes, albeit under different names, have been found in other cultures as well and may date back to antiquity. For example, the *al-mi'raj* is a mythical horned rabbit (albeit with a single horn on its head, à la the unicorn, rather than a pair of horns), which was originally documented in a Persian story about Alexander the Great, who may have been given a gift of a horned rabbit (or a rhinoceros). A photo and description of the creature can be found in Zakariya Ibn Muhammad al-Qazwini's *Marvels of Things Created and Miraculous Aspects of Things Existing,* a thirteenth-century Persian scientist and writer, where it was described as extremely aggressive and dangerous.

Horned rabbits or hares, sometimes known as *lepus cornutus* (horned hare), were also mentioned as far back as the Middle Ages. Images and descriptions of these creatures can be found in natural history texts, such as in the sixteenth-century books, *Animalia Quadrupedia et Reptilia,* by Joris Hoefnagel, and *Historiae animalium,* by Conrad Gesner, as well as in two texts from the seventeenth century: *Animalium Quadrupedum* by Adriaen Collaert and *A Description of the Nature of Four-Footed Beasts: With Their Figures Engraven in Brass,* by Joannes Jonstonus. It continues to show up in artwork and texts through the eighteenth century. By the end of the eighteenth century, however, scientists were less likely to see this animal as a real animal.

In all of these cases, the stories of the horned rabbit may have derived from a very real disease that afflicts both rabbits and hares called shope papilloma, which causes bony protuberances to grow out of a rabbits' head and sometimes body.

It seems as if every well-known American cryptid has a song dedicated to it, and the jackalope is no exception. The best known of these songs is just called *Jackalope,* and it was released by the Okee Dokee Brothers in 2016. This song might have been written about any number of cryptids, as the Okee Dokee Brothers sing:

> Some say they're fast, some say they're slow
> I've heard they're big, I've heard they're small
> Seems like no one can ever agree
> The chorus continues:
> It's almost like they don't exist at all

See also: Skvader, Wolpertinger

Further Reading:

Furst, J. L. (1989). Horned Rabbit: Natural History and Myth in West Mexico. *Journal of Latin American Lore,* 15(1), 137–49.

KELPIE

A kelpie is a Scottish water cryptid that looks like a horse but can shapeshift, taking on the form of a human when it wants to. They live in the lochs (or lakes) of Scotland, although some people think that they are associated more with rivers than lochs, but tracking kelpie stories shows that they are primarily found in Lochs (especially Loch Ness) and have been a feature of Scottish folklore for hundreds of years.

Horses were extremely important animals in Scandinavia, which may explain why water horses are found in not just Scandinavian countries but also areas where Norse invaders and settlers traveled and settled—especially Scotland and the northeastern coast of England.

Kelpies first showed up in print in the seventeenth century as place names in Scotland, but they were certainly a feature of Scottish folklore for long before that time. In the countries of northern Europe, which would have had the most connection with Scotland, nixies are the most analogous to the kelpie in that they are mischievous and sometimes dangerous water spirits, although they are not horses. Other horse water spirits include the ceffyl dŵr of Wales, the nuggle of Orkney, and the nykur of Iceland, all shapeshifting water horses.

Kelpie stories can emphasize the positive, helpful nature of the kelpie, or the negative destructive nature. The following story is an example of a helpful kelpie:

> A man, in carting home his peats for winter fuel, was in habit of seeing a big black horse grazing on the banks the Ugie, at Inverugie Castle, near Peterhead, ea morning as he passed to the "moss." He told some his neighbours. They suspected what the horse was, and advise man to get a "waith-horse" bridle, approach the animal wi care and caution, and cast the bridle over his head. The man knew the nature of the creature, and followed the advice. Kelpi secured, and did good work in carrying stones to build the bridg the Ugie at Inverugie. When his services were no longer needed was set at liberty. As he left he said: "Sehr back an sehr behns Cairryt a' the Brig o' Innerugie's stehns." The old man, who handed down this story to his children, from of whom I have now got it, used to say to any of them that c plained of being tired after a hard day's work: "Oh, aye, ye're the kelpie that cairryt the stehns to big the brig o' Innerugie, 'back an sehr behns'." (Gregor 1883: 292)

Kelpies are black, or another dark color, with a flowing mane that appears to be either made of seaweed or is intertwined with it. The hooves of the kelpie are backward, a feature found in other water horses as well (Iceland's nykur has backward hooves and ears).

As a shapeshifter, kelpies can turn into humans. In some accounts, if a kelpie is in its human form, it must keep its feet well hidden, because rather than human feet, the kelpie retains its hooves while human. In addition, a kelpie in its human guise can sometimes be detected because of the presence of seaweed or kelp in the person's hair.

One tale featuring a shapeshifting kelpie goes like this:

> A man was crossing the Burn of Strichen, at the same place, the farm of Braco. On approaching a dyke he had to pass over, he heard, as he thought, some one speaking. He walked quietly towards the spot from which the sound of words came, and peeped over the dyke. He saw an old man mending his trowsers, and, as he was mending, he kept saying, "That clout 'ill dee here; and this ane 'ill dee there." The man looked, and listened for a little. At last he inflicted a blow on the old man's head, saying, "An this clout 'ill dee there." In a moment the kelpie was in his true form, and off with loud neighing to his deep pool. (Gregor 1883: 293–4)

One of the functions of water cryptids, regardless of the culture that they are found in, is they act as warnings to children who live near large, fast-moving, or dangerous bodies of water.

But they also have importance to fishermen, and indeed, water cryptids are found in virtually every culture with a strong fishing tradition. Creatures that share some of the same physical or behavioral characteristics of kelpies are also found in a wide variety of cultures, but again, only those with strong connections to the water.

Like mermaids, another water creature, kelpies are dangerous but seductive creatures. They lure men (mostly fishermen) to them and encourage them to climb onto their back for a ride, only to ride them to the bottom of the water where they drown. Children too would be tempted to ride kelpies, and if they did, they would also end up at the bottom of the loch, where sometimes they would be eaten.

In some legends, male kelpies take on human form and seduce young women into marrying them. As with other animal bride stories featuring selkies or swan maidens, if a human finds the kelpie's bridle, they can control the kelpie; removing it will send the kelpie back to the water in its horse form, just as it is the selkie's seal skin that allows it to return to its seal form. This difference can be explained by the fact that kelpies are male while selkies are female; the kelpie bridle can be removed, which forces the kelpie to return to the water, while the selkie skin can be removed by the human, which forces it to stay in its human form. Without his bridle, however, a kelpie can be captured and forced to do hard labor.

See also: Merfolk, Selkie, Siren

Further Reading:

Gregor, W. (1883). Kelpie Stories From the North of Scotland. *The Folk-Lore Journal*, 1(1), 292–4.

Kruse, J. T. (2020). *Beyond Faery: Exploring the World of Mermaids, Kelpies, Goblins & Other Faery Beasts.* Llewellyn Worldwide.

Parsons, E. C. M. (2004). Sea Monsters and Mermaids in Scottish Folklore: Can These Tales Give us Information on the Historic Occurrence of Marine Animals in Scotland? *Anthrozoös*, 17(1), 73–80.

KISHI

The kishi is a two-faced evil spirit found among Bantu-speaking people in Angola and Zambia. M'kishi, the plural word for multiple creatures, refers to a tribe of such creatures that live in the hills and hunt and eat humans.

They are a form of were-hyena: shapeshifters that normally look like hyenas, sometimes with two heads, but that transform into human men. These men, like the Brazilian encantado, a dolphin that turns into an attractive man at night, target young women, charming them and manipulating them in order to get what they want. Also like the encantado, which wears a hat so as not to expose the blow hole on top of its head, the kishi must wear its hair long as a human in order to hide its second face—the hyena face.

Once a kishi has charmed and caught its prey, it will turn its head so that its hidden face, with the powerful jaws of the hyena, jaws that evolved to crush even the largest of bones, can tear the victim apart and devour her. Sometimes a kishi will take a woman as its bride, and after she provides it a son, it kills her and raises its son to be a kishi like it. There are countless stories about the terror that a pack of m'kishi can cause, many of which include information on how to kill it, which is difficult because if you cut off its head (or one of its heads), another will grow back.

While kishi primarily means spirit, it can also refer to the amulets and talismans that people may carry to protect them from a kishi or to cure disease. In addition, magical practitioners known as nganga can trap a kishi in an object or bag, disarming them. But the only way to lure a kishi to you is with human flesh—specifically that of one of your relatives, who you must kill yourself.

In much of sub-Saharan Africa where witchcraft beliefs still operate as a religious practice and a form of social control, witches are believed to be people who are born with an evil spirit inside them; some witches may not even know they are witches. One of the most common attributes of African witches, like European witches, is the ability to shapeshift into animal form. In Africa, that animal is most always the hyena. Other witches keep hyenas as familiars, or "knight cattle," which they would send out to do their evil bidding.

Hyenas are feared predators in those parts of Africa where they still live. While they do not hunt humans, they are primarily scavengers, so they live at the outskirts of human society, eating the waste that humans leave behind—including human corpses. This is one reason for the fear and even disgust that most Africans have toward hyenas, which are seen as brutish, dangerous, and secretive as well as sacred. Some people think that all hyenas are owned or claimed by a hyena, reinforcing the fear and hatred of these animals.

See also: Encantado, Zanzibar Leopard

Further Reading:

Knappert, Jan (1977). *Bantu Myths and Other Tales*. Brill Archive.
Mack, C. K., Mack, C., & Mack, D. (1999). *A Field Guide to Demons, Fairies, Fallen Angels and Other Subversive Spirits*. Macmillan.

KITSUNE

Kitsune are Japanese magical white foxes that sometimes take on human form and marry and seduce men. These fox-maidens, however, can be detected by other animals, and when they are caught, they must transform back into foxes and leave their human husbands.

One of the most famous versions of this story is *The Fox-Woman Kuzunoha Leaving Her Child*. It tells of a man named Abe no Yasuna who saved a white fox that was being pursued by hunters and who later, unknowingly, married the fox (who was a shapeshifter) in the form of a beautiful girl named Kuzunoha. After having a son together, Kuzunoha had to leave her husband and son when he found out that she was, in fact, a fox.

Kitsune are an example of the prominence of foxes in the lore of people around the world.

While foxes in Europe were known as trickster animals, in Asia, they tended to be associated with love, marriage, and sex. In the Asian tradition, foxes are typically represented as female while they are primarily male in Europe.

Kitsune were viewed positively in Japan, unlike in China, where foxes (and where these beliefs probably emerged) were seen as evil.

Kitsune are able to bring wealth to humans. If a man sees a beautiful woman in the woods, she is most likely a kitsune. Even though kitsune refers to foxes, the term *kitsu-ne* means "come and sleep" in Japanese, as the following story illustrates:

> A certain man in the reign of Emperor Kimmei (540–571) had waited many years to find a beautiful wife. Finally, one day, as he was walking across a field he met a beautiful woman. He asked her to marry him and she agreed. Eventually, a son was born to them. On the same day, a pup was born to the man's dog. As the pup grew up it became very hostile to the mistress of the house—snarling at her and frightening her. The man refused to kill the dog, however, and one day it attacked the woman so fiercely that, in despair, she returned to fox form and fled. The man was crushed, as he loved his wife in spite of her being a fox, and he cried out to her to ki tsu ne (come and sleep), and because she returned to him at night she is called ki tsune. (Skibyak 2020)

In some cultures, foxes are associated with gods. Because foxes kill mice that wreak havoc on the rice crops, in Japan, they have long been associated with Inari Ōkami, the Shinto spirit of the harvest. The kitsune act as Inari's messengers.

In China, foxes were once thought to steal people's breath while they were sleeping. They were also believed to be able to shapeshift into humans and then have sexual relationships with women—a belief that translated directly into the kitsune. These relationships could be beneficial to the humans involved, because the foxes were able to bring great wealth to their human partners and their families (often through stealing). These stories date back hundreds of years and often involve the fox/kitsune begging a human into letting him stay with the family, in exchange for riches. In the Chinese folktale, "Jenshih, the Fox Lady," a soldier falls in love with a beautiful woman, who confesses to him that she is actually a fox. During their marriage, she brought him many riches, but one day some dogs in the market smelled her scent and attacked and killed her. Chinese foxes also took on a human woman's appearance in order to seduce men, but in these stories, the fox-woman typically married (rather than simply seduced) the man.

Foxes can also possess women, in both China and Japan. Known as *kitsune-tsuki*, the victim is taken by the fox and is transformed, both emotionally and physically, by the presence of the creature. The human may act like they are insane, yip like a fox, or eat what foxes are thought to eat. Sometimes they learn to read when they are illiterate or learn a new language while possessed. Xiaofei Kang suggests (2007) that women said that they were possessed by a fox in order to escape from some of the constraints of their intensely patriarchal lives. Victims could be cured by a Shinto exorcism.

See also: Selkie

Further Reading:

Batthgate, Michael R. (2004). *The Fox's Craft in Japanese Religion and Folklore: Shapeshifters, Transformations, and Duplicities*. Routledge.

Kang, Xioofei (2007). Spirits, Sex, and Wealth: Fox Lore and fox Worship in Late Imperial China. In D. Aftandilian (Ed.), *What are the Animals to us?: Approaches From Science, Religion, Folklore, Literature, and art*. University of Tennessee Press, 21–36.

Skibyak, G. (2020). Kitsune: A Look Into the Lasting Presence of the Fox Spirit in Japanese. Doctoral dissertation, New Mexico State University.

LAVELLAN

The lavellan is a large rodent-like creature (although it has also been described as a reptile) with breath and saliva that is toxic when a victim is exposed to it. It has agouti fur, a large mouse- or rat-like head, with bright flashing eyes and it is said to be a very quick runner, and lives in the rivers and ponds of Scotland.

The lavellan's most dangerous attribute is its extremely toxic breath and saliva—it is said that the breath can kill a person or animal from as far as 100 feet away, but drinking water that has had either preserved lavellan skin or the head of a lavellan can cure a victim. On the other hand, drinking from water that a lavellan has been in is deadly; for this reason, finding dead cattle or other animals is probably a good sign that there's a lavellan in the area. In addition, it is a blood sucker.

The lavellan is that relatively rare cryptid that is most likely a regular animal. In this case, the appearance, ecology, and behavior of the lavellan are just an exaggerated version of the Eurasian water shrew, a small mammal found throughout Europe and Asia, including Scotland, where the lavellan lives, and whose saliva (but not breath) is in fact venomous (but only slightly). Other candidates for the lavellan include the water vole or a stoat, which at one time had also been thought to produce a venomous substance. On the other hand, some people think it may just be a childhood bogeyman—a creature created by parents to warn children away from bodies of water or to keep them close to home as the lyrics of this children's song demonstrate: "Let him not go away from the houses, to moss or wood, lest the Lavellan come and smite him."

See also: Bunyip, Mamlambo

Further Reading:

Campbell, J. G. (1900). *Superstitions of the Highlands and Islands of Scotland*. James MacLehose and Sons.
Fleming, J. (1814). Contributions to the British Fauna. *Memoirs of the Wernerian Natural History Society*, II(Part I), 238–51.
Raye, L. (2018). Robert Sibbald's Scotia Illustrata (1684): A Faunal Baseline for Britain. *Notes and Records: The Royal Society Journal of the History of Science*, 72(3), 383–405.

MILK HARE

A milk hare (or sometimes in Scandinavia, a troll cat) is a special type of witch, who survives (and does mischief) by turning herself into a rabbit or hare and drinking the neighbors' cows dry. She usually brings the milk back to her home in her mouth, where she then spits it up into a bowl, as depicted in a fifteenth-century wall painting in Uppsala, Sweden. Milk hares were known throughout Sweden, Norway, and Iceland, and the tradition dates back to at least the fifteenth century. Tales involving the milk hare are a variant of the English and Scottish tale "The Daughter of the Witch," about a girl who innocently displays her magical abilities by magically milking a neighbor's cow.

In the Irish folktale, "The Coming of Oscar," a rabbit magically transforms into a man and is only discovered after the rabbit, whose tail was severed during a chase, turns back into a man with a suspiciously bleeding backside. This motif is found in folktales throughout the British Isles and Scandinavia, although in most such tales, the rabbit generally starts out as a woman. In another Irish tale called "The Old Woman as Hare," for example, an old woman lives alone in a cabin. Nearly every week some of her neighbors' cows are dry. When a suspicious neighbor sees a hare come out of the old woman's cabin, he shoots the hare, hitting her in the shoulder. Upon entering the woman's cabin the next morning, the neighbor finds the old woman, her bloody shoulder wrapped in cloth.

In the German tales "Witch as Hare" and "Girl Who Transformed Herself into a Hare," a hunter sees a hare in the forest and shoots at it; when his shots fail to kill the hare, the man assumes that the hare is magical and loads his gun with consecrated powder and shoots again. But instead of killing a hare, the hunter finds a woman, shot dead in the breast. A related tale from England, "Witch and Hare," involves a witch who assumes the shape of a hare in order to trick a local hunter. Eventually, the witch is caught (bleeding and covered with wounds from an almost successful hunt) and burned at the stake. Other European tales also echo this theme of hares transforming into humans (usually women) and ending up wounded—or dead—as punishment for their crimes. In the Welsh story, "The Shot Hare," for instance, a witch used to transform herself into a hare to tease a poacher. The poacher, frustrated that he could not kill the hare, talked to a doctor who told him to take a piece of mountain ash and vervain and place it beneath his gun and to read from a piece of paper when encountering the hare again. The next time he saw the hare, the poacher did as he was told and was able to shoot at the hare's legs, injuring her. When next he saw the hare, she was running into a woman's house, where he found her groaning with blood running from her legs. And finally, in the English tale, "A Witch-Hare at Sedgefield," a hunting party was chasing a hare and followed the animal as it ran into a small hole in a house but not before being grabbed on the leg by a dog. When they entered the house to find the hare, instead they found an old woman with a broken leg.

Scandinavian tales feature the milk hare as well, as in the Swedish folktale "Milking Others' Cows," which opens like this:

> Magnus Tilda's mother was certainly an Easter-hag, she was. and she had two milk-hares, a big one and a little one. people said she had made them out of knitting-needles and heddle-withes and rags. they would milk other people's cows and then run home and spit up the milk. she had a kettle in the barn and every morning it was full. (Lindow 1978: 170)

The perceived association between witches and rabbits (or hares) may have had to do with the reputation both shared for being evil and lustful. Some of the association, too, may have been rooted in the very real context of rural people in medieval and Renaissance Europe, where women were the primary caretakers of rabbits and so were frequently seen tending, talking to, and handling the animals. Still, the sheer number of stories and images in which women become rabbits, rabbits become women, or creatures are half-rabbit, half-woman is striking.

While these tales may seem like nothing more than ancient folklore, it's worth pointing out that there are a handful of legal cases in England in which women were accused of witchcraft based on "eyewitness" testimony that they had transformed into hares. In at least one of those cases, in 1663, the defendant, a woman named Julian Coxe, was executed. It's also worth noting that all of the milk hare cases that resulted in prosecution occurred in England, where witches were generally thought to be more threatening, than Ireland or Scandinavia.

See also: Black Dog

Further Reading:

Kvideland, R., & Sehmsdorf, H. K. (1988). *Scandinavian Folk Belief and Legend* (Vol. 15). University of Minnesota Press.

MINNESOTA ICEMAN

The Minnesota iceman is a creature that was once purported to be the "missing link" between apes and humans but turned out to be a hoax.

In 1967, Frank Hansen, a retired Air Force pilot and promoter, began exhibiting a frozen carcass that he called the Minnesota iceman. This was the year that the Patterson-Gimlin film was released, kicking off a new wave of interest in Bigfoot, so the public was primed to accept the idea of a human-like creature that somehow survived the extinction of all of its relatives to live in Minnesota.

It was about 6 feet tall, covered in hair, with very large appendages. It appeared to have a bullet hole in the skull and perhaps one in one of its arms, which was misshapen or broken. It also gave off a terrible odor.

Hansen's initial story was that the creature was found by fishermen (in one telling, they were Russian; in another, Japanese) floating in an ice block in the Bering Strait; it was then purchased by a secretive California millionaire (rumored to be actor Jimmy Stewart) and given to Hansen to care for and display. Later his story changed, and he said that he encountered three live creatures in Minnesota while out hunting, and that one of them attacked him, leading him to shoot it to defend himself. He said that he returned to the spot months later and retrieved the carcass from the snow where it had been buried. After meeting a carnival showman, Hansen decided to take his new find on the road.

Hansen exhibited the iceman at carnivals and state fairs, taking advantage of the last gasp of the freak show in America. A freak show is an exhibition of odd or unusual people and animals, in order to shock, and sometimes educate, viewers. Freaks include "born freaks" (those with disfiguring diseases or disabilities as well as, in the Western context, "native" people), "made freaks" (such as tattooed or heavily pierced people), as well as "novelty acts," which would include sword swallowers and fire eaters. Often known as monsters, those with different or extraordinary bodies have been ostracized, ridiculed, put on display, and sometimes killed for their physical appearance.

Traveling shows in which human oddities were displayed alongside exotic animals, deformed animals, musicians, jugglers, and other attractions have been popular throughout the Western world, going back to the Middle Ages. In the West, freaks were displayed as single attractions in inns, taverns, and at local fairs throughout medieval Europe. In the mid-nineteenth century, human oddities joined what became known as the freak show or ten-in-one, in which multiple attractions were joined together into one show, as part of a stationary or traveling exhibit.

To a modern eye, not only do freak shows rub us wrong, but the idea of displaying what was purported to be a Neanderthal who survived into the modern era in a freak show where patrons pay twenty-five cents to look at it seems off to us.

But freak shows were expected to be both entertaining and educational. Each attraction was discussed by a barker, who related all of the interesting and exotic facts about the attraction. In the nineteenth century, human freaks were thought of as monsters; without an understanding of genetics, how those monsters came to be was the subject of a great deal of academic and popular talk. One theory suggested that mothers may give birth to children with abnormalities if they were startled while pregnant; being frightened of an elephant while pregnant, for example, could make the woman's baby look elephant-like.

In the eighteenth century, the science of teratology developed, which was the scientific study of "monsters" or those born with disabilities. This led to a new understanding of freaks that saw them as part of God's natural order, a belief that was later discarded in favor of the missing link theory that developed after Darwinism, which saw freaks as being a literal half-human, half-animal creature, which gave rise to the freak known as the "wild man."

One of the more famous wild men attractions was P. T. Barnum's long running "What Is It?" exhibit. The monster was portrayed by two African American men—one who was born with very short legs and one who was said to be "mentally retarded" and also possessed a sharply sloping forehead. Both men portrayed wild men, or missing links between animals and humans.

The Minnesota iceman is a deceased version of the freak show wild man. Hansen kept it encased in ice, and carnival-goers could pay a quarter to see it through glass. He was also the barker; he promoted the iceman, giving it a biography and positioning it within the now trendy discourse surrounding human evolution and "missing links."

Because of the exploding popularity of Bigfoot in the United States and the Chinese interest in two Asian ape-men, the Chinese yeren and the Himalayan yeti, ape-men were in the media, along with language like the "missing link." Jane Goodall was working in Tanzania and news of her findings about chimpanzee behavior was just starting to enter public consciousness. It was in this mix that Hansen's iceman became a sensation.

Hansen first began showing the creature in 1967, visiting not just circus, carnival, and world's fair sideshows but also shopping malls and other public places. It was originally called The Siberskoye Creature, per Hansen's first story. While being displayed at Chicago's International Livestock Exhibition in 1968, a zoology student named Terry Cullen saw the creature and thought it needed to be investigated. Cullen contacted Ivan Sanderson and Bernard Heuvelmann, two zoologists who pioneered the field of cryptozoology, Heuvelman giving it its name.

In one of the worst instances of a cryptozoologist being fooled by a hoax, both Bernard Heuvelmans and Ivan Sanderson, the two most well-known and respected cryptozoologists and zoologists of their time, visited Hansen at his home in Rollingstone, Minnesota, in winter 1968 in order to investigate the body, kept in a refrigerated trailer, at length. The men stayed in Rollingstone for three days, taking photos and making sketches and notes, and concluded that the creature was from Vietnam, where Hansen served, where it was shot and then brought back to the United States. Heuvelmans claimed that it was a new species of Neanderthal, even though

Neanderthals had not been found in Vietnam (the closest known Neanderthals to Vietnam were found in China). Heuvelmans named the specimen Homo pongoides, positioning it into our own genus, Homo, while Sanderson (who nicknamed it Bozo after Bozo the Clown), in a 1969 article in which he included the missing link theory, wrote, "Let me say, simply, that one look was actually enough to convince us that this was—from our point of view at least—the 'genuine article.'"

Besides the yeren, there are other ape-men in Asia that were starting to be known, at least among cryptozoologists, outside of Asia. One of those is the batatut, or rock ape, a hairy wild man or ape-man thought to live in the jungles of Vietnam. American soldiers picked up stories about the creature from South Vietnamese contacts, leading to a number of instances where soldiers blamed an unexpected sound or occurrence on the batatut.

With the stamp of approval of Heuvelmans and Sanderson, Hansen's iceman gained even more popularity. Eventually, thanks to the media attention—it had reached London's *Sunday Times* in 1969—the Smithsonian became interested in Hansen's body, but Hansen refused to let scientists from that institution see it. Perhaps Hansen shunned this new publicity (it was later speculated) because his body contained two bullet holes, which might get Hansen in trouble.

Eventually, people began to suspect that the iceman was a hoax. In order to dispel those rumors, Hansen said that he switched out the actual corpse for a latex model, in order to protect the body, although the body—if there ever was one—was never seen again. (In 2013, the purported latex replica was sold on eBay to Steve Busti, who has it on display at the Museum of the Weird in Austin, Texas.)

Primatologist John Napier, while not allowed to see the body, did conduct an investigation of sorts on behalf of the Smithsonian and discovered that Hansen commissioned the building of the creature in 1967, which suggested that there was never a real body, nor was a latex model ever substituted for that body. Instead, there was only ever a hoax.

Even though the consensus today is that there was no real body, and that the latex model now being housed in Texas is in fact the iceman, the iceman, thanks to its promotion by Heuvelmans and Sanderson, became another piece of evidence supporting the evolutionary relic theory and, in particular, the idea that there are these "crypto-hominids" living today throughout Asia.

See also: Bigfoot, Yeren

Further Reading:

Meldrum, J. (2016). Neanderthal: The Strange Saga of the Minnesota Iceman by Bernard Heuvelmans, Translated by Paul LeBlond, With Afterword by Loren Coleman. *Journal of Scientific Exploration*, 30(4), 604–6.

Regal, B. (2011). Bigfoot, the Anti-Krantz, and the Iceman. In B. Regal (Ed.), *Searching for Sasquatch*. Palgrave Macmillan, 55–79.

MOA

The moa is a large, extinct flightless bird, measuring up to 12 feet in height. Native to New Zealand, the moa was once thought by Europeans to be a mythical animal.

It turns out, however, that the moa was once a very real bird. Like the emu and the ostrich, the moa was a very large, flightless, and even wingless bird that was hunted to extinction by the Maori, the indigenous people of New Zealand. It is thought that there were once as many as 50,000 or 60,000 moa, but by 1440, they were wiped out. By the time that Captain James Cook arrived in New Zealand in 1769, no birds were visible, although Europeans began to hear stories about these giant birds, stories that suggested that the moa was real; other stories, on the other hand, suggested that they occupied a supernatural realm, rather than the world of people. Starting in the mid-nineteenth century, moa fossils began to appear, adding to the lore about these mysterious birds.

But could any moa have survived into the present day? Some Maoris, as well as some cryptozoologists like Rex Gilroy, who is also involved in the search for Yowie, suggest that, according to legend, they did not kill all of the birds but allowed some to survive on the shore of Lake Rotorua.

Is the moa a cryptid? That depends on who is being asked. Most scientists would say (and do say) that the moa was once a very real animal and is now, thanks to easily documentable activities, extinct. But there are some who think that the moa may in fact have survived into the present era. Those who believe that the moa has survived point toward the number of documented encounters with what are believed to be real birds; these encounters began to be reported in the nineteenth century and are seen by cryptozoologists as proof that the creature continued to exist.

One explanation for the persistence of moa sightings, hundreds of years after scientists maintain that all nine species went extinct, has to do with New Zealand's unusual animals. New Zealand has no native land mammals; because of this, New Zealand's animals evolved in an environment with very little predation, allowing very large birds like the moa, or any of New Zealand's other flightless birds, to thrive. Today, it is thought that a few individuals may be found in the isolated wilderness of South Westland and Fiordland.

Today, the moa, like Australia's thylacine, operates as a hopeful antidote to the destruction caused by humans on this planet. If the thylacine, or the moa, or any of the other unique creatures that humans have eliminated from the planet are thought to have survived, that means that perhaps humans are not the blight on nature that we appear to be; perhaps there is hope for the planet after all.

See also: Thylacine

Further Reading:

Anderson, A. (2003a). The Beast Without: The moa as a Colonial Frontier Myth in New Zealand. In Roy Willis (Ed.), *Signifying Animals*. Routledge, 248–56.

Anderson, A. (2003b). *Prodigious Birds: Moas and moa-hunting in New Zealand*. Cambridge University Press.

Spittle, Bruce (2010). *Moa Sightings*. Paua Press Ltd.

Worthy, T. H., & Holdaway, R. N. (2002). *The Lost World of the moa: Prehistoric Life of New Zealand*. Indiana University Press.

MONKEY MAN OF DELHI

The monkey man of Delhi refers to a series of events that occurred in May 2001 in the city of Delhi, India (it also made an appearance in Mumbai). What occurred has since been referred to as a mass hysteria event.

One May day, rumors started circulating through the city that there was an ape-man or monkey man running loose and attacking people and property. In particular, the creature scratched and bit dozens of people over an approximately two-week period. The attacks coincided with a hot spell, which forced residents out of their steamy homes to sleep on their roofs (where they were vulnerable to attack). A group of concerned citizens even beat up a short Hindu mystic, thinking that he was the creature, and two people, including a pregnant woman, supposedly lost their lives after they were so frightened that they fell. Reports conflicted in terms of the creature's appearance and behavior, with some witnesses describing it as a dark, muscular, hairy ape-man and others describing it as a short, slight man with glasses. Others described a shapeshifter; one person reported that it was a 4-feet-tall monkey that turned itself into a cat. All told, the police received almost 400 calls from citizens who reported a strange primate-like creature was attacking—not just stealing from—humans.

Delhi, like cities throughout South Asia, is host to thousands of free-roaming monkeys that fight for food and other resources with other monkeys as well as with the millions of humans who live in the city. So residents are familiar with monkeys. Even so, many people reported that they were monkeys, others thought they were monkey men, and a few thought they were from outer space. No matter what the explanation was, there is no question that people were hurt; according to one study, 63 percent of witnesses had experienced a physical attack and ended up in the hospital, while 95 percent experienced some type of injury.

As with similar stories from other parts of the world, the media reporting on the sightings helped to spur other sightings and witness accounts as well as, for a short time, a series of hoaxes. They also spurred the creation of multiple vigilante groups whose armed and unarmed members attempted to hunt down and kill the monster.

Ultimately, after two weeks during which there were a flurry of witness sightings as well as a growing sense of fear and dread in the community, the reports stopped as did the news coverage.

In addition, the monkey man did not have one or two key witnesses advocating for it; so when press coverage started to decline, there was no one to quickly have another experience that they could then recount.

Besides the eyewitness accounts and the physical injuries on the bodies of many of the victims, there was no other evidence for the existence of the creatures and ultimately, scientific experts and the police alike suggest that the entire hysteria was based on the anxieties of the primarily poor residents of Delhi, residents who were sleeping uneasily on their roofs because their apartments were too hot. The anxiety, combined with the heat, the loss of power, and the presence of monkeys, may have contributed to the event.

See also: Orang Pendek, Deloy's Ape

Further Reading:

Bartholomew, R. B. (2001). Monkey man Delusion Sweeps India. *Skeptic (Altadena, CA)*, 9(1), 13.
Verma, S. K., & Srivastava, D. K. (2003). A Study on Mass Hysteria (monkey men?) Victims in East Delhi. *Indian Journal of Medical Sciences*, 57(8), 355–60.

MONTAUK MONSTER

The Montauk monster is the name given to a carcass that was found on the beach in Long Island, New York, in July 2008. The body was found at the far eastern end of the island, at Ditch Plains Beach in Montauk. It is an example of a globster, an unidentified, and often unidentifiable, lump of flesh that ends up washed up on a beach. Cryptozoologist Ivan Sanderson coined the term to refer to an unknown carcass found washed ashore in Tasmania that would be called the Tasmanian globster.

Three young women, Jenna Hewitt, Rachel Goldberg, and Courtney Fruin, went to the Ditch Plains Beach on July 12, where they stumbled upon the body.

It was about the size of a cat or small dog, dead, hairless, and terribly bloated. It had four legs, like a mammal, but the face seemed to have a large beak on it—a beak with teeth. It also looked like it had bindings or cloth wrapped around at least a couple of its legs (which some people thought were the bindings used on fighting dogs). Hewitt photographed the creature and shared it on her social media, where it went viral.

The first name that the creature received was the Hound of Bonacville, a tongue-in-cheek play on the Hound of the Baskervilles combined with Bonackers, a word that refers to the working-class residents of nearby East Hampton. It was used in the first newspaper report on the creature, the July 23 issue of the *East Hampton Independent*. Soon after, the story was picked up by Gawker on July 29, kicking off the international media frenzy that converged on Long Island that summer.

What was the Montauk monster?

Scientists and laypeople alike had theories as to what the creature could possibly be. Perhaps it was created in some kind of terrible experiment, maybe at the nearby Plum Island Animal Disease Center? Or perhaps it was the result of a nuclear disaster? Perhaps it was an alien that had somehow landed on our planet and then died a lonely death on the beach?

It was also suggested that the monster could have been a hoax, manufactured in order to market something, although no one ever came forward and admitted to creating the creature.

Cryptozoologist Loren Coleman traveled to New York to investigate it, but by the time he arrived, it had been removed from the beach by someone connected to Hewitt and was allegedly taken "into the woods," so he was never able to see the body, although he did give it its name: the Montauk monster. The pictures Hewitt took, however, are clear enough to give people a good look at the creature.

Biologist William Wise suggested that it was a dog or coyote that had been in the ocean for quite some time. Because of what looked like a beak on the face, some people suggested that it could be a type of turtle, but turtles don't have teeth. (In addition, there was no beak; while the first picture taken by Hewitt seems to show a beak, the angle of that picture obscures what is clear in subsequent photos: that it is a mammal's head with much of the soft tissue of the face gone, leaving what looks like a bony beak.)

One unusual theory was that the animal was the subject of a "Viking funeral" during which the dead animal was placed on a wooden raft and set alight. Apparently someone had set up a Viking burial for a dead racoon just one month before the monster washed ashore. Others—including Loren Coleman himself—have since echoed this theory. Because the carcass disappeared before it could be examined, the mystery may remain a mystery—although the consensus today is that it really was a raccoon. But whether it was a racoon that underwent a Viking burial is a question that is much harder to answer.

See also: Mermaid

Further Reading:

Hallenbeck, B. G. (2013). *Monsters of New York: Mysterious Creatures in the Empire State*. Stackpole Books.

NITTAEWO

The Nittaewo refer to a legendary tribe of hominid creatures that lived in the deep forests of Sri Lanka.

The indigenous people of Sri Lanka, known as the Veddahs, have long discussed these creatures, which were described as bipedal ape-men with short strong arms, covered in reddish fur and standing only about 3–4 feet tall. They had long, curved nails or claws, and because they used no known tools, they used their claws to tear apart their prey. They were thought to sleep in caves, coming out at night to hunt animals or steal meat from, or even harm, the Veddahs. The Veddahs believe that their ancestors killed the last of the Nittaewo in the eighteenth century by barricading them in a cave and setting it on fire.

There has been no evidence, other than the stories told by the Veddahs, as well as retelling by Europeans, that the Nittaewo exists, although in 1984, a Spanish anthropologist named Salvador Martinez claimed to have briefly seen one. The word Nittaewo may derive from niṣāda (nigadiwa in Sinhalese, the language of Sri Lanka), a term which the Indo-Aryan invaders who arrived in the fifth century BCE used to describe the indigenous Sri Lankans (the Veddahs). If this is true, then that means that the creature known to the Veddahs as Nittaewo is actually just a misrepresentation of the Veddahs themselves.

What or who were the Nittaewo? It is possible that the Veddahs simply encountered another animal, most likely a gibbon or orangutan, Asia's only two ape species. While neither ape is native to Sri Lanka, they can both be found on the islands of Indonesia, and gibbons can be found much closer to Sri Lanka, in India itself. (However, Sri Lanka is located off the southernmost coast of India but the hoolock gibbon, the only ape in India, only lives in the far northeast of the country.) Gibbons are an especially good fit given the size and locomotion (gibbons spend more time walking on two legs than any other ape) of that species, although the Nittaewo was said to have short arms, while gibbons have long arms to help them brachiate. Orangutans have the right coloring but are far too big.

The other major theory is that the Nittaewo could have been a living hominin species—related to Home sapiens sapiens, our own species, but not quite human. As outlandish as this sounds—that there was a population of human-like creatures living in the forests of Sri Lanka tens of thousands of years after any other Homo species went extinct—in nearby Indonesia, that exact situation did occur.

Homo floriensis is a species of now-extinct hominins who lived on the Indonesian island of Flores and who were wiped out by or became absorbed into the population of Homo sapiens who settled the area about 50,000 years ago. Like the Nittaewo, Homo floriensis fossils (less than a dozen partial skeletons have so far been found) indicate that they were very short—probably 3–4 feet—but that they did use stone tools. For years after their discovery in 2003, paleoanthropologists debated whether this was in fact an extinct species of near-humans or simply a population of short modern humans suffering from a genetic abnormality and living in isolation. Today, the consensus is that they were indeed a separate species from us. This offers a great deal of support to the theory that the Nittaewo were not just real but were another species of hominin, wiped out as recently as the late eighteenth century. Unlike Homo floriensis, however, there have been no fossil discoveries of Nittaewo—even though the last living members may have been alive as recently as 250 years ago.

See also: Vietnam Rock Ape

Further Reading:

Heuvelmans, Bernard (1955). *On the Track of Unknown Animals*. Routledge.

Nevill, Hugh (1886). The Nittaewo of Ceylon. *The Taprobanian*, 1(3).

Rambukwella, A. T., & Kadirgamar, S. J. (1963). The Nittaewo—The Legendary Pygmies of Ceylon. *The Journal of the Ceylon Branch of the Royal Asiatic Society of Great Britain & Ireland*, 8(2), 265–90.

Streumer, P. (1997). The Leaf-clad Vedda: An European Contribution to Sri Lankan Folk-lore. *Journal of the Royal Asiatic Society of Sri Lanka*, 42, 59–78.

POPOBAWA

Popobawa is the name of an evil spirit or creature that is said to inhabit the islands of Zanzibar as well as the coastal areas of East Africa. The name popobawa is Swahili for bat wing, which refers to the shadow cast by the creature while it flies. But many residents just call it a jinni or djinni, the Muslim term for a spirit that can be good or evil. Some think that the popobawa started out as a jinni that became evil, and the legend most certainly comes from Islam, which has been the dominant religion in the region for hundreds of years. In fact, reciting the Quran is one way to protect oneself from the popobawa, and smearing pig's oil onto one's body can keep it away.

It is a shapeshifter and appears sometimes like a human, sometimes like a bat, and sometimes like another animal form. It sometimes announces itself with a terrible smell and attacks people, causing them physical and emotional damage. It also will sexually assault both women and men, who are often too ashamed of the attack, or afraid that the popobawa will return, to report it. (Jinn, too, can and will rape people.) Because the creature attacks families within their homes, during attacks, people will sleep outside to keep themselves safe.

It is most well known thanks to a major event in 1995, which caused mass hysteria, but was first reported in 1965 when some villagers on the island of Pemba reported seeing the creature. In the 1995 case, and subsequent cases, a number of different villagers reported that something attacked them while in their bed sleeping. It would cause pressure on their chests, often causing them to lose consciousness. This is when the sexual attacks would occur; sometimes an entire household's members could be attacked in one night. It has appeared every few years, with the last mass sighting in 2007, and its appearance seems to be connected with political unrest.

See also: Zanzibar Leopard

Further Reading:

Radford, Benjamin (2008). Popobawa. *Fortean Times*, October 15.

Thompson, K. D. (2017). *Popobawa: Tanzanian Talk, Global Misreadings*. Indiana University Press.

Walsh, M. (2009). The Politicisation of Popobawa: Changing Explanations of a Collective Panic in Zanzibar. *Journal of Humanities*, 1(1), 23–33.

QUAGGA

The quagga is an extinct zebra from South Africa. Today, there are three species of zebra—the plains zebra, the Grévy's zebra, and the mountain zebra.

All zebras are native to the African continent, with the plains zebra the most common variant, found throughout the eastern and southern parts of Africa. The quagga is an extinct subspecies of plains zebra, which was hunted to extinction in the nineteenth century. Other extinct zebra species went extinct much earlier; Equus koobiforensis, for example, is a fossil species from the early Pleistocene and went extinct over 2 million years ago. The quagga had a stripe pattern that was distinct from those of the other zebra species; brown rather than black stripes were found primarily on the front part of the body. Unlike the moa of New Zealand, which was eliminated thanks to indigenous overhunting, the quagga, like Australia's thylacine, disappeared over a very short period of time after European settlement. For the quagga, which lived for 2 to 3 million years, the discovery of gold in South Africa in the mid-nineteenth century triggered a gold rush, which ultimately led to the establishment of Johannesburg and, within just a few years, the elimination of the quagga from the landscape. By 1878, the quagga was functionally extinct, only existing in a handful of captive specimens, the last of which died in 1883. Like the thylacine, the quagga has had its DNA analyzed and is one of the few species that scientists feel can be a good candidate for possible cloning in order to resurrect the species—although this is not yet possible with current technology. Other scientists are trying to bring back the species by selectively breeding plains zebras to develop the special striped pattern found on the quaggas. Because the quagga was a subspecies of a currently extant species, the plains zebra, and contains identical mitochondrial DNA to that species, it may be possible to recreate the quagga through this process. Today, there are at least two dozen preserved quagga skins as well as a smaller number of skeletons, bones, and other materials in research facilities around the world, many of which are being used in various "breeding back" projects.

See also: Moa, Thylacine

Further Reading:

Higuchi, R., Bowman, B., Freiberger, M., Ryder, O. A., & Wilson, A. C. (1984). DNA Sequences From the Quagga, an Extinct Member of the Horse Family. *Nature*, 312(5991), 282–4.

Leonard, J. A., Rohland, N., Glaberman, S., Fleischer, R. C., Caccone, A., & Hofreiter, M. (2005). A Rapid Loss of Stripes: The Evolutionary History of the Extinct Quagga. *Biology Letters*, 1(3), 291–5.

RAT KING

A rat king, or Rattenkönig, refers to the phenomenon whereby a number of rats become intertwined by their tails. But it also refers to an actual rat king, that is, a rat that is king of the rats.

In the primary sense of the term, a rat king is a collection of rats linked together by their tails. Usually, there is something else involved, which helps the tails to adhere to each other, like sap or glue or another sticky or messy substance like urine or feces, often combined with twigs, leaves, and trash. There's no way to know how often this occurs naturally, as opposed to a person catching a group of rats, immobilizing them in some way, and then tying their tails together, but there have been enough well-documented examples to indicate that it is a real phenomenon, no matter how rare. It has also been observed in squirrels, whose tails can get tangled up together while they are still in the nest. Whether rats or squirrels, if no one intervenes to separate the animals, they will die.

Why would this occur? It is relatively easy to understand that it might develop when baby rats are together in their nests, but given that most rat kings that survived are of adult animals, the nest explanation doesn't make much sense, because the individuals could not survive till adulthood. Another explanation suggests that during winter, rats will sleep in tighter quarters to keep warm, and the combination of multiple bodies squeezed together in a tight space, with various bodily secretions, food, and other materials, may cause their tails to stick together.

Why would such an odd, and for most people, deeply unsettling phenomenon be called a rat king? Rats are very common folkloric animals where they often act as stand-ins for humans, thanks to their prehensile hands, gregarious nature, and human-like characteristics.

Folktales about rats are common in cultures around the world, but in Europe, where rats took the blame for the Black Death of the fourteenth and seventeenth centuries, they have a uniquely terrible reputation.

According to Marten Hart, there have been fifty-seven documented cases of rat king discoveries since the sixteenth century and all were in Central Europe. Today, there are preserved rat kings in natural history museums throughout Europe, with the most extraordinary specimen of all—featuring thirty-two individual rats—being housed in a natural history museum in the German town of Altenburg. In fact, Germany has more rat kings than any other country, which suggests that at least some of Germany's rat kings were created as hoaxes, or else there is something about Germany that specifically encourages the formation of rat kings, or more likely, their promotion. It was not until 1862 that the term "rat king" entered the English language, and it could be that this only occurred because of a growing international press and rising rates of literacy.

The first time the rat king appeared in print was in the sixteenth century. In 1564, in Johannes Sambucus's Emblemata, the rat king was included as both a natural phenomenon and the source of a moral lesson, with the rats symbolizing some aspect of human society. A few years before the Emblemata was published, Konrad Gesner published his *Historia animalium*, which included the following description: "Some would have it that the rat waxes mighty in its old age and is fed by its young: this is called the rat king." But the concept of the rat king was certainly well known in Germany before that time, because in 1535, in his treatise *Against Catholicism*, Martin Luther wrote, "The friars were the pope's columns, they carried him as the rats carry their king." This suggests the idea of the rat king as an actual king of rats. This idea of a rat that rules all of the rats is obviously a metaphor for the pope and his servants, but it may stem from a misinterpretation of the rat king. Perhaps it is not made up of the tangled bodies of multiple rats but might instead be one animal with multiple appendages or even multiple bodies. This monstrous creature could easily be called a king rat or rat king, based on just the size alone.

Rat kings are almost always found long after the rats died, usually from starvation or a combination of starvation and injuries, often in a hidden location, such as in attics, basements, or within the walls or beneath the floorboards. If they were found alive, at least according to the reports that have survived, they would be killed—both because they were repellent and because they were an omen of ill tidings to come.

While rat kings remain very rare, and live rat kings are almost unheard of, in 2021 a farmer in Estonia found a live rat king made up of thirteen rats (two of whom were already dead). The animals were filmed, euthanized, and are now on display at the Tartu University Museum of Zoology in Estonia.

But rat kings are still with us, in the ballet The Nutcracker, where the mouse king and its army are clearly the descendants of the German rat king. Before The Nutcracker was a ballet, it was a story called "Nussknacker und Mausckönig" (Nutcracker and Mouse King), written by German author ETA Hoffman in 1816 and featured an evil mouse king with seven heads, all with their own crowns.

See also: Coney Island Sea Rabbit, Deloy's Ape

Further Reading:

Hoffmann, E. T. A., & Dumas, A. (2007). *Nutcracker and Mouse King and The Tale of the Nutcracker*. Penguin.
Miljutin, A. (2007). Rat Kings in Estonia. *Proceedings of the Estonian Academy of Sciences Biology Ecology*, 56(1), 77œ81.

ROLLING CALF

In Jamaican folklore, a duppy is the ghost of a dead person. As with many Afro-Caribbean traditions, the duppy is a combination of beliefs from West Africa and Europe but particularly England. A rolling calf is a type of duppy.

Duppies are spirits of the dead, who stay in this world to torment the living; like the English ghost, duppies are unhappy or restless, which keeps them stuck on this plane. In the Obeah tradition, which comes from Ghana and the Ivory Coast, each person is born with two souls. Upon death, the good or holy soul will go to heaven whereas the earthly soul will stay with the body for three days, after which, if the appropriate burial practices are not observed, the soul will leave the body, becoming a restless, malicious spirit: a duppy.

Duppies are nocturnal, coming out at night from their homes in the bamboo and cottonwood groves where they harass people and cause mischief. They harm both people and property, and can take many forms, with their own appearance, origin story, and characteristics. They are not mindless beings but retain the agency and memories of the dead. And historically, Jamaica has produced more than its fair share of death.

Like all of the West Indian islands settled by Europeans, Jamaica was founded on the sugar trade, which depended on slavery for its lifeblood. Between 1513, when the first captured Africans arrived in Jamaica, and 1834, when slavery there was abolished, millions of African men, women, and children were brought to Jamaica, and millions died there, without ever seeing their homelands again—and for most, not getting the proper burial rites after they died. This means that there must have been many millions of duppies in Jamaica for well over 200 years.

While there are many forms that duppies take, the most common is to look like a human being, albeit one with feet that point backward—a common characteristic of both cryptids and witches.

There are a variety of ways to stop a duppy; duppies are afraid of light, so shining a light on them will cause them to flee; throwing rice at a duppy will also stop it as it will stop whatever it is doing in order to try to count the rice grains. Because they can't count above three, the rice will confuse them, allowing a victim to escape. In addition, twins and people born with a caul, both spiritually significant occurrences, cannot be harmed by a duppy.

One of the most unusual, and highly feared, duppy is the rolling calf.

This duppy is highly unusual in that it is a giant cow. Americans will recognize the legend of Babe the Blue Ox, companion to Paul Bunyan, and bovine deities were once very common in the ancient world, but cow monsters are highly unusual.

The rolling calf is a surprisingly frightening creature. According to legend, the rolling calf was "born" as the ghost of a cow killed by a cruel butcher, which came back to exact revenge. It is now the ghost of anyone who was particularly cruel or immoral in life such as a murderer. It is a frightening sight, dragging its heavy iron collar and chains like one of the ghosts from *A Christmas Carol*, chasing its victims, and shooting fire from its nostrils and poison from its mouth. (Rolling, here, does not refer to the calf's locomotion but refers to the fact that it wanders or roams from place to place.)

Like other duppies, the rolling calf takes on multiple forms, including a bull, a cat, a dog, a horse, and even a goat with blazing red eyes and the legs of four different creatures. Even when it takes on the shape of a small cat, it can still harm someone—through their breath.

The rolling calf, like all duppies, is a product of West African beliefs, as they evolved in the New World. Most of Jamaica's enslaved people were taken from West Africa, and in particular Ghana and Nigeria, and brought with them their beliefs in a variety of spirits and ghosts, which were then translated in this new environment, allowing new duppies to appear. Also, because the rolling calf appears at night, wandering along rural roads, quiet paths, and dark woods, it is linked to a wider tradition of roadside creatures, such as England's black dog, creatures that roam lonely roads at night, scaring travelers and often signaling an imminent death.

See also: Cuero

Further Reading:

Henriques, J. F. (2019). Duppy Conquerors, Rolling Calves and Flights to Zion. In Steve Goodman, Toby Heys and Eleni Ikoniadou (Eds.), *AUDINT—Unsound:Undead*. Urbanomic Media Ltd., 147–50.
Lawrence, R. (2008). The Third-World Duppy. *JCLs; Journal of Caribbean Literatures*, 5(3), 98–103.
Leach, M. (1961). Jamaican Duppy Lore. *The Journal of American Folklore*, 74(293), 207–15.

SARIMANOK

The sarimanok is a colorful mythical bird that is found under different names throughout Southeast Asia. This specific bird is found on the Philippine island of Mindanao, where the Maranao, one of the Philippine's many indigenous groups, live.

While the sarimanok is not a specific species of bird, in the art and ceremonial materials from the region, it is usually depicted as a hornbill, birds with important ritual and symbolic functions in many of the cultures of Southeast Asia. In fact, many of the indigenous peoples of the area share similar beliefs and practices regarding hornbills, including a taboo on killing and eating them, and the use of hornbills in funerary practices. The sarimanok is usually depicted with a fish in its beak, which represents the offering made to the creature.

Even though the sarimanok is associated primarily with the Maranao people, images of the bird are found throughout the Philippines. There is no real way to determine when the sarimanok developed and whether it or beliefs in the bird predate the fourteenth century, when Islam arrived on Mindanao. Given the fact that mythical birds are found among many of the indigenous peoples of Southeast Asia, many of whom were, like the Maranao, converted to Islam, it could be that beliefs and practices surrounding mythical birds spread as Muslim missionaries traveled throughout the islands. On the other hand, prior to the arrival of Islam in the fourteenth century, the Maranao people spoke of another sacred bird, called Itotoro, that, through its spiritual counterpart and sibling Inikadowa, was able to connect this world with the afterlife. After the conversion to Islam, it may be that the Itotoro merged with Muslim beliefs and formed the sarimanok. Whether or not the sarimanok arrived on Mindanao before or after the Islam, we know that some of the legends about the bird, including origin stories, feature the Prophet Mohammed.

See also: Thunderbird, Ahool

Further Reading:

Cañete, R. R. (2015). Avian Spirit Iconography Among the Dayak and Other Peoples of Southeast Asia. *Borneo Research Journal*, 9, 114–45.

Gonzalez, J. C. T. (2011). Enumerating the Ethno-ornithological Importance of Philippine Hornbills. *Raffles Bull Zool*, 24, 149–61.

SEA RABBIT OF CONEY ISLAND

The sea rabbit of Coney Island is a fictional sea creature that is part rabbit, part fish, which lives, according to the mythology, around New York's Coney Island. It is a type of mer-rabbit.

Coney Island most likely got its name thanks to the population of wild rabbits that once lived on the island. Coney Island was originally established by the Dutch in the seventeenth century, and the Dutch name for rabbits is *konijn*; thus the island's name was originally Kojijn Eiland. The old English name for rabbits is coney (originally spelled, and pronounced, "cunny"), from the Latin *cunnus*, which means pudendum (i.e., a woman's external genitals), and *cuniculus*, which means rabbit (technically, it means "underground passage," since rabbits live underground). Coney, then, refers to rabbits and was once slang for a woman's genitals. The English took the colony from the Dutch in 1644, replacing Kojijn Eiland with Coney Island. (The original pronunciation of Coney Island—cunny island—was changed in the Victorian era to the current "coney" because its pronunciation was too easily confused with slang for female genitals.)

Rabbits no longer live on the island, but, according to artist Takeshi Yamada (born 1960), the sea rabbit still lives there. According to Yamada (who goes by Dr.), who created the mythology for this animal, Henry Hudson first discovered the sea rabbit when exploring the region around modern-day New York City, prior to the arrival of the Dutch colonists. Today, there are two species of sea rabbits in North America: the Coney Island Sea Rabbit (*Monafluffchus americanus*) and Coney Island Tiger-Striped Sea Rabbit (*Monafluffchus konjinicus*), and both are endangered.

Yamada, a rogue taxidermist and "gaffe master" who creates fantastical animals out of a variety of materials, came up with the concept of the sea rabbit, which is about the size of a medium-size dog and has a torso and head from a rabbit, the webbed front feet of a duck, and the lower body and tail of a fish. His website includes not only photos of the rabbits in a variety of poses and settings but also drawings of the animals that allegedly were published in natural history texts from the past two centuries and a huge amount of natural history about the species.

For example, in the wild, the male sea rabbit lives with a harem of twenty to twenty-five female rabbits, and females give birth to from eight to ten pups at a time, while on shore. These animals, which were once plentiful, were almost driven to extinction by Dutch hunters, who ate their meat and sold their fur overseas. According to Yamada, the only animals that exist today do so in breeding centers such as at the Coney Island Aquarium and Coney Island University where "Dr. Yamada" teaches, while the research about the animals is conducted at the Coney Island Sea Rabbit Repopulation Center, which is devoted to the captive breeding of the species and of which Dr. Yamada is executive director.

Yamada has popularized the sea rabbits through both his website and interviews and performances featuring one of the sea rabbits he created. He also frequently walks on the beaches and boardwalk of Coney Island with one of his creatures, telling the public about them.

See also: Feejee Mermaid, Skvader

Further Reading:

Shanly, C. D. (2014). Acconey Island. In *A Coney Island Reader: Through Dizzy Gates of Illusion*. Columbia University Press, 54–6.

SELKIE

In Celtic folklore, selkies are seals that can, upon removal of their skin, take on human form and marry humans. The human generally is unaware of the real identity of their spouse, until they find the seal skin. Discarding the skin means the selkie will never be able to return to the sea.

The name "selkie" is a derivation of the Scots word for seal (selk or selch), and the Scots have long been surrounded by seals—both gray seals and harbor seals. One suggestion for the origin of the selkie has to do with the arrival of Norse invaders, who wore heavy fur-covered clothing, but, given the prevalence and importance of seals to the lives of early Celts, it may be more simple than that. Seals, like whales or elephants in other cultures, may have been seen as the reincarnation of dead humans—or more specifically, fishermen who drowned at sea, which is one of the understandings of selkies.

Stories about selkies are part of a larger set of folktales about human-animal shapeshifting and human-animal weddings. There are dozens of folklore motifs that describe the transformation of animals to people, and people to animals, depending on which kind of animal is in the tale. In a large number of transformation tales, if the creature is injured while in its animal guise, that injury will later be found on the human, giving their secret away.

Selkie tales are very similar to mermaid tales and are clearly related, as are the beings themselves. The Mermaid Wife is the name that folklorists have given to tales that feature either mermaids or selkies being married to human men. These legends are found throughout the British Isles and in Iceland. Tales of men who married mermaids (human-fish females), or selkies (seal-women; very occasionally are selkies male), are commonly found in this region and involve a motif found in the swan maiden tales: the mermaid or selkie is often held captive by the husband as long as he has her skin. If she finds it, she will often swim away, abandoning him forever. Selkies, while they are married to their human husbands, give birth to human children who are part selkie; usually they have webbed hands and feet.

Like mermaids, selkies are almost always represented as female, and it is the capture of the selkie by a man by virtue of stealing her skin that is the most central dramatic point to every selkie tale. Selkie tales, in this way, tell us much about the gendered nature of marriages and the ways in which marriage can, for a woman, offer family and satisfaction but may also represent a loss of freedom and a loss of connection to her own family. It is this tension that selkie tales highlight.

In one such story, "The Silkie Wife" from the Shetland Islands, it turns out that the selkie was already married to one of her own kind in the sea, and she makes her escape from her human husband in order to reunite with her first husband. In the Icelandic tale "The Sealskin," the selkie mourns the loss of her seven selkie children, to whom she later returns after finding her skin. In one variant, "Herman Perk and the Seal," also from the Shetland Islands, the man in the story does not end up marrying a selkie; instead, he helps a selkie husband to recover the skin of his wife, returning her to the sea and earning himself riches. Usually, in all of these tales, the husband, if he had been a hunter or fisherman, never hunts seals again. Occasionally, as in the Irish tale "Tom Moore and the Seal Woman," the children of the selkie and her husband have webbed feet; in fact, people with webbed feet were once thought to be descended from selkies.

Selkies are most well known in Ireland and Scotland (and especially Orkney), both countries with heavy ties to the sea, and feature not only in Irish and Scottish folklore but in contemporary poetry and literature as well. Selkies are not only creatures capable of transforming between their true, seal appearance and their human appearance, which is attained through the loss of her skin, but they, like mermaids, occupy the realm between land and sea.

Irish and Scottish folk creatures are well represented, not just in the folktales and legends of those regions but the songs as well. In Scotland, there have been ballads about selkies for hundreds of years. Perhaps the most well known of all is a song called *The Great Silkie of Sule Skerry*, which refers to the relatively rare male selkie from Orkney, in the North of Scotland, where Norse invaders and settlers had a lasting impact on the culture. While there are as many versions of the song as there are singers, it opens something like this:

In Noroway there lived a maid,
"Bye-loo my baby," she begins,
"Oh know not I my babe's father

Or if land or sea he's living in."
Then there arose at her bedfeet,
And a grummlie guest I'm sure was he,
Saying, "Here am I thy babe's father
Although I be not comely.
I am a man upon the land,
I am a silkie in the sea,
But when I'm in my own coutrie
My dwelling is in Sule Skerry."
Then he has taken a purse of gold
And he has put it upon her knee,
Saying, "Give to me my little wee son
And take thee up thy nurse's fee."
And it shall pass on a summer's day
When the sun shines hot on every stone,
That I shall take my little wee son
And teach him for to swim in the foam.
"And you shall marry a gunner good,
And a proud good gunner I'm sure he'll be,
And he'll go out on a May morning
And kill both my young son and me."
And she did marry a gunner good,
And a proud good gunner I'm sure 'twas he,
And the very first shot he ever did shoot
He killed the son and the great silkie.

See also: Merfolk, Swan Maiden

Further Reading:

Jøn, A. A. (1998). Dugongs and Mermaids, Selkies and Seals. *Australian Folklore*, 13, 94–8.
Lunge-Larsen, L. (2004). *The Hidden Folk: Stories of Fairies, Dwarves, Selkies, and Other Secret Beings.* Houghton Mifflin Harcourt.

SKVADER

The skvader is a rabbit-like creature found in Sweden. It has the head and legs of a hare, combined with the wings, tail, and back of a wood grouse.

The original skvader was created by Rudolf Granberg, a Swedish taxidermist, and it now lives at the Norra Berget Museum in Sundsvall. According to Swedish legend, in 1874, a hunter named Håkan Dahlmark told his friends that he shot a skvader. Years later, in 1907, Dahlmark's maid gave him a painting of such an animal, created by her nephew, which was later donated to the Norra Berget Museum, which in 1916 contracted the taxidermist Granberg to make the animal, based on the painting. Today, the skvader is a popular exhibit at the museum and the unofficial symbol for the town of Sundsvall, where a statue of the animal was erected in 1994. (There is another skvader at the Biologiska Museet in Djurgården, Stockholm.)

The idea of a skvader would not have been outlandish to the earliest natural historians in the West. Pliny the Elder described a half-rabbit-half bird, which supposedly lived in the Alps.

See also: Jackalope

Further Reading:

Nordlund Edvinsson, T. (2021). The Game/s that Men Play: Male Bonding in the Swedish Business Elite 1890–1960. *Business History*, 1–17.

STELLER'S SEA APE

The Steller's sea ape is relatively unique among cryptids in that it is an aquatic ape. It was discovered in 1741 by naturalist George Steller, while on Vitus Bering's Second Kamchatka Expedition to America.

Steller saw his first sea ape off the Shumagin Islands off of Southwest Alaska. He recorded this account in his diary:

> The animal was about two ells [six feet] long. The head was like a dog's head, the ears pointed and erect, and on the upper and lower lips on both sides whiskers hung down which made him look almost like a Chinaman. The eyes were large. The body was longish, round and fat, but gradually became thinner toward the tail; the skin was covered thickly with hair, grey on the back, reddish white on the belly, but in the water it seemed to be entirely red and cow-colored. The tail, which was equipped with fins, was divided in two parts, the upper fin being two times as long as the lower one, just like on sharks. However, I was not a little surprised that I could perceive neither forefeet, as in marine amphibians, nor fins in their place. For more than two hours it stayed with our ship looking at us one after the other with admiration. it now and then came closer and often so close it could have been touched with a pole. then as soon as we moved it retired away.

He continued:

When I had observed it a long time I had a gun loaded and fired at the animal intending to get possession of it and make an accurate description but the shot missed. although it was somewhat frightened it reappeared right away and approached our ship gradually but when another shot at it was in vain or perhaps only slightly wounded, it and retreated into the sea and did not come back. (Steller 2011: 72–3)

What did Steller see? He may have seen a sea cow, a now-extinct animal that lived in the Bering Sea, where Steller was. In fact, these animals were wiped out by hunters only thirty short years after Steller described the sea ape. Another possibility is that he saw a northern fur seal, also known as the Alaska fur seal. Its head looks like a dog's head, it has the whiskers just as Steller noted, its size and shape match his description. While Steller certainly would have seen seals before, he would not have had the chance to see a northern fur seal, which live, like the sea cow once did, in the Bering Sea. The split tail that Steller described was probably the two rear legs.

See also: Mermaid

Further reading:

Ford, C. (2003). *Where the Sea Breaks Its Back: The Epic Story-Georg Steller & the Russian Exploration of AK.* Graphic Arts Books.
Steller, G. (2011). *De Bestiis Marinis.* Lulu. com.
Steller, G. W., & Frost, O. W. (1993). *Journal of a Voyage With Bering, 1741–1742.* Stanford University Press.

SWAN MAIDEN

A swan maiden is a swan-human hybrid or, more specifically, a creature that primarily lives as a swan but can transform into a human upon command. Swan maidens are most well known through folklore, and folktales about the creature are found throughout Asia, Africa, Europe, and the Americas.

Swan maiden tales involve a man tricking a swan maiden—a creature that takes on a human appearance when not wearing her robe of feathers—into becoming his wife by stealing her feather robe. Eventually, one of the maiden's children finds her robe and shows it to her, whereby she puts it on, turns into a swan, and disappears. What makes the swan maiden tales different from other stories in which the animal bride reverts to her animal form is that in some (but not all) of these stories, she wants to become a permanent human; her husband must go through a variety of steps in order to achieve this for her.

For example, in one European tale, "The Swan Maidens," collected by Joseph Jacobs, a man sees a swan maiden when out hunting:

But instead of ducks there appeared seven maidens all clad in robes made of feathers, and they alighted on the banks of the lake, and taking off their robes plunged into the waters and bathed and sported in the lake. They were all beautiful, but of them all the youngest and smallest pleased most the hunter's eye, and he crept forward from the bushes and seized her dress of plumage and took it back with him into the bushes.

After the swan maidens had bathed and sported to their heart's delight, they came back to the bank wishing to put on their feather robes again; and the six eldest found theirs, but the youngest could not find hers. They searched and they searched until at last the dawn began to appear, and the six sisters called out to her, "We must away; 'tis the dawn; you meet your fate whatever it be." And with that they donned their robes and flew away, and away, and away.

When the hunter saw them fly away he came forward with the feather robe in his hand; and the swan maiden begged and begged that he would give her back her robe. He gave her his cloak but would not give her her robe, feeling that she would fly away. And he made her promise to marry him, and took her home, and hid her feather robe where she could not find it. So they were married and lived happily together and had two fine children, a boy and a girl, who grew up strong and beautiful; and their mother loved them with all her heart. (Jacobs 1916: 98–105)

This tale is similar to many animal brides tales in that when the husband finds, and either destroys or hides, the wife's animal skin, she must stay a human; but when the wife puts the skin back on, she returns to being an animal. In some versions of the swan maiden, the wife wants to be reunited with her husband after she becomes a swan again. In other versions, she does not; for instance, the Swedish tale "The Swan Maiden" ends with the wife flying off and the husband being left bereft.

In the Japanese tale, "The Crane Wife," a man cares for a wounded crane, which later, unbeknownst to him, turns into a beautiful woman whom he marries. She makes her husband promise to never peek into her weaving room, where she makes beautiful clothes that he sells to support them. After looking into the room one day, he finds that it is a crane, not a woman, who is weaving, and she is using her own feathers as thread. But because the man saw the wife's true form as a crane, she flew off, leaving him forever.

Swan maidens have been found in a number of different cultures, although they are most commonly found in northern Europe. Variants of the story have been found as far east as China and possibly derived originally from India. It is thought that the tales feature whatever migratory bird is most prominent in the region where the tale is told—swans (and also cranes) in Eurasia, doves in the Middle East, and geese in North America.

Historian Boria Sax (1998) suggests that swan maidens, which illustrate both our once close relationship to nature through practices like totemism and our alienation from the natural world (when the bride returns to her original, animal form), originated in the serpent cults of the ancient Mediterranean. In that area, the bride often took the guise of a serpent, while as the story moved north into Europe, a swan became the primary animal form.

See also: Selkie, Tanuki

Further Reading:

Gaster, M. (1915). *Rumanian Bird and Beast Stories*. Folk-Lore Society, no. 83, 249–54.
Hofberg, H. (1980). *Swedish Fairy Tales*. Translated by W. H. Myers. Belford-Clarke Company.
Jacobs, Joseph (1916). *Europa's Fairy Book*. G. P. Putnam's Sons.
Miller, A. L. (1987). The Swan-Maiden Revisited: Religious Significance of Divine-Wife. Folktales With Special Reference to Japan. *Asian Folklore Studies*, 46(1), 55–86.
Sax, B. (1998). *The Serpent and the Swan: The Animal Bride in Folklore and Literature*. University of Tennessee Press.

TANUKI

The *tanuki* is a Japanese animal that resembles a raccoon or a badger but is a member of the dog family; in English, it is known as a raccoon dog (Nyctereutes procyonoides). But the tanuki is also the name of a mythical Japanese creature.

Tanukis in the latter sense are shapeshifters—creatures that can turn into humans (or even inanimate objects) to get what they want. For example, according to Japanese folklore, tanuki can even transform into Buddhist monks in order to beg for food. In order to shapeshift, it is said that the tanuki must first place a leaf on its head; tanuki are often depicted in art that way.

The tanuki (in the folkloric sense) arrived in Japan from China, where it was a shapeshifting fox known as Huli Jin. After arriving in Japan in the thirteenth century, it shifted from a fox to a raccoon dog, while still retaining its shapeshifting and trickster characteristics. In addition, while the Huli Jin was evil, the tanuki is not; they are tricksters but are also linked with the divine. Both of Japan's great religions, Buddhism and Shintoism, predate the arrival of the tanuki, but after its arrival, it was gradually incorporated into both religions as yōkai animal spirits that are responsible for protecting nature. The first written account of the tanuki was in a thirteenth-century collection of stories called Uji Shūi Monogatari, and by the sixteenth century, the tanuki was well integrated into Japanese folklore.

One popular folktale is called the "Farmer and the Badger"—the tanuki was mistranslated and became a badger. Other similar tales are called "The Crackling Mountain." In *The Japanese Fairy Book*, translated into English in 1908, the story begins like this:

Long, long ago, there lived an old farmer and his wife who had made their home in the mountains, far from any town. Their only neighbor was a bad and malicious badger. This badger used to come out every night and run across to the farmer's field and spoil the vegetables and the rice which the farmer spent his time in carefully cultivating. The badger at last grew so ruthless in his mischievous work, and did so much harm everywhere on the farm, that the good-natured farmer could not stand it any longer, and determined to put a stop to it. So he lay in wait day after day and night after night, with a big club, hoping to catch the badger, but all in vain. Then he laid traps for the wicked animal.

The farmer's trouble and patience was rewarded, for one fine day on going his rounds he found the badger caught in a hole he had dug for that purpose. The farmer was delighted at having caught his enemy, and carried him home securely bound with rope. When he reached the house the farmer said to his wife:

"I have at last caught the bad badger. You must keep an eye on him while I am out at work and not let him escape, because I want to make him into soup to-night." (Ozaki 1908)

Later, after catching the badger/tanuki, the wife freed the creature, thinking it was cruel to hang it like that. After gaining his freedom, the badger cried out, "I'll be revenged for this" and escaped. The story goes on to tell how the badger got its revenge by killing the woman and then taking on her form.

The badger meanwhile assumed the old woman's form, and as soon as he saw the old farmer approaching came out to greet him on the veranda of the little house, saying:

"So you have come back at last. I have made the badger soup and have been waiting for you for a long time."

The old farmer quickly took off his straw sandals and sat down before his tiny dinner-tray. The innocent man never even dreamed that it was not his wife but the badger who was waiting upon him, and asked at once for the soup. Then the badger suddenly transformed himself back to his natural form and cried out:

"You wife-eating old man! Look out for the bones in the kitchen!" (Ibid.)

Unlike most shapeshifters, the tanuki can also change the physical world by transforming into inanimate objects like rocks; that's one way that they like to trick humans, by altering the environment in order to confuse people.

Today, the tanuki straddles the border between the natural world and the world of magic. It is a magical Chinese creature that transmogrified into both a very real creature, which is now evolving away from the other species of raccoon dog, and a magical trickster shapeshifter. The tanuki continues to transform, as in the last century it has begun to lose most of its negative associations, and is now more cute than troublesome.

Stories of the tanuki are not limited to Japanese folklore. They have also made it into mainstream media, as this 1889 story published in the *Tôô Nippô* newspaper, which discussed a train leaving Tokyo on its way to Okegawa:

Just before arriving in Okegawa . . . a steam train that had left Ueno encountered another train, with its whistle a-blowing, advancing along the same tracks from the opposite direction. The train driver was surprised; he hastily reduced his speed and blew his own whistle wildly.

The oncoming train did the same, continuing to toot its whistle repeatedly. However, whilst it initially had appeared very close, it did not seem to come any closer. When the driver fixed his eyes on it, the train seemed to be there, but it also seemed not to be there—a figment—it was very unclear, so he increased his speed to the point that he should have crashed into the other train. But that other train just disappeared like smoke, leaving not one trace.

But where it had been, two old *tanuki* were found lying dead on the tracks, having been run over. Thinking they were terrible nuisances and now they would get their comeuppances, the driver skinned them and used the meat for *tanuki* soup. What a surprise that such a thing could occur these days, during the Meiji period. (Foster 2012: 15)

This story is an old legend known as the Counterfeit Steam Train, Phantom Train, or Ghost Train, and the tanuki refers to the old Japanese ways, while the train embodies progress, modernity, and the future. The story, then, is about the tanuki's attempt to halt the march of progress. Why it was published in the paper as news is unclear, however.

See also: Kitsune, Tengu

Further Reading:

Burton, A. (2012). The Transformations of Tanuki-san. *Frontiers in Ecology and the Environment*, 10(4), 224–4.
Ortabasi, Melek (2013). (Re)animating Folklore: Raccoon Dogs, Foxes, and Other Supernatural Japanese Citizens in Takahata Isao's Heisei Tanuki Gassen Pompoko. *Marvels & Tales*, 27(2), 254–75. Project MUSE. Web. February 17, 2015.
Ozaki, Y. T. (1908). *Japanese Fairy Tales*. A.L. Burt Company.

TENGU

The tengu is a mythological creature in Japanese folklore. It is an example of a yōkai, which are spirits that date back to when Japan's religious beliefs were animistic but that remain a part of Japanese society today.

While yōkai are as old as Japan, and have been found in Japanese art and literature for centuries, today one can find yōkai in manga, anime, and other modern media forms, demonstrating that even ancient religious beliefs and practices are still relevant today. In the past, when religion played a much stronger role in Japan, a wide variety of unfortunate events might be blamed on yōkai, which are not evil but, like spirits in many cultures, can be quite mischievous, although they can also be helpful. There are at least three dozen different yōkai, which differ in form, appearance, the areas that they inhabit, and more. Yōkai have different supernatural powers, including shapeshifting and the ability to possess a human.

The tengu is one type of yōkai. It is a shapeshifter as well as a hybrid creature: it has a humanoid body, with the head of a dog, bird, or occasionally monkey. It occasionally has wings and always is depicted with a long red nose (which itself is based on a bird's beak) and (since the thirteenth century) wearing the clothing of a yamabushi, which is a kind of monk. Tengu literally means "sky dog" and is most commonly translated as "heavenly dog" or "heavenly sentinel." These terms point to one of the tengu's abilities, which is seeing the future. (They are also said to be good sword fighters.) But the idea of a dog in the heavens, which has some insight into the afterlife, is strikingly reminiscent of the Native American and old Norse beliefs about dogs guarding the gate to the afterworld. Even more reminiscent of these beliefs, in the Nihon Shoki, an eighth-century Japanese text, the tengu is called "heavenly dog" and is depicted as a shooting star. In this world, another function of the tengu is that they are guardians of the mountains.

One explanation for the origin of tengu suggests that when a proud or arrogant person dies, they are reincarnated as a tengu, while other folktales suggest that tengu are the spirits of dead priests. Like so much of Japanese culture, the tengu could have derived originally from China; the tiāngǒu is a Chinese demon with a vaguely canine appearance. Another possible link is the Indian god Garuda, also depicted with the body of a man and the wings as well as the head or face of a bird. In Japan, the first time the tengu appeared in print was in the eighth century, well after both Chinese and Indian influence arrived in Japan.

In the folklore about the tengu, they are mischievous and troublesome and, in particular, cause problems for Buddhist priests; they are sometimes seen as an enemy of Buddhism.

Tengu live in forests, mountains, rivers, or streams, and a group of tengu is organized like a clan or tribe, with a chief tengu at the head. Like the yōkai, there are many different types of tengu. For example, daitengu ("greater divine dog") are large humanoid tengu with large wings; the kotengu or karasutengu (lesser divine dog) is a smaller version that looks more like a bird. The kawa tengu is the river tengu that is often invisible to humans. In art, tengu are depicted with a number of tools that are associated with them, including a staff called a khakkhara, a fan called a hauchiwa, and a sandal often called tengu-geta. Some tengu are not anthropomorphic or zoomorphic at all. For example, the tengu dioshi is the sound of a large tree falling in the forest, while the Tengu tsubute is the phenomenon of rocks falling from the sky, and Tengubi is a fireball in the sky.

The tengu has changed significantly as Japanese society has changed. By the seventeenth century, much of the evil nature of the old tengu was discarded in favor of a more positive portrayal as well as one that is kinder to Buddhism. They are still an important part of a number of smaller religious practices in Japan, not associated with Buddhism or Shintoism.

See also: Tanuki

Further Reading:

Knutsen, R. (2011). *Tengu: The Shamanic and Esoteric Origins of the Japanese Martial Arts*. Global Oriental.

Sari, I. A. L. (2020). The Figures and Meanings of Tengu: Semiotic Study of Mythological Creatures in Japanese Folklore. *Humanus*, 19(2), 217–29.

TIKBALANG

The tikbalang is a monster from the folklore of the Philippines. It is a human-horse hybrid, one of the rarer hybrid forms, sometimes known as a werehorse. In Western mythology, the centaur is an equivalent horse-human being.

The tikbalang lives in the high mountains and forests of the Philippines. Unlike most werehorses that have the body of a horse with the head of a human, combining the most salient characteristics of both—the human head emphasizes the human intellect while the horse body highlights the equine strength and power—tikbalangs have the head and hooves of a horse and a human—or humanoid—body. They are neither graceful nor strong; instead, they are freakish, misshapen, and ugly, with a mane of spikes. For the people who live in the mountainous regions of the country, the tikbalang was one of many named and unnamed spirits that occupied the forests, rivers, and other natural environments where they lived. These spirits could be good or bad or neutral and did not correspond to either the Christian god or the Christian devil.

The tikbalang in particular traveled to the Philippines on a circuitous route from India. Since the first century, much of Southeast Asia was under the influence of Hinduism, which probably reached the Philippines through Indonesia and affected both the religious beliefs and the folklore of the islands. Indian folklore—both Hindu and Buddhist—in particular has had a significant influence on folklore throughout Asia and Europe.

The *Jātaka* (sometimes known as the Pali Jātaka because of the language in which they were written) is a collection of fables, anecdotes, poems, and other stories, about the many lives (or Jātaka, which means "birth") of Siddhartha Gautama in India, before he was known as the Buddha. The tales were written down between the third and fourth centuries BCE, and compiled by the first century CE, although it is not known how old the tales actually are, and spread around the world, influencing the folklore of countries from Ireland to Japan.

Hinduism is notable for its pantheon of gods and goddesses, each of whom has an animal that serves as a "vehicle" for them, literally carrying the gods around. Known as vahanas, these include a variety of animals that symbolically represent the power of the god or goddess. Other gods are part animal themselves, such as Ganesh, the elephant god, or Hanuman, the monkey god. Finally, some gods have avatars, which are animals that the god uses when they visit earth. One such god is Hayagriva, the avatar of Lord Vishnu, and appears as a man with four arms and the neck and head of a horse. It is Hayagriva, known in India as a source of wisdom, who most likely provided the foundation for the Philippine Tikbalang.

Because the first horses arrived to the Philippines with the Spanish in the sixteenth century, horses were unknown to Filipinos, and early descriptions of the tikbalang did not describe it as having any horse-like characteristics. These were probably added to the creature as horses became incorporated into the country.

The first European account of the tikbalang comes to us from a Catholic missionary named Juan de Plasencia, in 1589, just two decades after the Spanish first arrived on the islands. He described it as a "ghost, goblin or devil" and remarked on the fear of the indigenous people toward them, which led to the use of amulets and talismans to protect themselves. For the next three centuries, Spanish religious authorities would continue to lament the fact that the local people continued to hang on to this "superstition" and reject Catholicism. While we cannot take Plasencia's account on its face—the Spanish were famous for describing the religious beliefs of indigenous peoples they encountered as demonic—it is notable that Plasencia's description does not mention horses at all.

Today, belief in tikbalangs is still found among some Filipinos. Today, they are thought to be guardians of the forest but are also seen as similar to sprites or goblins from other cultures— trickster creatures that are not evil but play tricks on humans, causing havoc for them. In particular, the tikbalang will hang out on roads or beneath bridges and will lead travelers astray. There is also a belief that if you catch a tikbalang, and pluck one of his spikes (or one of the golden hares that makes up his mane in other accounts), you can control the tikbalang and make it serve you. This belief parallels beliefs in animal brides like selkies or swan maidens, who can be controlled by a human who is in possession of their animal skin.

See also: Selkies

Further Reading:

Eugenio, D. L. (Ed.). (2007). *Philippine Folk Literature: An Anthology* (Vol. 1). UP Press.
Ratcliff, L. K. (1949). Filipino Folklore. *The Journal of American Folklore*, 62(245), 259–89.

ZANZIBAR LEOPARD

The Zanzibar leopard (Panthera pardus adersi) is a subspecies of leopard, which is native to Zanzibar, an island chain off the coast of the African country of Tanzania. The Zanzibar leopard is thought by scientists to be extinct.

It is smaller than most leopards but was the largest nonhuman predator species in Zanzibar. It appears that it was hunted to extinction, a process that was probably exacerbated by the small size of the animal's habitat (the island of Unguja, the largest island in the chain, is only 646 square miles in size), which, thanks to population growth, offered even less space for the leopards.

Prior to its extinction, Zanzibar locals had had numerous conflicts with the leopards, which resulted in them being both feared and hated. They were responsible for killing livestock and were blamed for fatal attacks on people as well, which led to, in 1964, an organized government-sponsored effort (led by a witch finder) to hunt and eradicate the animals. By the 1990s, scientists believe that the last of the leopards was killed. Like many big cats, leopards are solitary, only interacting with other leopards for mating. This makes them much harder to spot than gregarious species like lions.

The Zanzibar leopard has a similar history to the thylacine, or Tasmanian tiger, which went extinct in 1936 after a similar campaign of demonization followed by eradication. The last remaining member of the species, an animal known today as Benjamin, was captured in 1933, and just before his death in 1936, when it was clear that the thylacine had been hunted to near extinction, it received protection from the state against hunting. Unfortunately, that was too late, as after Benjamin's death, there were no more thylacines to be found. While a similar attempt to save the Zanzibar leopard was initiated in the 1990s, it was most likely too late. While the thylacine was demonized and accused of killing livestock that it probably did not kill, the Zanzibar leopard is associated with witchcraft, making it much more than a natural threat.

In much of Africa where witchcraft beliefs are present, witches are thought to keep big cats as animal familiars. The Zanzibar leopard is thought to be one such species. Locals speak of two kinds of leopards: wild leopards, which did not attack and kill people, but also what were called kept leopards, which were the familiars that were owned and controlled by witches. It was these leopards that locals thought had attacked and killed people, on the orders of whatever witch controlled them. These familiars are said to live in caves on the island, and tourists today can visit those caves with local tour guides in order to try to get a glimpse of one. It is this belief that is most likely responsible for the loss of the species.

Goldman and Walsh (2002) conducted a survey of the residents of Unguja, the largest of Zanzibar's islands, and found that locals had been seeing what they believe to be Zanzibar leopards as late as 1996. However, there has been no verification of their existence beyond that year, and camera traps and other methods used by scientists have provided just the smallest clues. In 2018, a camera trap left by the Animal Planet television show *Extinct or Alive* did catch what looked to be a leopard in Jozani-Chwaka Bay National Park, but that identification has not been confirmed, nor does it indicate whether there is more than one leopard, much less enough of a population to maintain enough genetic diversity for survival. Most recently, Weier (2019) conducted a survey of residents and placed a camera trap in the same location, the Jozani-Chwaka Bay National Park, where the last camera had allegedly caught a leopard. Weier reported, however, that he found no sign of a leopard. He also searched for biological evidence, including scat, fur, the bodies of prey, or even claw marks, but found nothing. One discovery that Weier made was that local people think there are two varieties of Zanzibar leopard. Besides the wild versus kept distinction, locals also saw physical differences between what they call the

Kisutu variant (yellow with red or black spots) and the Konge variant (smaller, with a gray coat with black stripes). In fact, in 2019, what the locals called a Kisutu leopard carcass was found on a road, but it seems clear that it was just a stray domestic cat.

See also: Kishi, Milk Hare, Thylacine

Further Reading:

Goldman, H. V., & Walsh, M. T. (2002). Is the Zanzibar Leopard (Panthera Pardus Adersi) Extinct. *Journal of East African Natural History*, 91(1), 15–25.
Walsh, M. T., & Goldman, H. V. (2016). Cryptids and Credulity: The Zanzibar Leopard and Other Imaginary Beings. In S. Hurn (Ed.), *Anthropology and Cryptozoology*. Routledge, 70–106.
Weier, A. (2019). Leopards Are Good to Think With: Spotting the Zanzibar Leopard in Jozani Forest. Independent Study Project (ISP) Collection. 3146. https://digitalcollections.sit.edu/isp_collection/3146.

Appendix

Cryptozoology Podcasts

- ABC Cryptozoology
- Alien Zoo
- All Day Paranormal
- Atlas Obscura
- Beastly Theories
- Bigfoot—Terror in the Woods
- Bigfoot and Beyond with Cliff and Bobo
- Bigfoot for Breakfast
- Bigfoot Society
- Conspiracies & Cryptids
- Counting Cryptids
- Cracking Cryptids and Curios
- Cryptic
- Cryptid Campfire
- Cryptid Zone
- Cryptids
- Cryptids Decrypted
- Cryptids On Cryptids
- Folklore on the Rocks
- From The Shadows
- Ghosts-n-Heauxs
- Kevin's Cryptids
- Monster Tales: a cryptid adventure
- Monsters Among Us
- MonsterTalk
- Mysteries and Monsters
- Mysterious Creatures Program
- Sasquatch Chronicles
- The Amateur Cryptid Survival Guide
- The Cryptid Factor
- The Cryptonaut Podcast
- Wild Thing
- Yowie Central

Cryptozoology Organizations

- Big Cat Monitors
- Bigfoot ABCs

- Bigfoot Chronicles
- Bigfoot Encounters
- Bigfoot Field Researchers Organization
- Bigfoot in New York?
- Bigfoot News Wire
- British Columbia Scientific Cryptozoology Club
- Chattahoochee Bigfoot Organization
- Cryptid Zoo
- East Texas Bigfoot Independent Study
- Friends of Bigfoot
- Gulf Coast Bigfoot Research Organization
- International Bigfoot Society
- Loren's CryptoZooNews
- Mad River Sasquatch Study
- Michigan Bigfoot Information Center
- Monster Tracker
- Monsters and Mysteries in America
- Nessie's Grotto
- New Jersey Bigfoot Reporting Center
- North American Bigfoot
- North East Sasquatch Researchers Association
- Operation Nightscream: Sasquatch and Bigfoot Researchers
- Oregon Bigfoot
- Pennsylvania Bigfoot Society
- Sasquatch Information Society
- Sasquatch Watch
- Texas Bigfoot Research Center
- TexLa Cryptozoological Research Group
- The Bigfoot Research Network
- The British Big Cats Society
- The British Columbia Scientific Cryptozoology Club
- The Cryptozoology Emporium
- The International Society of Cryptozoology
- The Northwest Bigfoot Research Foundation
- The Official Loch Ness Monster Site
- The Ohio / Pennsylvania Bigfoot Research Group
- The Vietnam Cryptozoic and Rare Animals Research Centre
- West Coast Sasquatch Research
- Winnipeg River Sasquatch Association

Well-Known Cryptozoologists and Those Who Write Regularly on Cryptozoology

- Ada Arney
- Adrienne Mayor
- Al Hodgson
- Albert Samuel Gatschet (1832–1907)
- Aleksandr Kondratov (1937–1993)
- Alexander Rempel
- Alexei Sitnikov
- Alton Higgins

- Andrei Kozlov
- Andrew D. Gable
- Andrew Sanford
- Angel Morant Forés
- Ann Richardson Davis
- Anthonie Cornelis Oudemans (1858–1943)
- Arnošt Vašíček
- Austin Whittall
- B. Ann Slate
- Benjamin Radford
- Bernard Heuvelmans (1916–2001)
- Bob Garrett
- Bob Gimlin
- Bob Rickard
- Bob Titmus
- Boris Porshnev (1905–1972)
- Brian Brown
- Brian Regal
- Bruce A. Champagne
- Bruce L. Owens
- Byambyn Rinchen (1905–1977)
- C. M. Kosemen
- Charles Cordier
- Charles Pitman
- Charles William Hobley
- Charlie Estepp
- Charlie Jacoby
- Chester Moore Chris Moiser
- Chris Stringer
- Christian Le Noël
- Christine Janis
- Christine M. Kirkland
- Christopher Murphy
- Claude Gagnon
- Clemente Onelli
- Cliff Barackman
- Clive Gamble
- Constance Whyte
- Craig Heinselman
- D. Zevegmid
- D. G. Gerahty
- Dale Drinnon
- Dallas Tanner
- Dan Houser
- Daniel Loxton
- Daniel O. Schmitt
- Daniel Perez
- Daris Swindler (1925–2007)
- Darren Naish
- David C. Xu
- David Hatcher Childress
- David J. Daegling
- David O'Reilly
- David Oren
- Denys Tucker
- Derek Randles
- Di Francis
- Dick Raynor
- Dmitri Bayanov
- Don Hunter

- Don Sherman
- Donald Baird
- Donald Prothero
- Doug Hajicek
- Ed Schillinger
- Édouard Louis Trouessart (1842–1927)
- Eduard Seler (1849–1922)
- Edward Newman
- Ernst Bartels
- Esteban Sarmiento
- Eugene Thomas
- Eugene Yost
- Ezekiel Stone Wiggins (1839–1910)
- Ferdinand Anders
- Florentino Ameghino
- Frank Gordon
- Frank Searle
- Frank Turk (1911–1996)
- Fredrick William Holiday (1921–1979)
- Fritz Dieterlen
- G. P. Dement'ev
- Gary J. Galbreath
- Gary Opit
- Gathorne Gathorne-Hardy
- George Eberhart
- George M. Eberhart
- Gerald Russell
- Greg "Squatchman" Yost
- Gregory Forth
- Grover Krantz (1931–2002)
- Harlan Ford (d. 1980)
- Harry Johnston
- Henry H. Bauer
- Henry Newman
- Herbert Francis Fenn
- Herman Regusters
- Howard Hill
- I. F. Tatzl
- Igor Burtsev
- Ingo Krumbiegel
- Ivan Ivlov
- Ivan T. Sanderson (1911–1973)
- J. Richard Greenwell (1942–2005)
- Jacqueline Roumeguère-Eberhardt
- James "Bobo" Fay
- James F. Robinson
- James Terry (1844–1912)
- Jamsrangiin Tseveen (1880–1942)
- Janice Carter
- Jaroslav Mareš
- Jarret Ruminski
- Jean-Louis Brodu
- Jeffrey Cassar
- Jeffrey Meldrum
- Jennifer Marshall
- Jerome Clark
- Jim Hiers
- Jim McClarin
- Jimmy Chilcutt
- Joe Nickell

- John Bindernagel (1941–2018)
- John Blashford-Snell
- John Colarusso
- John Conway
- John E. Roth
- John Freitas
- John H. Duffy
- John Keel (1930–2009)
- John Kirk
- John MacKinnon
- John R. Napier (1917–1987)
- John Robert Colombo
- John Stamey
- John W. Burns (1888–1962)
- John Willison Green (1927–2016)
- Jonathan Downes
- Jonathan Whitcomb
- Jon-Erik Beckjord (1939–2008)
- Josh Gates
- Joshua Blu Buhs
- Kai Roath
- Karen Mutton
- Karl Shuker
- Kathy Moskowitz Strain
- Ken Gerhard
- Kevin Kehl
- Lars Thomas
- Lee Frank
- Leonid Yershov
- LeRoy Fish
- Liu Minzhuang
- Loren Coleman
- Lucien Blancou
- M. A. Wetherell (1883–1939)
- Malcolm Smith
- Manuel Jesús Molina
- Marc Rowley
- Marc van Roosmalen
- Marc Wolfgang Miller
- Marcello Truzzi (1935–2003)
- Marcus Scibanicus
- Marie-Jeanne Koffmann
- Marjorie H. Halpin
- Mark A. Hall (1946–2016)
- Mark Chorvinsky (1954–2005)
- Mary Sutherland
- Matt Crowley
- Matthew Delph
- Matthew Moneymaker
- Maurice Burton (1898-1992)
- Maya Bykova (d. 1995 or 1996)
- Melba Ketchum
- Michael Bradley
- Michael Heaney
- Michael M. Ames (1933–2006)
- Michael Trachtengerts (1937–2017)
- Michael Williams
- Michel Meurger
- Michel Raynal
- Mike Quast

- Mikhail Sergeyevich Yeltsin
- Monique Watteau
- Muaed Mysyrjan
- Myra Shackley
- Neville Bonney
- Nicholas Witchell
- Nigel Brierly
- Nikolai Damilin
- Odette Tchernine (1897–1992)
- Pat Spain
- Patrick Huyghe
- Paul Cropper
- Paul Freeman (1943–2003)
- Paul Sieveking
- Paul Willis
- Percy Fawcett
- Peter Byrne
- Peter Hocking
- Peter Scott (1909–1989)
- Philip Henry Gosse
- Philippe Coudray
- R. G. Burton
- Ranae Holland
- Randy Filipovic
- Rebecca Lang
- Reinhold Messner
- René Dahinden (1930–2001)
- Rex and Heather Gilroy
- Richard Ellis
- Richard Freeman

- Richard Noll
- Richard S. Lambert (1894–1981)
- Richard Terry
- Rick Dyer
- Robert "JavaBob" Schmalzbach
- Robert H. Rines (1922–2009)
- Robert Michael Pyle
- Robert Todd Carroll (1945–2016)
- Robin McCray
- Roderick Sprague (1933–2012)
- Roger Patterson (1933–1972)
- Ronald Binns
- Rory Nugent
- Roy Mackal (1925–2013)
- Rudy Breuning
- Rula Lenska
- Rupert Gould (1890–1948)
- Ryan Bergara
- Scott Herriot
- Scott Marlowe
- Sergei Turkin
- Stueart Campbell Sylvain Pallix
- Tim Dinsdale (1924–1987)
- Tim E. Cassidy
- Tim Fasano (1956-2019)
- Tim Mendham
- Todd Standing
- Tom Biscardi
- Tom Slick (1916–1962)
- Tom Steenburg

- Tony "Doc" Shiels
- Tony Healy
- Tony Pratt
- Trader Horn (1861–1931)
- Trevor Beer
- Ulrich Magin
- Valentin B. Sapunov
- Véronique Campion-Vincent
- Vine Deloria Jr. (1933–2005)
- Vladimir Markotic (1920–1994)
- W. M. Gerald Russell
- Ward Reed
- Wenzcislaw Plawinskiy
- Wes Germer
- William Beebe
- William Charles Osman Hill (1901–1975)
- William Hichens (d. 1944)
- William Jevning
- William R. Corliss (1926–2011)
- William Rebsamen
- Willy Ley (1906–1969)
- Wolf Henner Fahrenbach
- Woody Pratt
- Zachary Barwise
- Zhugdariyn Damdin

Cryptozoology Television Series

- Alaska Monsters
- Animal X
- Arthur C. Clarke's Mysterious World
- Beast Hunter
- Beast Legends
- Destination Truth
- Expedition Mungo
- Extinct or Alive
- Finding Bigfoot
- Freak Encounters
- Gravity Falls
- Harry and the Hendersons
- In Search of . . .
- Is It Real?
- Kagewani
- Lost Tapes
- MonsterQuest
- Monsters and Mysteries in America
- Mountain Monsters
- Sasquatch
- So Weird
- Terror in the Woods
- The Proof Is Out There
- The Secret Saturdays
- The UnXplained
- The X-Creatures
- Weird Travels

Cryptozoology Museums

- International Cryptozoology Museum

Cryptozoology Journals

- The Journal of Cryptozoology

Cryptozoology Festivals and Conventions

- Beast Fest
- Braxxie Bazaar
- Chilo Cryptid Festival
- Covington Cryptid Block Party
- Cryptid Con
- Flatwoods Monster Fest

- Lizard Man Festival
- Mothman Festival
- Ohio Bigfoot Conference
- Texas Bigfoot Conference
- Sasquatch Music Festival

Cryptozoology Training and Certificate Programs

- Cryptozoology Diploma Course (Centre of Excellence)
- Cryptozoology 101 (Universal Class)
- Cryptozoology and Bigfoot (Outschool)

- Cryptozoology/Hominology Degree (IMHS Metaphysics Institute)
- Cryptozoology Certificate Course (Courses for Success)

Bibliography

Afinogenov, G., & Roeder, C. (2018). Cold War Creatures: Soviet Science and the Problem of the Abominable Snowman. *Ice and Snow in the Cold War*, 236–52.

Agentweatherby (2020). Does Anyone Have any Stories of the Barmanou. *Reddit, R/Pakistan*, May 12, https://www.reddit.com/r/pakistan/comments/hplbrd/does_anyone_have_any_stories_of_the_barmanou/.

Aguirre, S. M. (2003). *Mitos de Chile*. Editorial Sudamericana Chilena.

Akerbyrgg (2020). Does Anyone Have any Stories of the Barmanou. *Reddit, R/Pakistan*, May 12, https://www.reddit.com/r/pakistan/comments/hplbrd/does_anyone_have_any_stories_of_the_barmanou/.

Anderson, A. (2003). The Beast Without: The moa as a Colonial Frontier Myth in New Zealand. In *Signifying Animals*. Routledge, 248–56.

Anderson, A. (2003). *Prodigious Birds: Moas and Moa-Hunting in New Zealand*. Cambridge University Press.

Appel, G. (2022). *The Cryptid Beast of the Dark Forest*. Page Publishing Inc.

Are the Legends True? Man Claims he Spotted Fabled Loveland Frogman: Legend of Humanoid Frog Lives on. (2016). *KWLT5*, August 4.

Argue, D. (2018). Does the Yahoo in Gulliver's Travels Represent an Eighteenth Century Description of the Sasquatch? *The Relict Hominoid Inquiry*, 7, 97–106.

Arment, C. (2004). *Cryptozoology: Science & Speculation*. Coachwhip Publications.

Ashley-Montagu, F. M. (1929). The Discovery of a New Anthropoid Ape in South America? *The Scientific Monthly*, 29(3), 275–9.

Bacon, A.-M., & Long, V. (2001). The First Discovery of a Complete Skeleton of a Fossil Orang-utan in a Cave of the Hoa Binh Province, Vietnam. *Journal of Human Evolution*, 41, 227–41.

Bartholomew, R. B. (2001). Monkey man Delusion Sweeps India. *Skeptic (Altadena, CA)*, 9(1), 13.

Bartholomew, R. E. (2012). *The Untold Story of Champ: A Social History of America's Loch Ness Monster*. SUNY Press.

Bauer, H. (2014). Cryptozoology and the Troubles with "Skeptics" and Mainstream Pundits. *Journal of Scientific Exploration*, 27(4), 690–704.

Bauer, H. H. (1987). Society and Scientific Anomalies: Common Knowledge About the Loch Ness Monster. *Journal of Scientific Exploration*, 1(1), 51–74.

Bauer, H. H. (2002). The Case for the Loch Ness Monster: The Scientific Evidence. *Journal of Scientific Exploration*, 16(2), 225–46.

Bay Monster (1982). *Washington Post*, July 12.

Bayanov, D. (2012). Historical Evidence for the Existence of Relict Hominoids. *The Relict* Hominoid Inquiry, 1, 23–50.

Beattie, H. (1918). Traditions and Legends Collected from the Natives of Murihiku. (Southland, New Zealand.) Part XI. *The Journal of the Polynesian Society*, 27(3), 107.

Bhutto, A. (2018). Invisible Monster: A Compromised Zoologist in Pakistan. *TLS. Times Literary Supplement*, 6024, 29–30.

Big Cats Caught on Camera in Arkansas (2009). *4029 TV*, May 18.

Bindernagel, John A. (2010). *The Discovery of the Sasquatch*. Beachcomber Books.

Black, G. F., & Thomas, N. W. (1903). *Examples of Printed Folk-Lore Concerning the Orkney and Shetland Islands*. London. https://archive.org/details/examplesprinted00thomgoog

Blackburn, L. (2012). *The Beast of Boggy Creek: The True Story of the Fouke Monster*. Anomalist Books.

Blackburn, L. (2013). *Lizard Man: The True Story of the Bishopville Monster*. Anomalist Books.

Bord, Janet and Colin (2006). *Bigfoot Casebook*. Pine Winds Press.

Borges, J. L., & di Giovanni, N. T. (Trans.). (2002). *The Book of Imaginary Beings*. Vintage Classics, Random House.

Bousfield, E. L., & LeBlond, P. H. (1992). Preliminary Studies on the Biology of a Large Marine Cryptid in Coastal Waters of British Columbia. *American Zoologist*, 32, 2A.

Bousfield, E. L., & LeBlond, P. H. (1995). An Account of Cadborosaurus Willsi, new Genus, new Species, a Large Aquatic Reptile from the Pacific Coast of North America. *Amphipacifica*, 1(suppl_1), 3–25.

Brantlinger, P. (1985). Victorians and Africans: The Genealogy of the Myth of the Dark Continent. *Critical Inquiry*, 12(1), 166–203.

Bronson, E. B. (1910). *In Closed Territory*. AC McClurg & Company.

Brown, C. (1982). Creature Feature. *Washington Post*, July 16.

Brown, R. (2009). *The Lake Erie Shore: Ontario's Forgotten South Coast*. Dundurn.

Bubandt, N. (2019). Of Wildmen and White Men: Cryptozoology and Inappropriate/d Monsters at the Cusp of the Anthropocene. *Journal of the Royal Anthropological Institute*, 25(2), 223–40.

Buhs, J. B. (2011). Tracking Bigfoot Through 1970s Children's Culture: How Mass Media, Consumerism, and the Culture of Preadolescence Shaped Wildman Lore. *Western Folklore*, 70(2), 195–218.

Buhs, Joshua Blu. (2009). *Bigfoot: The Life and Times of a Legend*. University of Chicago Press.

Burgkmair, H. *The Folk Zoology of Southeast Asian Wildmen*. The Newsletter of the International Institute for Asian Studies, no. 52.

Burton, A. (2013). Gone Fishing. *Frontiers in Ecology and the Environment*, 11(9), 516.

Cape Ann Serpent on Lake Champlain (1819). *Plattsburgh Republican*, July 24.

Carpenter, Scott. (2014). *The Bigfoot Field Journal*. Independently published.

Carroll, C. M. (2021). *Missouri Ozarks Legends & Lore*. Arcadia Publishing.

Cartmill, Matt. (2008). Bigfoot Exposed: An Anthropologist Examines America's Enduring Legend/Sasquatch: Legend Meets Science. *American Journal of Physical Anthropology*, 135(1), 118.

Cassady, C. (2009). *Paranormal Great Lakes: An Illustrated Encyclopedia*. Schiffer.

Chakravorty, A. (2021). Wild Men of Central Asia: A Cryptozoological Analysis of Jonathan Swift's Yahoo. *Research Journal Of English (RJOE)*, 6(3), 1–5.

Champlain, L. (2003). The Measure of a Monster. *Skeptical Inquirer*, 2, 5.

Cheezum, E. A. (2007). *Discovering Chessie: Waterfront, Regional Identity, and the Chesapeake Bay Sea Monster, 1960–2000*. Doctoral dissertation, University of South Carolina.

Chessie, the Chesapeake Bay Sea Monster (1980). *Richmond Times Dispatch*.

Christiansen, R. (Ed.). (1964). *Folktales of Norway*. University of Chicago Press.

Citizens Cheer Bobcat Killing (1954). *The Robesonian*, January 13, 1, 7.

Coleman, Christopher K. (2011). *Dixie Spirits: True Tales of the Strange and Supernatural in the South*. New York: Fall River Press Feschino, Frank C. 2004. *The Braxton County Monster*. Quarrier Press.

Coleman, L., & Huyghe, P. (1999). *The Field Guide to Bigfoot, Yeti, and Other Mystery Primates Worldwide*. Avon Books.

Coleman, L. (2003). *Field Guide to Lake Monsters, Sea Serpents, and Other Mystery Denizens of the Deep*. Penguin.

Coleman, L. (2003). *Bigfoot!: The True Story of Apes in America*. Simon and Schuster.

Collins, D. (1984). Chessie and his Ilk; De-Monstrably Shy. *Washington Post*, December 9, https://www.washingtonpost.com/archive/sports/1984/12/09/chessie-and-his-ilk-de-monsterably-shy/78e115db-2f7b-4982-8b80-166ba2112b14/.

Colombo, J. R. (1982). *Windigo, an Anthology of Fact and Fantastic Fiction: An Anthology of Fact and Fantastic Fiction*. University of Nebraska Press. Print.

Conway, J., Koseman, C. M., & Naish, D. (2013). *Cryptozoologicon* (Vol. 1). Irregular Books.

Cornell, F. C. (1920). *The Glamour of Prospecting*. T. Fisher Unwin Ltd.

Cowan, J. (1925). *Fairy Folk Tales of the Maori*. Whitcombe & Tombs Limited.

Crabtree, Julius E. (1974). Smokey. In *Smokey and The Fouke Monster*. Day's Creek Production Corp.

Cribb, R. (2009). Nature Conservation and Cultural Preservation in Convergence: Orang Pendek and Papuans in Colonial Indonesia. In Stella Borg Barthet (Ed.), *Sea of Encounters: Essays Towards a Postcolonial Commonwealth*. Editions Rodopi B.V., 221–42.

Cribb, R., Gilbert, H., & Tiffin, H. (2014). *Wild Man from Borneo*. University of Hawaii Press.

Croker, T. C., & Croker, T. F. D. (1862). *Fairy Legends and Traditions of the South of Ireland*. William Tegg.

Crouch, J. N. (2021). *Goatman: Flesh or Folklore?* Createspace.

Cunningham, G., & Coghlan, R. (2011). *The Mystery Animals of Ireland*. CFZ Press.

Curtin, J. (1895). *Tales of the Fairies and of the Ghost World: Collected from Oral Tradition in South-west Munster*. David Nutt in the Strand.

Daegling, D. J., & Schmitt, D. O. (1999). Bigfoot's Screen Test. *Skeptical Inquirer*, May/June, 20–5.

Daegling, David J. (2004). *Bigfoot Exposed: An Anthropologist Examines America's Enduring Legend*. Altamira Press.

Dagnall, N., Denovan, A., Drinkwater, K., Parker, A., & Clough, P. J. (2017). Urban Legends and Paranormal Beliefs: The Role of Reality Testing and Schizotypy. *Frontiers in Psychology*, 8, 94.

Dash, M. (1993). The Dragons of Vancouver. *Fortean Times*, 70, 46–8.

Debenat, J.-P. (2014). *The Asian Wild Man*. Translated by Paul LeBlond. Hancock House.

Dederen, J. M., & Mokakabye, J. (2018). Negotiating Womanhood: The Bird Metaphor in Southern African Folklore and Rites of Passage. *Tydskrif vir Letterkunde*, 55(2), 91–103.

Dendle, P. (2006). Cryptozoology in the Medieval and Modern Worlds. *Folklore*, 117(2), 190–206.

Department of Primary Industries, Parks, Water and Environment (2019). *Thylacine Sighting Reports*, September 1, 2016 to September 19, 2019, https://dpipwe.tas.gov.au/Documents/RTI%20025%20-%202019-20.pdf (Accessed October 8, 2020).

Derby, L. (2008). Imperial Secrets: Vampires and Nationhood in Puerto Rico. *Past and Present*, 199(suppl_3), 290–312.

Derby, R. (2005). Vampiros del Imperio, o por qué el Chupacabras Acecha las Américas? In Salvatorre Ricardo (Ed.), *Culturas Imperiales: Experiencia y Representación en América, África y Asia*. Beatriz Viterbo Editora, 317–44.

Desjarlais, J. (2020). *The Florida Skunk Ape: A Complete History* [self-published].

Dikötter, F. (1998). Hairy Barbarians, Furry Primates, and Wild men: Medical Science and Cultural Representations of Hair in China. In G. Obeyesekere (Ed.), *Hair: Its Power and Meaning in Asian Cultures*. State University of New York Press, 51–74.

Dresser, N. (2022). American Vampires. In D. Puglia (Ed.), *North American Monsters: A Contemporary Legend Casebook*. University Press of Colorado, 118.

Eberhart, G. M. (1983). *Monsters, a Guide to Information on Unaccounted for Creatures, Including Bigfoot, Many Water Monsters, and Other Irregular Animals*. Garland Pub.

Eberhart, G. M. (2002). *Mysterious Creatures: A Guide to Cryptozoology*. ABC-CLIO.

Edgar, M. (1940). Imaginary Animals of Northern Minnesota. *Minnesota History*, 21(4), 353–6.

Eggs, C. C., Large, S., & Shipping, F. (2004). Villagers Speak of the Small, Hairy Ebu Gogo. *Daily Telegraph*, November 18, 2004.

Elliott, D. M. (2021). *West Virginia Urban Legends and Their Impact on Cultures Both Local and Abroad*. Bowling Green State University.

Emmer, R. (2010). *Mokele-mbembe: Fact or Fiction?* Infobase Publishing.

Erdoes, R., & Ortiz, A. (1984). *American Indian Myths and Legends*. Pantheon Books.

Erdoes, R., & Ortiz, A. (2013). *American Indian Myths and Legends*. Pantheon Books.

Ettinghausen, R. (1950). *The Unicorn*. Studies in Muslim Iconography, Freer Gallery of Art Occasional Papers Vol. 1, No. 3, Washington.

Eugenio, D. L. (Ed.). (2007). *Philippine Folk Literature: An Anthology* (Vol. 1). University of Pennsylvania press.

Fahrenbach, W. H. (1988). Sasquatch: Size, Scaling and Statistics. *Cryptozoology*, 13, 47–75.

Fee, C. R., & Webb, J. B. (Eds.). (2016). *American Myths, Legends, and Tall Tales: An Encyclopedia of American Folklore [3 Volumes]: An Encyclopedia of American Folklore (3 Volumes)*. Abc-Clio.

Fennell, J. (2020). *Rough Beasts: The Monstrous in Irish Fiction, 1800–2000* (Vol. 82). Liverpool University Press.

Ferry, J. (1992). Sea Serpent Glides into Folklore of Canadians. *Los Angeles Times*, August 23.

Fixico, D. L. (2017). *"That's what They Used to Say": Reflections on American Indian Oral Traditions*. University of Oklahoma Press.

Fleming, B. E. (2017). The Ojibwe Who Slew the Wiindigo. *Tribal College*, 28(3), 51.

Fleming, J. (1814). Contributions to the British Fauna. *Memoirs of the Wernerian Natural History Society*, II(Part I), 238–51.

Ford, C. (2003). *Where the Sea Breaks Its Back: The Epic Story-Georg Steller & the Russian Exploration of AK*. Graphic Arts Books.

Forth, G. (2005). Hominids, Hairy Hominoids and the Science of Humanity. *Anthropology Today*, 21(3), 13–17.

Forth, G. (2008). *Images of the Wildman in Southeast Asia: An Anthropological Perspective*. Routledge.

Forth, G. (2009). Symbolic Birds and Ironic Bats: Varieties of Classification in Nage Folk Ornithology. *Ethnology*, 48(2), 139–59.

Forth, G. (2014). Gugu. Evidence from Folk Zoological Nomenclature and Classification for a Mystery Primate in Southern Sumatra. *Anthropos*, 109(1), 149–60.

Forth, G. (2021). Ambiguous Birds: Ideas About Bats on Flores Island and Elsewhere. *Journal of Ethnobiology*, 41(1), 105–20.

Foster, M. D. (2012). Haunting Modernity: Tanuki, Trains, and Transformation in Japan. *Asian Ethnology*, 71(1), 3.

France, R. L. (2016). Historicity of Sea Turtles Misidentified as Sea Monsters: A Case for the Early Entanglement of Marine Chelonians in pre-plastic Fishing Nets and Maritime Debris. *Coriolis: Interdisciplinary Journal of Maritime Studies*, 6, 1–24.

France, R. L. (2017). Imaginary Sea Monsters and Real Environmental Threats: Reconsidering the Famous Osborne, "Moha-moha," Valhalla, and "Soay beast" Sightings of Unidentified Marine Objects. *International Review of Environmental History*, 3(1), 63–100.

France, R. L. (2017). *Imaginary Sea Monsters and Real Environmental Threats from International Review of Environmental History* (Vol. 3). Edited by James Beattie. Canberra: The Australian National University, Australia retrieved from ANU press on the June 24, 2019.

Freeman, C. (2010). *Paper Tiger: A Visual History of the Thylacine*. Brill.

Freeman, R. (2004). In Search of Orang-Pendek. *Fortean Times*.

Freeman, R. (2019). *Adventures in Cryptozoology: Hunting for Yetis, Mongolian Deathworms and Other Not-So-Mythical Monsters*. Mango Media Inc.

French, C. C., & Stone, A. (2013). *Anomalistic Psychology: Exploring Paranormal Belief and Experience*. Palgrave Macmillan.

Friedman, R. (1996). The Chupacabra Becomes a Recurring Legend. *The San Juan Star*. https://www.princeton.edu/~accion/chupa27.html.

Galeano, J. C., & Morgan, R. (2009). *Folktales of the Amazon*. Libraries Unlimited.

Gallehugh, J. F. (1976). The Vampire Beast of Bladenboro. *North Carolina Folklore Journal*, 24, 53–8.

Gardner, R. (1950). Caddy, King of the Coast: A Sea Serpent That's as Real as the Flying Saucer and Just as Harmless Still Churns the Pacific for its Favored Fans. *Macleans*, June 15.

Gasparini, Z., Salgado, L., & Casadío, S. (2003). Maastrichtian Plesiosaurs from Northern Patagonia. *Cretaceous Research*, 24(2), 157–70.

Gaster, M. (1915). *Rumanian Bird and Beast Stories*. Folk-Lore Society, no. 83, 249–54.

Gillespie, A. K. (2022). The Jersey Devil. In D. J. Puglia (Ed.), *North American Monsters: A Contemporary Legend Casebook*. University Press of Colorado, 102–17.

Godfrey, L. S. (1991). Tracking Down the Beast of Bray Road. *The Week*, December 29.

Goldman, H. V., & Walsh, M. T. (2002). Is the Zanzibar Leopard (Panthera Pardus Adersi) Extinct. *Journal of East African Natural History*, 91(1), 15–25.

Gow, A. S. F., & Page, D. L. (Eds.). (1965). *The Greek Anthology: Hellenistic Epigrams* (Vol. 2). CUP Archive.

Grandjean, K. (2021). The Secret History of the Jersey Devil: How Quakers, Hucksters, and Benjamin Franklin Created a Monster by Brian Regal and Frank J. Esposito. *Pennsylvania History: A Journal of Mid-Atlantic Studies*, 88(1), 137–9.

Grant, J. (1867). The Wild Beast of Gevaudan. *The Argosy: A Magazine of Tales, Travels, Essays, and Poems*, 4(1), 54–62.

Green, J. (1984). The Search in China for Unknown Hominoids. In V. Markotic (Ed.), *The Sasquatch and Other Unknown Hominoids*. Western Publishers, 88–93.

Green, John. (2004). *The Best of Bigfoot/Sasquatch*. Hancock House Publishers.

Green, John. (2006). *Sasquatch: The Apes Among Us*. Hancock House Publishers.

Green, L. G. (1948). *Where Men Still Dream*. Standard Press Ltd.

Greenwell, R. (1985). A Classificatory System for Cryptozoology. *Cryptozoology*, 4, 1–14.

Gregor, W. (1883). Kelpie Stories From the North of Scotland. *The Folk-Lore Journal*, 1(1), 292–4.

Grey, S. F. (2018). Cosmology, Psychopomps, and Afterlife in Homer's Odyssey. In R. Mattila, S. Ito, & S. Fink (Eds.), *Imagining the Afterlife in the Ancient World*. Springer VS, 101–16.

Groves, C. P. (1984). But How Many Large, Terrestrial Animal Species Remain to be Discovered? *Cryptozoology*, 3, 111–15.

Guimont, E. (2019). Hunting Dinosaurs in Central Africa. *Contingent Magazine*.

Guoxing, Z. (1982). The Status of the Wildman Research in China. *Cryptozoology*, 1, 14.

Hagenbeck, C. (1909). *Beasts and Men*. Longmans, Green, and Company.

Hairr, J. (2013). *Monsters of North Carolina: Mysterious Creatures in the Tar Heel State*. Stackpole Books.

Hall, M. A. (2004). *Thunderbirds: America's Living Legends of Giant Birds*. Cosimo, Inc.

Hallenbeck, B. G. (2013). *Monsters of New York: Mysterious Creatures in the Empire State*. Stackpole Books.

Halloy, A., & Servais, V. (2014). Enchanting Gods and Dolphins: A Cross-cultural Analysis of Uncanny Encounters. *Ethos*, 42(4), 479–504.

Harris, N. (1981). *Humbug: The art of PT Barnum*. University of Chicago Press.

Harte, J. (2011). Shock! The Black Dog of Bungay: A Case Study in Local Folklore. *Folklore*, 122(3), 347–8.

Hawkins, J., Ryan, J. S., & Adams, P. (2007). The Folklore of Awe: Elements and Influences Involved in the Construction of Tales Concerning Strange Creatures and Phenomena Arising in the Australian Environment and Culture. Unpublished thesis. https://rune.une.edu.au/web/bitstream/1959.11/6442/2/open/SOURCE03.pdf.

Hazel, R. (2019). *Snakes, People, and Spirits, Volume One: Traditional Eastern Africa in its Broader Context* (Vol. 1). Cambridge Scholars Publishing.

Healy, T., & Cropper, P. (1994). *Out of the Shadows: Mystery Animals of Australia*. Ironbark.

Heaney, M. (1983). The Mongolian Almas: A Historical Re-Evaluation of the Sighting by Baradiin. *Cryptozoology*, 2, 40–52.

Heinselman, C. (2001). *Eastern Sasquatch Analysis: Potential Patterns or Dubious Data?* Paper presentation for the 3rd Annual East Coast Bigfoot Researchers Meeting, September 2002.

Henriques, J. F. (2019). Duppy Conquerors, Rolling Calves and Flights to Zion. In S. Goodman, T. Heys, & E. Ikoniadou (Eds.), *Unsound/Undead. UNSPECIFIED*.

Heuvelmans, B. (1958). *On the Track of Unknown Animals*. Rupert Hart-Davis.

Heuvelmans, B. (1968). *In the Wake of the Sea-Serpent*, trans. R. Garnett. Hill & Wang.

Heuvelmans, B. (1982). What Is Cryptozoology. *Cryptozoology*, 1(1), 12.

Heuvelmans, B. (1983). How Many Animal Species Remain to be Discovered? *Cryptozoology* 2, 1–24.

Heuvelmans, B. (1984). The Birth and Early History of Cryptozoology. *Cryptozoology* 3, 1–30.

Heuvelmans, B. (1986). Annotated Checklist of Apparently Unknown Animals with Which Cryptozoology Is Concerned. *Cryptozoology*, 5, 1–26.

Heuvelmans, B. (1988). The Sources and Method of Cryptozoological Research. *Cryptozoology* 7, 1–21.

Heuvelmans, B. (1990). The Metamorphosis of Unknown Animals into Fabulous Beasts and of Fabulous Beasts into Known Animals. *Cryptozoology*, 9, 1–12.

Heuvelmans, B. (2007). *The Natural History of Hidden Animals*. Kegan Paul.

Heuvelmans, B. (2016). *Neanderthal: The Strange Saga of the Minnesota Iceman*. Anomalist Books.

Heuvelmans, B., & Garnett, R. (Trans.). (1958). *On the Track of Unknown Animals*. Rupert Hart-Davis.

Higuchi, R., Bowman, B., Freiberger, M., Ryder, O. A., & Wilson, A. C. (1984). DNA Sequences From the Quagga, an Extinct Member of the Horse Family. *Nature*, 312(5991), 282–4.

Hobley, C. W. (1913). On Some Unidentified Beasts. *East African Geographical Review*, 3(6), 48–52.

Hoefle, S. W. (2009). Enchanted (and Disenchanted) Amazônia: Environmental Ethics and Cultural Identity in Northern Brazil. *Ethics Place and Environment (Ethics, Place & Environment (Merged with Philosophy and Geography))*, 12(1), 107–30.

Hofberg, H. (1980). *Swedish Fairy Tales*. Translated by W. H. Myers. Belford-Clarke Company.

Hofreiter, M., Siedel, H., Van Neer, W., & Vigilant, L. (2003). Mitochondrial DNA Sequence From an Enigmatic Gorilla Population (Gorilla Gorilla Uellensis). *American Journal of Physical Anthropology: The Official Publication of the American Association of Physical Anthropologists*, 121(4), 361–8.

Holden, R., & Holden, N. (2001). *Bunyips: Australia's Folklore of Fear*. National Library Australia.

Holyfield, D. (1999). *Encounters with the Honey Island Swamp Monster*. Honey Island Books.

Howard, A. J. (2021). *Wild man, Cannibal, Trickster: The Wendigo in Literature and Media*. Doctoral dissertation, University of Leeds.

Hurn, S. (Ed.). (2016). *Anthropology and Cryptozoology: Exploring Encounters with Mysterious Creatures*, New York: Routledge.

Jøn, A. A. (1998). Dugongs and Mermaids, Selkies and Seals. *Australian Folklore*, 13, 94–8.

Jacobs, Joseph. (1916). *Europa's Fairy Book*. G. P. Putnam's Sons.

Jankiewicz-Brzostowska, M. (2020). Depictions of Animals in the Satirical War Prints of Kobayashi Kiyochika. *Art of the Orient*, 9(1), 134–54.

Jayatilaka, S. (1881). Siṇhalese Omens. *The Journal of the Ceylon Branch of the Royal Asiatic Society of Great Britain & Ireland*, 7(24), 147–61.

Jenkins, G. (2010). *Chronicles of the Strange and Uncanny in Florida*. Pineapple Press Inc.

Jennings, P. (2014). *Pagan Portals-Blacksmith Gods: Myths, Magicians & Folklore*. John Hunt Publishing.

Jifang, Z. (2007). Hubei Bigfoot—Fact or Fiction? *Beijing Review*, (51), 16, December 20. http://www.bjreview.com/print/txt/2007-12/17/content_90934.htm.

Jordan, J. A. (1956). *Elephants and Ivory: True Tales of Hunting and Adventure*. Rinehart and Co.

Jorgenson, K. P. (2001). *Very Crazy, GI: Strange but True Stories of the Vietnam War*. Random House Digital, Inc.

Joyner, G. (2012). *Monster, Myth or Lost Marsupial? - The Search for the Australian Gorilla in the Jungles of History, Science and Language*. Hayes and Thomas.

Joyner, G. C. (1980). *More Historical Evidence for the Yahoo, Hairy Man, Wild Man or Australian "Gorilla."* National Library of Australia, MS 3889.

Joyner, G. C. (1984). The Orang-utan in England: An Explanation for the use of Yahoo as a Name for the Australian Hairy man. *Cryptozoology: Interdisciplinary Journal of the International Society of Cryptozoology*, 3, 55–7.

Joyner, G. C. (2003). Scientific Reaction to Evidence for the Yahoo or "Australian ape," 1882–1912. *Journal of the Royal Australian Historical Society*, 89(2), 162–78.

Joyner, G. C., & Joyner, G. C. (1977). *The Hairy Man of South Eastern Australia*. GC Joyner.

Jusiak, K. (2015). The Embodiment of the Taboo: The Images of Wendigo in Literature and Their Rendition in Modern Media. Doctoral dissertation, bachelor's thesis, Adam Mickiewicz University in Poznań.

Jylkka, K. (2018). "Witness the Plesiosaurus": Geological Traces and the Loch Ness Monster Narrative. *Configurations*, 26(2), 207–34.

Kallen, S. A. (2008). *The Loch Ness Monster*. Capstone.

Kang, Xioofei. (2007). Spirits, Sex, and Wealth: Fox Lore and fox Worship in Late Imperial China. In D. Aftandilian (Ed.), *What are the Animals to us?: Approaches From Science, Religion, Folklore, Literature, and art*. University of Tennessee Press, 21–36.

Kato, S., Miyamoto, H., Takahashi, M., & Kamahora, J. (1963). Shope Fibroma and Rabbit Myxoma Viruses. II Pathogenesis of Fibromas in Domestic Rabbits. *Biken Journal*, 6, 135–43.

Kearney, L. S. (1928). *The Hodag and Other Tales of the Logging Camps*. LS Kearney.

Keel, J. A. (2002). *The Mothman Prophecies*. Macmillan.

Kimbrough, K., & Shirane, H. (Eds.). (2018). *Monsters, Animals, and Other Worlds: A Collection of Short Medieval Japanese Tales*. Columbia University Press.

Knappert, Jan. (1977). *Bantu Myths and Other Tales*. Brill Archive.

Knutsen, R. (2011). *Tengu: The Shamanic and Esoteric Origins of the Japanese Martial arts*. Global Oriental.

Kojo, Y. (1991). Some Ecological Notes on Reported Large, Unknown Animals in Lake Champlain. *Cryptozoology*, 10, 42–54.

Kolan, M., Leis, K., Baska, A., Kazik, J., & Gałązka, P. (2019). Wendigo Psychosis. *Current Problems of Psychiatry*, 20(3), 213–16.

Kortenhof, K. D. (2006). *Long Live the Hodag!: The Life and Legacy of Eugene Simeon Shepard, 1854–1923*. Hodag Press.

Krantz, Grover. (1992). *Big Footprints*. Johnson Printing Company.

Kruse, J. T. (2020). *Beyond Faery: Exploring the World of Mermaids, Kelpies, Goblins & Other Faery Beasts*. Llewellyn Worldwide.

Kvideland, R., & Sehmsdorf, H. K. (1988). *Scandinavian Folk Belief and Legend* (Vol. 15). University of Minnesota Press.

Кузнецова, O. (2021). Birds' Eden: Birds of Paradise in Early Modern Russian Culture. *Acta Universitatis Lodziensis. Folia Litteraria Rossica*, 1(14), 9–16.

Lake Erie Sea Serpent: Said to Have Been Seen by Fishermen Near Oak Harbor (1892). *Cleveland Plain Dealer*, May 21.

Landrum, C. (2011). Shape-Shifters, Ghosts, and Residual Power: An Examination of Northern Plains Spiritual Beliefs, Location, Objects, and Spiritual Colonialism. In C. E. Boyd & C. P. Thrush (Eds.), *Phantom Past, Indigenous Presence: Native Ghosts in North American Culture and History*. University of Nebraska Press, 255–79.

Laurance, B. (2013). *Yetis, Yowies and Dinosaur Trees: Amazing Finds in the Hunt for Living Legends*. The Conversation.

Lawrence, R. (2008). The Third-World Duppy. *JCLs; Journal of Caribbean Literatures*, 5(3), 98–103.

Laycock, J. (2008). Mothman: Monster, Disaster, and Community. *Fieldwork in Religion*, 3(1), 70.

Leach, M. (1961). Jamaican Duppy Lore. *The Journal of American Folklore*, 74(293), 207–15.

Leary, F. (2003). *The Honey Island Swamp Monster: The Development and Maintenance of a Folk and Commodified Belief Tradition*. Doctoral dissertation, Memorial University of Newfoundland.

LeBlond, P. H. & Bousfield, E. L. (1995). *Cadborosaurus: Survivor from the Deep*. Horsdal & Schubart.

Lees, C. A., & Overing, G. R. (2018). Women and Water: Icelandic Tales and Anglo-Saxon Moorings. *GeoHumanities*, 4(1), 97–111.

Legendary Big Cat' Seen Prowling Countryside Sparks Claims Mythical Beast's Been Found (2022). *Daily Star*, January 5.

Lenik, E. J. (2010). Mythic Creatures: Serpents, Dragons, and Sea Monsters in Northeastern Rock Art. *Archaeology of Eastern North America*, 38, 17–37.

Leonard, J. A., Rohland, N., Glaberman, S., Fleischer, R. C., Caccone, A., & Hofreiter, M. (2005). A Rapid Loss of Stripes: The Evolutionary History of the Extinct Quagga. *Biology Letters*, 1(3), 291–5.

Letnic, M., Fillios, M., & Crowther, M. S. (2012). Could Direct Killing by Larger Dingoes Have Caused the Extinction of the Thylacine from Mainland Australia? *PLoS One*, 7(5), e34877.

Lewis, T., & Kahn, R. (2005). The Reptoid Hypothesis: Utopian and Dystopian Representational Motifs in David Icke's Alien Conspiracy Theory. *Utopian Studies*, 16(1), 45–74.

Ley, W. (1987). *Willy Ley's Exotic Zoology*. Random House Value Publishing.

Lindow, J. (1978). *Swedish Legends and Folktales*. University of California Press.

Living, V. (2012). *Monsters of West Virginia: Mysterious Creatures in the Mountain State*. Stackpole Books.

Lloyd, E. (1846). *A Visit to the Antipodes: With Some Reminiscences of a Sojourn in Australia (No. 22)*. Smith, Elder.

Lockyer, C. (1990). Review of Incidents Involving Wild, Sociable Dolphins, Worldwide. In S. Leatherwood & R. R. Reeves (Eds.), *The Bottlenose Dolphin*. Academic Press, 337–53.

Lombard, Jean. (2004). Waterslangverhale in Afrikaans: die Relevansie van Mitisiteit. *Literator: Journal of Literary Criticism, Comparative Linguistics and Literary Studies*, 25(1), 113+.

Lopez, Barry H. (1978). *Of Wolves and Men*. J. M. Dent and Sons Limited.

Loxton, D. (2004). The Loch Ness Monster. *Skeptic (Altadena, CA)*, 11(1), 96B.

Loxton, D. (2012). Mokele Mbembe! *Skeptic (Altadena, CA)*, 17(3), 65A.

Loxton, D., & Prothero, D. R. (2013). *Abominable Science: Origins of the Yeti, Nessie, and Other Famous Cryptids*. Columbia University Press.

Lunge-Larsen, L. (2004). *The Hidden Folk: Stories of Fairies, Dwarves, Selkies, and Other Secret Beings*. Houghton Mifflin Harcourt.

MacDermot, E. T. (1911). *The History of the Forest of Exmoor*. Barnicott & Pearce, Wessex Press.

Mack, C. K., Mack, C., & Mack, D. (1999). *A Field Guide to Demons, Fairies, Fallen Angels and Other Subversive Spirits*. Macmillan.

Mackal, R. P. (1987). *A Living Dinosaur?: In Search of Mokele-Mbembe*. Brill Archive.

Mackerle, I. (2001). *Mongolské Záhady [Mongolian Mystery]* (in Czech) (1st ed.). Ivo Železný.

Magin, U. (2016). Necessary Monsters: Claimed "Crypto-Creatures" Regarded as Genii Locii. *Time and Mind*, 9(3), 211–22.

Magraner, J. (2018). Relic Hominids of Central Asia: Extracts from the Report – Notes on Relic Hominids of Central Asia. *The Relict Hominoid Inquiry*, 7, 16–68.

Márquez Calle, G. (2008). El hábitat del Hombre Caimán y otros estudios sobre ecología y sociedad en el Caribe. Universidad Nacional de Colombia, Sede San Andrés.

Mart, T. S. (2021). *A Guide to Sky Monsters: Thunderbirds, the Jersey Devil, Mothman, and Other Flying Cryptids*. Indiana University Press.

Martín, J. (2001). *Vieques Poligono Del 3er. Tipo*. Cedicop.

Marvin, G. (2012). *Wolf*. Reaktion Books Ltd.

Maseko, B. (1984). Mamlambo. *Kunapipi*, 6(3), 13.

May, A. (1984). Legend of Chessie Alive, Well, in Maryland. *WBALTV*, https://www.wbaltv.com/article/legend-of-chessie-alive-well-in-maryland/13126354#.

McCloy, J. F., & Miller, R. (1976). *The Jersey Devil*. B B & A Publishers.

McCoy, N. (2005). *New Zealand Mysteries: Secrets, Spooks, Conspiracies and con Artists*. Whitcouls.

McEwan, G. J. (1986). *Mystery Animals of Britain and Ireland*. Robert Hale.

McGrath, A. (2022). *Beasts of the World: Hairy Humanoids* (Vol. 1). Untold Publishing.

McKinstry, L. (2019). *Possible Champ Sighting Near Westport*. Press-Republican.

McLeod, Michael. (2009). *Anatomy of a Beast: Obsession and Myth on the Trail of Bigfoot*. University of California Press.

McNamee, G. (Ed.). (2000). *The Serpent's Tale: Snakes in Folklore and Literature*. University of Georgia Press.

Meldrum, J. (2012). Adaptive Radiations, Bushy Evolutionary Trees, and Relict Hominoids. *Relict Hominoid Inquiry*, 1, 51–6.

Meldrum, J. (2016). Neanderthal: The Strange Saga of the Minnesota Iceman by Bernard Heuvelmans, Translated by Paul LeBlond, With Afterword by Loren Coleman. *Journal of Scientific Exploration*, 30(4), 604–6.

Meldrum, J. (2013). *Sasquatch Field Guide*. Paradise Cay Publications, Inc.

Meldrum, J. (2016). *Sasquatch, Yeti, and Other Wildmen of the World. A Field Guide to Relict Hominoids*. Paradise Cay Publications.

Meldrum, J. (2006). *Sasquatch: Legend Meets Science*. Tom Doherty Associates, LLC.

Mentz, S. (2012). "Half-Fish, Half-Flesh": Dolphins, the Ocean, and Early Modern Humans. In J. E. Feerick & V. Nardizzi (Eds.), *The Indistinct Human in Renaissance Literature*. Palgrave Macmillan, 29–46.

Messner, R. (2001). *My Quest for the Yeti: Confronting the Himalayas' Deepest Mystery*. Macmillan.

Métraux, A. (1944). South American Thunderbirds. *The Journal of American Folklore*, 57(224), 132–5.

Meurger, M., & Gagnon, C. (1998). *Lake Monster Traditions: A Cross-Cultural Analysis*. Fortean Tomes.

Miles, J. (2000). *Weird Georgia: Close Encounters, Strange Creatures, and Unexplained Phenomena*. Cumberland House Publishing.

Miljutin, A. (2007). Rat Kings in Estonia. *Proceedings of the Estonian Academy of Sciences Biology Ecology*, 56(1), 77–81.

Miller, A. L. (1987). The Swan-Maiden Revisited: Religious Significance of Divine-Wife. Folktales with Special Reference to Japan. *Asian Folklore Studies*, 46(1), 55–86.

Minard, P. (2018). Making the "Marsupial Lion": Bunyips, Networked Colonial Knowledge Production Between 1830–59 and the Description of Thylacoleo Carnifex. *Historical Records of Australian Science*, 29(2), 91–102.

Mnensa, M. (2010). Mamlambo's Helping Hand. *Journal of Pan African Studies*, 4(2), 249–50.

Molina, M., & Jaramillo, R. (Trans.). (1986). *Ensayo sobre la Historia Natural de Chile*. Ediciones Maule, Santiago de Chile.

Monster Serpent Lurks in Muddy American River (1981). *Weekly News of the World*, March 23.

Mouritsen, O. G., & Styrbæk, K. (2021). Strange Beings from the Depths of the Sea. In O. G. Mouritsen, K. Styrbæk, J. D. Mouritsen, & M. Johansen (Eds.), *Octopuses, Squid & Cuttlefish: Seafood for Today and for the Future*. Springer, 5–16.

Mullis, J. (2019). Cryptofiction! Science Fiction and the Rise of Cryptozoology. In *The Paranormal and Popular Culture*. Routledge, 240–52.

Mulvane, J. (1994). The Namoi Bunyip. *Australian Aboriginal Studies*, 1, 36.

Murray, C. E. (2019). Locating the Wild Man: Rain Forest Enchantments and Settler Colonial Fantasies Amid the Ruins of the Anthropocene. *Journal of Historical Sociology*, 32(1), 60–73.

Mynott, J. (2018). *Birds in the Ancient World: Winged Words*. Oxford University Press.

Mystery Creature Lurks in Baltimore County (2004). *WBAL TV*, July 27.

Naish, D. (1995). Cryptocetology: Introducing a New Branch of Cryptozoology. *Animals & Men*, 7, 19–27.

Naish, D. (1996a). Ancient Whales, Sea Serpents and Nessies Part One: Pros and Cons. *Animals & Men*, 9, 16–23.

Naish, D. (1996b). Ancient Whales, Sea Serpents and Nessies Part 2: Theorising on Survival. *Animals & Men*, 10, 13–21.

Naish, D. (1996c). Analysing Video Footage Purporting to Show the "Migo" – A Lake Monster from Lake Dakataua, New Britain. *The Cryptozoology Review*, 1(2), 18–21.

Naish, D. (1997a). The Migo Is (Probably) a Crocodile. In J. Downes (Ed.), *The CFZ Yearbook 1997*. CFZ, 51–67.

Naish, D. (1997b). Another Caddy Carcass? *The Cryptozoology Review*, 2(1), 26–9.

Naish, D. (2000). Where be Monsters? *Fortean Times*, 132, 40–4.

Naish, D. (2001a). Sea Serpents, Seals and Coelacanths: An Attempt at a Holistic Approach to the Identity of Large Aquatic Cryptids. In I. Simmons & M. Quin (Eds.), *Fortean Studies* (Vol. 7). John Brown, 75–94.

Naish, D. (2001b). How to Approach a Winged Humanoid. http://www.forteantimes.com/exclusive/naish_01.shtml

Naish, D. (2016). *Hunting Monsters: Cryptozoology and the Reality Behind the Myths*. Arcturus Publishing.

Naish, D. Knatterud, E. & Hedley, S. L. (2004). Cetaceans, Sex and Sea Serpents: An Analysis of the Egede Accounts of a "Most Dreadful Monster" Seen Off the Coast of Greenland in 1734. *Archives of Natural History*, 32, 1–9.

Naish, D., & Tattersdill, W. (2021). Art, Anatomy, and the Stars: Russell and Séguin's Dinosauroid1. *Canadian Journal of Earth Sciences*, 58(9), 968–79.

Napier, J. R. (1973). *Bigfoot: The Sasquatch and Yeti in Myth and Reality*. E. P. Dutton.

Nevill, Hugh. (1886). The Nittaewo of Ceylon. *The Taprobanian*, 1(3).

Neville, S. (2020). Midwestern Strange: Hunting Monsters, Martians, and the Weird in Flyover Country by BJ Hollars. *Indiana Magazine of History*, 116(1), 87–8.

Newton, M. (2005). *De Loys's Ape. Encyclopedia of Cryptozoology: A Global Guide*. McFarland & Company, Inc.

Noel, C. (2019). *Midspeak: Tapping into Sasquatch and Science*. Independently published.

Nord, J. (1933). Letter to the Editor. *Victoria Daily Times*, October 11.

Novitskaia, V. (2015). *Tanuki in Folklore as a Mirror of Japanese Society*. Anomalist Books. https://conservancy .umn.edu/bitstream/handle/11299/212104/thesis.pdf?sequence=3.

Nugent, R. (2016). *Drums Along the Congo: On the Trail of Mokele-Mbembe, the Last Living Dinosaur*. Open Road Media.

Nunnelly, B. (2007). *Mysterious Kentucky*. Whitechapel Productions.

O'Bryen, R. (2020). Untangling the Mangrove: Slow Violence and the Environmentalism of the Poor in the Colombian Caribbean. In L. Blackmore & L. Gomez (Eds.), *Liquid Ecologies in Latin American and Caribbean Art*. Routledge, 73–88.

O'Flaherty, R. (1846). *A Chorographical Description of West or H-Iar Connaught: Written AD 1684* (Vol. 15). For the Irish Archaeological Society.

Ogude, J., & Nyairo, J. (2007). *Urban Legends, Colonial Myths: Popular Culture and Literature in East Africa*. Africa World Press.

Okonowicz, E. (2012). *Monsters of Maryland: Mysterious Creatures in the Old Line State*. Stackpole Books.

Oren, D. C. (1993). *Did Ground Sloths Survive to Recent Times in the Amazon Region?* Departamento de Zoologia do Museu Paraense Emílio Goeldi.

Oren, D. C. (2001). Does the Endangered Xenarthran Fauna of Amazônia Include Remnant Ground Sloths? *Edentata*, 4, 2–5.

Ortabasi, Melek. (2013). (Re)animating Folklore: Raccoon Dogs, Foxes, and Other Supernatural Japanese Citizens in Takahata Isao's Heisei Tanuki Gassen Pompoko. *Marvels & Tales*, 27(2), 254–75. Project MUSE. Web. February 17, 2015.

Oswald, F. (1915). *Alone in the Sleeping-Sickness Country*. Kegan Paul, Trench, Trubner & Co.

Oudemans, A. C. (1892). *The Great Sea-Serpent. An Historical and Critical Treatise*. Luzac.

Ozaki, Y. T. (Ed.). (1903). *The Japanese Fairy Book*. Archibald Constable & Company.

Paddle, R. (2002). *The Last Tasmanian Tiger: The History and Extinction of the Thylacine*. Cambridge University Press.

Pan, Yu-Yen, Nara, Masakazu, Löwemark, Ludvig, Miguez-Salas, Olmo, Gunnarson, Björn, Iizuka, Yoshiyuki, Chen, Tzu-Tung, & Dashtgard, Shahin E. (2021). The 20-million-year old Lair of an Ambush-Predatory Worm Preserved in Northeast Taiwan. *Scientific Reports*, 11(1), 11.

Parsons, E. C. M. (2004). Sea Monsters and Mermaids in Scottish Folklore: Can These Tales Give us Information on the Historic Occurrence of Marine Animals in Scotland? *Anthrozoös*, 17(1), 73–80.

Paxton, C. G. M., & Naish, D. (2019). Did Nineteenth Century Marine Vertebrate Fossil Discoveries Influence Sea Serpent Reports? *Earth Sciences History*, 38, 16–27.

Paxton, C. G. M. (2002). In Search of Monster? A Defence to Cryptozoology. *The Skeptic*, 15(3), 10–14.

Paxton, C. G. M. (2004). Giant Squids are Red Herrings: Why Architeuthis Is an Unlikely Source of Sea Monster Sightings. *The Cryptozoology Review*, 4(2), 10–16.

Paxton, C. G. M. (2011). Putting the "Ology" into Cryptozoology. *Biofortean Notes*, 1, 7–20.

Peng, Z. (2000). The Image of the "Red-Haired Barbarian" in Chinese Official and Popular Discourse. In H. Meng & S. Hirakawa (Eds.), *Images of Westerners in Chinese and Japanese Literature*. Brill.

Picasso, F., (1998). South American Monsters and Mystery Animals. *Strange Magazine*, 20, 28–35.

Piippo, M. (2020). Loch Ness Monster and Her Impact on Culture. INSPIRE Student Research and Engagement Conference. 16. https://scholarworks.uni.edu/csbsresearchconf/2020/all/16.

Pohanka, R. (2013). *Tatzelwurm und Donauweibchen: Österreichs Naturgeister und Sagengestalten*. Amalthea Signum Verlag.

Powell, J. (1971a). Monster Is Spotted by Texarkana Group. *Texarkana Gazette*, May 3.

Powell, J. (1971b). Hairy "Monster" Hunted in Fouke Sector. *Texarkana Gazette*, May 3.

Powell, J. (1981). On the Trail of the Mokele-Mbembe: A Zoological Mystery. *Explorers Journal*, 59(2), 84–90.

Proyart, L. B. (1776). *Histoire de Loango, Kakongo, et autres royaumes d'Afrique: rédigée d'après le mémoires des préfets apostoliques de la mission françoise; enrichie d'une carte utile aux navigateurs: dédiée a Monsieur*. éditeur non Identifié.

Radford, B. (2011). *Tracking the Chupacabra: The Vampire Beast in Fact, Fiction, and Folklore*. UNM Press.

Radford, B., & Nickell, J. (2006). *Lake Monster Mysteries: Investigating the World's Most Elusive Creatures*. University Press of Kentucky.

Radford, Benjamin. (2008). Popobawa. *Fortean Times*, October 15.

Rambukwella, A. T., & Kadirgamar, S. J. (1963). The Nittaewo—The Legendary Pygmies of Ceylon. *The Journal of the Ceylon Branch of the Royal Asiatic Society of Great Britain & Ireland*, 8(2), 265–90.

Rasmus, S. M. (2002). Repatriating Words: Local Knowledge in a Global Context. *American Indian Quarterly*, 26(2), 286–307.

Ratcliff, L. K. (1949). Filipino Folklore. *The Journal of American Folklore*, 62(245), 259–89.

Raye, L. (2018). Robert Sibbald's Scotia Illustrata (1684): A Faunal Baseline for Britain. *Notes and Records: The Royal Society Journal of the History of Science*, 72(3), 383–405.

Raynal, M. (1989). Cryptozoology: Science or Pseudoscience? *Cryptozoology*, 8, 98–102.

Raynor, D. (2001). Eyewitness Evidence and the Remains of the Loch Ness Monster. In C. Heinselman (Ed.), *Dracontology Special Number 1: Being an Examination of Unknown Aquatic Animals*. Francestown, New Hampshire: Craig Heinselman, 127–8.

Regal, B. (2011). *Searching for Sasquatch*. Palgrave Macmillan.

Regal, B. (2011). *Searching for Sasquatch: Crackpots, Eggheads, and Cryptozoology*. Springer.

Regal, B. (2015). The Jersey Devil: A Political Animal. *New Jersey Studies: An Interdisciplinary Journal*, 1(1), 79–103.

Regal, B., & Esposito, F. J. (2018). *The Secret History of the Jersey Devil: How Quakers, Hucksters, and Benjamin Franklin Created a Monster*. JHU Press.

Regusters, H. A. (1982). *Mokele-Mbembe: An Investigation into Rumors Concerning a Strange Animal in the Republic of the Congo, 1981*. Munger Africana Library Notes, ISSUE 64, JULY 1982. https://authors.library.caltech.edu/25708/1/MALN_64.pdf.

Renner, J. (2012). *It Came from Ohio: True Tales of the Weird, Wild, and Unexplained*. Gray & Company.

Ridley, W. (1875). *Kamilaroi, and Other Australian Languages*. T. Richards, Government printer.

Rinčen, P. R. (1964). Almas Still Exists in Mongolia. *Genus*, 20, 186–92.

Rines, R. H., & Dougherty, F. M. (2003). Proof Positive-Loch Ness Was An Ancient Arm of the Sea. *Journal of Scientific Exploration*, 17(2), 317–23.

Roberts, A. (1987). *Cat Flaps! A Survey of Mystery Cats in the North of England*. Brigantia Books.

Roberts, R. (2004). Villagers Speak of the Small, Hairy Ebu Gogo. *Daily Telegraph*, November 18, 2004.

Roesch, B. S. (1997). A Review of Alleged Sea Serpent Carcasses Worldwide (Part One–1648-1880). *The Cryptozoology Review*, 2(2), 6–27.

Roesch, B. S. (1998a). A Review of Alleged Sea Serpent Carcasses Worldwide (Part Two–1881-1896). *The Cryptozoology Review*, 2(3), 25–35.

Roesch, B. S. (1998b). A Review of Alleged Sea Serpent Carcasses Worldwide (Part Three–1897-1906). *The Cryptozoology Review*, 3(1), 27–31.

Roesch, B. S. (1999). A Review of Alleged Sea Serpent Carcasses Worldwide (Part Four-1907-1924). *The Cryptozoology Review*, 3(3), 15–22.

Roman, C. (2019). Indigenous Beliefs About Little People. *Ab-Original: Journal of Indigenous Studies and First Nations and First Peoples' Cultures*, 3(1), 124–9.

Roman, Joe. (2013). Fishing with Dolphins: An Astonishing Cooperative Venture in Which Every Species Wins but the Fish. *Slate Magazine*, January 31, slate.com/technology/2013/01/fishing-with-dolphins-symbiosis-between-humans-and-marine-mammals-to-catch-more-fish.html.

Romero, G. S., & Schwalb, S. R. (2016). *Beast: Werewolves, Serial Killers, and Man-Eaters: The Mystery of the Monsters of the Gévaudan*. Skyhorse.

Rose, C. (2000). *Giants, Monsters, and Dragons*. W. W. Norton and Co.

Rossi, L. (2016). A Review of Cryptozoology: Towards a Scientific Approach to the Study of "Hidden Animals". In F. M. Angelici (Ed.), *Problematic Wildlife, A Cross Disciplinary Approach*. Springer International Publishing, 573–88.

Rudkin, E. H. (1938). The Black dog. *Folklore*, 49(2), 111–31.

Russell, D. A., & Séguin, R. (1982). Reconstruction of the Small Cretaceous Theropod Stenonychosaurus Inequalis and a Hypothetical Dinosauroid. *Syllogeus*, 37, 1–43.

Ryan, A. V. (1958). The Jersey Devil. *New York Folklore*, 14(1), 55.

Ryan, J. S. (2002). *The Necessary Other, or "When One Needs a Monster": The Return of the Australian Yowie*. Australian Folklore.

Saggase, P. (2005). Cadborosaurus Willsi: Attributive Inquiry. *Bipedia*, 24, 5.

Sanderson, I. T. (1967). The Wudewása or Hairy Primitives of Ancient Europe. *Genus*, XVIII: 1–4, 109–27.

Sanderson, I. T. (1972). *Investigating the Unexplained: A Compendium of Disquieting Mysteries of the Natural World*. Prentice-Hall.

Sari, I. A. L. (2020). The Figures and Meanings of Tengu: Semiotic Study of Mythological Creatures in Japanese Folklore. *Humanus*, 19(2), 217–29.

Saville-Kent, W. (1893). *The Great Barrier Reef of Australia*. W. H. Allen & Co.

Sax, B. (1998). *The Serpent and the Swan: The Animal Bride in Folklore and Literature*. University of Tennessee Press.

Sax, B. (2001). *The Mythical Zoo: An Encyclopedia of Animals in World Myth, Legend, and Literature*. Abc-Clio.

Schembri, E. (2011). Cryptozoology as a Pseudoscience: Beasts in Transition. *SURG Journal*, 5(1), 5–10.

Schmalzer, S. (2009). *The People's Peking Man*. University of Chicago Press.

Scott, P., & Rines, R. (1975). Naming the Loch Ness Monster. *Nature*, 258(5535), 466–8.

Sea Serpent has Head Like a Horse and Pants Like a Dog, Says Witness (1933). *Capital Journal*, December 6.

Sea Serpent Seen Again Saturday: Cadborosaurus Cited by Officers of Ocean Liner (1933). *Edmonton Journal*, October 23.

Sergent, D., & Wamsley, J. (2002). *Mothman: The Facts Behind the Legend*. Marks Phillips Pub.

Shackley, M. (1983). *Still Living? Yeti, Sasquatch and the Neanderthal Enigma*. Thames and Hudson Inc.

Shuker, K. P. (1989). *Mystery Cats of the World: From Blue Tigers to Exmoor Beasts*. Robert Hale.

Shuker, K. P. N. (1995). *In Search of Prehistoric Survivors*. Blandford, 192.

Shuker, K. (1996). *The Unexplained: An Illustrated Guide to the World's Natural and Paranormal Mysteries*. Barnes & Noble Books.

Shuker, K. P. (2005a). Taxonomic Niceties. *Fortean Times*, 194, 72.

Shuker, K. P. (2005b). Taxonomic Comeback: Dr Karl Shuker Replies. *Fortean Times*, 196, 76.

Shuker, K. P. N. (1995). *In Search of Prehistoric Survivors*. Blandford.

Shuklin, V. V. (2001). *Russian Mythological Dictionary*. Yekaterinburg.

Simpson, G. G. (1984). Mammals and Cryptozoology. *Proceedings of the American Philosophical Society*, 128, 1–19.

Simpson, J. (1972). *Icelandic Folktales and Legends*. University of California.

Skibyak, G. (2020). *Kitsune: A Look into the Lasting Presence of the Fox Spirit in Japanese Culture*. Doctoral dissertation, New Mexico State University.

Slater, C. (1996). Breaking the Spell: Accounts of Encantados by Descendants of. In A. J. Arnold (Ed.), *Monsters, Tricksters, and Sacred Cows: Animal Tales and American Identities*. University of Virginia Press, 157–84.

Smith, J. M. (2011). *Monsters of the Gévaudan: The Making of a Beast*. Harvard University Press.

Smith, M. (1982). Review of the Thylacine (Marsupialia, Thylacinidae). In M. Archer (Ed.), *Carnivorous Marsupials Volume 1*. Royal Zoological Society of New South Wales, Sydney, vi.

Smith, O. D. (2021). The Wildman of China: The Search for the Yeren. SINO-PLATONIC PAPERS Number 309, 1–20.

Something About the Dingonek (1918). *Macleans*, January, 31, 3.

Soustelle, G., & Soustelle, J. (1938). *Folklore Chilien*. Paris: Institut International de Coopération Intellectuelle.

Spittle, Bruce. (2010). *Moa Sightings*. Paua Press Ltd.

Srinivasan, A. (2017). The Sucker, the Sucker! *London Review of Books*, 39(17), 23–5.

Ståhlberg, S., & Svanberg, I. (2017). Wildmen in Central Asia. *Anthropos*, 112(1), 51–62.

Steller, G. (2011). *De Bestiis Marinis*. Lulu.com.

Steller, G. W., & Frost, O. W. (1993). *Journal of a Voyage With Bering, 1741–1742*. Stanford University Press.

Stephany, T. J. (2007). *The Great Thunderbird: Source of the American Indian Symbol*. http://timothystephany.com/papers/Article-Thunderbird_rev09b.pdf.

Sterling, E., Hurley, M., & Le, M. (2006). *Vietnam: A Natural History*. Yale University Press.

Stewart, R. (2019). *Diction in the Description of Dragons in Icelandic Texts from c. 871 1600*. Master's thesis.

Strachan, A. E. (2003). *Chasing Chupacabras: Why People Would Rather Believe in a Bloodsucking red-eyed Monster from Outer-space Than in a Pack of Hungry Dogs*. Doctoral dissertation, Massachusetts Institute of Technology.

Strain, Kathy Moskowitz. 2008. *Giants, Cannibals, & Monsters: Bigfoot in Native Culture*. Hancock House Publishers.

Strange Hairy Creature Reported on the East Coast Believed by Some to be a Gorilla (1952). *The Taranaki Daily News*, February 5, Press Assoc. Auckland, NZ.

Strassberg, R. *A Chinese Bestiary: Strange Creatures from the Guideways though Mountains and Seas*. University of California Press.

Streumer, P. (1997). The Leaf-clad Vedda: An European Contribution to Sri Lankan Folk-lore. *Journal of the Royal Asiatic Society of Sri Lanka*, 42, 59–78.

Stuckwish, D. (2009). *Biblical Cryptozoology Revealed Cryptids of The Bible*. Xlibris Corporation.

Swift, J. (1726). *Reprinted as Gulliver's Travels into Several Remote Nations of the World*. Lee & Shepard, 1876.

Sykes, B. (2016). *Bigfoot, Yeti, and the Last Neanderthal: A Geneticist's Search for Modern Apemen*. Red Wheel Weiser.

Sykes, B. C., Mullis, R. A., Hagenmuller, C., Melton, T. W., & Sartori, M. (2014). Genetic Analysis of Hair Samples Attributed to Yeti, Bigfoot and Other Anomalous Primates. *Proceedings of the Royal Society B: Biological Sciences*, 281(1789), 20140161.

Taylor, D. C. (2018). *Yeti: The Ecology of a Mystery*. Oxford University Press.

Thay, E. (2001). *Ghost Stories of Ohio*. Ghost House Books.

The Bundahishn (2019). Dalcassian Publishing Company.

The Devil of Leeds (1887). *Elkhart Sentinel*, October 15, 8.

The Epic of Gilgamesh (1972). Penguin Books.

The Moha-Moha (Chelo-Sauria Lovelli.) A Sandy Cape Curiosity (1894). *Maryborough Chronicle*, September 22, 2–3.

Thibodeau, S. (2001). The Fouke Monster 30 Years Later: Ex-Journalists Recall Sifting Fact from Fouke Fiction after Sighting. *Texarkana Gazette*, June 24.

Thompson, K. D. (2017). *Popobawa: Tanzanian Talk, Global Misreadings*. Indiana University Press.

Thompson, R. H. (1991). *Wolf-hunting in France in the Reign of Louis XV: The Beast of the Gévaudan*. Edwin Mellen Press.

Thurston, Mary Elizabeth. (1996). *The Lost History of the Canine Race*. Andrews McMeel Publishing.

Thwaites, R. G. (Ed.). (1901). *The Jesuit Relations and Allied Documents: Travels and Explorations of the Jesuit Missionaries in New France, 1610–1791; the Original French, Latin, and Italian Texts, with English Translations and Notes* (Vol. 73). Burrows Bros. Company.

Timbs, J. (1869). *Eccentricities of the Animal Creation*. Seeley, Jackson and Halliday.

Todd, V. (2012). Tribal Beliefs About Bigfoot. *The Journal of Chickasaw History and Culture*, 13(1), 70.

Tohall, P. (1948). The Dobhar-Chú Tombstones of Glenade, Co. Leitrim (Cemeteries of Congbháil and Cill-Rúisc). *The Journal of the Royal Society of Antiquaries of Ireland*, 78(2), 127–9.

Turner, D. H. (1977). Windigo Mythology and the Analysis of Cree Social Structure. *Anthropologica*, 19(1), 63–73.

United States Congress Senate. Committee on Environment and Public Works. Subcommittee on Environmental Protection (1988). *Effectiveness of Programs for the Protection of Chesapeake Bay* (Vol. 4).

Urbani, B., & Viloria, Á. L. (2008). *Ameranthropoides loysi Montandon 1929: The History of a Primatological Fraud*. LibrosEnRed.

"Vampire" Charges Woman (1954). *The News and Observer*, January 6, 1, 6.

Van Herwaarden, J. (1924). Een ontmoeting met een aapmensch. *De Tropische Natuur*, 13, 103–6.

Van Valen, L. M. (1983). Cryptozoology, Paleontology, and Evidence. *Cryptozoology*, 2, 155–7.

Varner, G. R. (2007). *Creatures in the Mist: Little People, Wild Men and Spirit Beings Around the World: A Study in Comparative Mythology*. Algora Publishing.

Varricchio, D. J., Hogan, J. D., & Freimuth, W. J. (2021). Revisiting Russell's Troodontid: Autecology, Physiology, and Speculative Tool Use1. *Canadian Journal of Earth Sciences*, 58(9), 796–811.

Velden, F. F. V. (2016). Reality, Science and Fantasy in the Controversies About the Mapinguari in Southwestern Amazonia. *Boletim do Museu Paraense Emílio Goeldi. Ciências Humanas*, 11, 209–24.

Verma, S. K., & Srivastava, D. K. (2003). A Study on Mass Hysteria (Monkey Men?) Victims in East Delhi. *Indian Journal of Medical Sciences*, 57(8), 355–60.

de Vidaurre, F. G. (1861). *Historia Geográfica, Natural y Civil del Reino de Chile* (Vol. 14). Impr. Ercilla.

Wágner, Karel. (2013). *Bigfoot Alias Sasquatch*. Independently published.

Walls, R. E. (1984). Relict Neanderthals: A Folkloristic Comment. *Antiquity*, 58(222), 52.

Walsh, M. (2009). The Politicisation of Popobawa: Changing Explanations of a Collective Panic in Zanzibar. *Journal of Humanities*, 1(1), 23–33.

Walsh, M. T., & Goldman, H. V. (2016). Cryptids and Credulity: The Zanzibar Leopard and Other Imaginary Beings. In S. Hurn (Ed.), *Anthropology and Cryptozoology*. Routledge, 70–106.

Ward, M. (1997). Everest 1951: The Footprints Attributed to the Yeti-myth and Reality. *Wilderness and Environmental Medicine*, 8, 29–32.

Watson, W. G. W. (1920). *Calendar of Customs, Superstitions, Weather-lore, Popular Sayings, and Important Events Connected with the County of Somerset*. Somerset County Herald.

Weerawardane, P. (2004). Ebu Gogo-the Little People of Flores. *SPAFA Journal (Old Series 1991-2013)*, 14(3), 45–9.

Wenzel, N. (2009). The Legend of the Almas: A Comparative and Critical Analysis. Independent Study Project (ISP) Collection. 801. https://digitalcollections.sit.edu/isp_collection/801.

Wilkosz, I. (2019). Aztec Dogs: Myths and Ritual Practice. In R. Mattila, S. Ito, & S. Fink (Eds.), *Animals and Their Relation to Gods, Humans and Things in the Ancient World*. Springer VS, 367–87.

Williams, G. (1912). An Unknown Animal on the Uasingishu. *Journal of the East Africa and Uganda Natural History Society*, 3(5), 123–5.

Witcutt, W. P. (1942). The Black Dog. *Folklore*, 53(3), 167–8.

Wong, K. (2005). The Littlest Human. *Scientific American*, 292(2), 56–65.

Wood, F. (2008a). Aspects of the Wealth-Giving Mamlamgo. *Southern African Journal for Folklore Studies*, 18(2), 96–109.

Wood, F. (2008b). The Mermaid Woman in the 21st Century: Oral Narratives Concerning the Wealth-Giving Mermaid Woman, the Mamlambo, in Their Contemporary South African Context. *International Journal of the Humanities*, 6, 30–6.

Wood, F., & Lewis, M. (2007). *The Extraordinary Khotso: Millionaire Medicine man from Lusikisiki*. Jacana Media.

Woodley, M. A., Naish, D., & Shanahan, H. P. (2008). How Many Extant Pinniped Species Remain to be Described? *Historical Biology*, 20, 225–35.

Wood-Martin, W. G. (1886). *The Lake Dwellings of Ireland: Or, Ancient Lacustrine Habitations of Erin, Commonly Called Crannogs*. Hodges, Figgis & Company.

Woods, B. A. (1954). The Devil in Dog Form. *Western Folklore*, 13(4), 229–35.

Worthy, T. H., & Holdaway, R. N. (2002). *The Lost World of the moa: Prehistoric Life of New Zealand*. Indiana University Press.

Zabihi, M., Salim-Zadeh, M. J., & Farrokhfar, F. (2020). A Comparative Study on Characterization of Imaginary-Synthetic Beings in The Miniatures of the Wonders of Creation, by Zakariya al-Qazwini, Schools of Painting in the Ilkhanid and Mughal Eras. *Negareh Journal*, 15(55), 35–47.

Zhenxin, W., & Wanpo, H. (1981). A Challenge to Science: The Mystery of the Wildman. In S. Moore (Ed.), *Wildman: China's Yeti*. Fortean Times Occasional Papers no. 1, 5–15.

Zipes, Jack. (2008). What Makes a Repulsive Frog So Appealing: Memetics and Fairy Tales. *Journal of Folklore Research*, 45(2), 109–43.

Zmarzlinski, A. (2020). The Black Dog: Origins and Symbolic Characteristics of the Spectral Canine. *Cultural Analysis*, 18(2), 35–73.

Index

About the Author

Margo DeMello received her PhD in Cultural Anthropology from UC Davis in 1995 and is an Assistant Professor in the Anthrozoology program at Carroll College. She served as the Program Director for Human-Animal Studies at Animals & Society Institute from 2004 to 2019 and is the past president of House Rabbit Society.

Her books include *Bodies of Inscription: A Cultural History of the Modern Tattoo Community* (2000), *Stories Rabbits Tell: A Natural and Cultural History of a Misunderstood Creature* (with Susan Davis, 2003), *Low-Carb Vegetarian* (2004), *Why Animals Matter: The Case for Animal Protection* (with Erin Williams, 2007), *The Encyclopedia of Body Adornment* (2007), *Feet and Footwear* (2009), *Teaching the Animal: Human-Animal Studies across the Disciplines* (2010), *Faces around the World* (2012), *Animals and Society: An Introduction to Human-Animal Studies* (2012), *Speaking for Animals: Animal Autobiographical Writing* (2012), *Inked* (2014), *Body Studies: An Introduction* (2014), *Mourning Animals: Rituals and Practices Surrounding Animal Death* (2016), *On the Job: An Encyclopedia of Unique Occupations around the World* (2021), and a second edition of *Animals and Society: An Introduction to Human-Animal Studies* (2021). She lives in Montana with a husband, four Chihuahuas, four cats, and four house rabbits.

www.ingramcontent.com/pod-product-compliance
Lightning Source LLC
Chambersburg PA
CBHW080413270326
41929CB00018B/3004